Genius and Eminence

THE SOCIAL PSYCHOLOGY OF
CREATIVITY AND EXCEPTIONAL ACHIEVEMENT

INTERNATIONAL SERIES IN EXPERIMENTAL SOCIAL PSYCHOLOGY

Series Editor: Michael Argyle, University of Oxford

NOTICE TO READERS

Dear Reader

An Invitation to Publish in and Recommend the Placing of a Standing Order to Volumes Published in this Valuable Series.

If your library is not already a standing/continuation order customer to this series, may we recommend that you place a standing/continuation order to receive immediately upon publication all new volumes. Should you find that these volumes no longer serve your needs, your order can be cancelled at any time without notice.

The Editors and the Publisher will be glad to receive suggestions or outlines of suitable titles, reviews or symposia for editorial consideration: if found acceptable, rapid publication is guaranteed.

ROBERT MAXWELL
Publisher at Pergamon Press

Genius and Eminence

THE SOCIAL PSYCHOLOGY OF
CREATIVITY AND EXCEPTIONAL ACHIEVEMENT

Edited by

ROBERT S. ALBERT

PERGAMON PRESS
OXFORD · NEW YORK · TORONTO · SYDNEY · PARIS · FRANKFURT

U.K.	Pergamon Press Ltd., Headington Hill Hall, Oxford OX3 0BW, U.K.
U.S.A.	Pergamon Press Inc., Maxwell House, Fairview Park, Elmsford, New York 10523, U.S.A.
CANADA	Pergamon Press Canada Ltd., Suite 104, 150 Consumers Road, Willowdale, Ontario M2J 1P9, Canada
AUSTRALIA	Pergamon Press (Aust.) Pty. Ltd., P.O. Box 544, Potts Point, N.S.W. 2011, Australia
FRANCE	Pergamon Press SARL, 24 rue des Ecoles, 75240 Paris, Cedex 05, France
FEDERAL REPUBLIC OF GERMANY	Pergamon Press GmbH, Hammerweg 6, D-6242 Kronberg-Taunus, Federal Republic of Germany

First edition 1983

Library of Congress Cataloging in Publication Data

Main entry under title:
Genius and eminence.
(International series in experimental social psychology)
1. Genius. 2. Creative ability. 3. Social psychology.
I. Albert, Robert S. II. Series.
BF412.G43   1983   153.9'8   82–16510

British Library Cataloguing in Publication Data

Genius and eminence. — (International series in experimental social psychology)
1. Intellect
I. Albert, Robert S. II. Series
155.9 BF431
ISBN 0-08-028105-2

Printed in Great Britain by A. Wheaton & Co. Ltd.

THIS BOOK IS DEDICATED TO MY BROTHER LOUIS
AND THOSE FRIENDS AND COLLEAGUES
WHO MAKE UP PITZER COLLEGE

Preface

OF COURSE, in the final analysis, books must stand or fall by their contents, regardless of what the author says about them. Yet I cannot resist a few words about this one.

Its articles were selected on the basis of several criteria: mainly that they are well-written, cogently argued, and are not idiosyncratic statements by the author. Equally important, they should fit together, both as a whole and within their separate sections. The reader, moving from beginning to end, should be presented with an integrated set of statements about the state of the art and the issues at hand. In a word, there should be nothing "idiosyncratic" about the book. Although the book obviously represents the manner in which I view these topics, my own particular bias, I hope, is less visible than it otherwise might be. Because it is important to the intent of the book, a few words about the book's organization.

The seven topics, although not fully comprehensive, are intended to give readers a firm base from which to move on their own. The sections are arranged to give an historical overview and a contemporary reckoning of the basic concepts, major research techniques, and continuous issues involved in understanding exceptional achievement. The careful reader will notice that there are places within sections as well as across them where articles do not agree. This is deliberate. I recommend that the reader take them all seriously.

This may be the intent and yet one might still ask why compile such a book as this. The reason for me is as simple as this: because human relationships are essential to the survival of each of us, this gives tremendous significance to the behaviors that we have focused upon in this book. As the philosopher Whitehead noted, relationship is significance; where relationships are essential, they obviously carry great significance. The wish, the drive for achievement as several authors point out, is the prime motive to progress in everyday affairs. And although the title of the book rightfully stresses socio-psychological factors, its implicit theme is that of development. Development is change. But not all change is progressive. The type of development with which this book is concerned is that which facilitates or enhances a gifted person's change and progress which therefore may have a positive, meliorating influence in the lives of many others. For these reasons, the book is meant not only for social scientists, or the medical profession, but also for parents, educators, and legislators.

Various articles show us that it is possible to appreciate the differences between important ideas regarding exceptional achievement without necessarily over-dramatizing or stereotyping them. (In fact that is just the way not to understand them.) Although the transitions from potential to actual abilities depicted are extremely complicated and arduous, they certainly can be undertaken by more than the few we recognize as geniuses, if we understand the human qualities behind them. Thus, we do not say that because persons of exceptional achievement (geniuses) are so infrequent it does not pay us to bother, but rather because such persons are rare *and* important, we should try to understand them, and through our understanding to promote the development of others. I, for one, am not afraid of geniuses nearly as much as I am of those persons and institutions that are afraid.

Several ideas occurred to me while considering the articles for this book which I would like to pass on, although they may be "old hat" to some readers. Taken together, these conclusions offer further evidence of the social and psychological nature of creativeness and achievement, placing their emphases in a wider context. The first realization has to do with the early recruitment of scientists and artists. Contrary to popular opinion that scientists are, as Einstein described, "rather odd, uncommunicative, solitary fellows," and that artists are flamboyant, gregarious, and outgoing, their careers are opposites. Scientists – young and old – are the most watched over, supported group of professionals I know of. Adam Smith's invisible hand may not operate in economics but it certainly does in the higher echelons of science. There is nothing comparable to its "invisible" selection and channeling of scientific gifts; especially not among the arts. If this apparent paradox does hold, it has widespread importance for our educational systems as well as the early identification of talent in other fields besides mathematics and science.

There is one immediate implication of this imbalance and it is evident in this book. There are comparatively fewer empirical articles regarding artists or eminents in other fields than there are on science and scientists. The larger truth is that we know much more about scientists and their careers than of persons with careers in business, law, sports, medicine, etc. Since what we know obviously depends upon who is available for study as well as our techniques, interests, and values, this raises the possibility that the model we construct concerning creativity and eminence may be of limited generality. Perhaps a reader or two of this book will rectify this.

It is therefore extremely misleading and short-sighted to think of creativity as primarily an individual entity, ability, or activity. Although such performances require individual participation, as several readings show, whether or not any gifted person becomes creative depends heavily on the career he embarks upon. Different fields offer different opportunities and have their own built-in injunctions for their members to be creative, to attempt the original. Progress in science, as Merton tells us, is predicated upon scientists attempting to be original and as an institution, science does not leave such important matters to chance or whim. The sciences recognize and reward such efforts only when undertaken in the solution of what has been institutionally determined as significant and difficult. Novelty of response, or whim, or a highly idiosyncratic perspective alone do not make a person creative.

This points to the fact that creativity taking place in the real world may be significantly different from the creativity observed in the laboratory or measured by psychometric tests. Real-world creativity is most often a deliberate assertive response to the difficulty *and* significance of problems one is aware of. Only rarely is it to something set in front of us. The creative individual is a confronting person who feels confronted, often with little initial recognition of by what or why. Frequently these individuals willfully seek out opportunities to be creative. Because of this, real-world creativity, for all the analogies made between it and play, has its own set of consistent, long-term purposes and strenuousness.

Such effort is moral as well as psychological. Although it may surprise some readers to describe such efforts as moral, I believe this to be the case. The person who is creative accepts, and commits himself, to a period if not a life of difficulty, constrained by criteria that are shared, maintained, and honored by history and by peers alike. This too makes "novelty," at best, a minor consideration and meaningful only when it is stimulated by the particulars of the problem attempted.

Viewed from this perspective one can say that it is as much the problems faced that generate one's "creativeness" as it is the person involved. For it is these shared demands and criteria which tell us when and which of our efforts are truly creative. Thus, the set of personality attributes that many eminent persons possess in common are at best dispositions to be creative. By themselves they are not creative or creativity.

In line with the above is a question: Are the particular kinds of development and commitments that eminent persons undergo and meet reversible? Once started, can they be dissuaded, given up, blunted, turned back? Can such people decide deliberately to stop being creative, stop being ambitious? I doubt it because the developments and the behaviors we find in such people are sustained by a triple helix of family, education, and career. Such participation appears highly unidirectional and demanding. Because of these silent imperatives, in some ways for some people, creative behavior does share a certain potential for psychopathology since both are predicated upon the resolution of difficult, painful, personal, and at times, disorienting problems. This is not to say that creative behavior *is* itself psychopathological but that it often shares certain developmental features and existential outcomes with psychopathology. My own hunch is that creativeness, rather than destroy the soul, is more likely to anneal it as it subjects one to these stresses and responsibilities. Creativeness is most dangerous when denied.

Although this book begins broadly, it ends with a very personal statement by the great mathematician, G. H. Hardy, that is extremely germane to many of its issues. Hardy describes with great simplicity the tremendous pulling power of great ability when coupled to ambitions, both professional and personal. But for all their power, Hardy poignantly reminds us that such gifts work under limitations, very human limits; time and age erode the greatest gifts, they harness the strongest ambitions. With this erosion may come frustration; and perhaps later, a bitter melancholy.

Nonetheless, it is clear from reading Hardy that he derived an equally profound, longer satisfaction and pride from his efforts and achievements. Although Hardy writes about the limits of choice and the presence of obligations imposed by great gifts, he declares, in the final analysis, that "A man's first duty . . . is to be ambitious. Ambition is a noble passion which may . . . take many forms . . . the noblest is that of leaving behind something of permanent value. . . . Ambition has been the driving force behind nearly all the best work of the world. . . ." Can one ask for a more equitable exchange?

Robert S. Albert
Pitzer College
Claremont, CA

Acknowledgements

BOOKS, like children, do not come into existence without the aid of others and this collection of readings is no exception. I wish now to acknowledge the help that others have given me in putting this collection together and seeing it into print.

Because this book of readings grows out of my teaching as well as my research, I certainly must thank those students who have had to endure years of my enthusiasm and hectoring for them to read, read, read. The articles that I have included in this volume, like my students, are the objects of those enthusiasms and concerns. Students' comments made the selection of articles more confident. A little closer to home I want to thank Ms. Katie Wheeler who was my Research Assistant during much of this project. Her cheerful alacrity was indeed an asset. I am indebted to Mrs. Stella Vlastos for her assistance and encouragement not only during the earliest stages of this book but throughout the larger research project from which much of it grew. My appreciation goes also to Mrs. Norma Miller who calmly met several, very harshly imposed, deadlines.

To my own editor, Dr. Michael Argyle, whose apt suggestions have made this book a more versatile and representative collection than it might otherwise have been, my gratitude. Particular thanks must go to Mrs. Barbara Barrett, Publishing Manager of Pergamon Press for her patience and comprehensive replies to my, at times desperate, letters. I did not believe the enterprise could be as enjoyable or as efficient as it has been, working at such a long distance.

All of the authors contacted were quick in their response to my inquiries and made this work that much easier. I wish to thank especially Professor Robert Merton for his professional generosity and involvement.

I thank my wife, Julie, and sons John and Jess, each of whom had to sacrifice some personal ease while this book was in process.

Last, but far from least, is my appreciation of Pitzer College and its representatives on the Research and Development Committee over the years. Without their repeated encouragement and votes of confidence through grants and sabbaticals my research project as well as this book would never have come into being. Happily, this book now gives me a proper opportunity to make this public.

Contents

Introduction to the series

MICHAEL ARGYLE

SOCIAL psychology is in a very interesting period, and one of rapid development. It has survived a number of "crises", there is increased concern with external validity and relevance to the real world, the repertoire of research methods and statistical procedures has been greatly extended, and a number of exciting new ideas and approaches are being tried out.

The books in this series present some of these new developments; each volume contains a balance of new material and a critical review of the relevant literature. The new material consists of empirical research, research procedures, theoretical formulations, or a combination of these. Authors have been asked to review and evaluate the often very extensive past literature, and to explain their new findings, methods or theories clearly.

The authors are from all over the world, and have been very carefully chosen, mainly on the basis of their previous published work, showing the importance and originality of their contribution, and their ability to present it clearly. Some of these books report a programme of research by one individual or a team, some are based on doctoral theses, others on conferences.

Social psychologists have moved into an increasing number of applied fields, and a growing number of practitioners have made use of our work. All the books in this series will have some practical application, some will be on topics of wide popular interest, as well as adding to scientific knowledge. The books in the series are designed for advanced undergraduates, graduate students and relevant practitioners, and in some cases for a rather broader public.

We do not know how social psychology will develop, and it takes quite a variety of forms already. However, it is a great pleasure to be associated with books by some of those social psychologists who are developing the subject in such interesting ways.

I

Overview: Issues and History

NO SUBJECT with as long a history as genius can survive without acquiring a multitude of questions and misconceptions. In over 2000 years of history, the topic of genius has become riddled with fact and fantasy, truth and error, awe and fear, as well as appreciation. It has been the nature of genius and geniuses to spark some of our best thinking along with some of our more base emotions. Raising critical issues of nature and nurture from the beginning, the topic also has kept before us the question of what constitutes freedom of thought and the significance of the individual in human events. Much that was written about genius prior to Galton was literary and philosophical and centered on the limits of human power, the distinction between talent and genius, and whether or not either or both are controllable through education and legislation. If genius was not, it was to be feared and envied as a law unto itself.

This chapter begins with Addison's fertile essay on genius (I-1). An early version of a much longer pamphlet Addison wrote in 1719, it is a model of Augustan writing and highly representative of the articles and books by many writers which followed. The distinctions presented in Addison's essay and many of the questions they raise remain important to this day and still to be resolved.

Addison's essay is followed by two papers by Albert. The first (I-2) describes how the allied concepts of genius, giftedness, and creativity have each been of particular interest to different professions at different times in more recent history. The results show that each profession, because of its own special background, has looked to one of the three concepts in its effort to observe and understand originality and/or exceptional achievement. The reader who is concerned with research and educational strategies may find interesting the differing operational definitions implicit among these professional emphases and the developmental implications that each contains. Several articles in the book point to a decidedly clear "age of ascent" (about age 25) for persons of high achievement, pointing to the involvement of the maturational process.

Albert's second article (I-3) synthesizes contemporary research and thinking on the twin topics of genius and eminence. It points out that Galton's earlier wish that he had used the term *eminence* instead of *genius* in the title, "Hereditary Genius" has come true in the past thirty years, with important results. Much of the research conducted on exceptional achievement is now centered on the performances of living eminent persons. Anticipating section III on Giftedness, this paper attempts to put in perspective early developmental and emotional differences often observed between gifted children and eminently creative adults.

The last articles of this section are discussions on the myths of genius from two very different perspectives. Becker (I-4) takes a sociological approach and analyzes the labelling process as it is used by both adversaries of genius and persons of genius, each for their own purposes. Becker describes a number of social and political implications that have attached themselves to the label genius, especially during the romantic nineteenth century. He is particularly acute in pointing out the motivation for labelling oneself as a "genius" by many artists. Chapter I ends with a short paper by Lenneberg drawing from the world of music a number of examples of how the often unfounded myth of the unappreciated, struggling artist has been exploited and allowed to persist in the face of contradictory evidence. At the end of the paper the author raises the important question of the methods and responsibility of the historical researcher in challenging such myths and setting the record straight.

1

On Genius*

J. ADDISON

> — Cui mens divinior, atque os
> Magna sonaturum, des nominis hujus honorem.
> HOR. I Sat. iv. 48.
> On him, confer the Poet's sacred name,
> Whose lofty voice declares the heavenly flame.

THERE is no character more frequently given to a writer, than that of being a genius. I have heard many a little sonnetteer called a fine genius. There is not an heroic scribbler in the nation that has not his admirers who think him a great genius; and as for your smatterers in tragedy, there is scarce a man among them who is not cried up by one or other for a prodigious genius.

My design in this paper is to consider what is properly a great genius, and to throw some thoughts together on so uncommon a subject.

Among great geniuses those few draw the admiration of all the world upon them, and stand up as the prodigies of mankind, who by the *mere strength of natural parts,* and without any assistance of art or learning, have produced works that were the delight of their own times and the wonder of posterity. There appears something nobly wild and extravagant in these great natural geniuses, that is infinitely more beautiful than all the turn and polishing of what the French call a *bel esprit,* by which they would express a genius refined by conversation, reflection, and the reading of the most polite authors. The greatest genius which runs through the Arts and Sciences, takes a kind of tincture from them, and falls unavoidably into imitation.

Many of these great natural geniuses that were never disciplined and broken by rules of art, are to be found among the ancients, and in particular among those of the more eastern part of the world. Homer has innumerable flights that Virgil was not able to reach; and in the Old Testament we find several passages more elevated and sublime than any in Homer. At the same time that we allow a greater and more daring genius to the ancients, we must own that the greatest of them very much failed in, or, if you will, that they were very much above the nicety and correctness of the moderns. In their similitudes and allusions, provided there was a likeness, they did not much trouble themselves about the decency of the comparison: thus Solomon resembles the nose of his beloved to the tower of Lebanon which looketh towards Damascus;

The Spectator: a new edition, Vol. 2. New York: D. Appleton & Co. (1879), 329–333.

as, the coming of a thief in the night, is a similitude of the same kind in the New Testament. It would be endless to make collections of this nature; Homer illustrates one of his heroes encompassed with the enemy, by an ass in a field of corn that has his sides belaboured by all the boys of the village without stirring a foot for it: and another of them tossing to and fro in his bed and burning with resentment, to a piece of flesh broiled on the coals. This particular failure in the ancients opens a large field of raillery to the little wits, who can laugh at an indecency, but not relish the sublime in these sort of writings. The present emperor of Persia, conformable to this eastern way of thinking, amidst a great many pompous titles, denominates himself "the sun of glory", and "the nutmeg of delight". In short, to cut off all cavilling against the ancients, and particularly those of the warmer climates, who had most heat and life in their imaginations, we are to consider that the rule of observing what the French call the *bienseance* in an allusion, has been found out of later years, and in the colder regions of the world; where we would make some amends for our want of force and spirit, by a scrupulous nicety and exactness in our compositions. Our country man Shakspeare was a remarkable instance of this first kind of great geniuses.

I cannot quit this head without observing that Pindar was a great genius of the first class, who was hurried on by a natural fire and impetuosity to vast conceptions of things and noble sallies of imagination. At the same time, can anything be more ridiculous than for men of a sober and moderate fancy to imitate this poet's way of writing in those monstrous compositions which go among us under the name of Pindarics? When I see people copying works, which, as Horace has represented then, are singular in their kind, and inimitable; when I see men following irregularities by rule, and by the little tricks of art straining after the most unbounded flights of nature; I cannot but apply to them that passage in Terence:

> – Incerta hæc si tu postules
> Ratione certâ facere, nihilo plus agas,
>   Quàm si des operam, ut cum ratione insanias.
> *Eun*. Act. 1. Sc. 1

You may as well pretend to be mad and in your senses at the same time, as to think of reducing these uncertain things to any certainty by reason.

In short, a modern Pindaric writer, compared with Pindar, is like a sister among the Camisars compared with Virgil's Sibyl: there is the distortion, grimace, and outward figure, but nothing of that divine impulse which raises the mind above itself, and makes the sounds more than human.

There is another kind of great geniuses which I shall place in a second class, not as I think them inferior to the first, but only for distinction's sake, as they are of a different kind. This second class of great geniuses are those that have formed themselves by rules, and submitted the greatness of their natural talents to the corrections and restraints of art. Such among the Greeks were Plato and

Aristotle; among the Romans, Virgil and Tully; among the English, Milton and Sir Francis Bacon.

The genius in both these classes of authors may be equally great, but shows itself after a different manner. In the first, it is like a rich soil in a happy climate, that produces a whole wilderness of noble plants rising in a thousand beautiful landscapes, without any certain order or regularity: in the other, it is the same rich soil under the same happy climate, that has been laid out in walks and parterres, and cut into shape and beauty by the skill of the gardener.

The great danger in the latter kind of geniuses is, lest they cramp their own abilities too much by imitation, and form themselves altogether upon models, without giving the full play to their own natural parts. An imitation of the best authors is not to compare with a good original; and I believe we may observe that very few writers make an extraordinary figure in the world, who have not something in their way of thinking or expressing themselves that is peculiar to them, and entirely their own.

It is odd to consider what great geniuses are sometimes thrown away upon trifles.

"I once saw a shepherd," says a famous Italian author, "who used to divert himself in his solitudes with tossing up eggs and catching them again without breaking them: in which he had arrived to so great a degree of perfection, that he would keep up four at a time for several minutes together playing in the air, and falling into his hand by turns. I think," says the author, "I never saw a greater severity than in this man's face; for by his wonderful perseverance and application, he had contracted the seriousness and gravity of a privy-counsellor; and I could not but reflect with myself, that the same assiduity and attention, had they been rightly applied, might have made him a greater mathematician, than Archimedes."

2

The Concept of Genius and Its Implications for the Study of Creativity and Giftedness*

R. S. ALBERT

WHILE this article refers to creativity and giftedness as well as genius, its major focus is upon genius. The history of the concept is as long and as checkered as any in psychology. It has been a concept that not only has had a long history but that unwittingly has been the meeting ground for such diverse fields of interest as literature, philosophy, intellectual history, and differential psychology.

Historically, it is not clear just when the concept of genius first developed, although it surely is spoken of by the early Greek philosophers, especially Plato (Anastasi, 1965). The word "genio" appears to have been used first during the middle sixteenth century when it referred primarily to a great artist, denoting specifically such a person's great but *not* unique abilities. Specifically, the term "genio" was used first in the sixteenth century primarily to denote the "newly created" (Nahm, 1956). Uniqueness was not introduced as an important aspect of genius until the late seventeenth century, nor a preoccupation regarding creativity until the early twentieth century (Berenson, 1952). As an attribute of, or the necessary condition for, creativity, genius appears to have assumed some of its modern meanings around the end of the seventeenth century. There is evidence of tremendous interest in genius among early eighteenth-century English writers (Albert and Barton, 1969). Toward the middle of the nineteenth century the term genius assumed additional meanings that were less clear for being more mystical or overly speculative. Lange-Eichbaum (1932) suggested that whenever used, the term genius "never loses its religious subflavor." Among popular references there always has been this aura of the mystical attached to the idea of genius (Terman, 1940), and popular autobiographies and biographers often have helped to preserve the atmosphere.

While a historical view of psychological concepts, in terms of their development and their usage, is interesting and often necessary to clear away superficial meanings, it is unfortunate that the concept of genius has been used somewhat indiscriminately to anchor intelligence and creative continua at their highest points, usually with the implication that few people could ever approach these heights or have much in common with those persons who do. For along with the

*American Psychologist, 1969, 24, 743–753 (edited). Copyright 1969 by the American Psychological Association. Reprinted by permission of the publisher and author.

belief that geniuses represent the ultimate in intelligence and creativity (Anastasi, 1965; Terman, 1940; Tyler, 1965), there also has been the subtheme that such people are unexplainable by contemporary models of behavior or personality development among the social sciences, a point similar to one Freud made for psychoanalysis in 1914, although earlier, in 1909, he had suggested the more influential point that there existed a common imaginative activity of neurotics "and also of all comparatively highly gifted people."

Such views lead to scientific impasses, for, on the one hand there is the need for a model of one of the basic psychological activities, the appearance and the development of creativity, and on the other hand there is no study of persons who demonstrate it in rather unambiguous measures.

Nowadays when one thinks of such behavioral attributes as creative, novel, or original, the main emphasis is upon the personality and behavior of moderately intelligent contemporary persons, especially students and young children who, along with their accessibility, bring with them "psychological" health. This may be, in part, a reaction to earlier research on the extreme or clinical case, and is seen as part of the effort to develop a psychology of the "normal." While there is much to be said for such a strategy, the study of intelligence and creativity may have suffered. For along with this move from the extreme case, the concept of genius not only has been used to anchor the extreme ends of both intelligence and creativity, but there has been a continued, relatively unchallenged, acceptance of the earlier ideas that genius or a genius is basically "mad," inspired, or so distinctly peculiar as to be hardly understandable through behavioral and social science techniques. There has been, with some conceptual consistency, the attendant tendency to assume that the proper study of a person designated as a genius is through clinical or psychiatric concepts and methods. That is where a large amount of the early study of genius began and from that originated much of the social sciences' dislike for the use of extreme cases as general models of behavior. . . .

Present Study

The present research investigated the bibliography concerning genius and some allied concepts to gain a sense of the comprehensiveness of behavioral, medical, and social sciences interests in genius. Thus, one of the purposes of this project was to see whether or not there has been sustained interest in the concept of genius. A second aim of the study was to determine the conceptual emphases placed in the study of genius, creativity, and giftedness as well, and how these three topics might be related in the literature. . . .

Results and Discussion

The period of major interest in genius was prior to 1945. The topic of genius and the allied concepts of distinction, eminence, and fame accounted for only a small amount of the published psychological literature for the period 1927–1965. Of the four concepts, that of genius accounted for 70% of the publications devoted to the general area of exceptionalness (135 papers). While 135 papers is not a small number devoted to any topic in professional literature, these 135 papers comprise a very small and diminishing proportion of published work (and interest?) on genius in the behavioral, medical, and social sciences during the period in question. . . . 67% of the references on genius, distinction, eminence, and fame occurred prior to 1944, whereas only 33% were published in the period 1945–1965, showing a definite decline in such work. . . .

In the period 1927–1944, only 23% of the literature concerned with creativeness, gifted children, or giftedness was published, whereas from 1945 to 1965, 77% of this literature was published. The major acceleration of interest appears after 1954, a point discussed below. When one examines the figures for the areas of creativity, giftedness, and gifted children, one can see that a greater change in professional interest has occurred. For the period from 1927 to 1965, 1126 articles abstracted were mainly concerned with creativity, giftedness, or gifted children, but of these 1126 articles, only 20% were published during 1927–1944, while 80% were published during 1945–1965. Obviously, over the past four decades there has been a slight reversal in the proportion of entries for the two general areas, genius and creativity–giftedness. Of the two areas, that of creativity–giftedness accounts for the majority (86%) of publications dealing with high level attainment and creative behavior. Genius, etc., accounted for only 14% of the 1318 entries.

There is not only a difference among the areas of creativity, giftedness, and gifted children, in terms of the total number of publications for each, but also differing rates of growth in professional interest, as measured by number of publications. Over the 1927–1965 period, creativity had the largest number of publications. Dividing the period into pre- and post-World War II eras, the topic of giftedness shows the greatest growth in publications in the 1945–1965 period; 80% of its publications occurred during 1945–1965, especially from 1954 on.

So much for the overall figures. They show that the published interest in genius never has been large in proportion to the overall published work in the behavioral, medical, and social sciences as these appear in *The Psychological Abstracts*. Moreover, what interest there was prior to World War II seems to have been devoted since then to creativity, giftedness, and gifted children. The area of genius *per se* as a focus of professional interest appears very much a thing of the past. Yet, as stated above, the idea of there being such a thing as genius or such people as geniuses still intrigues some persons interested in personality development and creativity, for example, McCurdy and Follett (1966).

Examining the specific facets of the various concepts tells us what was of interest in the past regarding genius, fame, etc., and something of why there was the shift in publications to that of creativity and giftedness.

Content Analysis of Areas

Genius

The content of the articles gives some idea of the major points of emphasis in past work on genius. The major focus of interest is the oldest one, the psychopathology assumed in genius or so closely related to genius, as to be a necessary condition for genius (Bett, 1952; Freud, 1947; Hitschmann, 1956; Lombroso, 1895), making genius one among many forms of psychopathology (22%). The second major focus of interest (19%) somewhat surprisingly is with the conditions and characteristics related or contributing to genius. In this category, general health as distinct from mental health is important. Also involved here is a subtheme discussing the moral strength of character of genius as well as goodness or badness of character. A surprising distant (to the author) third focus in terms of the few papers (13%) are those that dealt with the background of genius, namely, heredity and/or eugenics much in the fashion of Galton's (1869) earlier work; for example, Bramwell (1948), or those in which the evidence of national or racial characteristics of geniuses or genius were viewed as a product or a culmination of large national or racial forces. This, too, was a point mentioned by Galton, but plays much more a role in Kretschmer's (1931) work. This area appears related to another, both in intent and in the proportion of articles devoted to it — 12% of the articles discussed, analyzed, or attempted to define the meaning of genius. Most often this was in nonobservables such as inspiration, or terms that would be extremely difficult to operationalize. A few papers did make such an effort, for example, Terman (1940), defining genius as high level conceptual ability, or papers that were direct descendants of Galton's work in qualifying eminence. However, most of the interest in the problem disappears by the middle 1920s. There were only 13 papers (10%) discussing the demographic and family—social background of geniuses. These articles had more of a social interest than a hereditary interest to them insofar as they were concerned with the kinds of social—cultural conditions that helped or hindered the occurrence of geniuses. It should be noted that the development of genius as a function of psychological process was seldom mentioned, McCurdy (1957) being an important exception. Occurrence or appearance have been decidedly the two major issues regarding genius. A last substantive category, concerning artistic and literary rather than empirical interest in genius, is consistent with the very earliest discussion of genius in Western literature. Only 6% of the entries dealt with either the various arts or issues of aesthetics. The remaining 18% were miscellaneous books, papers, reviews, biographies, not clearly classifiable in terms of the other categories.

Summarizing, roughly 64% of the papers published during 1927—1965 on the subject of genius concerned themselves with identifying traits or characteristics of genius. If there is a major question about genius, it is how to *recognize* one rather than how to understand what the development of such a person might be, or requires, psychologically and culturally. Surprisingly few questions asked what contributes to the designation of a person as a genius. Most of the papers concerned with the meaning or the nature of genius assumed that there is such a thing or attribute as genius, and go on to discuss the national, racial, religious, or supernatural forces involved. Little or no effort is made to analyze the implications that the study of genius might have for the behavioural, medical, or social sciences. A case in point are clinical studies of famous persons that tended to reduce their genius to being either the manifestation of abnormality or to present it as an example of highly efficient, but nevertheless neurotic, defenses that while protecting the individual were also driving him to his productivity, for example, Lowenfeld (1941). Rarely is anything said of possible psychological health or the evidence of psychological health that the combination of high quality and continued productivity might manifest. Early exceptions are White's (1930, 1931) two papers. For some understanding of the potential psychological health and the dynamics involved, one must go to the writings of Erikson (1950, 1958, 1959, 1966), Kubie (1958), and Maslow (1959), although there is a very strong interest in creativity being an attribute of positive ego-strength in more recent psychological literature. Somewhat surprisingly, within the last few years historians have presented a number of interesting papers on the interplay of personality and historical factors (cf. Mazlich, 1963). Along with their quality, such works are noticeable for their growing number (Bushman, 1966; Strout, 1968; Wyatt and Willcox, 1959). . . .

Eminence, distinction, and fame

These categories represent a group of concepts that are quite ancillary to that of genius. As mentioned above, very few articles are devoted to these concepts. Together, the three concepts accounted for 29% of the abstracted articles regarding genius and allied issues. In searching the papers, there appears little difference between distinction and eminence. Of the two, eminence appears to be a more highly social concept, most articles pertaining to it discussing origin, race, or the particular social class of eminent men rather than analyzing the psychological or social conditions or processes making for eminence, or raising questions of how one evaluates it. Basically, the three — eminence, distinction, fame — are concerned with demography, not development. A minor theme to this cluster of concepts is the question of age at which eminence is achieved, or even more specifically, the month of birth of eminent persons.

Creativity and giftedness

The two other major concepts investigated were creativity and giftedness. Because there were distinctions made in the literature between gifted children and giftedness, they will be discussed separately at times. It appears that as interest in genius and its allied areas diminished, interest in creativity, giftedness, and gifted children accelerated, especially after 1954. This growth was spurred by the tremendous concern in this country for the education and the use of gifted intelligence in scientific training and research after the launching of Russia's sputnik. But there also were academic reasons for this growth in interest. These were the major papers of Barron (1955), Guilford (1959), Roe (1953), and Terman (1954a, 1954b), all within a span of a few years.

From 1949 through 1953, Anne Roe published a series of papers and monographs on eminent scientists. The major emphases of her papers appear to be twofold: on possible relationships between family background and career choice, and on the psychological characteristics that might be related to the attainment of eminence in different sciences. . . . These monographs were important for their centering attention upon eminence, not genius (in somewhat the same manner in which Galton hoped he had done, as stated in his preface to the second edition of *Hereditary Genius*); their emphasis away from psychopathology as a major basis of eminence; and their indication of certain dynamic and developmental processes as they underlie productive careers in the *different* sciences, rather than simply upon the attainment of eminence among scientists who happen to be in different fields. Barron's experimental work on the way personality correlates to creativity was first published in 1952, after which there were four papers published in 1953, all in the same general area, with other publications since that time (cf. Barron, 1968). The point to be emphasized is the tremendous burst of experimental work on dynamic, personality factors in creativity, an approach sorely lacking before. Barron was working in an area that previously had been approached through psychoanalytically oriented case material. It is historically important to note that many of the important theoretical concepts that Barron worked with were psychoanalytic. What Barron brilliantly showed was a productive *rapprochement* between experimental method and psychoanalytic theory, which shows how much of a meeting of mind there had been in the ensuing 32 years since the Terman—Chase paper. Three of Guilford's works (Guilford, 1950, 1959; Wilson, Guilford and Christensen, 1953) made popular his work on divergent thinking to a growing professional audience, offering another model of research possible in the area of creativity. Undoubtedly, Guilford's papers helped to put the area of creativity further into the mainstream of psychology. Although more of a summation of his earlier work but a stimulant to this growth are Terman's (1954a, 1954b) two monographs. Each represents not only the important research findings of the major American psychologist investigating genius and the gifted, but were two of the clearer statements of some of the family and personal factors important for the development and utilization (or not) of talent among the gifted, a topic most congruent with the educational interests of the times. . . .

Creativity

There are eight categories into which most of the published work on creativity fall. But one area predominates: Articles concerned with personality dynamics and cognitive processes accounted for 21% of the published work. Environmental conditions and specific personality characteristics that might facilitate or hinder creativity compose the next largest group of entries − 16%. The third largest area of interest − 15% − consisted of articles discussing the meaning of creativity or offering definitions or theories about it. Such publications have been less frequent as the number of treatises dealing with the motivational dynamics and the cognitive processes involved in creative behavior have increased, a trend suggesting that a field's ability to establish operational definitions may profitably precede theoretical definitions.

The fourth most frequently published articles (11%) dealt with the more traditional problems of psychological health or psychopathology and creative behavior. Interestingly, only one-fifth of *these* papers were concerned specifically with the effect of psychotherapy on creative behavior.

The fifth largest category of publications (10%) were articles relating creativity as a personality attribute to artistic behavior or to work in the various arts. A common feature in this category is a comparison of the creative processes involved in arts and in science. Most often the question is posed as one of differences rather than of similarities, and too often the comparisons do not consider the possibilities of behavioral or background differences among the different art forms or among the different sciences. As mentioned above, Roe's studies are exceptions.

For a number of obvious reasons one would expect that the problems of identifying what creativity is or who are creative people would represent a sizable interest in the social sciences. Yet, writings directed to these problems are just under 10% of the total publications, with very few papers concerned with the problem of predicting creative behavior from either test or observational data. In spite of the great public concern with training and education for highly complex research (cf. Joncich, 1964), only 7% of the treatises were concerned with the education for or the training of creativity. Anticipating some of the data reported below, one should mention that this is quite distinct from the tremendous concern with education of the gifted, for the issue of education of the gifted accounted for 43% of the publications regarding giftedness or gifted children. This difference between the frequencies in the two areas raises the interesting question of whether or not social scientists think of giftedness as implying creativity, much in the way that they once assumed an IQ of 140 or better reflected genius.

The smallest identifiable category (4%) regarding creativity concerned itself with demography, which was one of the early interests concerning genius. This 4% compared to the 21% of articles related to dynamics and processes amounts to a change of interest from static external traits, seen in much writing prior to 1945, to interest in the more dynamic internal conditions within the individual, seen in post-1945 articles. The remaining 6% of the articles in the area of creativity constitutes a miscellany of biographies, textbooks, and reviews.

Giftedness. . . . There are different growth rates for giftedness and creativity, with giftedness showing the largest post-1945 growth. As already indicated, the largest group of published works for this category concerns itself with the education or training for gifted persons (43%). The rest of the articles spread rather evenly among the remaining five categories. The second largest category, accounting for 13% of the publications, was concerned with test performances, or measures of skills or achievements of the gifted. When the compositions in this category are coupled with those papers dealing with the identification of the gifted (12%), one-quarter of the publications related to giftedness or the gifted child are concerned with the identification of giftedness or gifted children. For the topic of giftedness there are basically two highly related areas of interest — the education and training of giftedness and the identification of the gifted. Together these two issues account for 68% of the publications. The remaining publications are concerned with personality dynamics or personality traits (12% compared to the 21% of such publications in creativity), social and cultural conditions as factors related to giftedness (7%), and, lastly, the question of health (3%). Health is discussed more as a question of school adjustment than as a question of psychodynamics related to creative behavior or psychopathology, as in the case of genius. The remaining 10% of the articles not categorizable in the above areas makes up a miscellany of textbooks, reviews, etc.

Summary and Conclusions

Table I.1 offers a comparison of major published emphasis regarding creativity, genius, and giftedness.

The early interest in genius not only has lessened over the years, but that interest has differed considerably from professional interest in creativity and giftedness. Whereas a large part of the literature on genius considered questions of pathology, heredity, and demography, the interest in creativity related more to personality dynamics and cognitive processes and much less to the question of psychopathology, pathology, or ill health. A look at the publications on giftedness discloses that the emphasis is very much upon the education, the training, or the identification of the gifted. Again interest in psychopathology or racial and national origins is quite minimal. Since all interests in the areas under consideration have changed drastically during the 38-year period under examination, it seems appropriate to characterize the changes as historical changes as well as professional emphases. As such, these data fall within the concern of a social history of science as well as within the more specific fields of interests traditionally involved.

TABLE I.1 *Comparative Percentages of Psychological Abstracts Relating to Common Topics for Genius, Creativity, and Giftedness*

Category	Genius (%)	Creativity (%)	Giftedness (%)
Demography and heredity	23	4	1
Health-psychopathology	22	11	3
Conditions and characteristics related or contributing to	13	16	7
Meaning and theories of	12	15	5
Education of, training for	2[a]	7	43
Traits, skills, measures important in the identification of	2	10	25
Personality cognitive dynamics	–	21	12

Note.—Percentages do not equal 100% as only those categories important to the concepts of genius, creativity, and giftedness are shown.

[a]Because so few articles dealt with the category, these articles were originally included in the miscellany category.

Such changes in interest suggest that one of the important features of early works on genius was to alert social scientists to the presence of productive, although at times unusual, people, who, by their very achievements had continuously raised questions concerning the social and personal bases of such productivity and the psychological meaning and processes of achievement. If anything, this early work was one of the first efforts to link motivation to creative behavior. However, the first questions were not directed where such early efforts were made, for example, Galton (1869) and Terman (1906); these efforts were devoid of queries of motivation and high achievement. These came with and, of course, after Freud's introductory writings. Unfortunately, the precursory linking of genius to the exceptional or the pathological case probably kept the topic of genius from being a major focus of most social scientists, since interest in psychopathology generally has been left to psychiatry or the clinically-oriented investigator. Over the years social science research increasingly has eschewed dealing with comparisons between extreme groups. The idea of genius for many years focused attention on the highest types of creative behavior of one sort or another. It raised questions of origin of development and of costs for such behavior. If one changes the label from genius to eminent, as is rapidly becoming the case, then questions of genius qua eminence offer many opportunities for an interdisciplinary investigation of high level creative behavior and achievements from many points of view, on many levels, and by means of many techniques. If one can imagine the ingredients of a model of eminent achievement combining the psychological and sociological approaches, the sociological approach of Barber (1961) and Merton (1968) — and eminence is very much sociological — and the psychological approaches of Barron, Erikson, and Roe, one can see the various psychological levels of development and behavior being studied in both historical and social contexts. The psychological levels could disclose more about the interplay of family dynamics and cognitive styles (Bing, 1963; Dyk and Witkin, 1965; Ferguson and Maccoby, 1966). The historical and social contexts may reveal why only a small proportion of gifted children reach full productivity, the ways in which they are most likely to be heard, favorably, and why only in certain fields.

One line of research that might enhance our knowledge and diminish our disappointments is to make a distinction between levels of giftedness, for example, the level of giftedness that allows some to graduate from college and the level of exceptional giftedness that aids some to graduate from college and complete other preparatory experiences while in their teens or early twenties. Such distinctions would balance the discriminations made on the lower end of the intelligence continuum (Kebbon, 1965; Matthews, 1963; Sloan and Birch, 1955; Taylor, 1964; Thompson and Margaret, 1947), with finer discriminations at the upper end. While at best suggestive, there are data pointing to achievement and professional differences among subjects at different levels of giftedness (e.g., Albert and Barton, 1969; Fowler, 1962; Frierson, 1965; Gallagher and Lucito, 1961; Getzels and Jackson, 1962; Hildreth, 1954; Hollingworth and Cobb, 1928; Lucito and Gallagher, 1960).

There is the additional need to investigate differences among the various levels and forms taken by creativity and eminence. Where MacKinnon (1964) and his co-workers generally found that creativity and eminence do not require IQs beyond those of most college graduates, Cox's (1926) research showed that persons of such eminence as to be called geniuses had average IQs of 160 or better. Two aspects to these data should be remembered: They were estimated; and the average IQs in the different fields, for example, soldiers or scientists, differed considerably from one another. Without weighting IQs too heavily in this strategy, one must recognize that for all its predictive limitations, the IQ does predict academic *learning* capacity quite well (other things being equal). And it is their learning, formal and informal, very early (Fowler, 1962) and very determinedly (Cox, 1926; McCurdy, 1957; Roe, 1953; Terman, 1940), that characterizes persons labeled genius or eminent. Of course, there are other factors besides intelligence and other forms of intelligence than those required for effective performance on standard intelligence tests (cf. Hudson, 1967; Vernon, 1965). This, too, is at issue. Roe showed that eminent scientists in the different sciences think somewhat differently, for example, biologists using visual imagery, psychologists using verbal modes. They also seem to undergo somewhat different psychosexual developments, a finding that fits to some extent with the more recent studies of Bing (1963), Dyk and Witkin (1965), and Ferguson and Maccoby (1966). Is the same true of the eminent in non-science fields, or of those who achieve eminence in different cultures (cf. Ferguson, 1954; Vernon, 1965) or during different historical periods (cf. Hughes, 1964, chs. 2 and 3; Huizinga, 1954, chs. 1 and 18; Wyatt and Willcox, 1959,

p. 19)? These and other uncertainties need investigation and could be searched by changing the labels and lowering the sights from genius to eminence.

There is one other crucial issue in this area of investigation: the prediction from giftedness to eminence. Few studies have attempted this. For the most part, scientists do not know the levels or types of achievement attained by Hollingworth's (1942) children with IQs above 180 or Terman's (Terman and Oden, 1947) gifted group. Yet each study's subjects are now at an age when their achievements and their eminence (or lack) would be discernible. While much has been discovered about creative behavior, giftedness, and genius *qua* eminence by working backward, a fully scientific understanding of them will be achieved only by working forward and predicting their occurrences.

References

ALBERT, R. S. and BARTON, D. (1969) Studies in early cognitive development among the exceptionally gifted.

ANASTASI, A. (1965) *Differential psychology*. New York: Macmillan.

BARBER, B. (1961) Resistance by scientists to scientific discovery. *Science*, 134, 596–602.

BARRON, F. (1952) Personality style and perceptual choice. *Journal of Personality*, 20, 385–401.

BARRON, F. (1953) Complexity-simplicity as a personality dimension. *Journal of Abnormal and Social Psychology*, 48, 163–172.

BARRON, F. (1955) The disposition toward originality. *Journal of Abnormal and Social Psychology*, 51, 478–485.

BARRON, F. (1968) *Creativity and personal freedom*. Princeton: Van Nostrand.

BERENSON, B. (1952) *Rumor and reflection*. New York: Simon & Schuster.

BETT, W. R. (1952) *The infirmities of genius*. New York: Philosophical Library.

BING, E. (1963) The effect of child rearing practices in development of differential cognitive abilities. *Child Development*, 34, 631–648.

BRAMWELL, B. S. (1948) Galton's "hereditary genius"; and the three following generations since 1896. *Eugenics Review*, 39, 149–153.

BUSHMAN, R. L. (1966) On the uses of psychology: Conflict and conciliation in Benjamin Franklin. *History and Theory*, 5, 225–240.

COX, C. M. (1926) *Genetic studies of genius*. Vol. 2: *The early mental traits of three hundred geniuses*. Stanford: Stanford University Press.

Cumulated subject index, 1927–1960 (1960) *Psychological Abstracts*. Boston: G. K. Hall.

DOOLEY, L. (1916) Psychoanalytic studies of genius. *American Journal of Psychology*, 27, 363–417.

DYK, R. and WITKIN, H. (1965) Family experiences related to the development of differentiation in children. *Child Development*, 36, 21–55.

ERIKSON, E. H. (1950) *Childhood and society*. New York: Norton.

ERIKSON, E. H. (1958) *Young man Luther: A study in psychoanalysis and history*. New York: Norton.

ERIKSON, E. H. (1959) Identity and the life cycle. *Psychological Issues*, 1, 101–164.

ERIKSON, E. H. (1966) Gandhi's autobiography: The leader as a child. *The American Scholar*, 35, 632–646.

FERGUSON, G. A. (1954) On learning and human ability. *Canadian Journal of Psychology*, 8, 95–112.

FERGUSON, L. and MACCOBY, E. (1966) Interpersonal correlates of differential abilities. *Child Development*, 37, 549–571.

FOWLER, W. (1962) Cognitive learning in infancy and early childhood. *Psychological Bulletin*, 59, 116–152.

FREUD, S. (1947) *Leonardo da Vinci*. New York: Vintage Books.
FREUD, S. (1948) Formulations regarding the two principles in mental functioning. In, *Collected papers*. Vol. 4. London: Hogarth Press.
FRIERSON, E. C. (1965) Upper and lower status gifted children: A study of differences. *Exceptional Children*, 32, 83–90.
GALLAGHER, J. J. and LUCITO, L. J. (1961) Intellectual patterns of gifted compared with average and retarded. *Exceptional Children*, 27, 479–482.
GALTON, F. (1869) *Hereditary genius*. New York: Macmillan.
GETZELS, J. W. and JACKSON, P. W. (1962) *Creativity and intelligence: Explorations with gifted students*. New York: Wiley.
GUILFORD, J. P. (1950) Creativity. *American Psychologist*, 5, 444–454.
GUILFORD, J. P. (1959) Three faces of intellect. *American Psychologist*, 14, 469–479.
HILDRETH, G. (1954) Three gifted children: A developmental study. *Journal of Genetic Psychology*, 85, 239–262.
HITSCHMANN, E. (1956) *Great men: Psychoanalytic studies*. New York: International Universities Press.
HOLLINGWORTH, L. S. (1942) *Children above 180 IQ Stanford-Binet*. New York: World Book.
HOLLINGWORTH, L. S. and COBB, M. V. (1928) Children clustering at 165 I.Q. and children clustering at 145 I.Q. compared for three years in achievement. *Yearbook of National Social Studies Education*, 2, 3–33.
HUDSON, L. (1967) *Contrary imaginations*. Middlesex: Penguin Books.
HUGHES, H. S. (1964) *History as art and as science*. New York: Harper & Row.
HUIZINGA, J. (1954) *The waning of the middle ages*. Garden City: Anchor Books.
JONCICH, G. (1964) A culture-bound concept of creativity: A social historian's critique, centering on a recent American report. *Educational Theory*, 14, 133–143.
KEBBON, L. (1965) *The structure of abilities at lower levels of intelligence*. Stockholm: AB Broderg and Soner.
KRETSCHMER, E. (1931) *The psychology of men of genius*. New York: Harcourt Brace.
KUBIE, L. S. (1958) *Neurotic distortion of the creative process*. Lawrence: University of Kansas Press.
LANGE-EICHBAUM, W. (1932) *The problem of genius*. New York: Macmillan.
LOMBROSO, C. (1895) *The man of genius*. New York: Scribner.
LOWENFELD, H. (1941) Psychic trauma and productive experience in the artist. *Psychoanalytic Quarterly*, 10, 116–130.
LUCITO, L. J. and GALLAGHER, J. J. (1960) Intellectual patterns of highly gifted children on the WISC. *Peabody Journal of Education*, 38, 131–136.
MacKINNON, D. W. (1964) The nature and nurture of creative talent. In R. E. Ripple (Ed.), *Readings in learning and human abilities*. New York: Harper & Row.
MASLOW, A. H. (1959) Creativity in self-actualizing people. In H. H. Anderson (Ed.), *Creativity and its cultivation*. New York: Harper.
MATTHEWS, C. G. (1963) Relationship of differential abstraction ability levels to psychological test performances in mentally retarded subjects. *American Journal of Mental Deficiency*, 68, 235–244.
MAZLICH, B. (1963) *Psychoanalysis and history*. Englewood Cliffs: Prentice-Hall.
McCURDY, H. G. (1957) The childhood pattern of genius. *Journal of the Elisha Mitchell Scientific Society*, 73, 448–461.
McCURDY, H. G. and FOLLETT, H. (Eds.) (1966) *Barbara: The unconscious autobiography of a child genius*. Chapel Hill: University of North Carolina Press.
MERTON, R. K. (1968) The Matthew effect in science. *Science*, 159, 56–63.
NAHM, M. (1956) *The artist as creator*. Baltimore: Johns Hopkins Press.
PHILLIPS, W. (Ed.) (1963) *Art and psychoanalysis*. Cleveland: World.
PROJECT ON SCIENTIFIC INFORMATION EXCHANGE IN PSYCHOLOGY (1963) *Reports*. Vol. 1. Washington, DC: American Psychological Association.
ROE, A. (1951a) A psychological study of eminent biologists. *Psychological Monographs*, 65(14, Whole No. 331).

ROE, A. (1951b) A psychological study of physical scientists. *Genetic Psychology Monographs*, **43**, 121–235.

ROE, A. (1953) A psychological study of eminent psychologists and anthropologists, and a comparison with biological and physical scientists. *Psychological Monographs*, **67**(2, Whole No. 352).

ROE. A. (1961) The psychology of the scientist. *Science*, **134**, 454–459.

SLOAN, W. and BIRCH, J. W. (1955) A rationale for degrees of retardation. *American Journal of Mental Deficiency*, **60**, 258–264.

STROUT, C. (1968) Ego psychology and the historian. *History and Theory*, **7**, 282–297.

TAYLOR, J. B. (1964) The structure of ability in the lower intellectual range. *American Journal of Mental Deficiency*, **68**, 766–774.

TERMAN, L. M. (1906) Genius and stupidity. *Pedagogical Seminary*, **13**, 307–373.

TERMAN, L. M. (1940) Psychological approaches to the biography of genius. *Science*, **92**, 293–301.

TERMAN, L. M. (1954a) The discovery and encouragement of exceptional talent. *American Psychologist*, **9**, 221–230.

TERMAN, L. M. (1954b) Scientists and nonscientists in a group of 800 gifted men. *Psychological Monographs*, **68**(7, Whole No. 378).

TERMAN, L. M. and CHASE, J. M. (1920) The psychology, biology and pedagogy of genius. *Psychological Bulletin*, **17**, 397–409.

TERMAN, L. M. and ODEN, M. (1947) *The gifted child grows up*. Stanford: Stanford University Press.

THOMPSON, C. W. and MARGARET, A. (1947) Differential test responses of normals and mental defectives. *Journal of Abnormal and Social Psychology*, **42**, 285–293.

TYLER, L. E. (1965) *The psychology of human differences*. New York: Appleton-Century-Crofts.

VERNON, P. E. (1965) Ability factors and environmental influences. *American Psychologist*, **20**, 723–733.

WHITE, R. K. (1930) Note on the psychopathology of genius. *Journal of Social Psychology*, **1**, 311–315.

WHITE, R. K. (1931) The versatility of genius. *Journal of Social Psychology*, **2**, 460–489.

WILSON, R. C., GUILFORD, J. P. and CHRISTENSEN, P. R. (1953) The measurement of individual differences in originality. *Psychological Bulletin*, **40**, 362–370.

WYATT, F. and WILLCOX, W. B. (1959) Sir Henry Clinton: A psychological exploration in history. *William and Mary Quarterly*, **16**, 3–26.

3

Exceptional Creativity and Achievement*

R. S. ALBERT

OF ALL the many ideas about exceptional persons and unusual achievement, the oldest active explanation is the concept of *genius*. It is over two thousand years old. Over this long period of time, it has undergone a number of changes in what it connotes, but it has been remarkably stable as to whom it refers. The major change in this history has come during the past one hundred twenty-five years, the period during which persons interested in the subject of genius and geniuses have become much more willing to subject their opinions and hypotheses to critical empirical observation. From this increased scientific vigor has come a greater reliance upon the study of two rather distinct populations: eminent adults (living and dead) and gifted youth. With the introduction of social science methodology into the study of genius, the important questions regarding the connections, if any, between creative abilities and exceptional intellectual development and the role of educational, social, and family factors in such development have become more sharply focused and less open to value-laden judgments and loose speculation. The end product of this important historical change has been the beginning of a compact field of research interest focused upon the study of eminent persons and the factors and the experiences contributing to their eminence. This line of investigation, initiated by Galton (1869), has developed links to a diverse number of important topics. Without an understanding of the origin and early applications of the concept of genius, it is difficult to adequately appreciate the great strides made and the great promise inherent in the increasingly robust state of the contemporary study of genius.

Historically, "genius" has designated persons and/or styles of thinking and performances that clearly break with the past; alter radically the customary means of attack on problems in art, philosophy, politics, science, and welfare; or represent the essence of high performance in these areas. The main emphasis has been on the unexpected, the unpredicted, and the almost unfathomable occurrence and results of "genius." Two key experiential manifestations of genius are (1) the rare but radical *disruption* of preceding manners, attitudes, customs, or cognitive habits; and (2) the performance of complex tasks in

*Encyclopedia of Clinical Assessment, Vol. 2. (1980) San Francisco, Jossey-Bass, Reprinted by permission.

manners and styles very rarely observed. Although not always in aspect of these two manifestations, adult-level artistic or scientific works that are extremely precocious are also taken as manifestations. At the same time, persons of genius are often considered extremists or potentially disruptive forces militating against personal and social tranquility. Genius is also held to be untutored and beyond the influence of conventional education – a product of nature rather than nurture. Such persons have been viewed with much ambivalence and suspicion and are as often stigmatized as praised with the appellation of "genius."

Background and Current Status

The exact origin of the concept of genius is not clear. The concept has been in use for more than 2000 years. During this time, genius has been generally associated with the mystical, as opposed to a more human and mundane process of development or use of abilities. Although there is no exact Greek word parallel to the word *genius,* the Greeks placed great emphasis on an individual's *Daimon,* a guardian spirit. The term *Daimon* thus implied an individual's own natural abilities, as well as motivations and appetites. Over time, it became progressively associated with an individual's character and therefore was an intrinsic moral or social quality of that person. Everybody has some individual genius or *Daimon*, which was honored and worshipped on birthdays. This democratic notion of genius disappeared over the years, to be supplanted by connotations of exceptionality, deviancy, or elitism. Ironically, this second notion came about because, in addition to their idea of an individual *Daimon,* the early Greeks also linked genius with madness. In Aristotle's view, there is "no great genius without madness," madness being frenzied inspiration from the gods. This viewpoint became quite influential during the late eighteenth, nineteenth, and early twentieth centuries.

In Roman history, genius was associated more with households than with individuals. Specifically, it came to designate Roman emperors and their households, palaces, and spheres of influence – and, ultimately, whole civilizations and geographical regions, even continents. Among Romans, genius was also regarded as a male creative force. Each important man brought genius with him, was protected and guided by his own genius, and passed it on through the birth of his children as part of his illustrious family's history. Genius for Romans was not a democratic attribute.

During the Middle Ages, the idea developed that special talent or unusual ability in an individual (almost always a male) is a manifestation of some outside "spirit" using this person as a conduit, acting through him. In the early Renaissance, the *divine* quality of great artists and artisans was emphasized, but later in this period genius became associated more closely with unusual and powerful *human* talent or creativity. In the eighteenth century, the differences between genius and talent, and their respective roles in human affairs, were debated.

The central issues of "natural," untutored ability and the purposes and means of education also were widely discussed. Writers in this period tried to find "rational" means for understanding persons referred to as geniuses. They also tried to determine whether the manifestations and the sheer number of persons of genius could be changed, controlled, or deliberately enhanced. This century-long debate, part of the English Enlightenment's championing of scientific methods of inquiry over religious and monarchial dogmas, broke off early in the nineteenth century. However, it was instrumental in raising before the public the issues of educational policy and its impact upon differently-endowed children and of the place and goals of education in democratic societies. These issues are still involved in our discussions of gifted children and the necessity of special educational programs versus mainstream educational programs for the gifted.

There was very little interest in or new ideas about genius between the end of the eighteenth century and the middle of the nineteenth century. Sir Francis Galton's *Hereditary Genius* (1869) is a landmark for several reasons. First, it successfully applied statistics and empirical reasoning to a major problem in human affairs: the possibility and extent to which hereditary processes determine human capacity and careers. A second important feature is Galton's effort to measure the allusive and speculative concept "genius." Galton focused his interest not only on living persons but on the observable achievements of their lives. For the first time, genius was treated as an observable, measurable human attribute. Although there was an apparent social-class bias in Galton's selection of persons of genius, and although evidence of racial prejudice appears in the later chapters, Galton did clarify the concept of genius and render it amenable to empirical investigation.

A third important feature of Galton's work is his methodology. It is the psychometric tradition and continues to this day. Its major practitioner in the study of genius, other than Galton, is Lewis Terman, who undertook the monumental study entitled *Genetic Studies of Genius*. In 1925 he published the first of five volumes regarding the prevalence and developmental characteristics of over one thousand intellectually-gifted children. Volume 2, authored by Catherine Cox and entitled *The Early Mental Traits of Three Hundred Geniuses* (Cox, 1926), describes the intellectual development and personal characteristics of historically famous persons. One of Cox's major achievements is to show that persons who have achieved great fame in various fields differ in *both* their intellectual development (as represented by IQ) and their salient personality characteristics. This finding has been elaborated in subsequent research (Barron, 1969). Between the 1920s and the 1950s, the psychometric study of genius concentrated primarily on the behavioral, cognitive, and personality concomitants of high IQ scores. Some leaders in this effort were Terman and his co-workers (Terman, 1925; Burks, Jensen, and Terman, 1930; Terman and Oden, 1947, 1959), Hollingworth (1926, 1942; Hollingworth and Cobb, n.d.), Burt (1975), Pressey (1949), and Torrance (1971). More recently, Stanley and his group at Johns Hopkins (Stanley, 1976; Stanley, George, and Solano, 1977; Stanley, Keating, and Fox, 1974) have attempted to identify and understand the mathematically gifted preadolescent, while synthesizing many of the early insights into a pioneering educational research program.

A second major tradition in the study of genius is the linking of genius to madness. This view has survived into the present, although it languished until the nineteenth century (when it became the predominant view of genius). Some famous expositions are those of Kretschmer (1931), Lange-Eichbaum (1932), Lombroso (1895), Moreau de Tours (1885), Morel (1857), and Freud (1913). It should be noted that the one person, Freud, who did more than anyone else to give a rational and empirical basis to this view of genius also produced a book typical of this genre. Although Ellis (1904) published a study showing that only 4% of his 1030 genius-like subjects could be classified clearly as insane or psychologically pathological, many persons, lay and professional have remained relatively unconvinced. Later, one of Terman's students, White (1930), investigated the incidence of psychopathology among Cox's and Ellis's subjects, again with little evidence for equating genius and psychopathology. . . .

Like Galton, Freud brought new techniques and concepts to the study of genius. Freud's monumental breakthrough is that he was able to show that persons of genius can be "rationalized." That is to say, their earliest development and much of their career can be understood in psychological terms, rather than by invoking highly inflammatory labels or preternatural forces for purposes of explanation. Moreover, both Freud and Galton contributed to our present perspective of eminent persons as being different from other persons in degree rather than in their nature. After Freud, all persons' development was to be understood as lawful and more or less alike. Both men focused on famous men's families as the most critical set of psychological factors involved in high-level achievement. Thus, Freud, like Galton, helped to bring geniuses into alignment with less extraordinary persons, although Freud assumed that they were necessarily neurotic. In his study of genius, Freud focused on the individual's efforts — consciously and unconsciously — to overcome personal and interpersonal obstacles. After Freud, it has been a standard practice in the study of important and/or highly creative persons to investigate their intrapersonal dynamics and interpersonal conflicts for clues to their unusual motivation and careers (see, for example, Lowenfeld, 1941).

Overall, one can say that beginning from the middle of the nineteenth century to this day, most persons deeply interested in the study of genius have worked in the empirical tradition. The study of genius has taken a definite turn toward studying *living* eminent persons, a major change from speculations and predominantly literary studies of the famous. Quite recently, however, with the application of some very imaginative statistical analysis to archival data, Simonton (1975a, 1975b, 1976, 1977) has developed important information on some of the basic historical and sociological parameters to extraordinary achievement.

As part of the methodological change over the years, most researchers have quietly dropped the term *genius* and replaced it with *eminent person.* In addition, two different traditional orientations have based their research on different populations. Psychoanalysts have mainly studied famous artists, and researchers with a psychometric and more eclectic viewpoint have mainly studied eminent scientists. It is becoming clear that the findings on one population are not necessarily applicable to the other population and that their early family experiences as well as their cognitive talents differ from one another.

This historical review has shown us a number of significant changes in our thinking about and the techniques for studying persons of genius. But it does not indicate what we have learned because of these changes. For this one must look closely at the work of the past thirty years.

Much of the work in this area has been to rectify the early problems of thinking and fact regarding genius. An excellent example of the constructive nature of the changes undergone and the types of information generated from them is Anne Roe's research in the early 1950s. Instead of studying "genius" or geniuses, Roe (1951a, 1951b, 1953) selected a number of unquestionably eminent living scientists for extensive observation and interview regarding their early development and careers. While confirming some of Cox's (1926) earlier work, Roe's research clearly showed for the first time that, while high intelligence is a necessary ingredient to first-rate scientific work, a complex pattern of deep commitment and long work hours is equally essential. She also notes among her samples a preponderance of middle-class professional fathers, 72% first borns or only sons, a large percentage of early parental deaths, early social isolation from subjects' peers, and the importance of doing research in high school or college with a sympathetic teacher. Together, these data strongly suggest that a cognitive style of thinking congruent with science; a family that esteems work and success; a family experience, such as early parental death, that requires coming to terms in the early years with strong feelings of loss; estrangement; and the discovery and confirmation of one's talents to do and to enjoy research in an area of interest are critical in getting one in a career position for achieving later eminence. Roe also found that eminent scientists in biology, physics, and the social sciences differ in their early home life (social scientists come from more emotionally binding homes), time of career decisions (social scientists decide later and after seriously considering literature), and peer relationships (social scientists are more involved with peers and data much earlier than physical scientists). Eiduson (1962) and Chambers (1964) have elaborated on Roe's research, exploring in more depth and detail the personality dimension of scientific eminence. For example, Eiduson found that researchers had few strong positive ties to either parent and enjoyed fantasy and intellectual pursuits at an early age. Chambers (1964) studied scientists in different fields and, like Roe, found differences among them. For example, he found that pscyhologists are more impulsive and introverted than chemists and tend to come from more involving, affectionate families — even though these homes, as Roe had reported earlier, were at times emotionally binding.

MacKinnon (1962, 1963, 1965, 1975), in his work with architects, also has elaborated on Roe's work, exploring more extensively the personality dimension of their eminence. He found that architects are not asocial but do value their independence and autonomy, their productivity, their commitment to intellectual matters and esthetically enjoyable experiences, and their creativity. Like the research scientists studied by Roe and by Eiduson, they did not all come from tranquil homes; some homes were marked with tension or brutality. They are able to tolerate tension, are emotionally expressive and uninhibited, and came from homes which one or both parents were artistic in interest and skill.

In their research, both Roe and MacKinnon relied on their subjects' retrospection; therefore, their results are prone to the problems in such efforts. Nonetheless, each solidified one important change in the study of genius: a merging of psychometric analysis with a concern for the dynamics of an eminent person's development, career choices, and professional performances.

There is one important point to keep in mind regarding such research. Although it offers many interesting insights into the lives and careers of eminent persons, it does not inform us about the persons in the same field or vocation who do not achieve eminence. Without sufficient control groups and longitudinal designs in the study of geniuses, we shall always lack substantial information about the factors and experiences that influence one person's successful career and another's lack of success.

Additionally, there is the problem of important lines of investigation being initiated only to be prematurely dropped. One unfortunate example is the possibility of significant cognitive and educational differences operating among children of different levels of giftedness. Such possibilities were suggested in Cox's (1926) research and discussed even earlier by philosophers for centuries. . . .

Overall, the bulk of these studies demonstrate five salient points: (1) children of exceptionally gifted IQ often go through their cognitive development faster than children of "average giftedness"; (2) exceptionally gifted children can be identified by both the accelerated rate and range of abstract academic subjects they can master; (3) exceptionally gifted children usually began to speak and learned to read at very early ages; (4) there appears more heterogeneity among gifted children than is often acknowledged (Albert, 1971; Willerman, 1979); and (5) the exceptionally gifted are no more distinguished by their originality than are the gifted (giftedness being primarily a matter of intelligence and academic ability). In recent years,there has been an unfortunate application of "giftedness" not only to high IQ scores but to creative ability — unfortunate because research has shown that intelligence and creative ability are almost entirely independent of one another when subjects' IQs are in the gifted or higher range and that neither can be measured adequately by the same instruments (Albert, 1969; Guilford, 1959; MacKinnon, 1962; Wallach, 1971).

Another influential line of research has followed from Guilford's (1959, 1966, 1967) distinction between convergent and divergent cognitive styles. Convergent processes are involved mostly in one's search for clear, specific answers, processes probably most clearly instrumental in answering multiple-choice questions. Divergent processes generate more associational, less restricted, more personal responses; these most clearly operate in answering open-ended questions, for which there is no one best answer. A number of researchers into originality or creativity were inspired by Guilford's work; perhaps the most prominent are Getzels and Jackson (1962), Hudson (1967), Wallach and Kogan (1965), and Wallach and Wing (1969). Guilford's work encouraged professionals to rethink definitions of creativity and to consider whether creativity differs from intelligence and how the two concepts are to be measured.

Critical Discussion

General Areas of Concern

. . . Two forces brought "creativity" to the fore: the arrival of psychoanalysis right after World War II as a major theory in child psychology as well as in clinical psychology and the development of measurement techniques during World War II. Psychoanalysis brought an interest in the lives of famous persons through its use of them as examples of the power of the theory to explain many facets of human development and different types of behavior, especially of geniuses. Their creative behavior was the most intriguing aspect under scrutiny. The questions of the source of creative ability and of why only some persons were noticeably creative led to an interest in the antecedents of this ability. Although the topic of genius and geniuses were then of little professional interest, creativity and its nurturance was an area of very high professional interest. Along with this interest occurred an awareness that it was difficult to measure adequately the highest levels of intelligence among groups of eminent persons. Barron, MacKinnon, and Roe soon discovered that eminent persons were creative *and* exceptionally gifted intellectually. (One is tempted to say this was a rediscovery, for Cox, 1926; Jones, 1923; and Rockwell, 1927, had made somewhat the same point earlier but with much less data.) To put the matter simply, it was repeatedly shown that it takes high intellectual abilities and other skills to be unusually creative and to become eminent.

The low, often insignificant, correlations between some measures of creativity and intelligence for homogeneous high-ability groups soon led to the belief that creativity and intelligence were almost completely distinct from one another and, of all things, that intelligence might be less important than creativity in the production of original products and the solution of complex problems. This proposition is difficult to accept when one realizes that the median IQ for eminent persons in a variety of fields appears to be in the range of 145–150, an IQ significantly higher than (1) the 120 IQ accepted as the threshhold above which creativity and intelligence are believed to become separate cognitive domains and (2) . . . the 130 IQ often used as the measure of giftedness by state educational programs. However, it is well below the time IQs of Cox's 300 historical geniuses; according to her calculations that was 160 IQ, with many of her subjects having IQs above 180 and only a few with an IQ below 140. Some years later, Hollingworth (1942) agreed that 180 IQ was most likely the level for "true genius."

It is important to be clear on one fact here: the IQ is an index, one score representing a subject's performances on a variety of measures of different aptitudes. Increasingly, it is becoming harder to hold that a single IQ test can either measure all of the essential cognitive processes involved in what we commonly think of as intelligent behavior or that its final score can adequately give us all the critical information we hope to ascertain from it. Galton long ago made intelligence − not IQ − an initial feature to the achievement of eminence and every major researcher in eminence since has supported his viewpoint. Unfortunately, what was not being asked in the 1950s or 1960s often enough or forcefully enough was a serious question, namely what facilitates the creative use of intelligence. . . .

Elaboration on Critical Points

Part of the present difficulty in sorting out what is intelligence and what is creativity originates in some major research by Getzels and Jackson (1962); unfortunately, many read it as supporting the emphasis upon nonintellectual abilities in the production of original responses and a belittlement of intelligence's role in such performance among groups of extremely intelligent adolescents (mean IQ 150) and extremely creative adolescents (mean IQ 127). Getzels and Jackson's measure of convergent processes (which they took to represent intelligence) and divergent processes (representing creativity), as well as their description of their two experimental samples, led initially to the belief that there are substantial differences between those subjects who perform well on divergent tests and those who perform well on convergent tests. When one realizes that *all* of Getzels and Jackson's subjects were intellectually gifted and that the academic achievement of both experimental groups was higher than that of their school controls and equal to one another's, some of their main points became more questionable than enlightening. Without any follow-up of these subjects there is no way of knowing whether any of the reported differences among their subjects have long-term career or personal significance.

We would suggest, along with Hudson (1967), that what has been demonstrated is that there are different sets of interest, personal values, and cognitive styles operating among highly intelligent persons who achieve eminence in a variety of fields. If this is true, a number of research findings fall into place, including those of Getzels and Jackson. There are some important personality fators and differences in the development and careers of creative persons, as opposed to their less creative controls. One long-term project on the empirical correlates of genius (Albert, 1969, 1971, 1975, 1978, 1980) has shown that time after time (1) persons who attain outstanding eminence usually are involved in their future careers early in adolescence (recall the previous statement that the higher the IQ, the earlier this foreshadowing); (2) that such persons, as a group, not only begin their careers earlier than their peers, but are more productive in them for longer periods of time; and (3) that this lengthy, continuous, innovative productivity involves such personality attributes as moderately high needs to achieve, to be independent, and to be innovative, as well as high persistence, self-reliance, a sense of responsibility to one's own interests and career, and with a sense of social responsibility. Many of these traits are recognizable as aspects of the high ego strength that Barron (1969) clearly identified among his samples of eminent persons. What we find, when putting these research findings together, is that eminent persons are very intelligent, well-educated and informed, hard-working, and willing to take risks of being wrong and/or different in order to be independent and innovative. These are abilities and characteristics that twenty-five years of research has shown to be characteristic of eminent persons and rarely found in combination.

This complexity of ability and personality also appears to be the result of long development in rather distinctive family environments (Barron, 1969; MacKinnon, 1962, 1963, 1965; McCurdy, 1957; Oden, 1968; Roe, 1951a, 1951b, 1953; Simonton, 1976). When we look closely at these family environments, we notice several recurrent characteristics. Many eminent persons do not have close or stable relationships with their parents, or their parents with one another, a factor more apparent for persons achieving eminence in non-scientific fields than for those eminent in the sciences. A complicated, tense parent–child relationship helps the eminent-to-be person learn how to cope with tensions, complexity, and a sense of being quite special to usually one, but sometimes both, parents (Albert, 1978, 1980). In cases where the eminent-to-be person is highly scientific or mathematically gifted, he or she is likely to describe their parent–child relationship as one of distance more than of hostility; where the gifts are more artistic, the child is likely to have been extremely involved with one or both parents, usually at different points in the child's development, and this closeness was in some cases reinforced by the early death of an older sibling, usually a brother (Albert, 1980). Because these experiences in a family occur together infrequently, one can appreciate why the combination of high intelligence, abundant talent, and strong personality found among many eminent persons is itself something of a rarity. Among the frequently noted characteristics of geniuses and eminent persons from Galton's original work (1869) to the present has been their extraordinarily high level of "natural ability" or intelligence (Barron, 1969; Cox, 1926; Roe, 1951a, 1951b, 1953;

Willerman, 1979). There is no substantial reason for disparaging intelligence's contribution in such productive, creative persons.

Many studies during the 1950s, 1960s and early 1970s have shown that it is a relatively rare combination of gifted intelligence and cognitive flexibility — coupled with strong, clear interests, moderately high needs for achievement and independence, and long-term family stimulation and support for such development and thinking — that underlies an adolescent's ability to perform well academically and "creatively". What Getzels and Jackson showed within a cross-sectional study of adolescents, Oden (1968) later demonstrated in a major 40-year follow-up of Terman's gifted children. Perhaps the two most striking differences between the most and the least successful of these subjects were (1) their families' stance on education and cultural experience and (2) the different degrees of family stability and cohesion. The more successful subjects came from relatively more stable families, and their parents were better educated and clearly valued education and cultural experience for themselves and their children. It appears that authoritative, career-successful parents with high self-esteem generally have children who also are generally competent and academically successful and show promise of some adult achievement and success. Where parents are themselves noticeably creative, this ability too gets carried into the children's development, so that it is also a mistaken idea that families cannot tolerate more than one creative member. To the contrary, as Galton first showed, many families — for example, the Churchills and Kennedys in politics, the Comptons in science, and the Bachs in music — appear to be fertile environments for developing creative abilities. Since one often observes the presence of similar abilities and talents among members of a family, it is possible that hereditary factors are involved in talents and cognitive aptitudes.

From the earliest research of Terman, then, various characteristics have been consistently identified with intellectually-gifted children. In recent years this research, like that describing creative persons, has presented very few surprises (see Stein, 1974). Good summaries of these "standard" findings are by Carroll and Larring (1974) and Torrance (1971). And, as was noted earlier, a composite has begun to be developed for geniuses (Albert, 1971, 1975, 1978; Simonton, 1978).

Intellectually-gifted children are healthier physically and psychologically than less gifted children. They walk, speak, and tend to read earlier, often with much less tutorage. Other characteristics that identify gifted children are their variety of interests and long pursuit of them. Another finding of particular note is gifted children's early ability to organize, to structure, and to synthesize complex and abstract ideas. A stable finding, since Barron (1969), among noticeably creative persons of all ages is their pursuit and use of stimulus material that is complex, initially in disorder, and unclear in its meaning. The similarities between the gifted and the creative in this regard should be evident. Research on eminent adults presents some of the above characteristics plus others, usually emphasizing a daring independent mindedness; a tolerance of differences, and an intuitiveness in selection of problems and methods of solution. Creative persons also are less stereotyped in their sexual identities than less creative men or women, although neither homosexuality nor lesbianism has been strongly associated with creativity or eminence. Theoretical and aesthetic values appear to guide creative behavior; religious, political, and economic values are quite secondary.

Thus, one sees in the behavior of the creative adult that some of the early cognitive traits of the intellectually gifted child have come to fruition, along with the progressive acquisition of a specific set of personality attributes, highly focused motivations, and values that guide and facilitate a fuller employment of gifted cognitive skills (see Welsh, 1977). Such a constellation often puts a strain on creative persons internally and creates cleavage between them and some significant part of their environments. Thus, it is not surprising to find that creative persons *are* tense, irritable, and "pulled in" while engaged in creative operations. Clearly, it is in the *emotional* domain that creative, eminent persons are most distinctive from their equally intelligent but less creative and less eminent controls. Nonetheless, another personality trait shown by creative persons is their unusual ability to withstand long periods of loneliness, tension, and emotional strain while in pursuit of their interests and careers; they rarely become severely psychologically ill. Moreover, creative persons, from late childhood on, often exhibit an explicit sense of responsibility to both their careers (or interests) and to others. They are rarely as irresponsible or impulsive as often described in popular literature. In none of the above descriptions does one find justification for the instability and irresponsible, bizarre behavior that was often attributed as the mark of genius.

Personal Views and Recommendations

What is now most needed are longitudinal studies of exceptionally gifted children and their families, for these are apparently the richest source of future eminent persons. Only such research can reveal what, in the long run, significantly contributes to or impedes such development. Without such research, there will be but piecemeal knowledge of some very important persons and processes. Also, Stanley (1976) has shown that whenever research has asked specific questions of a specific population and used reliable instruments specific to the behaviors in question, scientific progress occurs. Progress in the study of genius has come only through this effort and not through the more dramatic earlier descriptions of putative genius, no matter how entertaining or well written they may be (Sarton, 1921).

Application to Particular Variables

Age

The more precocious the child is in his intellectual development, display of talent, or artistic performance, the earlier one usually finds that these are reliable and valid signs of giftedness (Albert, 1971; Willerman and Fiedler, 1977). In terms of eminent persons, it has been found that they, too, often show these signs of early giftedness *and* also often begin their careers in which they achieved eminence at a younger than usual age (Albert, 1971, 1975; Cox, 1926; Lehman, 1953; Simonton, 1975a). The rule appears to be: "the more gifted the child, the younger the career starts and the higher the attainment."

Sex

Far more men appear to have achieved high eminence and are studied in regard to it. What is known of genius is overwhelmingly male oriented. All major works on genius or eminence have been, until recently, much more concerned with men of eminence than with eminent women.

Education

The idea persists that geniuses need little or no formal education. This notion stems from an unclear idea of what is a genius and from the "unexpected" quality of many important discoveries and artistic creations. Although there is no one standard research to refute this proposition, case studies and empirical observations of eminent persons in many fields invariably show that such persons are usually better educated than the average person of their time and socioeconomic circumstances. What one often finds is the presence of a highly involved parent or other family member starting the eminent-to-be person in his or her field, followed by a significantly involved teacher or tutor who continues the instruction and also encourages the ambitions of the pupil (see Zuckerman, 1977). There is no evidence for believing that ignorance leads to eminence or worthwhile careers; there is evidence for believing that a sound but not binding education will give substance to early interests and direction to giftedness.

Socioeconomic Status

Although one often hears or reads dramatic stories of the poverty-stricken child who becomes a great person, the evidence regarding the socioeconomic backgrounds of eminent persons — evidence from Galton (1869) through Cox (1926) to Roe (1951a, 1951b, 1953), MacKinnon (1963), and Oden (1968), up to more recent research on eminent persons (Simonton, 1975b; Zuckerman,

1977) — shows that most eminent persons come from middle- or higher-placed families. Eminent persons usually come from families that are aware of the opportunities for further advancement and/or service to their communities. This characteristic fits with the theme of prosocial responsibility so often noticed in the careers of eminent persons, although their products may disturb the equanimity of their field or times. When one looks closely into the history of the families of eminent persons, one often finds that there has been a "build-up" of specific talents and interests over several generations. This "build-up" is through the marriage of talented persons and their sharing of interests, ambitions, and values. The child who becomes an eminent person in later life is often the recipient of both this hereditary and family-trained high ability as is the case of Sir Francis Galton himself (Albert, 1980; Burt, 1975; Galton, 1869). Once one uses other criteria besides income, one sees that the families from which most eminent persons come are psychologically stimulating *and* relatively stable. These familes appear to be well educated and well above the poverty level of subsistence. It is true that some great men and women (mainly in the arts and in sports) have been orphans or from poor families; when one connects what has already been said of education as well as age and sex, it should be clear that the family is not only a genetic pool for intelligence and talents but an educational environment of immense complexity and power.

Vocation

It has been pointed out that eminent persons are not merely lucky but represent the end product of many complicated long-term developmental processes. Such persons, as mentioned, are more than intelligent; they are usually exceptionally involved and educated in their field and well suited psychologically to its requirements and stresses. Intelligence alone will not lead to eminence, nor will an interest in something. Instead, a combination of gifted cognitive abilities, personality traits, and values energizes and sustains eminent careers.

It is evident that different general fields have different cognitive and personality requirements for success in them and draw their more successful recruits from different types of early backgrounds and temperaments. The better the match between the requirements of a particular field and an interested person with high intelligence, the more likely eminence will occur in that career. One confounding factor in making this vocational choice is the fact that gifted persons, children and adults, have a wider range of interests than most of their less gifted contemporaries and usually more than one strong talent. Because of this, one would think it would be difficult for a very gifted person to choose the best vocation. Perhaps so, but one notices in the histories of eminent persons a steady, active search for the vocation that will allow them to integrate their interests and talents. The careers of some very famous persons (for instance, Darwin and Freud) are the outcome of such endeavors over several decades.

In the main, eminent persons in the physical sciences and the performing arts appear to show clear indications of requisite abilities early in life. They also make earlier career decisions and thus earlier career starts than persons who become eminent in other fields. To a large extent this is a function of the clearer, earlier, spontaneous appearance of most mathematical and artistic talents than is the case for general giftedness. Talents other than mathematics or the performing arts appear to reach their more mature levels of development later and to be more "open" to the vicissitudes of experience, education, and opportunity than either mathematical or artistic giftedness in attaining the necessary levels of development for achieving eminence; they appear to require a wider range of experience in their development and for their proper early identification. The attainment of genius, rare as it is, is much more a function of early giftedness being nurtured, well educated, and specifically encouraged than it is a gift of the gods, a product of madness, or a matter of luck, as was commonly believed through the first half of this century.

References

ALBERT, R. S. (1969) Genius: present-day status of the concept and its implication for the study of creativity and giftedness. *American Psychologist,* 24, 743–753.
ALBERT, R. S. (1971) Cognitive development and parental loss among the gifted, the exceptionally gifted and the creative. *Psychological Reports,* 29, 19–26.
ALBERT, R. S. (1975) Toward a behavioural definition of genius. *American Psychologist,* 30, 140–151.
ALBERT, R. S. (1978) Observations and suggestions regarding giftedness, familial influence and the attainment of eminence. *Gifted Child Quarterly,* 22, 201–211.
ALBERT, R. S. (1980) Family positions and the attainment of eminence: a study of special family positions and special family experiences. *Gifted Child Quarterly,* 24, 87–95.
ANASTASI, A. and SCHAEFER, C. E. (1971) Note on the concepts of creativity and intelligence. *Journal of Creative Behavior,* 5, 113–116.
BARRON, F. (1969) *Creative Person and Creative Process.* New York: Holt, Rinehart and Winston.
BAUMRIND, D. (1967) Child care practices anteceding three patterns of preschool behavior. *Genetic Psychology Monographs,* 75, 43–88.
BAUMRIND, D. (1971) Current patterns of parental authority. *Developmental Psychology Monographs,* 1(1), 1–103.
BURKS, B. S., JENSEN, D. W. and TERMAN, L. M. (1930) *Genetic Studies of Genius.* Vol. 3: *The Promise of Youth.* Stanford: Stanford University Press.
BURT, C. (1975) *The Gifted Child.* London: Hodder and Stoughton.
CARROLL, J. L. and LARRING, L. R. (1974) Giftedness and creativity: recent attempts at definition: a literature review. *Gifted Child Quarterly,* 18, 23–29.
CHAMBERS, J. (1964) Relating personality and biographical factors to scientific creativity. *Psychological Monographs,* 78(7, Whole No. 584).
COX, C. M. (1926) *Genetic Studies of Genius.* Vol. 2: *The Early Mental Traits of Three Hundred Geniuses.* Stanford: Stanford University Press.
DAVIDSON, H. (1931) An experimental study of bright, average, and dull children at the four year mental level. *Genetic Psychology Monographs,* 9, 119–289.
EIDUSON, B. T. (1962) *Scientists: Their Psychological World.* New York: Basic Books.
ELLIS, H. (1904) *A Study of British Genius.* London: Hurst and Blackett.
ERIKSON, E. H. (1958) *Young Man Luther: A Study in Psychoanalysis and History.* New York: Norton.

ERIKSON, E. H. (1969) *Gandhi's Truth.* New York: Norton.
FREUD, S. (1947) *Leonardo da Vinci: A Study in Sexuality* [1913]. New York: Random House.
GALLAGHER, J. J. (1975) *Teaching the Gifted Child.* Boston: Allyn & Bacon.
GALTON, F. (1869) *Hereditary Genius: An Inquiry Into Its Laws and Consequences.* New York: Macmillan.
GETZELS, J. W. and JACKSON, P. W. (1962) *Creativity and Intelligence: Explorations with Gifted Students.* New York: Wiley.
GRAY, C. E. (1966) A measurement of creativity in Western Civilization. *American Anthropologist,* 68, 1384–1417.
GUILFORD, J. P. (1950) Creativity. *American Psychologist,* 5, 444–454.
GUILFORD, J. P. (1959) Traits of Creativity. In H. H. Anderson (Ed.), *Creativity and Its Cultivation,* New York: Harper & Row.
GUILFORD, J. P. (1966) Intelligence: 1965 model. *American Psychologist,* 21, 20–26.
GUILFORD, J. P. (1967) Creativity, Yesterday, today and tomorrow. *Journal of Creative Behavior,* 1, 3–14.
GUILFORD, J. P. (1971) Some misconceptions regarding measurement of creative talents. *Journal of Creative Behavior,* 5, 77–87.
HILDRETH, G. (1938) The educational achievement of gifted children. *Child Development,* 9, 365–371.
HILDRETH, G. (1954) Three gifted children: a developmental study. *Journal of Genetic Psychology,* 85, 239–262.
HOLLINGWORTH, L. S. (1926) *Gifted children: The Nature and Nurture.* New York: Macmillan.
HOLLINGWORTH, L. S. (1942) *Children Above 180 IQ Stanford-Binet.* New York: World Book.
HOLLINGWORTH, L. S. and COBB, M. W. (undated) Children clustering at 165 IQ and children clustering at 145 IQ compared for three years in achievement. In *Twenty-Seventh Yearbook of the National Society for the Study of Education.* Pt. 3. Chicago, IL.
HUDSON, L. (1967) *Contrary Imaginations.* Middlesex: Penguin Books.
JONCICH, G. (1964) A culture-bound concept of creativity: a social historian's critique, centering on a recent American report. *Educational Report,* 14, 133–143.
JONES, A. M. (1923) The superior child: a series of case studies. *Psychological Clinic,* 15, 1–8, 116–123, 130–137.
KRETSCHMER, E. (1931) *The Psychology of Men of Genius.* New York: Harcourt Brace Jovanovich.
KROEBER, A. (1944) *Configurations of Culture Growth.* Berkeley: University of California Press.
LANGE-EICHBAUM, W. (1932) *The Problem of Genius.* New York: Macmillan.
LEHMAN, H. D. (1953) *Age and Achievement.* Princeton: Princeton University Press.
LOMBROSO, C. (1895) *The Man of Genius.* New York: Scribner.
LORGE, I. and HOLLINGWORTH, L. (1936) Adult status of highly intelligent children. *Journal of Genetic Psychology,* 63, 215–226.
LOWENFELD, H. (1941) Psychic trauma and productive experience in the artist. *Psychoanalytic Quarterly,* 10, 116–130.
McCURDY, H. G. (1957) The childhood pattern of genius. *Journal of Elisha Mitchell Science Society,* 73, 448–462.
MacKINNON, D. W. (1962) The nature and nurture of creative talent. *American Psychologist,* 17, 484–495.
MacKINNON, D. W. (1963) Creativity and images of the self. In R. W. White (Ed.), *The Study of Lives.* New York: Atherton.
MacKINNON, D. W. (1965) Personality and the realization of creative potential. *American Psychologist,* 20, 273–281.
MacKINNON, D. W. (1975) IPAR's contribution to the conceptualization and study of creativity. In I. A. Taylor and J. W. Getzels (Eds), *Perspectives in Creativity.* Chicago: Aldine.

MEEKER, M. (1968) Differential syndromes of giftedness and curriculum planning: a four-year follow-up. *Journal of Special Education*, 2, 185–194.

MILLER, M. B. and BIALER, I. (1970) Intellectual deviancy. In H. C. Haywood (Ed.), *Psychometric Intelligence*. New York: Appleton-Century-Crofts.

MOREAU DE TOURS, P. (1885) *Fous et Bauffons*. Paris: Baillière.

MOREL, A. (1857) *Traité des Dégénérescenses de l'Espèce Humaine*. Paris: Baillière.

NAHM, M. C. (1956) *The Artist as Creator: An Essay of Human Freedom*. Baltimore: Johns Hopkins University Press.

NAROLL, R. and others. (1971) Creativity: a cross-historical pilot survey. *Journal of Cross-Cultural Psychology*, 2, 181–188.

ODEN, M. (1968) The fulfillment of promise: 40-year follow-up. *Genetic Psychology Monographs*, 77(1), 3–93.

PRESSEY, S. L. (1949) *Educational Acceleration: Appraisals and Basic Problems*. Columbus: Ohio University Press.

ROCKWELL, J. G. (1927) Genius and the IQ. *Psychological Review*, 34, 377–384.

ROE, A. (1951a) A psychological study of eminent biologists. *Psychological Monographs*, 65(14, Whole No. 331).

ROE, A. (1951b) A psychological study of physical scientists. *Genetic Psychology Monographs*, 43, 121–235.

ROE, A. (1953) A psychological study of eminent psychologists and anthropologists, and a comparison with biological and physical scientists. *Psychological Monographs*, 67(2, Whole No. 352).

SARTON, G. (1921) Evariste Galois. *Scientific Monthly*, 13, 363–375.

SIMONTON, D. K. (1975a) Age and literary creativity: a cross-cultural and transhistorical survey. *Journal of Cross-Cultural Psychology*, 6, 259–277.

SIMONTON, D. K. (1975b) Sociocultural context of individual creativity: a transhistorical times-series analysis. *Journal of Personality and Social Psychology*, 32, 1119–1133.

SIMONTON, D. K. (1976) Biographical determinants of achieved eminence: a multivariate approach to the Cox data. *Journal of Personality and Social Psychology*, 33, 218–226.

SIMONTON, D. K. (1977) Creative productivity, age, and stress: a biographical time-series analysis of 10 classical composers. *Journal of Personality and Social Psychology*, 35, 79–804.

SIMONTON, D. K. (1978) The eminent genius in history: the critical role of creative development. *Gifted Child Quarterly*, 22, 187–195.

STANLEY, J. C. (1976) Test better finder of great math talent than teachers are. *American Psychologist*, 31, 313–314.

STANLEY, J. C., GEORGE, W. C. and SOLANO, C. H. (Eds.). (1977) *The Gifted and the Creative: A Fifty-Year Perspective*. Baltimore: Johns Hopkins University Press.

STANLEY, J. C., KEATING, D. P. and FOX, L. H. (Eds.) (1974) *Mathematical Talent: Discovery, Description, and Development*. Baltimore: Johns Hopkins University Press.

STEIN. M. I. (1974) *Stimulating Creativity*. Vol. 1: *Individual Differences*. New York: Academic Press.

TERMAN, L. M. (1925) *Genetic Studies of Genius*. Vol. 1: *Mental and Physical Traits of a Thousand Gifted Children*. Stanford: Stanford University Press.

TERMAN, L. M. and ODEN, M. (1947) *Genetic Studies of Genius*. Vol. 4: *The Gifted Child Grows Up*. Stanford: Stanford University Press.

TERMAN, L. M. and ODEN, M. (1959) *Genetic Studies of Genius*. Vol. 5: *The Gifted Child at Mid-Life*. Stanford: Stanford University Press.

TORRANCE, E. P. (1971) Psychology of gifted children and youth. In W. M. Cruickshank (Ed.), *Psychology of Exceptional Children and Youth*. (3rd ed.) Englewood Cliffs: Prentice-Hall.

WALLACH, M. A. (1971) *The Intelligence/Creativity Distinction*. Morristown: General Learning Press.

WALLACH, M. A. and KOGAN, N. (1965) *Modes of Thinking in Young Children: A Study of the Creativity-Intelligence Distinction*. New York: Holt, Rinehart and Winston.

WALLACH, M. A. and WING, C. W. (1969) *The Talented Student: A Validation of the Creativity-Intelligence Distinction*. New York: Holt, Rinehart and Winston.

WELSH, G. S. (1977) Personality correlates of intelligence and creativity in gifted adolescents. In J. C. Stanley, W. C. George and C. H. Solano (Eds), *The Gifted and the Creative: A Fifty-Year Perspective*. Baltimore: Johns Hopkins University Press.

WHITE, R. K. (1930) Note on the psychopathology of genius. *Journal of Social Psychology*, **1**, 311–315.

WILLERMAN, L. (1979) *The Psychology of Individual and Group Differences*. San Francisco: Freeman.

WILLERMAN, L. and FIEDLER, M. F. (1977) Intellectually precocious preschool children: early development and later intellectual accomplishments. *Journal of Genetic Psychology*, **131**, 13–20.

ZUCKERMAN, H. (1977) *Scientific Elite*. New York: Free Press.

4

The Mad Genius Controversy*

G. BECKER

THE "MODERN" conception of genius — as the manifestation of the highest degree of innate original ability in individuals — was popularized at the start of the eighteenth century and marks the culmination of an intermittent intellectual debate that had its beginnings with the Renaissance. . . .

It was the evolvement of the modern conception of genius during the eighteenth century that, perhaps more than any other single factor, was central to the eventual victory of the moderns, and made originality the definitive mark of all superior intellectual production. The definition of the genius as an innately gifted individual with an extraordinary capacity for imaginative creation, original thought, invention, and discovery, established him as the foremost enemy of tradition, imitation, and the conventional order. . . . This stress on originality — the foremost attribute of the truly great man — established the genius as the relentless destroyer of tradition and the enemy of conventional forms. In this sense, he could be seen as an agent of change and revolution. The Romantics, whether or not they were aware of the perils of his role, sought to legitimatize the prestige and power of the genius by suggesting that the extraordinary man was somehow destined to perform a sacred function. . . .

In his critical reply to Nordau's *Degeneration,* George Bernard Shaw sought to demonstrate the wholesomeness and sanity of modern artistic and literary expression, and proposed that the genius, far from being dangerously out of step with contemporary values, is overwhelmingly conservative by nature. He observed (Shaw, 1908: 18–19):

> The greatest possible difference in conduct between a genius and his comtemporaries is so small that it is always difficult to persuade the people who are in daily contact with the gifted one that he is anybody in particular: all the instances to the contrary (Gorki scandalizing New York, for example) being cases in which the genius is in conflict, not with contemporary feeling in his own class, but with some institution which is far behind the times, like the institution of marriage in Russia (to put it no nearer home). In really contemporary situations, your genius is ever 1 part genius and 99 parts Tory.

Because the genius, in his conduct and expression of opinion, is typically in conflict only with some institution that is "far behind the times," observed

*Reprinted from George Becker, *The Mad Genius Controversy* pp. 107–121, 126–129, copyright (*ca.*) 1978 by Sage Publications, with permission of the publisher and the author.

Shaw (1908: 19), "it is necessary for the welfare of society that genius should be privileged to utter sedition, to blaspheme, to outrage good taste, to corrupt the youthful mind, and, generally to scandalize its uncles.". . .

What distinguished those assessments of genius that defined the great man as a "blessing" and a responsible agent of progress and modernity from those that viewed him as a fundamentally dangerous and unstable element in the history of man, was the tendency of the latter to regard the genius' alleged propensity for dangerous thought and action as rooted in a pathological condition. The genius, more than most other men, was seen as a victim of compulsion — a compulsion dictated by his own particular constitution. His works were, therefore, the expressions not of well-reasoned intention or choice, but, instead, the products of a mind — bent on originality — which lacked the elements necessary to impose "responsible" direction. . . .

This tendency, common in the mad genius literature, to link certain types of artistic and intellectual expression with various forms and degrees of pathology, deserved to be seen as an attempt to control or monitor the direction of intellectual change and innovation. . . .

However, the post-Napoleonic period, informed by the "excesses" of the French Revolution and experiencing the revolutionary activity of 1820, 1830, and 1848–1849, saw the emergence of an increasingly reactionary mood and a growing tendency to view the *"Originalgenie"* as a potentially dangerous and unstabilizing force. . . . Tocqueville, for example, commenting specifically on the role of the French men of letters in "fermenting" the Revolution of 1789, made the following observation in *The Old Regime and the French Revolution:*

> Their very way of living [the men of letters] led these writers to indulge in abstract theories and generalizations regarding the nature of government, and to place a blind confidence in these. For living as they did, quite out of touch with practical politics, they lacked the experience which might have tempered their enthusiasms. Thus they completely failed to perceive the very real obstacles in the way of even the most salutary revolutions. [in Huszar, 1960: 13]

> Our revolutionaries [the men of letters] had the same fondness for broad generalizations, cut-and-dried legislative systems, and a pedantic symmetry; the same contempt for hard facts; the same taste for reshaping institutions on novel, ingenious, original lines. . . . The result was nothing short of disasterous; for what is a merit in the writer may well be a vice in the statesman and the very qualities which go to make great literature can lead to catastrophic revolutions.

The start of the mad genius controversy toward the middle of the nineteenth century, then, appears tied to the revolutionary unrest of the period and, more specifically, to the recognition that those identified as geniuses often tended to occupy a central position in fermenting social, political, and intellectual unrest. The evaluation of the men of genius in terms of sanity and madness constituted one response to the perceived influence of many of these individuals. . . .

The Labeling Paradigm

The conception of deviance as an on-going, continuously shifting product of dynamic social processes between rule-violators and others has led to a shift in emphasis from the individual "flaws" or attributes of the deviant to a concern with the societal reaction to those attributes. Accordingly, the questions raised are how, why, and with what consequences certain individuals or groups define given behaviors as deviant, abnormal, or criminal. . . .

What receives little or no attention in the labeling literature is a view of the rule-violator preceding the act of labeling and processing by agents of social control. Hence, omitted are data pertaining to the activities, motivations, and self-view of the individual rule-breakers prior to formal or informal acts of stigmatization (Lorber, 1967: 302). . . .

Far from having been the passive victims or responders to negative typing, a sizable proportion of, in particular, Romantic geniuses acted as the initiators of their "victimization," and more or less deliberately conveyed an impression that contributed to the "imposition" by others of the "madness" label. These Romantic men of genius underscored by their actions and the numerous instances of self-labeling that the ancient commentators had indeed been correct in their observation that the "demon of madness" was no stranger to the extraordinarily gifted individual. These "confessions" and the largely willful projection of the image of madness were motivated, so it has been argued, by at least two dominant and interrelated factors: the need for an affirmed identity, and the need to break from the dependence on the past.

Generally impoverished and deprived of political power and a privileged class status following the demise of the *ancien régime*, the Romantic artists and men of letters revived the classical notion of "divine mania" or "inspiration" and established it as a defining mark of the extraordinary individual. . . .

The need, then, to seek a sense of identity by appropriating certain qualities of the ancients and the need, simultaneously, to establish their own intellectual and artistic independence led them to adopt a system of premises and logic that left them defenseless against the label of madness. Trapped by their own logic, they had no recourse — they assumed the label themselves.

The findings derived from this study of the genius—madness controversy, then, demonstrate the fact that the individual may possess a "deviant" identity prior to form or informal acts of stigmatization by others and, more or less deliberately, may seek to convey an impression of himself that he hopes will lead to the imposition of a particular label by his audience. The identity that had been sought by especially the Romantics was in terms of the sacred and inspired "mania" of the ancients. While these Romantics seemed successful in establishing this particular image of the genius during their age, their expressed doubts and trepidation helped foster, in subsequent years, a nonmystical and "scientific" assessment that stressed not "mania," but clinical pathology as the condition of genius. What is significant about the genius—madness controversy, however, for purposes of this discussion, is not that the attempt to negotiate a particular identity had "backfired," but that the genius was clearly not the helpless "victim" of philistine labelers — he not only contributed heavily to his "victimization," he even, to a degree, instigated it. . . .

References

HUSZAR, G. B. de (Ed.), (1960) *The Intellectuals: A Controversial Portrait.* Glencoe: Free Press.
LORBER, J. (1967) Deviance as performance: The case of illness, *Social Problems*, **14**(3), 303–310.
SHAW, G. B. (1908) *The Sanity of Art (1895).* New York: B. R. Tucker.

5

The Myth of Unappreciated Genius*

H. LENNEBERG

"I REALLY have no idea what is meant by that so-called misunderstanding from which I am supposed to be suffering. Your journal frequently proves that I enjoy the opposition quite often. . . . As I said, I am quite content with the ever growing recognition I have been receiving."

Thus wrote Robert Schumann at thirty-nine to Franz Bendel who succeeded him as editor of the *Neue Zeitschrift für Musik.* This statement, from a man who denounced vulgarity in a period when the notion of the unappreciated genius was coming into full bloom, is quite astonishing, especially in view of the biographies that imply that his early music was not favorably received. . . .

In Schumann's case, it appears that the first work he was willing to publish was issued with a commitment to underwrite any loses that the publisher, Kistner, might incur. For the next few years, Schumann continued either to guarantee sales or to pay for publication. Not until 1837 was he successful enough for Breitkopf und Härtel to publish *Carnaval* (Op. 9) – already accepted by Schlesinger in Paris – without any written guarantee against losses. How well Schumann thought he was doing is indicated in an amusing sidelight to his continuing battle with Clara Wieck's father. He informed Clara:

> You told me that your father said that nobody buys my stuff. I recently remembered that while I was at Härtel's and asked them about it. They looked it up in their books where everything is minutely recorded. I can now tell you they sold 250–300 copies each of my *Carnaval* and *Fantasiestücke* and 300–350 of my *Kinderscenen* which have only been out for half a year. Well, that's not so bad, I said to myself and went contentedly on my way (October 27, 1839).

. . . In the Romantic tradition, great composers are usually depicted as not only destined to be gifted, but also innovative or radical and of extraordinary integrity. Generally they are moody, sometimes to the point of insanity, and almost inevitably unappreciated or misunderstood.

Today this notion that the artist is a misunderstood prophet has been encouraged by artists themselves. The more *avant-garde* of our authors, painters, and musicians, those who have not attracted a large audience, have persuaded themselves and us that this is the way it has always been; that no serious artist

*The myth of the unappreciated (musical) genius, by H. Lenneberg, in *The Musical Quarterly* (1980) **54**, pp. 219–231. Used by permission.

can win instant recognition and immediate reward, and that therefore he creates solely for the future. Some even deride those colleagues who receive popular acclaim and consider their success as virtual proof of superficiality or lack of seriousness. . . . -

The neglect of Schubert's music was largely commercial. His friends and the professional musicians to whom the technical demands of his style presented no obstacle perceived his works as the masterpieces they are and performed them repeatedly, although within their limited circle.

But even this statement is an oversimplification. To what extent was Schubert's music neglected? Some of his songs were immediately successful. *Erlkönig, Heidenröslein,* and the notorious so-called *Trauerwalzer* would have brought him considerable wealth had the legal rights of composers been established as they are now. Composers often received only small sums for their best-loved or most successful works primarily because early copyright (insofar as it became gradually established) benefited only the publisher; not until the middle of the nineteenth century did the *droit d'auteur* begin to make headway. (This is one of the reasons why popular composers such as Hummel and Pleyel became publishers themselves.) The actual number of works by Schubert published during his lifetime was considerable. The approximately 100 opus numbers which were published represent nearly 300 individual compositions in the catalogues of a few publishers (Deutsch, 1946). . . .

Berlioz had a similar problem. He cannot be called unappreciated simply because he supported himself as a journalist or as a "librarian". "He was an acclaimed musician at twenty-seven, a leader, as we should say now, of the *avant-garde*," says Jacques Barzun (1977), the most rational of Berlioz's biographers.

But it cannot be denied that Berlioz had perpetual financial difficulties and that several of his works provoked highly controversial responses. For the most part, however, his financial problems were the result of the unusually heavy burden of supporting his wife's family, as well as his own, the political turbulence in Paris, the intrigues of various rivals at the opera, and a barbaric indifference on the part of government officials. But his status as a composer was never in doubt since the creation of the *Symphonie fantastique.* . . .

As if it were not tragic and heroic enough for Beethoven to have continued composing music that he would never hear, he must also be made into a titanic battler against ill will and poverty; this in spite of having had a lifelong stipend and being the shrewd equal of the publishers of his day and of their dubious practices. The legend that Mozart was poisoned by his rival Salieri has long been laid to rest, but the story that he was *poor and unappreciated* by his Viennese audiences persists even in scholarly circles. Only recently, a popular critic attributed the serious C-Minor Piano Concerto (K. 491) to Mozart's tragic failure as a concert artist in 1784 (*sic*), the same year that Mozart wrote to his father that he had been offered twenty-four ducats for one of his most recent concertos but preferred to retain it for his own exclusive use (letter of May 25, 1784) (Rich, 1977).

Mozart's case may be the most stubborn of the unappreciated composer. Let us hope that Uwe Kraemer's (1976) attempt to account for the huge sums Mozart tried to borrow in the last three years of his life will finally put an end to the myth. The author tries to prove that Mozart was a secret gambler, a plausible notion, but without a shred of direct evidence. But in the process of analyzing Mozart's finances, Kraemer computes his income and expenditures insofar as they are available and concludes that Mozart earned very large sums of money which he spent as fast as he received them. While Mozart's income waxed and waned as does that of any freelance artist, Kraemer estimates Mozart's earnings in his best years to have been as high as 10,000 guilders. Compared to the salary of 2000 guilders of the Director of Vienna's Allgemeine Krankenspital, a 2000-bed hospital, this is hard to reconcile with unappreciated artistry. Even the seemingly modest stipend of 800 guilders bestowed upon him by the Court in exchange for a few composing duties does not look quite as bad as it is generally made out to be. And Mozart charged ten times the usual fee for piano lessons which his students had to pay whether they attended or not. While Alan Rich points out that Mozart gave few public concerts in 1784, he is apparently not aware of his frequent appearances in private homes. (There has always been a rumor that Frau Mozart spent money as fast as Wolfgang could earn it. It was Mozart himself, however, who rented the most expensive apartment, kept a horse, bought many fancy clothes, and had a hairdresser come to his house every day.). . .

The widespread notion that artists must suffer for art and must make sacrifices is explained by Freud in his idea that creativity is a compensation. "As we have long known, art offers *substitute gratifications* [italics mine] for the oldest cultural renunciations, still the ones most deeply felt, and for that reason it serves as nothing else to reconcile men to the sacrifices made on behalf of culture." (Jones, 1953–57.) This seems to me to be a cautious and restrained way of a great man admitting his inability to fathom the psychological sources of art. I cannot dispute Freud whom I cite here only as an example of the high places in which the idea of renunciation and sacrifice on the part of creative genius prevails. Nor am I qualified to discuss what he says in psychoanalytic terms, though I wonder if he did not mean substitute gratification of the libido rather than cultural renunciations. [There is a book about the "diseases" of musicians, who, says the author, tend to be oversexed (Singer, 1960).] Neither do I fail to appreciate Thomas Mann's characterization of Adrian Leverkühn, the composer-protagonist of *Dr. Faustus,* who sells his soul to the devil in order to realize his artistic aims. Thomas Mann, himself an appreciated genius all his life, does not attribute Leverkühn's tragic life to a lack of audience response; audiences do not, in fact, figure very prominently in *Dr. Faustus.* Rather, Leverkühn is typical of the self-absorbed artistic personality that has come to dominate the cultural scene ever since the nineteenth century. . . .

A plausible if unspoken theory of why artists have come to be represented as martyrs may be found in Leonard Meyer's (1967) article on forgery. He suggests that we find even the most artistic and authentic-appearing forgery unacceptable because "we value — even revere — originality in art because the great artist challenged by the unknown or the partially understood (by the ambiguities in and incompleteness of our vision of the world) has dared to risk failure in order to reveal a new aspect of the universe to us." It takes little imagination to extend this willingness to risk failure and forge an image of the artist as inevitably taking chances against great odds.

It is a Romantic image difficult to apply to the earlier periods in which originality did not mean the overthrow of tradition and in which few artists needed to take immense risks. It is difficult, for example, to state unequivocally that Bach was a misunderstood genius. . . .

True objective history must always fight against long-cherished assumptions; the historian must occasionally be *avant-garde* himself and break with perhaps once-useful traditions that no longer serve him. But in doing so, he must not abandon the true and basic relationship an artist has to his times and his cultural history. He should not make every artist merely a long-suffering, impecunious martyr, an unappreciated genius.

References

BARZUN, J. (1977) Catalogue 208, *Musikantiquariat*, Hans Schrieder, Tutzing.
DEUTSCH, O. E. (1946) *Schubert: A Documentary Biography*. Eric Blom, London.
JONES, E. (1953–57) *The Life and Work of Sigmund Freud*. Vol. III, p. 414. New York.
KRAEMER, U. (1976) Wer hat Mozart verhungern lassen? *Musica*. **XXI** (3), 203.
MEYER, L. (1967) Forgery and the anthropology of art. *Music, the Arts and Ideas*. pp. 54, 60, Chicago.
RICH, A. (1977) *New York Magazine*, **21**, p. 81.
SINGER, K. (1960) *Berufskrankheiten der Musiker*. Berlin.

II

Genius: Signs and Outcomes

PERHAPS there is no field of research among the social sciences as that of exceptional achievement which can point as clearly to its major early contributions. The social sciences to a large extent began with Galton's mid-nineteenth century statistical studies of individual differences, the most obvious of which for Galton were those of human achievement. After Galton, in time, comes Freud with his theory of creativity and family dynamics. A little more than a quarter of a century later, we find Terman and his remarkable associate, Catharine Cox, laying the foundation for the psychometric study (and appreciation) of childhood intellectual giftedness. Cox more than any other researcher firmly linked exceptional achievement (genius) to equally exceptional early intellectual and characterlogical development. We often forget just how much emphasis she placed upon the necessary character of her 300 geniuses in explaining their extraordinary careers.

Appropriately, chapter II begins with her conclusions (II-1) for no book on genius and exceptional achievement would be complete without a representation of Cox's monumental research. A half a century old, it remains one of the most fertile pieces of research on the subject. Unmatched in the range and depth of their analyses, Cox's results foreshadow many later findings. Her work is followed by a recent research report by Walberg, Rasher, and Hase (II-2). By means of sophisticated statistics it confirms Cox's conclusions while contradicting the present-day belief that above an IQ threshold of 120, IQ does not correlate or contribute significantly to high achievement. The authors indicate that high IQ, while not a necessary factor, is a contributing factor to earned eminence. The chapter on Genius ends with Albert's effort (II-3) to clear away certain myths and presumptions linking genius and exceptional achievement. Based upon several different types of information regarding persons of exceptionally high and public achievement, the paper argues and gives evidence for staying close to an individual's performances before embarking on a deeper, more speculative understanding of genius and geniuses. It ends with a definition of genius that holds across many fields and many years.

1

The Early Mental Traits of 300 Geniuses*

C. M. COX

IS THERE a typical *youthful genius*? Does he differ from the average youth in other than intellectual traits? Does the character profile of the boy or young man who becomes a distinguished statesman differ from that of the youth who becomes an eminent musician? Are the profiles of these types more like each other than they are like that of the average youth of either type who achieves no more than average success in the field of his special interest or activity? In the following pages the evidence contained in the records of the early years of our eminent men is briefly summarized in so far as it bears upon these questions.

The trait profile for the group as a whole (Group C) is described and analyzed and certain typical subgroups are briefly characterized on the basis of their trait scores. . . .

The Trait Profile of 100 Youthful Geniuses (Group C)

We may assume that the trait profile for Group C is a typical historiometric trait profile of a group of youthful geniuses who become eminent men. The average rating of Group C for all of the 67 traits is +1.2, indicating that the members of the group are perceptibly above the common average in the possession of 67 good traits. Exceptions are in two *emotional* traits, . . . *absence of an occasional liability to extreme depression*, and . . . *absence of the liability to anger*; in one *negative self* trait, . . . *absence of eagerness for the admiration of the crowd*; and in one *social* trait, . . . *conventionality*, where the ratings are below the common average, but not significantly so. The averages for the trait groups for Group C as a whole and when arranged in order of magnitude, are as follows:

Trait	Ave. rating	Number of traits
Activity (persistence of motive)	+ 2.3	4
Intellectual activity	+ 2.0	2
Self (positive traits)	+ 2.0	5
Strength or force of character	+ 2.0	1
Intellectual	+ 1.8	8
Social	+ 1.2	15
Intellectual–Social	+ 1.1	2
Balance	+ 1.0	1
Emotional–Social	+ 1.0	5
Intellectual–Emotional	+ 0.9	2
Physical activity	+ 0.6	6
Emotional	+ 0.5	14
Self (negative traits)	+ 0.1	2

. . . It appears . . . that a trait profile characteristic of a group of youthful geniuses who become Eminent Men is (1) at or above the average in each of 67 good traits; (2) slightly above the average in favorable *emotional* traits; (3) noticeably above the average in *balance* and in *sociality*; and (4) distinctly above the average in *self* qualities, in *intellectuality*, in *activity* (including *intellectual activity* and *persistence*), and in *strength* or *force of character*. . . .

In conclusion, the trait profile of the youths of Group C indicates some boyhood characteristics of young geniuses. It indicates that they rate high in *intellectual, social,* and *activity traits,* while the *emotional* side of personality is, on the whole, not distinctly other than that of an unselected group. *Forcefulness* or *strength of character* as a whole, *persistence of motive*, and the *intellectual* traits rate conspicuously high. The high scores on all traits containing the *persistence of motive* factor, and the *intellective* factor indicate that young geniuses possess these traits to an unusual degree. These and the summation trait of *strength* or *force of character as a whole* are the traits in which our subjects score the highest ratings; they appear to be peculiarly characteristic of young geniuses. The estimates on the *self* traits and the *persistence* traits corroborate those on *forcefulness* or *strength of character* as a whole, emphasizing the presence of dynamic vigor of character and an innate assurance of superior ability in all of the members of the group. Finally, it is perhaps significant that the single trait that rates highest among our representative youthful geniuses is *desire to excel.*

We may conclude that the following traits and trait elements appearing in childhood and youth are diagnostic of future achievement: an unusual degree of persistence − . . . *tendency not to be changeable, tenacity of purpose*, and . . . *perseverance in the face of obstacles* − combined with *intellective* energy − . . . *mental work bestowed on special interests*, . . . *profoundness of apprehension*, and . . . *originality of ideas* − and the vigorous *ambition* expressed by the possession to the highest degree of . . . *desire to excel.* . . .

Characterization and Comparison of 15 Subgroups of Youthful Geniuses

We may now turn to the 15 subgroups of Group C, . . . characterizing and comparing them with the common average, with the average of group C (hereafter called Eminent Men) and with each other. (1) A group which represents greater eminence (First Ten) is compared with one which represents less eminence (Last Ten). A group which represents the "brightest" members of Group C (Highest IQs) is compared with one that represents the less "bright" (Lowest IQs). (2) The typical youthful behavior is described of each of 11 groups selected on the basis of the field or profession in which eminence was achieved and the 11 trait profiles are compared and contrasted. . . .

When the traits of the young geniuses in the subgroups are compared, the First Ten are conspicuous for their *persistence*; the Highest IQs for their *brightness*. When subgroups are arranged according to the field in which eminence was later achieved all are found to rate particularly high in *strength or force of character, intellectual* traits (except in the case of Soldiers), *self* traits, *activity* traits (except in the case of the two groups of Writers), and *persistence of motive*. It is the combination of superior traits that is particularly conspicuous in all of the subgroups and in the group as a whole.

The rare and striking personality of genius was, in the case of our subjects as a whole, manifested even in early youth by behavior that deviated from that of average individuals so pronouncedly that the record of its appearance was preserved in documentary form. The remarkable traits of youth were indicative of future greatness. The dynamic quality which, developing, raised performance to so high a level and won for the character it invigorated so large a sphere of influence was present and recognized even in childhood. And even in his earliest years the personality of the genius was something more than the sum of its extraordinary parts. . . .

Conclusions

. . . The primary concern of the investigation as a whole was this: What degree of *mental endowment* characterizes individuals of genius in their childhood and youth? Secondary in the present study, although otherwise of no less importance, was the question of the presence even in childhood of *traits of character other than "brightness"* which contribute to later high achievement. These two questions were the starting point for the discussions of the preceding pages. Each has been considered in detail. During the progress of the investigation it became evident that consideration of the main problem involved an additional question: What was the *hereditary background* of a group of young persons who later achieved very great distinction and what contribution was made by early *environment* to their development? The answer to this third question has been given a place because of the light it throws upon the problem as a whole.

Stated briefly in their logical order the three conclusions are as follows:

1. *Youths who achieve eminence have, in general, (a) a heredity above the average and (b) superior advantages in early environment.* It is evident that the forebears of young geniuses have made a definite contribution both physically and socially to the extraordinary progress of their offspring. The son of an eminent Lord High Treasurer of Ireland (Boyle), of an ambitious army general (Bulwer), of a president of the United States (Adams), of a king's first aide-de-camp (Hugo), of a British admiral (Penn), of one of the most eminent scholars of his age (Scaliger), of a president of the Parlement of Paris (Thou), of a Royal Chaplain (Addison), may be expected to rise to a position above the average. The inheritance of a child of able parents is undoubtedly superior, yet it is not sufficient in itself to account for genius. Indeed there have been many Lord High Treasurers, many ambitious generals, many presidents of the United States, whose sons did not, and apparently could not, achieve such eminence as our subjects; and there were other children of the same parents, the brothers and sisters of our young geniuses, who did not achieve eminence equal to that of the peculiarly gifted member of the family. The individual is the inheritor of ability, but he is unique with respect to the physiological and psychological organization of his inherited qualities. A favorable ancestral background is a definite asset; yet the peculiar combination of inherited traits which makes up a genius – the most favorable chance combination among many only less favorable ones – is an equally significant factor, and so an eminent man may be the son of a tinker (Bunyan), of a stonecutter (Canova), of a mason (Carlyle), of a strapmaker (Kant), of a day laborer (Cook), or a peasant (Jansen).

The average opportunity of our young geniuses for superior education and for elevating and inspiring social contacts was unusually high. Instruction by leading scholars of the day and friendly association with contemporary notables were not exceptional experiences. The extraordinary training for leadership received by Pitt the younger, John Quincy Adams, Niebuhr, and the Humboldt brothers; the specialized instruction of Mozart, Weber, and Michelangelo undoubtedly contributed to the rapid progress of these great men among the great. But again there were exceptions. The struggling cobbler Winckelmann was able to do little for his son, who, none the less, became an eminent archeologist. The opportunities offered to Faraday, Lincoln, or Blücher were apparently not favorable to success. Thus it appears that while individual chances for eminence are usually dependent upon a favorable hereditary background and are increased by favorable opportunity, eminence is not a function either of heredity or of environment alone.

2. *Youths who achieve eminence are distinguished in childhood by behavior which indicates an unusually high IQ.* Voltaire wrote verses "from his cradle"; Coleridge at 3 could read a chapter from the Bible. Mozart composed a minuet at 5; Goethe, at 8, produced literary work of adult superiority. Schelling at 11 was enrolled in a class with boys of 18 and 19 who recognized him as their equal in knowledge and ability. Accounts of the early years of our subjects are

full of examples of early mental maturity. In their reported interests, in their school standing and progress, and in their early production and achievement, the members of the group were, in general, phenomenal. Later achievement was foreshadowed in youthful behavior, and it is probable that early manifestations of superior intelligence would have been found in every case had the records of all been faithfully kept.

Since there is a constant relation between the sufficiency of the account and the estimated IQ of the subject (the IQ increasing with the reliability of the data), it appears that the true IQs of the subjects of the present study are even higher than the obtained estimates. A corrected estimate indicates that the true mean IQ for the group is not below 155 and probably at least as high as 165. The average of the obtained IQ estimates for a small group of cases more adequately reported than the others is 175 for the first 17 years of life. The corrected estimate, indicating a nearer approximation to a true IQ, is for the same group 184. It is probable that a number of the cases included among the 301 actually ranked in intelligence not far below the composition scores of several of their number and of these many are well above the 200 IQ mark. Arnauld, Comte, Goethe, Grotius, Laplace, Leopardi, Michelangelo, Newton, Pascal, the younger Pitt, Sarpi, Schelling, Voltaire and Wolsey probably rated at 200 IQ or even higher. Occasionally in our day a case is reported that ranks at this high level. Shall we expect in such an instance a Comte, a Grotius, a Newton, or a Michelangelo? We are probably warranted in expecting superior adult achievement wherever in childhood the IQ is above 150. But we may not be warranted in expecting a world genius even if the 200 IQ level is reached; for there are other factors involved in achieving greatness besides an essential degree of intellectual capacity. The tests — and it is in comparison with test performances that the IQs of our cases have been reckoned — cannot measure spontaneity of intellectual activity; perhaps, too, they do not sufficiently differentiate between high ability and unique ability, between the able individual and the extraordinary genius. The significant conclusion in the present study is derived from the evidence it presents that *the extraordinary genius who achieves the highest eminence is also the gifted individual whom intelligence tests may discover in childhood.* The converse of this proposition is yet to be proved.

3. That all equally intelligent children do not as adults achieve equal eminence is in part accounted for by our last conclusion; *youths who achieve eminence are characterized not only by high intellectual traits, but also by persistence of motive and effort, confidence in their abilities, and great strength or force of character.* The average score of all the good traits of the young geniuses is distinctly above the average score of the same traits in unselected individuals. The superior youths considered in the present study pursued high ideals, developed significant interests, and created new expressions of scientific and philosophical thought before they had reached the age of manhood. Schelling had outlined his philosophy at 20, Hume had defined his views before he was 25, Milton at 21

wrote an ode pronounced by an eminent critic to be perhaps the most beautiful in the English language. Peel at 24 was Chief Secretary for Ireland, Raphael at 21 painted the *Granduca Madonna*, Beethoven at 18 was appointed Chamber Musician to his princely ruler, Newton had unfolded his doctrine of light and colors before he was 20. Bacon wrote his *Temporis Partus Maximus* before the age of 20, Montesquieu had sketched his *Spirit of Laws* at an equally early age, and Jenner, when he was younger still, contemplated the possibility of removing from among the list of human diseases one of the most deadly scourges of the race. Achievements like these are not the accidents of a day. They are the natural outgrowth in individuals of superior general powers of persistent interest and great zeal combined with rare special talents.

These conclusions summarize the facts concerning a special group of geniuses, but the group concerned is representative of all those whose later achievements reach the highest level, and so conclusions true for its members are probably true for other similar, or approximately similar, individuals. Appearing usually in superior families (and the more usually so when educational and other early environmental inequality persists) young geniuses are found to display in childhood superior intelligence, superior talents, and superior traits of character. The converse has not been definitely demonstrated, but the appearance in childhood of a combination of the highest degree of general ability, special talent, seriousness of purpose, and indomitable persistence may well be greeted as indicating a capacity for adult achievement of the highest rank. The child is father of the man: the gifted youth will be the leader of the future.

2

IQ Correlates with High Eminence*

H. S. WALBERG, S. P. RASHER and K. HASE

Abstract

Indicators of eminence derived from word and citation counts in primary biographical articles in encyclopedias published at the turn of the century, in 1935, and 1974 correlate positively 0.33 overall with IQ estimates made from biographical sources on a select sample of 282 philosophers, scientists, non-fiction and fiction writers, musicians, artists, religious leaders, statesmen, revolutionaries, and soldiers. These results are striking since the sample is restricted to the higher end of the eminence distribution; the mean estimated IQ for the total group is 158.9. Indicators of eminence for some fields – philosophers, musicians, and artists – vary from one period to the next. Individuals also shift in estimated eminence during the three time periods examined.

REVIEWS (Chambers, 1969; Stein, 1968) and recent evidence (Walberg, 1969, 1971) indicate that eminence in various fields requires minimal levels of estimated intelligence; but that beyond these levels, that may vary from one field to the next, the degree of attained eminence is unlinked or weakly associated with intelligence, because perseverance, opportunity, and other factors may be relatively more important. The analysis of data reported below on 282 of the most eminent persons who lived in Western countries during the period of 1450 to 1850 show that IQ, estimated from biographical materials, and eminence correlate weakly but significantly at the highest levels of eminence.

According to the total space allotted to each, Cattell (1903) listed in rank order of eminence the top 1000 persons that were mentioned at the turn of the century in at least two of six American, English, French, and German biographical dictionaries. Cox (1926) eliminated from the list aristocracy and nobility, those born before 1450, and those beyond the 510th name on the original ranking. Cox and several associates combed more than 3000 sources including encyclopedias, biographies, and collections of letters in the Stanford and Harvard university libraries for information on the mental development of each person. From this information, Cox and two associates each independently estimated the IQs from information on two .periods in the life of each individual, before age 17 and between the ages of 17 and 26.

The correlations among the estimates made by the three estimators (inter-rater reliabilities) average between 0.71 and 0.75 (Cox, 1926); and our calculation

*Gifted Child Quarterly, (1978), 22, 196–200. Reprinted by permission.

of the correlation of the before-17 and after-17 mean estimates (a kind of stability reliability) is 0.82. The reliability of the estimates compares reasonably with that of intelligence tests now given to children in school classes (Cronbach, 1960).

The mean estimated IQ for the total group, 158.9 is far higher (three or four standard deviations) than the mean of about 100 which is found in unselected samples (the IQ score in the present analysis is the mean before-17 corrected estimate plus the mean of after-17 corrected estimate from Cox, 1926; divided by two). The variation within the group, however, is comparable to unselected samples, as indicated by a standard deviation of 14.0. The group ranges from Goethe, Leibnitz, and Grotius with estimated IQs between 195 and 200 and Masséna, Grant, and Drake between 120 and 125. Table II.1 shows philosophers higher and soldiers lower in estimated IQ than the other groups. The F-ratio for the differences among the IQ means for the 10 groups is 27.6 ($p < 0.001$).

For additional estimates of eminence, we counted the number of words in the primary biographical articles on each of the 282 persons in the 1935 *New International Encyclopedia* and the 1974 *Encyclopedia Britannica* and the number of citations to other articles mentioning the person at the end of the primary article in *Britannica*. Because the relations of eminence and IQ may vary in different fields and because IQ and eminence means vary significantly (the F-ratios on 1903, 1935, and 1974 word counts and 1974 citation counts are respectively 2.3, 3.7, 3.5, and 6.0 – all p's < 0.01), we calculated the means and correlations (Table II.1) for each field separately.

Table II.1 shows that 36 of the 40 correlations between IQ and the four indicators of eminence for the ten groups are positive. The mean of the 40 correlations (using Fisher's Z transformation) is 0.24 (Dixon and Massey, 1969); the limits of the 95% confidence interval for this within-group correlation for the total sample are 0.13 and 0.37. Generally then higher eminence is associated with higher intelligence for this sample of highly eminent persons; however, estimated IQ only accounts for about 5% of the variance in eminence in the total sample.

Table II.1 shows that the indicators of eminence for groups vary from one period to the next. Matched T-tests show four significant changes ($p < 0.05$): philosophers lost and musicians and artists gained in estimated eminence from 1903 to 1935; philosophers gained from 1935 to 1974. Individuals also shift in estimated eminence: for example, starting with the most eminent, the top ten on the 1903 estimates are Napoleon, Voltaire, Bacon, Goethe, Luther, Burke, Newton, Milton, Pitt, and Washington; on 1974 word counts the top ten in order are Samuel Johnson, Luther, Rembrandt, Da Vinci, Napoleon, Washington, Lincoln, Goethe, Beethoven, and Dickens; on 1974 citations, the top ten are Descartes (with 57 citations), Napoleon, Newton, Leibnitz, Luther, Hegel, Kant, Darwin, Galileo, and Da Vinci (with 36).

The total eminence estimate in Table II.1 averages out some of the random

TABLE II.1 *Means and Standard Errors of IQ and Eminence Estimates and the Correlations of IQ and Eminence*

Group	N	IQ	Means				Correlation with IQ				
			Standardized word counts			Citations[a]	Standardized word counts			Cita-tions	Total[b]
			1903	1935	1974	1974	1903	1935	1974	1974	
Philosophers	22	173.0 ± 2.2	110.6 ± 4.2	102.8 ± 3.5	108.2 ± 3.4	2.6 ± 0.3	0.02	0.05	0.07	0.17	0.05
Scientists	39	163.9 ± 1.7	99.7 ± 2.5	94.8 ± 2.2	98.2 ± 2.2	2.2 ± 0.2	0.34*	0.10	0.05	0.15	0.21
Non-Fiction Writers	42	162.3 ± 1.4	92.0 ± 3.2	92.0 ± 2.7	92.8 ± 3.5	1.5 ± 0.1	0.16	−0.08	−0.15	−0.04	−0.03
Fiction Writers	53	162.5 ± 1.6	103.3 ± 2.7	103.7 ± 2.8	102.1 ± 2.6	1.5 ± 0.1	0.15	0.36**	0.19	0.24*	0.28*
Musicians	11	153.4 ± 2.7	87.9 ± 5.1	112.9 ± 7.4	116.6 ± 2.6	2.4 ± 0.2	0.54*	0.51	0.34	0.51	0.63*
Artists	13	149.8 ± 3.0	105.1 ± 5.2	119.6 ± 4.9	116.0 ± 3.4	2.1 ± 0.2	0.70**	0.84***	0.46	0.54*	0.77***
Religious Leaders	23	159.2 ± 1.9	102.3 ± 4.8	95.5 ± 4.6	98.7 ± 3.8	1.6 ± 0.2	0.41*	0.21	0.13	0.36*	0.32
Statesmen	43	158.7 ± 1.8	100.0 ± 2.9	98.5 ± 2.6	96.4 ± 3.7	1.5 ± 0.1	0.09	0.13	0.13	0.20	0.11
Revolutionaries	9	163.1 ± 2.7	98.2 ± 6.2	100.2 ± 7.8	94.8 ± 5.4	1.2 ± 0.3	0.54	0.18	0.43	−0.69*	0.44
Soldiers	27	133.0 ± 1.2	99.0 ± 4.3	101.8 ± 4.8	99.6 ± 3.6	1.5 ± 0.2	0.15	0.13	0.05	0.02	0.12

[a]Citations is the logarithm of the number of citations.
[b]Total eminence is the mean of the standardized word counts for these time periods.

*$p \leqslant 0.05$
**$p \leqslant 0.01$
***$p \leqslant 0.001$

errors of the word counts for the separate years and provides more stable, reliable figures. The mean correlation of the total estimate with IQ (Dixon and Massey, 1969) is 0.33 (accounting for about 11% of the variance); the 95% confidence-interval limits are 0.21 and 0.42. Even the total estimate, however, contains some errors of measurement; and the correlation reported here underestimates the association of IQ and eminence. Moreover, as McNemar (1964) points out, when a sample is restricted to the high end (or any smaller part) of an eminence distribution, as in the present sample, the observed correlation underestimates the correlation that would be found in a less restricted sample. Because of two sources of underestimation, there seems little doubt that IQ and eminence are correlated positively.

On the other hand, it is possible that some unconscious bias entered the original IQ estimates of Cox and associates, and that they over-estimated to an unknown extent the IQs of the more eminent persons in the sample. Their careful work and independent checks on the IQ estimates suggests that they minimized such bias, but it cannot be completely discounted.

Although it may be concluded that IQ and eminence are positively correlated in the total sample, the analyses do not permit the confident inference that IQ is more critical in some fields. The categorization of people in fields (Cox, 1926) is somewhat arbitrary; for example, grouping Da Vinci with artists or Benjamin Franklin with statesmen ignores their contributions to science. Also, variations in the numbers of cases, means, and standard deviations in the ten fields as well as the instability of the eminence estimates disallow such an inference. Nor can it be inferred that IQ directly causes eminence since it may enable individuals to create opportunities in the family, schools, and other social institutions for ultimately attaining eminence (Stein and Meer, 1954). Moreover, as Cox (1926) originally pointed out, perseverance and other traits may compensate for less than genius-level IQ.

References

CATTELL, J. McK. (1903) A Statistical Study of Eminent Men. *Popular Science Monthly, 5,* 359–377.
CHAMBERS, J. A. (1969) A Multidimensional Theory of Creativity. *Psychological Reports, 25,* 779–799.
COX, C. M. (1926) *The Early Mental Traits of Three Hundred Geniuses.* Stanford: Stanford University Press.
CRONBACH, L. J. (1960) *Essentials of Psychological Testing.* New York: Harper.
DIXON, W. J. and MASSEY, F. J. (1969) *Introduction to Statistical Analysis.* New York: McGraw-Hill.
Encyclopedia Britannica (1974) Chicago: Encyclopedia Britannica.
GHISELLI, E. (1964) *Theory of Psychological Measurement.* New York: McGraw-Hill.
McNEMAR, Q. (1964) Lost: Our Intelligence? Why? *American Psychologist, 19,* 871–882.
New International Encyclopedia (1935) New York: Dodd, Mead.
STEIN, M. I. (1968) Creativity. In E. Borgatta and W. W. Lambert (Eds.), *Handbook of Personality Theory and Research.* Chicago: Rand McNally.

STEIN, M. I. and MEER, B. (1954) Perceptual Organization in a Study of Creativity. *Journal of Psychology,* 37, 39–43.

WALBERG, H. J. (1969) A Portrait of the Artist and Scientist as Young Men. *Exceptional Children,* 36, 5–12.

WALBERG, H. J. (1971) Varieties of Adolescent Creativity and the High School Environment. *Exceptional Children,* 38, 111–116.

3

Toward a Behavioral Definition of Genius*

R. S. ALBERT

> The idols imposed by words on the understanding are of two kinds. They are either names of things which do not exist (for as there are things left unnamed through lack of observation, so likewise are there names which result from fantastic suppositions and to which nothing in reality corresponds), or they are names of things which exist, but yet confused and ill-defined, and hastily and irregularly derived from realities.
>
> Francis Bacon, *Novum Organum*, 1939

THIS article discusses some of the troublesome issues involved in the concept of genius. An operational definition of genius is proposed; some of the implications for research on high achievement are presented; and supporting evidence is offered to indicate that it is possible to operationalize such an apparently global concept if one restricts its use to the behavioral, rather than to the sometimes superficially dramatic, components of high achievement. Because genius is typified by behavior that is exceptional, often unpredictable, and influential to many, it is not surprising to find genius a topic of concern for many eminent psychologists and social philosophers. . . .

Through the centuries, genius has been modeled after everything from demi-gods, heroes, prophets, martyrs, social activists, and supermen — "capable of re-creating the human cosmos, or part of it, in a way that was significant and not comparable to any previous recreation (Eissler, 1963)" — to the more mundane models such as children with very high IQ scores or persons with some inordinate "luck." Encompassing such a variety of specimens over so long a history, the idea of genius is basically an intriguing idea with a sad and overgenerous past. Most of the work on genius or exceptional creative behavior, has been a confusion of two classes of variables: factors of motivation (the "why" questions) and statements of consequences (the "effects" questions). The common behavioral denominators to this confusion have been rarity and social, as well as intellectual, consequences that are far out of proportion to, and of greater unpredictability than, most human endeavors. Because of such characteristics, theories of genius, like theories of history, have been used frequently as a means of selective bidding for a particular model of human nature (cf. Plumb, 1969). Seen from these vantage points, creative people are heroic, mysterious, and inexplicable. But they are also not the stuff of science or, often, of this world.

American Psychologist, (1975), 30, pp. 140–151. Copyright 1975 by the American Psychological Association. Reprinted by permission of the publisher and author.

Galton and Freud

The study of eminence and creative behavior needed the work of both Galton and Freud to get past many of the earlier, prohibitive attitudes and presumptions that bound thinking about creative behavior in such motley bundles of whole cloth.

Galton and Freud shared much of the nineteenth century's interest in biological and developmental processes; they agreed in more than principle that genius and creative behavior are primarily biological phenomena. Out of this shared perspective emerges what has become a contemporary focus on genius and creative behavior — emphasis on an individual's family as biological inheritance and as social-psychological influence. For Galton, the family was a genetic pool of talents that its progeny inherit, in different degrees, depending primarily on their biological distance from the center of the pool. For Freud, the family is a psychological reality in which conflicting, motivating processes are instigated and defensive patterns are shaped and interlocked. Out of the interrelationships between inherited talents and conflicts incited and shaped by the family, a person's capacity for creative behavior emerges. Just as important, by viewing both development and capacity as matters of degree, Galton and Freud made a monumental break from earlier views of genius that ascribed to each person distinct states of inspiration, of possession, of enthrallment, or of complete lack of genius.

Needless to say, how one defines genius is critical to how one will study it. It is the basic step. Galton's very effort to operationalize genius was itself extraordinary. Prior definitions has been remarkably varied, unanchored to observables, and almost always *post hoc*. Despite years of study, there had been a paucity of efforts toward agreement on what, why, or who genius was. Galton's definition was and remains one of the few detailed ones. It rests on five interlocking propositions: that a measure of an individual's genius can be derived from his degree of eminence; that on this rests a man's reputation; that this reputation, although based on contemporary critical opinion, is long-term in character; that critical opinion is focused on a real, extensively acknowledged achievement; and that such achievement is the product of natural abilities that are made up of a blend of intellect and disposition (or what is now termed *intelligence and personality*). The following excerpt from Galton makes this clear:

> Let it be clearly borne in mind, what I mean by reputation and ability. By reputation, I mean the opinion of contemporaries, revised by posterity ... the favourable result of a critical analysis of each man's character, by many biographers. I do not mean high social or official position, nor such as is implied by being the mere lion of a London season; but I speak of the reputation of a leader of opinion, of an originator, of a man to whom the world deliberately acknowledges itself largely indebted (Galton, 1869, p. 33).

It is interesting to note in this statement that genius *qua* eminence was historically bound and a matter of revision, not a once-for-all-time phenomenon.

There are several crucial implications to this definition. It deals in observable influences, not supposed ones or the momentary opinion of one or a few persons. In Galton's view, eminence is an objective attribute: it is known only after something occurs and influences a large number of persons over many years (at least long enough to be "revised by posterity"). An interesting correlate is that a person's genius may vary over the years although the substrate of natural abilities on which it is based need not vary. As for the nature of the relationship between a person's eminence and those abilities, Galton again was remarkably and refreshingly specific.

> By natural ability, I mean those qualities of intellect and disposition, which urge and qualify a man to perform acts that lead to reputation. I do not mean capacity without zeal, nor zeal without capacity, nor even a combination of both of them without an adequate power of doing a great deal of very *laborious work*. But I mean a nature which, when left to itself, will, urged by an *inherent stimulus*, climb the path that leads to eminence and has strength to reach the summit – on which, if hindered or thwarted, will fret and strive until the hindrance is overcome, and it is again free to follow its labouring instinct (Galton, 1869, p. 33, italics added).

Seemingly paradoxical for a view that puts so much emphasis on other persons' opinions and external acknowledgement, Galton subscribed heavily to the idea that the necessary condition to genius is intrinsic motivation, "an inherent stimulus" that urges and compels hard work. That one needs abilities to match the compulsion goes almost without saying but should be recognized. Given a combination of strong urges and exceptional natural abilities, Galton thought that the continued interaction *would* establish a noteworthy reputation, that genius "would out." None the less, a person's rank or eminence was always being judged, and he or she was placed by and among contemporaries. Galton, borrowing a very Darwinian proposition from his cousin Charles, looked upon

> social and professional life as a continuous examination. All are candidates for the good opinions of others, and for success in their several professions. . . . The world . . . [clearly a rather competitive one filled with candidates and judges] almost unconsciously, allots marks to men. It gives them for originality of conception, for enterprise, for activity and energy (pp. 5–6).

Of the personal attributes given marks, enterprise, activity, and energy suggest that *effort* is crucial to reputation and decidedly outweighs originality in Galton's opinion.

Galton's determination of the ranking of men is less satisfactory than his general model. His method was based on certain questionable assumptions, the major one being the source of accurate indexes of a person's reputation. For his rankings, Galton relied heavily (too heavily, some believe) on popular directories, such as *Men of the Times*, and on Foss' *Lives of the Judges* and *The London Times* obituaries. Although he placed an age requirement of 50 years or older as a gauge of a person's staying power in the world's good opinion, Galton did not appear concerned with the fact that the range of different types of noteworthy activities listed in such references was quite restricted and that such activities were very restricted socially in terms of likely candidates (cf. Annan, 1955, for a detailed discussion of how British families make up a prescribable network of talents, genetically and socially). Moreover, the basis for inclusion in such reference works appears to have been overly public, popular, and not always the most worthwhile, in spite of Galton's definition. None the less, Galton's technique of ranking men and their relatives, his main object in the first place, has been highly influential, and was taken up and modified by Ellis (1904) and Cox (1926) among others. Every major study of eminence does, to some degree, bear a methodological resemblance to Galton's original tenets and technique.

Galton assumed that a man's genius or his potential for it, though evidenced by the man himself, derived from genetic sources entirely external to him. Even if genius was within the genetic pool of his family, the locus of origin and the locus of control were outside the individual, since no one can choose his family of origin. Thus, Galton's position assigns importance to luck or chance as a determinant of genius. This bears a resemblance to the Greek view that a man of genius is one who, without choice, is touched by, inspired by, or visited by an outside god-spirit or daemon; one who is thereafter compelled or, in Galton's terms, "urged" to perform deeds that gain him a favorable reputation.

On the other hand, in Freud's view of creative behavior, while the locus of origin is external, the locus of control, like the major motives for creative behavior, is within the individual, allied to "madness" though it may be. Out of the meshing of the claims of biology and of society comes art. In Freudian theory, art, or creative behavior, is used in the service of protecting the individual and his primary groups, even if paradoxically it jeopardizes his reputation. Galton's creative individuals are not the potential enemies of society, that is, the "detonators of change" that Freud's are. Galton's world is more rewarding and accepting, "fairer," and less destructively critical than Freud's. Galton's social environment is Darwinian, judging the adaptive abilities and endurances of species through sheer capacity to survive. In Freud's world, survival is also at issue, but on a much different level.

Although he made a lifelong practice of studying men of genius — Leonardo Da Vinci (Freud, 1910/1953), Dostoevsky (Freud, 1928/1948), Moses (Freud, 1938/1955) — Freud never believed that he understood genius. In a later edition of *Hereditary Genius* Galton wished that he had used the word *ability* instead of *genius* in his title. Thus, Galton and Freud ended their studies of genius dissatisfied with it as an explanation.

Drawing a general conclusion at this point, one must confess that there is little that specifically helps in the understanding of genius or exceptional creative behavior. Pooling the work of Galton and Freud, we see genius as the esteemed *product* of high general abilities and continuous, energetic, highly personal effort over most of a lifetime. Implied in this conclusion are several aspects of interest. One does not have genius, one does genius-level work. High general abilities and prolonged, personal motivations are dispositional conditions to this level of performance. When we say a person has genius it is much like saying they have the 'flu — at best a descriptive label, superficial and begging questions. Genius is inferred from behavior having protracted influence; equally important, it is behavior that is eventually recognized as influential and esteemed by many of the influenced. We know that such behavior is itself considerably influenced by situational and environmental conditions, conditions which if left unacknowledged and unanalyzed give the appearance of luck or of genius to extraordinary achievement. Yet if one wishes to go beyond this general statement more is called for. Since historical eminence occurs in many different kinds of behavior, we need first to determine if there is a set of discriminating attributes common to this diversity of activities.

Definition of Genius

One should look to persons of recognized eminence for genius, since genius is evidenced in a consensus of peers and is operationalized through the various reward procedures that every society and profession has for acknowledging members' contributions (Cole and Cole, 1973; Zuckerman, 1967a). This statement follows Galton's wish to do away with the word *genius*. Furthermore, we should accept the fact that there is no one criterion, person, or group that can determine who has genius and who does not. Freud and others dealt with the motivational and personality correlates to creative behavior at levels and complexity deeper than Galton's "qualities of intellect and disposition." From them we take the idea that for the attainment of a great, enduring reputation, along with gifted cognitive abilities, there must be deep-seated, strongly persistent personality determinants operating, which are essentially developmental in nature, longitudinal in occurrence (rather than situationally determined and sporadic), and conducive to behavior of influence and consequence. These determinants urge men and women "to perform acts that lead to reputation" or eminence. Influence is a continuous phenomenon in every sense and is comparative and judgmental in part. Eminence is built on influence and is social, as well as individual, in origin and behavioral in nature. For these reasons, eminence is built only on public acts.

Therefore, a person of genius is anyone who, regardless of other characteristics he may possess or have attributed to him, produces, over a long period of time, a large body of work that has a significant influence on many persons for many years; requiring these people, as well as the individual in question, to come to terms with a different set of attitudes, ideas, viewpoints, or techniques before all can have "peace of mind," that is, a sense of resolution and closure.

The work associated with this person must be presented to others, for their use and evaluation; it is a public work and takes other talented men and women years to understand, to implement, and, equally important, to surpass. It is others' *necessary* effort that makes up the basic thrust of this person's impact. Others often spend their own careers working out the implications of this work, for in the end they must come to terms with it. It is this aspect that is so important, whether it is wanted by others or predictable.

Acknowledgement usually occurs through the work being referred to often and being explicitly incorporated in others' work. The individual most responsible for the work receives institutionalized awards, for example, the Nobel prize, and, lastly, he becomes the object of archival interest, first within a profession (*The Excitement and Fascination of Science*, 1965) and, if his influence is extraordinary, eventually among a wider, interested lay public (evidenced in popular and "serious" biographies).

The key ingredient to genius is productivity — large in volume, extraordinary in longevity, more or less unpredictable in content. The impact of the work is dislocation or sudden reorganization constituting a major shift, that is, productions of "originality" rather than of reasonable extension (cf. Ghiselin, 1963; Kuhn, 1962, for an important discussion of this process in the physical sciences). Productivity in any area is a continuous variable. Influential productivity is also continuous, but it is very rare within any field, a point originally made by Galton. Cole and Cole (1967) reported that of the quarter million scientists appearing in the 1961 *The Science Citation Index*, only 1.08% had received 58 or more citations, which is the physics Nobel laureates' average number of citations between 1955 and 1965. Another study (Garfield, 1970) showed that on the basis of number of citations, one can predict the most likely candidates for the Nobel prize in science, and, in fact, did locate both winners in physics! The basis of long-term influence, extraordinary productivity, can be observed for many persons of extraordinary influence in a variety of areas: Bach's 46 volumes of compositions; Binet's 277 publications (Dennis, 1954b); Darwin's 119 (Darwin, 1896), Einstein's 248 (Weil, 1960); Freud's 330 (Tyson and Strachey, 1956); Galton's 227 (Dennis, 1954b); Maslow's 165 (MacKinnon, 1972); and William James, who complained most of his life of work inhibition, produced 307 publications (Dennis, 1954a). Zuckerman (1967b) noted that laureates in science publish earlier, more, and longer than do matched scientists drawn from *American Men of Science*. The former have a median of 3.9 papers per year to the latter's 1.4 papers. Zuckerman noted even more prolific eminent mathematicians — Poincaré's 500 papers and 30 books over 34 years and the 995 papers of Arthur Cayley (who published a paper every two or three weeks).

Influential persons' productive longevity is also clearly observed: For example, Freud produced his psychoanalytic work over a 45-year span after shifting from neuropsychiatry in his late 30s; Picasso worked for over 75 years; Darwin and Einstein produced their work over periods of 51 years and 53 years, respectively. Raskin (1936) studied groups of eminent nineteenth-century scientists and writers and found that their periods of productivity averaged 34 years and 30 years, respectively (see also Lehman, 1953).

A number of studies have appeared over the years showing a close connection between extremely high productivity and the attainment of eminence in a variety of fields (Clark, 1957; Cole and Cole, 1967; Dennis, 1954a, 1954b; Lehman, 1953; Merton, 1961; Myers, 1970; Raskin, 1936; Zuckerman, 1967). Correlations between the number of citations (an empirical measure of influence) and peer ratings of eminence are 0.68 for psychologists (Clark, 1957) and 0.72 for physicists (Cole and Cole, 1967). In a report of psychologists (Myers, 1970), the correlation between the quality of a man's research and the number of citations to it is 0.89, extending Cole and Cole's (1967) observation on physical scientists that the number of citations is an exceptionally strong index of "the scientific significance" of a person's published work.

Taking influential, long-term productivity as the basis and hallmark of eminence, we can now put into sharper perspective several of the attributes that are often attached to genius. So-called "works of genius" may be the individual parts in a prolonged series of efforts made public over time. When examined closely, one finds that this voluminous series comprises a set of intricately linked core problems and an exceptionally large number of ideas about them (Merton, 1961), which, over time, lead to innovation. The term *innovation* is used here in the sense of "changes in something established" (*Shorter Oxford English Dictionary*, 1955) rather than the commonly held idea of "discovering" something never before seen or conceived − an apparent impossibility among humans. The individual work is the measurable unit in assaying influence; but it is the series that conveys the influence by being an interrelated body of work. It is its interrelatedness that makes for both its impact and its being identifiable as the work of one or few persons. Eponymy, therefore, is more than an act of respectful recognition; it is an act of historical bookkeeping. To call a major segment of a science or art Darwinian biology, Einsteinian physics, Freudian psychology, or Newtonian, Pavlovian, Picasso-like, Chagal-like, etc., is to state for the record that a discernible historical development has occurred, that major periods of change are traceable and identifiable rather than random, fated, and more or less unattributable. Sooner or later, for some of the reasons given above . . . the status of competing systems of thought or operations changes from major to minor, as was the case with hypnosis before and after psychoanalysis, or, more contemporarily, to the status of equality, as is the case with Pavlovian and Skinnerian models of learning phenomena.

So far we have spent a good deal of time discussing influence as one of the critical independent variables in the achievement of eminence. Yet, it would be misleading to suggest that the attainment of great influence, or impact, is what extraordinary creative behavior is all about, the aim of it all. It is not; it is the need to work on problems considered significant and troublesome by the individual. Influence is a highly personal, varied, and unpredictable adjunct to a man's work; man's specific aim for influence is erratic and its attainment out of his control. Influence and recognition may be sought, as they were with Freud (1925); or they may be explicitly repudiated, as they were by Wittgenstein whose voluminous work, both publications and lectures, has had an impact equal to few other men's in generating two major schools of philosophy, logical positivism and linguistic philosophy (Malcolm, 1966). Influence may be of some importance, even if played down, as it was for Darwin (Darwin, 1896; Eiseley, 1965), or of minor importance, as it was for Einstein (Frank, 1947; Michelmore, 1962; Schilpp, 1949). Influence might be unintended, being the "spin-off" of a more immediate set of interests and activities, as in the case of Sir Walter Scott, who thought of himself primarily as a novelist but who, in the process of research for his historical novels, radically changed the aim and some of the techniques in the study of history (Trevor-Roper, 1971). Eminent persons might be as keenly aware of their influence as, for example, Nobel laureate James Watson, who recently enumerated the influences that have resulted from his and Crick's development of the DNA double helix; "the working out of the whole pathway of DNA synthesis, protein synthesis, the cracking of the genetic code, the total conception of how a virus can multiply (Crick and Watson, 1972, p. 820)." Watson stated with assurance that "none of this research would have been possible without starting off with the structure of the genetic material. If you pick up biological journals and ask what percentage of the biology being done today is a direct product of what we were doing, it is maybe 25% (Crick and Watson, 1972, p. 820)."

Consequences of the Definition

The above definition, therefore, helps to clear up several misconceptions linked to the extraordinary influences which in the past have attracted somewhat romantic and even heroic explanations. "Undiscovered genius" is one common misconception. If our definition is valid, then one knows of persons of extra-ordinary abilities by the use of these abilities and by the subsequent influence they have. The proposed definition does not attempt in any way to second-guess history, for clearly there are no "might-have-beens," no undiscovered geniuses, no potential geniuses cruelly snuffed out or mysteriously prohibited (usually by an equally ill-defined fate). As we have seen, genius is, at best, a judgment placed on the degree of influence of a person's work and cannot be meaningfully placed on the origins or the style of that work, regardless of its appeal. Nor are there particular political, religious, social-economic groups, nationalities, races, or sexes with more genius than others, as others tried to demonstrate. Various groups of people may have more facilities, more opportunities, and even more motivation, predisposing them to concern themselves with certain phenomena, but none has intrinsically more genius *per se*, for there is no such thing. Areas of interest and the preferred means by which they work are a function of the resources and traditions available (Lehman, 1947), not of any inherent qualities to members of the groups. As Clark (1969) reminded us, "although circumstances and opportunities may vary, human intelligence seems to remain fairly constant . . . (p. 17)." Who has more "genius," the first men to harness fire or those who split the atom, those who developed the alphabet or those who used it to produce *Oedipus Rex, Hamlet*, or *War and Peace*? These are unanswerable questions that may call out preferences and prejudices but not meaningful answers. Nor can we put the tag of "genius" on work that is interesting to us or strikes us as unusual in some manner. This type of work obviously does not warrant the claim of genius unless such performances show the essentials of extraordinary creative behavior by being highly productive, influential, and generative over many years.

Some works are spoken of as being "ahead of their time" — a natural enough but not conclusive attribute to *potentially* significant work. This is not only *post hoc* but begs the question of what the merits are and for whom. Less dramatically stated, to call work "ahead of its time" means it was produced before it was well understood, as in the case of Mendel; before it could be technically confirmed, as in the case of Einstein; or before it could be appreciated and accommodated, as in the case of some major composers. If anything, these examples point to another facet of the generative capacity of influential work. Since it is simply not possible for a work to be done and, on that basis alone, to be judged accurately for its importance and/or the presence of genius, we turn to another index of extraordinary work of impact. It must be not only of large volume but it must be taken up, responded to (for and against), examined, and put to use by others. Its degree of "fit" with the field around it can only be determined empirically; this is one of the essential tests of its impact. Its endurance is another test, and this quality of work grows from and feeds into its generative capacity.

Important work, like all behavior, is *transactive*. Its capacity for developing and being significant over decades is necessary; by doing so, it attracts new generations of adherents. If endurance tests the validity of a person's work, then the ability to attract and hold new students attests to its educative and its intellectual significance as well as its more technical importance. The significance of the products of long-term creative behavior is on several levels: cognitive, cultural, educative, as well as political (cf. Hughes, 1958, for a detailed discussion), suggesting a variety of areas or levels of influence as indexes of significance. Along with its other consequences, long-term productivity helps overcome others' resistance, a resistance that is understandable if the work in question has any demand qualities to it. All that we have been discussing makes time a critical variable to the problem of eminence. It often takes a generation of education to overcome resistance through further explanation, new examples, new applications, etc., which is why the capacities to continue producing work, to endure and overcome resistances, and to educate are so important. Again we must emphasize these operations can only take place in "public" in order to be effective. Since most published work, at least in the social sciences, does not receive immediate or large-scale attention (American Psychological Association, 1963) the importance of persistence is clear. It is no accident that Freud and his early adherents established their own publishing house.

Such terms as *unique* and *de novo* are not only oversimplifications but grossly misleading. They make a very complicated and often contentious historical process appear ahistorical, split off from the rest of life, and, ironically, they belittle the very achievement they attempt to credit by conveying the false impression that the works in question occur in a relatively unchallenged field with few or no other persons working in the same area or even on the same problems. All that we know of important persons, work of influence, and eminence suggests just the opposite conditions hold true. That is why, in part, the works in question are significantly influential. If the issues involved are serious to begin with, so are the competitors and the resistances (cf. Ellenberger, 1970; Kuhn, 1962; Shakow and Rapaport, 1968, especially chapters 1 and 2 for very detailed discussions; Watson, 1968).

More Contemporary Issues and Evidence

Until now we have discussed the problems involved in defining genius. Within our concern for a proper definition has been a more basic, if implicit, concern: Can one predict who might become an eminent person? The importance of this question cannot be underestimated; related to its answer is our understanding of what the major facilitative variables and experiences are that contribute to the works that are underlying in the achievement of eminence. The essential issue is not eminence *per se* but the clues that indicate how we might increase the type of behavior that eminence results from.

Research on eminent persons has been conducted off and on over the many years since Freud's and Galton's pioneer efforts. The bulk of this research shows that persons who do achieve extraordinary eminence generally begin their productive careers significantly earlier than their less productive peers (Albert, 1971; Cox, 1926; Lehman, 1953; Raskin, 1936; Roe, 1952). More recent evidence on productive careers suggests that early starts are a solid index by which to estimate a person's productive ability. In several studies of University of Chicago PhDs, eight years after their receiving their degrees, Bloom (1963) showed that those more creative than matched controls had significantly more publications. In fact, the large majority of publications came from less than 10% of the subjects, which is consistent with Dennis' (1954a) earlier finding regarding eminent psychologists. Bloom concluded that "while productivity is clearly not synonymous with creativity, it seems quite likely that unless there is some minimum or *threshold of productivity* there is little probability or likelihood that the individual is creative (p. 256, italics added)." Bloom's second study extends this point. It indicates once again that higher productivity characterizes the more creative person among chemists and mathematicians. Samples were matched for age, education, intelligence, and work experience. After a ten-year period, the more creative subjects averaged four publications yearly whereas their less creative controls averaged slightly less than 0.5 publications. Harmon (1963) confirmed these data in an investigation of 157 biological and 347 physical scientists who were divided according to their experience and specialties. From a pool of grade point averages, intelligence, achievement, and aptitude scores, as well as from work records and ratings of the scientists' professional attainment (judged by at least three independent raters working in the individual's fields), the best objective indicator of scientific accomplishment was found to be the number of publications for an individual.

We know that genius is not a function of differences in measured intelligence: Many researchers have found that once the IQ is higher than 120, other variables become increasingly important (Barron, 1969; Bloom, 1963; Cox, 1926; Harmon, 1963; Helson and Crutchfield, 1970; MacKinnon, 1962, 1968; Oden, 1968; Roe, 1952; Terman, 1954), although it would be absurd to argue that more "intelligence" would make no difference!

There are also interesting data pertaining to the "age of ascent" in productive careers. A number of studies have independently reported almost identical ages of "creative" subjects' first productions. Raskin (1936) noted 25.2 years and 24.2 years for her select groups of nineteenth-century subjects; Helson and Crutchfield (1970) noted 24.8 years for their subjects. Like Bloom's (1963) and Harmon's (1963) creative subjects, Helson and Crutchfield's creative subjects published more, as well as earlier, than their controls. Even more telling was the fact that Raskin was able to determine that as far back as 1735 the average age for first publication was 25 years. When she separated her samples into the 25 highest ranking scientists and the 25 highest ranking men of letters (lists included Darwin, Faraday, Gauss, Maxwell and Pasteur; Balzac, Coleridge, Goethe, Poe, Tolstoi, and Wordsworth), the average age for first productions was reduced only to 22 years. The present study shows that Freud was 21 years old at the time of his first professional publication, and Darwin and Einstein each were 22 years old at the time of their first papers, ages almost identical to Raskin's most eminent samples. Across a variety of fields and a two-century time span, there is a stable age at which eminent persons begin to be actively and publicly influential.

Additional data are closer at hand. Examination of the publication careers of 48 psychologists who, up to 1971, were awarded The Distinguished Scientific Contribution Award (DSC) by the American Psychological Association shows that, diverse as their special interests are, they are not too far from the performances described above for other fields. Recipients first published at the average of 25.3 — almost identical to Raskin's (1936) and Helson and Crutchfield's (1970) subjects. Raskin also found that the productive careers of scientists and men of letters in her study averaged 34.2 years and 29.8 years, respectively. (We noted earlier that Darwin produced important work for over 51 years, Einstein for 53 years, and Freud for almost 55 years.) Recipients of the award have long productive careers before being honored — averaging almost 31 years of publishing up to the time of their recognition, although a few were in their forties and fifties when so awarded. Assuming that there might be a difference between the careers of those who received the DSC when it was instituted in 1956 and those more recently awarded, we analyzed data for the first and last 12 recipients. The median number of years between first publication and time of award was 25.5 and 26.5 years, respectively. With few exceptions, long productive careers precede psychology's highest acknowledgement of influential work.

This median number of years has been consistent, for over two centuries, for persons working in various sciences and different forms of literature. What factors are behind its stability? Although education, formal and otherwise, has changed tremendously over the past 200 years, the average age of first publications for young creative scientists and a variety of highly eminent people remains much the same. This fact leads one to speculate that the basis for the type of creative behavior leading to very high eminence requires a particular combination of cognitive and personality development and early family experiences, both of which begin early in childhood.

To test the rather obvious proposition that receiving the DSC is associated with professional influence, we compared the list of DSC winners with Myers' (1970) list of most-cited authors in psychology. The match is far from perfect. . . . It is interesting to find that the lists are almost independent. Only Skinner appears on both. Second, although Freud's high citation (98 percentile) ranks him as 37 among Myers' 62 most frequently cited authors in nonpsychiatric, psychological literature, and although he is first among the all-time influential psychologists (he also appeared among Garfield's 50 most-cited authors in the 1967 *Science Citation Index*), he is not listed among the most influential contemporary psychologists. (His citation percentile rank is higher than three others on the list; the fact that he is dead is not a valid explanation, for so are three other men on the list.) Simply stated, frequent citation does not necessarily indicate an influential contemporary psychologist: Even the most influential psychologist of all time is not necessarily influential in a contemporary sense (a finding that should protect us from "snap" judgments). . . .

Another aspect of this relationship can be demonstrated. By taking Myers' lists of most-cited and most influential psychologists and comparing them to Roeckelein's (1972) list of most-cited psychologists in eight of the most widely-used introductory psychology textbooks (which, by their nature, are intended to present the essentials of a field), one can see the educative influence that eminence carries with it. All of the most influential contemporary psychologists are listed by Roeckelein. In addition, Myers' ten all-time most influential psychologists were referred to almost twice as frequently as his ten most influential contemporaries (1053 times versus 596 times). . . .

The above evidence provides strong support for the basic contention in this article: Long-term creative behavior, as evidenced in influential productivity, is the "carrier" of genius *qua* eminence. The earlier a person starts and the more he does, the more likely will his impact on others be significant and, eventually, the higher his eminence will be. This does not say what, if any, special cognitive, cultural, personality, racial, religious, or social attributes are necessary or involved in such behavior. For the time being, we can say that injecting additional words like *genius* or *unique* into our thoughts on the matter does not appear at all necessary or helpful.

Final Observations

One aspect needs further consideration; in many respects it may be the most important; it is certainly the least understood. For creative behavior, or any behavior, to continue, there must be close congruence between some of the processes a person uses and some of the characteristics of the phenomenon dealt with. It would be difficult, if not impossible, at present to characterize such a "fit" as antecedent or consequence. What begins as a vague correspondence between process and phenomenon becomes progressively closer the more intensively and the longer a person does his work. Artists and scientists alike often speak of a dimly-conceived, intuited, "reality" to their early efforts, one that appears early in life and seems to guide much of their behavior as a concerted effort to apprehend, to symbolize, and to control such a reality. Polanyi (1967) and Holton (1971) discussed such a consequence in Einstein's career. A similar case can be made for Freud by going into his early family life and the cultural events surrounding him (Albert, 1973). Hollingsworth (1942) has shown that the interests and questions of the exceptionally gifted child are remarkably accelerated and border on the profound very early in childhood. With the "precocious" questioning and interest often comes an intense involvement with selected materials, problems, and cognitive processes that are consonant with later-discovered adult professions and life work. If one identifies his interests and special capacities early in life and discovers the existence of such possible enterprises, it follows that he is on his way earlier than most other persons (see Cox, 1926; Ellmann, 1959; Meschkowski, 1964; Roe, 1952; Schilpp, 1949).

The "realities" that make up the content of long-term creative behavior occur noticeably early and more or less independently. These parallels are not explicit and are far from exact; they require lifelong efforts to tease them out, not unique intelligence or aptitude.

Conclusion

The above arguments suggest that genius is not a blessing, a danger, or a fortuitous occurrence; it is not a trait, an event, or a thing. Rather, it is, and always has been, a judgement overlaid with shifting values. What genius has often been based on is far more solid — behavior. What it must be based on is creative behavior, which, although highly personalized, is made public and is eventually influential over many years and often in unpredictable ways. By being both productive and influential, this behavior can be measured, its influence traced, and the factors and events underlying it better understood. Of all the qualities attributed to persons of genius the most remarkable, along with perceptiveness, are continuity, endurance, productivity, and influence. Men and women with such attributes are usually esteemed and often honored. They are almost always eminent in comparison to others. But they do not have genius.

References

ALBERT, R. S. (1971) Cognitive development and parental loss among the gifted, the exceptionally gifted, and the creative. *Psychological Reports*, 29, 19–26.

ALBERT, R. S. (1973) *Genius, eminence and creative behavior*, Fort Lee: Behavioral Sciences Tape Library.

AMERICAN PSYCHOLOGICAL ASSOCIATION (1963) *Project on Scientific Information Exchange in Psychology. Reports.* Vol. 1. Washington, DC: Author.

ANNAN, N. G. (1955) The intellectual aristocracy. In J. H. Plumb (Ed.), *Studies in social history*. London: Longmans, Green.

ANNIN, E., BORING, E. and WATSON, R. L. (1968) Important psychologists, 1600–1967. *Journal of History of the Behavioral Sciences*, 4, 303–315.

BACON, F. (1939) *Novum organum*. In E. A. Burtt (Ed.), *The English philosophers from Bacon to Mill*. New York: Modern Library.

BARRON, F. (1969) *Creative person and creative process*. New York: Holt, Rinehart and Winston.

BLOOM, B. S. (1963) Report on creativity research by the examiner's office of the University of Chicago. In C. W. Taylor and F. Barron (Eds), *Scientific creativity: Its recognition and development*. New York: Wiley.

BUTCHER, J. J. (1968) *Human intelligence: Its nature and assessment*. London: Methuen.

CLARK, K. (1969) *Civilization: A personal view*. New York: Harper and Row.

CLARK, K. E. (1957) *America's psychologists: A survey of a growing profession*. Washington, DC: American Psychological Association.

COLE, J. and COLE, S. (1973) *Social stratification in science*. Chicago: University of Chicago Press.

COLE, S. and COLE, J. R. (1967) Scientific output and recognition: A study in operation of the reward system in science. *American Sociological Review*, 32, 377–390.

COX, C. (1926) *The early mental traits of three hundred geniuses: Genetic studies of genius*. Vol. 2. Stanford, CA: Stanford University Press.

CRICK, F. and WATSON, J. (1972) The double helix revisited. Francis Crick and James Watson talk to Paul Vaughan about their discovery of the molecular structure of DNA. *The Listener*, 88, (2281), 819–821.

DARWIN, C. (1896) *The life and letters of Charles Darwin* (including an autobiographical chapter). Francis Darwin (Ed.). Vol. 4. New York: Appleton.

DELLAS, M. and GAIER, E. L. (1970) Identification of creativity: The individual. *Psychological Bulletin*, 73, 55–73.

DENNIS, W. (1954a) Bibliographies of eminent psychologists. *American Psychologist*, 9, 35–62.

DENNIS, W. (1954b) Bibliographies of eminent scientists. *Scientific Monthly*, 79, 180–183.

EISELEY, L. (1965) Darwin, Coleridge and the theory of unconscious creation. *Daedalus*, 94, 588–602.

EISSLER, K. R. (1963) *Goethe: A psychoanalytic study* 1775–1786. Vol. 1. Detroit: Wayne State University Press.

ELLENBERGER, H. (1970) *The discovery of the unconscious*. New York: Basic Books.

ELLIS, H. (1904) *A study of British genius*. London: Hurst and Blackett.

ELLMANN, R. (1959) *James Joyce*. New York: Oxford University Press.

The excitement and fascination of science: A collection of autobiographical and philosophical essays (1965) Palo Alto, CA: Annual Reviews.

FRANK, P. (1947) *Einstein: His life and times*. New York: Knopf.

FREUD, S. (1948) Dostoevski and parricide (1928). In, *Collected papers*. Vol. 4. London: Hogarth Press.

FREUD, S. (1953) Leonardo da Vinci and a memory of his childhood (1910). In, *Standard Edition*. Vol. 2. London: Hogarth Press.

FREUD, S. (1955) *Moses and monotheism* (1938). New York: Vintage Books.

FREUD, S. (1959) *An autobiographical study* (1925). In, *The standard edition*. Vol. 20. London: Hogarth Press.

FREUD, S. (1969) *A general introduction to psychoanalysis* (1933). New York: Clarion Book.

GALTON, F. (1869) *Hereditary genius*. New York: Macmillan.

GARFIELD, E. (1970) Citation indexing for studying science. *Nature*, 222, 669–670.

GHISELIN, B. (1963) Ultimate criteria for two levels of creativity. In C. W. Taylor and F. Barron (Eds), *Scientific creativity: Its recognition and development*. New York: Wiley.

HARMON, L. R. (1963) The development of a criterion of scientific competence. In C. W. Taylor and F. Barron (Eds), *Scientific creativity: Its recognition and development*. New York: Wiley.

HAZARD, P. (1953) *The European mind, 1685–1715*. New Haven: Yale University Press.

HELSON, R. and CRUTCHFIELD, R. S. (1970) Mathematicians: The creative researcher and the average PhD. *Journal of Consulting and Clinical Psychology*, 34, 250–257.

HOLLINGSWORTH, L. (1942) *Children above 180 IQ*. Yonkers-on-Hudson: World Books.

HOLTON. G. (1971) On trying to understand scientific genius. *American Scholar*, 41(1), 95–110.

HUGHES, H. S. (1953) *Consciousness and society*. New York: Vintage Books.

JANIK, A. and TOULMIN, S. (1973) *Wittgenstein's Vienna*. New York: Simon and Schuster.

KLINEBERG, O. (1931) Genius. *Encyclopaedia of the social sciences*. Vol. 6. New York: Macmillan.

KUHN, T. S. (1962) *The structure of scientific revolutions*. Chicago: University of Chicago Press.

LEHMAN, H. C. (1947) National differences in creativity. *American Journal of Sociology*, 52, 475–488.

LEHMAN, H. C. (1953) *Age and achievement*. Princeton: Princeton University Press.

LEKACHMAN, R. (1968) *The age of Keynes*. New York: Vintage Books.

MacKINNON, D. W. (1962) The nature and nurture of creative talent. *American Psychologist*, 17, 484–495.

MacKINNON, D. W. (1968) Selecting students with creative potential. In P. Heist (Ed.), *The creative college student: An unmet challenge*. San Francisco: Jossey-Bass.

MacKINNON, D. W. (1972) Maslow's place in the history of psychology. *Journal of Creative Behavior*, 6, 158–163.

MALCOLM, N. (1966) *Ludwig Wittgenstein: A memoir*. Oxford: Oxford University Press.

MERTON, R. K. (1961) Singletons and multiples in scientific discovery. *Proceedings of the American Philosophical Society*, 105, 470–486.

MESCHKOWSKI, H. (1964) *Ways of thought of great mathematicians*. San Francisco: Holden-Day.

MICHELMORE, P. (1962) *Einstein: Profile of the man*. New York: Dodd, Mead.

MYERS, C. R. (1970) Journal citations and scientific eminence in contemporary psychology. *American Psychologist*, 25, 1041–1048.

NAHM, M. (1957) *The artist as creator*. Baltimore: Johns Hopkins Press.

ODEN, M. H. (1968) The fulfillment of promise: 40-year follow-up of the Terman gifted group. *Genetic Psychology Monograph*, 77, 3–93.

PEARSON, K. (1914) *The life, letters, and labours of Francis Galton*. Vol. 1. Cambridge: Cambridge University Press.

PLUMB, H. H. (1969) *The death of the past*. London: Macmillan.

POLANYI, M. (1955) From Copernicus to Einstein. *Encounter*, Winter, 54–63.

RASKIN, E. A. (1936) Comparison of scientific and literary ability: A biological study of eminent scientists and men of letters of the nineteenth century. *Journal of Abnormal and Social Psychology*, 31, 20–35.

ROE, A. (1952) *The making of a scientist*. New York: Dodd, Mead.

ROECKELEIN, J. E. (1972) Eponymy in psychology. *American Psychologist*, 27, 657–659.

SCHILPP, P. A. (Ed.) (1949) *Albert Einstein: Philosopher-scientist*. Evanston: Library of Living Philosophers.

SHAKOW, D. and RAPAPORT, D. (1968) *The influence of Freud on American psychology*. Cleveland: World Publishing.

Shorter Oxford English Dictionary (1955) (3rd ed.) Oxford: Clarendon Press.

TERMAN, L. M. (1954) The discovery and encouragement of exceptional talent. *American Psychologist*, 9, 221–230.

TREVOR-ROPER, H. (1971) Sir Walter Scott and history. *The Listener*, 86, 225–232.

TYSON, A. and STRACHEY, J. (1956) A chronological hand-list of Freud's works. *International Journal of Psycho-analysis*, 57, 19–33.

WATSON, J. D. (1968) *The double helix*. New York: Atheneum.

WEIL, E. (1960) *Albert Einstein: A bibliography of his scientific papers*. London.

ZUCKERMAN, H. (1967a) The sociology of the Nobel Prizes. *Scientific American*, 217, 5, 25–33.

ZUCKERMAN, H. (1967b) Nobel laureates in science: Patterns of production, collaboration and authorship. *American Sociological Review*, 32, 391–403.

III

Giftedness: Signs and Outcomes

NO CONCEPT has been more confused with genius than giftedness and for this reason no group of children than the gifted has been so disappointing in their adult achievement to their parents, teachers, and often themselves. The idea that children of gifted ability will inevitably become persons of genius has been an unfortunate belief since Terman's original five-volume *Genetic Studies of Genius,* for he somewhat inadvertently linked the two — IQ 140 or more with the label of "genius." Few recall that he later withdrew the tie. Nonetheless, the fact that Plato described such children as "golden" is indicative of the deep hopes that western society has held for such children. It also indicates the often misplaced aspirations with which they have been burdened. As Addison's article in chapter I shows, giftedness and education have been closely associated in the Western mind for centuries. It is a bond made of equal strands of optimism and the wish to control human fortunes. The fact that we cannot say that a gifted child will inevitably become a genius makes it essential to understand what constitutes giftedness and to appreciate it for its own sake. If we can do this, then perhaps there are educational and other strategies which will assist such children — as children — to fulfill their own unique promise. But to do this we must first disentangle creativity, giftedness, and genius.

Undoubtedly, there is no better known or more widely referred to study of giftedness than Terman's five volumes, *Genetic Studies of Genius.* Stein and Heinze (III-1) perform a great service for persons who are interested in giftedness by summarizing succinctly and accurately the highlights of Terman's comprehensive, longitudinal research with over 1000 intellectually gifted boys and girls. It is not only the foundation of the many special programs for gifted children but ironically, this project, in all its five volumes, is a basis for appreciating some of the reasons why giftedness and genius are *not* synonymous.

Because one's understanding of such an important type of development as giftedness is often beclouded by a lack of appreciation of some of the worthwhile achievements of gifted adults, this chapter is also devoted to the important problem of measurement and prediction. The second and third papers are devoted to such issues. Chauncey and Hilton (III-2) believe in the validity and predictive power of some aptitude tests whereas Wallach (III-3) questions their validity. It is interesting to note that not only do Chauncey and Hilton and Wallach argue from entirely different perspectives but they often refer to different types of giftedness and adult performances. How much of their disagreement is a result of this is a question each reader will want to think about. For upon its answer hinges what one believes are the most appropriate measures and proper roles of psychometric tests in identifying gifted persons. It might be interesting to follow Wallach with Nicholls' discussion (VI-1) on the measurement of creativity. These three papers and Albert (II-3) make up a subsection on the measurement of genius and exceptional achievement.

MacKinnon's paper (III-4) on effective persons draws a further distinction among gifted adults, one which is implicit in several other papers. In this case the differences are between what MacKinnon calls effective persons and those who are creative. A close reading suggests what may often become of gifted children who are gifted but not overly creative and those who are gifted and creative — a distinction later investigated by Getzels and Jackson (1962) and Wallach and Kogan (1965) among children. This paper also introduces us to some of the powerful influences that a gifted child's family can exert upon his development. The methodology MacKinnon describes, with appropriate alterations, was used also by Barron (VI-4). For those readers with a strong interest in family life and giftedness, we recommend following this paper with Oden's (IV-5) follow-up of Terman's gifted children in their middle age.

Chapter III ends with Keating's paper (III-5) asking — can we predict from early exceptional mathematical giftedness to adulthood achievement? The paper describes the salient personality and cognitive characteristics of a group of extremely mathematically precocious boys discovered by Julian Stanley and his associates at the Johns Hopkins University. For the past decade, his *Study of Mathematically Precocious Youth,* has been focused upon the early identification and appropriate education of mathematically gifted youth. It has had a substantial impact upon American education. Keating suggests that such early giftedness does often bring with it a degree of creativity *potential.* Because subjects were in their early adolescence, this study clearly raises the question of the most appropriate age at which we can measure and predict later real-life creativity, especially in the area of appropriate values. Such values, when they are strong, along with appropriate abilities and motivations make up the three basic ingredients to exceptional achievement.

1

A Summary of Terman's
Genetic Studies of Genius, *
Volumes I and III

M. I. STEIN and S. J. HEINZE

RESEARCH in the origin of genius, its development, and environmental influences which affect it have been postponed by beliefs that the Great Man is qualitatively different from the rest of humanity and not to be explained by the same laws of behavior; by beliefs that intellectual precocity is pathological, by the strength of democratic sentiment which de-emphasizes native differences in endowment; and by the late birth of the biological sciences, particularly genetics, psychology, and education.

The author sees three main problems in the study of genius: its nature, its origin, and its cultivation. In this volume, he deals mainly with the first, as seen in the mental and physical traits of intellectually superior children. The purpose of this study is to show "in what traits and to what extent, a representative group of intellectually superior children differs from a group of unselected normal children."

Data were collected on over 1400 children, each well within the top 1% of unselected school populations of corresponding age. Most of the report is based on a typical group of 643 children, for whom data were available. Control data for 600 to 800 unselected children were secured where possible. The children were from the public school system in California and were mostly from the larger urban centers.

In selecting the main group, the procedure was as follows: (a) Teachers were asked to nominate from one to three pupils whom they regarded as most intelligent in their classes. In addition to this procedure, others were also used, e.g., inquiries of teachers (especially in lower grades), siblings of those already selected, casual information, accident, etc. (b) These pupils were then studied with the National Intelligence Scale B, Form I, and those who scored at the 90th percentile (or as low as the 80th percentile in special cases, or among the younger children) were retained for further study. (c) Abbreviated forms (one for children of foreign parents and one for children of non-foreign parents) of the Stanford-Binet were administered. Students attaining an IQ of 125 or more (or 120 if

Creativity and the Individual. Glencoe: Free Press, (1960)

they were older pupils) on the abbreviated scale were given a complete Stanford-Binet. On the complete Stanford-Binet, those pupils below 11 years old who achieved an IQ of 140 and the older ones (13.5–14) who achieved an IQ of 132 (with appropriate decrements in IQ between these limits) were retained for the complete study.

This was the procedure in grades 3–8, and there were variations in it in grades 1 and 2. It is believed that between 80% and 90% of the total qualified population were canvassed by the procedure described above.

The data obtained for each child in intensive study included the following:

1. Both the Stanford-Binet and National B
2. The Stanford Achievement Test
3. A general information test in science, history, literature, and the arts
4. A test of knowledge of, and interest in, plays, games, and amusements
5. An interest blank to be filled out by the children
6. A reading record (for two months) kept by the children
7. A "Home Information Blank" and ratings on 25 traits filled out by parents
8. A "School Information Blank" and ratings on 25 traits (same as those rated by parents) filled out by the teachers
9. Ratings of the home wherever possible using the Whittier Scale
10. Medical examinations
11. Anthropometric measurements (thirty-seven)
12. Tests of character and personality.

In the selected groups, boys were more numerous than girls. This is not regarded as due to biased selection procedures, but either to variability or the differential death rate of embryos. Data on racial origin showed, in comparison with the population of the cities concerned, that the gifted children showed "a 100% excess of Jewish blood; a 25% excess of parents who are of native parentage; a probable excess of Scotch ancestry; a very great deficiency of Latin and negro ancestry." Half the parents came from cities of 10,000 or more and the grandparents were slightly more of rural origin. In terms of father's occupations, 31.4% were professionals; 50% were semiprofessional and businessmen; and the remainder were skilled, semiskilled, and unskilled labor. Social class in this study was highly correlated with intelligence in fairly early childhood. A random sample of family income yielded a mean of $4705 with a standard deviation of $3805. Ratings of homes by the Whittier Scale yielded a mean score above that of the unselected population. The schools reported unfavorable home conditions for 8.6% of the gifted and 24.1% of the control group. About 16% of the boys and 2% of the girls had had paid work outside the home at some time. In 5.2% of the cases, the parents had been divorced and in 1.9% they had been separated. These figures are lower than for the general California population. The parents of the gifted completed twice as many school grades (twelve) as the average adult. One-fourth of the subjects had at least one parent who was a college graduate and 17% of the parents held a college degree. Books in home libraries ranged from 0 to 6000 with a median of 202 and a mean of 328.

There was "considerable indirect evidence that the heredity of our gifted subjects is much superior to that of the average individual." The number of families with two children in the group was more than 1200 times chance expectancy. About one-quarter of the members of the Hall of Fame were related to the subjects. Forty-four known relatives had been listed in *Who's Who,* and 58 other relatives were considered eminent; one family had 34 known relatives listed in the *Cyclopedia of American Biography* or in *Who's Who.* Parents and grandparents in great number had held responsible posts.

The proportions of miscarriages and infant mortality in the families of the gifted children were extremely low. The ages of the parents at the time of the gifted child's birth (father = 33.6; mother = 29.0) was slightly lower than those reported by Cattell for parents of American men of science. Premature births were found in 4.4% of the cases. Birth weight was about three-fourths of a pound in excess of norm. Nineteen percent of the male births and 12% of the female births had been instrument deliveries. The proportion of those who had been breast fed was considerably higher than for the general population, and was higher for cases above 160 IQ than for the entire group.

The ages of learning to walk and talk were lower than for normal children. About half as many gifted as control children were reported by the school as having frequent headaches. Symptoms of "general weakness" were reported nearly 30% less frequently. More than half of the gifted had had tonsillectomies; about a quarter of the controls had. Mouth breathing was reported less frequently for the gifted child than for the control group. Defective hearing was reported two and one-half times more often for the control than for the gifted; defective vision, about a quarter more often among the gifted. Frequency of colds was about equal. Onset of puberty averaged somewhat earlier among the gifted than the control girls, for boys the same result is suggested but regarded as tentative due to the small number of boys above 12. The school reported nervousness in 13.3% of the gifted and 16.1 of the controls; stuttering in 2.6% of the gifted and 3.4% of the controls.

There was a preponderance of first-born gifted in families of two or more, and since this agrees with Cattell's data on adults it "suggests that the causes are to be sought in native endowment rather than in environment and education." Forty-two of the fathers and 13 of the mothers were deceased, and the causes of death were quite varied. Small proportions of both fathers and mothers had one or more chronic illnesses, and the figures were probably less than for corresponding ages in the general population. Longevity of grandfathers was greater than would be expected. There was a record of insanity in 0.4% of parents and 0.3% of grandparents, and 37 other relatives. Few other cases of hereditary defect were reported. As a whole, the gifted group was physically superior to comparison groups; in height, weight, and breathing standards, they surpassed norms for American-born children (but 63–73% deviated no more than ±10% from the norms); they surpassed other California children studied in height and weight. Physical traits of girls were more variable than those of boys. Various cephalic indices were found, but the majority were mesocephalic. Correlations beween all physical traits were positive and high.

Medical examinations were given and analysis made of the data for 591 children of the main experimental group. The results confirmed the belief that this group was physically superior to unselected children of the same age.

The average gifted child entered school at 6.25 years. About 85% were accelerated, not one retarded; the average acceleration was 14% of age. Eighty-two percent were said to deserve more promotion. Mean chronological age and mean mental age differed by 2.8 years in the first grade, and by nearly five years in the fifth grade. As a rule, teachers said gifted children were doing work of superior quality; the superiority was greatest in "thought" subjects. Two and a half times as many gifted as control children were rated as "very even" in mental ability, but twice as many of the gifted group were rated as "very uneven." By the age of 8, the gifted, on the average, had attended two different schools and by the age of 11, the average was 3. The average number of days absent from school was 12.

Only 1% were reported by parents as having a positive dislike for school. The school reported less than half as many gifted children displayed an undesirable attitude toward school.

Nearly half learned to read before starting school, most with little or no formal instruction. Roughly 70% of the parents had let the child set his own pace; 20% had encouraged rapid progress; and 10% had held him back. On the average, the gifted child spent two hours of homework per week on school lessons. More than half of the group had private lessons in special subjects and spent 6.5 hours per week on them.

Indications of superior ability in arithmetic were reported by parents of half the group; similarly, for a third in music; and for dramatics, drawing, or painting, it was somewhat less. Eight percent of the parents reported never having observed signs of superior intelligence in their children; for others, intellectual superiority was first noted at about 3.5 years. "The indications of superior intelligence most often noted were quick understanding, insatiable curiosity, extensive information, retentive memory, early speech, unusual vocabulary, etc." Few parents had a systematic child-training scheme, but a majority had encouraged the child by answering his questions and taking an interest in the things which concerned him. Nothing had been found that led Terman to conclude that the attainments of his gifted children were, in any considerable degree, "the product of artificial stimulation or forced culture."

For 543 of the main experimental group, Stanford Achievement Test scores were available in reading, arithmetic, and language usage. Scores on a 335-item, general information test were also obtained. The results revealed very great superiority of the gifted over the unselected children. The average gifted child mastered subject matter 40% above his chronological age, but he was held back to a grade that was only 14% beyond the norm for his age. Superiority of the gifted was most marked in general information, language usage, and reading. It was least marked in history and civics. "The accomplishment quotients of a considerable number of gifted children are higher than the teachers' marks . . . would lead one to expect. Presumably, in such cases, the teacher has either underestimated the child's accomplishment or has given low marks as a penalty for lack of application to the set tasks of the school."

For a given age, no correlation was found between educational accomplishment and the number of terms the gifted child had attended school. Terman suggests, "Both the gifted children and the unselected children who were investigated, show such real and varied differences between their abilities in school subjects as to warrant the statement that each child must be regarded as a unique individual with specific mental mechanisms." Unevenness of development was about equal for each group. Selected case studies of gifted children revealed examples of specialization. The unevenness in the ability to deal with school subjects "indicates differences which are too great to be accounted for by differences in training. The development of some of the mental abilities must be greatly facilitated by innate factors." The intelligence level of the gifted was higher than their achievement scores.

Gifted children were in general more interested in abstract subjects, and less in "practical" ones, than unselected children. Subject preferences of gifted boys and gifted girls were more alike than those of control boys and control girls; gifted boys resembled control boys in subject preference far more than gifted girls resembled control girls. The gifted, far more often than controls, rated as "very easy" subjects such as literature, grammar, debating, and ancient history. The controls rated as "very easy" far oftener than the gifted, subjects such as sewing, drawing, painting, general science, singing, folk dancing, penmanship, etc. Gifted boys found shop work easy more often than did control boys, and control girls found arithmetic easy somewhat oftener than gifted girls. Gifted girls showed a high correlation with gifted boys in subjects found easy, but no resemblance to control girls. One and three-quarters times as many gifted as control children had collections; twice as many had collections of a scientific nature.

The gifted preferred occupations that were rated higher on the Barr Scale (a method of rating occupations in terms of the demands they make on intelligence) than those preferred by the controls. Among the gifted, there was less distance between the occupational ambitions of the child and his father's occupational status than among the controls. In a list of twelve kinds of activities, nearly all were rated higher by the gifted than the controls. "Gifted children have more enthusiasms than average children, and their interests appear to be in general no less wholesome."

In play interests, gifted children had measurably greater interest in activities requiring thinking, and ones that were mildly social and quiet; they indicated slightly less interest in competitive games than did the controls. Gifted boys scored slightly higher in a masculinity rating of activity interests than did control boys at all ages except 13; gifted girls did not differ consistently from control girls. Gifted children scored higher on maturity of activity interests than controls. Sociability of activities was somewhat lower for gifted than controls. Gifted children played alone slightly more; they more often preferred older playmates; they showed much less sex preference in choice of playmates; and the girls showed far less sex preference than boys. The gifted child was usually sought as a companion to the same extent as control children. Little difference was found between control and gifted children in the extent to which they were teased by others or cried when they could not have their way. "However, somewhat more gifted than control are said to be regarded by other children as 'queer' or 'different.' " Gifted boys were more frequently said to have play interests that were not normal than was true among control boys, and the reverse was true for the girls. Many gifted children had imaginary playmates, but no comparable data were available for the controls.

Teachers reported that 88% of the gifted children and 34% of the control children read more than the average child. Gifted children, according to lists they kept themselves, read over a wider range, and read more science, history, biography, travel, folk tales, informational fiction, poetry, and drama, and a lower proportion of adventure, mystery, and emotional fiction. In both gifted and control groups, boys showed a wider range than girls.

Tests given to 689 gifted children and 609 controls showed that there is "considerable increase of intellectual interest with age, only a little increase in the case of social interests, and none with activity interest. . . . There are no differences of sex in intellectual interest, but girls surpass boys at nearly all ages in social interest, and boys surpass girls at most ages in activity interest." Gifted children scored decisively higher than control children in intellectual and social interests, and did not differ materially in activity interests.

On tests of "character" ("moral instability" and "incorrigibility") the gifted group ($N = 532$) scored decisively better than the control group ($N = 533$). The character development of a gifted 9-year-old was equal to a 14-year-old in unselected population. Gifted girls scored higher than gifted boys. Sex differences in the control group, when found, were considerably smaller. Boys of both groups scored higher on honesty.

In trait ratings by parents and teacher, the gifted ($N = 600$) excelled in all the following (listed in order of superiority of the gifted): intellectual, volitional, emotional, moral, physical, and social traits. On mechanical ingenuity, controls ($N = 500$) were rated higher. No consistent sex differences in the control or gifted groups were found in variability of trait ratings.

A separate study of 309 gifted California high school students (nominated by teachers, and tested by the Terman Group Test and regarded as "the brightest in two hundred taken at random," average age 15 years, 3.4 months) confirmed "in almost every detail the results of the main experimental group." In this group, the sex ratio shifted from 116 to 183 boys per 100 girls; and: "It is suggested that the proportion of high-scoring girls may decrease as adulthood is approached."

A follow-up study two years later showed *"that the gifted children have not lost in educational or general ability, and that gains have far outbalanced losses with respect to such traits as social adaptability and breadth of interests."*

In his concluding remarks, Terman points out that "superior intellectuality" in this study was defined as the ability to make a high score on such intelligence tests as the National, the Terman Group, and the Stanford-Binet tests. "It is not necessary to assume that the criterion of intellectual superiority is wholly adequate, or that the superiority itself is either hereditary or abiding." The adequacy of the criterion and the permanence of the superiority will be tested in follow-up studies. Nevertheless, the study is regarded as yielding considerable information about childhood traits which correlated highly with high scores.

Terman cautions that the groups have been described and not the persons in them. He also cautions regarding the limits of the field covered by the various tests and measures used, e.g., intelligence of the pupils cannot be regarded as measured in all its aspects. These limitations, however, should not detract from the objectivity and the verifiability of the obtained data.

Although the data do not provide convincing proof, there are several lines of evidence that suggest that it is difficult, if not impossible, to explain the deviation of the gifted from the unselected group in terms of intellectual and volitional factors by the environmental hypothesis. Two possible environmental causes have been definitely ruled out — formal schooling and parental income. The influence of endowment is strongly suggested by much of the data. In the gifted group, there were numerous exceptions, with respect to the findings on character, personality, and emotional stability. "The gifted are not free from faults and at least one out of five has more of them than the average child of the general population. Perhaps one out of twenty presents a more or less serious problem in one or another respect."

Although the intent of the book was not to focus on pedagogical problems, Terman observes, "The present neglect of superior talent is sufficiently indicated by the inability of teachers to recognize it. One of the most astonishing facts brought out in this investigation is that one's best chance of identifying the brightest child in a classroom is to examine the birth records and select the youngest, rather than to take the one rated as brightest by the teacher."

Prediction of the children's future is profitless. To expect a majority of them to achieve eminence is unwarranted. Eminence is a poor measure of success and is a product of chance combinations of personal merit and environmental factors. Furthermore, although the group studied is superior, it is not like the group of adult geniuses studied by Galton and others. A child in the gifted group had to rate as high as the first in two hundred, but in Galton's study, the subject ranked as the first in four thousand. "Only about one of our subjects in twenty, or about fifty in the group of one thousand, would rank as the first in four thousand of a random selection."

The problems of genius are regarded by Terman as outranked by few other problems and as requiring much additional research. . . .

Volume III: Follow-up Studies of a Thousand Gifted Children

This is a follow-up study, after approximately eight years, of subjects studied in Vol. I of the *Genetic Studies of Genius.*

Tests of intelligence, achievement, and non-intellectual traits were administered to the subjects. The following procedures were also utilized: an information blank on the home; an interest blank for subjects up to 19; an information blank for subjects 20 years or older; a blank of trait ratings to be filled out by parents and teachers; a blank for teachers concerning school information; a questionnaire for married students; and reports of conferences with teachers and with children, as well as reports of home visits. The medical examination and physical measurements included in the previous study were not repeated.

In summarizing his studies, Terman presents the following "Composite Portrait of the Gifted Child."

1. The gifted children come predominantly from families "of decidedly superior intellectual endowment and of slightly superior physical endowment."

2. During the last two generations, the fecundity of these families has decreased greatly.

3. The average IQ of the siblings of children with IQs above 140 is approximately 123.

4. As a group, the intellectually gifted children are slightly superior to other children in health and physique and tend to remain so.

5. As a group, children who are gifted are not intellectually one-sided, emotionally unstable, lacking in sociability or social adaptability, nor do they possess other types of maladjustments.

6. "Indeed in practically every personality and character trait such children average much better than the general school population."

7. As a group, the children in the study are normal or superior in social-intelligence ratings, social interests, and play activity.

8. The gifted boys are similar to other boys of corresponding age in mental masculinity and feminity. Gifted girls deviate significantly from the norm in the direction of masculinity.

9. In terms of measured character traits, the gifted child is on a par with the unselected child of 13 or 14.

10. In traits rated by teachers, gifted children show their superiority to the

average most in intellectual and volitional qualities and least in physical and social characteristics.

11. The average gifted child is accelerated by 14% of his age in school progress; but, as measured by achievement tests, he is accelerated by 40% of his age.

12. No correlation was found between achievement tests and the number of years the gifted have attended school by the age of 10.

13. Gifted boys "maintain or almost maintain their relative superiority to the common run in intelligence, at least through the period of adolescence."

14. "Girls somewhat more often than boys show a drop in IQ as adolescence is approached, or soon thereafter."

15. Achievement in high school and college continues in line with the IQ originally found in 1921–22.

16. The gifted children practically never fail high school subjects.

17. Three-quarters of the grades obtained by high school girls and almost half of those obtained by the boys are A's.

18. Gifted children in their senior years in high school score above the 90th percentile of all high school seniors on a high school content examination.

19. Among the gifted boys, 90%, and among the gifted girls, 80%, go to college. Most of them graduate.

20. The children who graduate from high-grade universities earn Phi Beta Kappa or other honors about three times as frequently as do other graduates.

Certain results of secondary importance were:

1. Although the gifted students in college are able to judge their occupational interests as accurately as other students, a good many of them are looking forward to occupations that are not in keeping with their interests as measured by the Strong Test of Occupational Interests.

2. High ratings of literary productions, by several of the gifted, stimulate several questions, of which two are considered. One is why the seven most talented were all girls, and the other is whether these children are as well endowed in literary ability as eminent authors whose early writings were of the same merit as theirs. Terman answers the first question by saying that "the most reasonable guess is that the sex difference is one of interest and preoccupation rather than ability." In answer to the second, he suggests that "only time can tell" whether the children will make the most of their abilities.

3. The group contains many hidden potentialities, but whether these ever will come to fruition depends on nurture factors.

4. The greater a child's intellectual gifts, the greater his difficulties in making the most of them because of the difficulties that may arise in social adjustment.

5. The Special Ability Group, made up of students who had outstanding talent but who did not have an IQ of 140 or above, turned out disappointingly. This suggests to Terman "the important role played by general intelligence in making possible superior accomplishment in a special field."

6. The spouses of the gifted children appear "in a majority of cases less well-endowed than the gifted subjects who have married them."

In his summary, Terman indicates, "It is to be hoped that the superstitions so commonly accepted relative to intellectually superior children have been permanently swept away by the factual data these studies have presented. It is simply not true that such children are especially prone to be puny, over-specialized in their abilities and interests, emotionally unstable, socially un-adaptable, psychotic, and morally undependable; nor is it true that they usually deteriorate to the level of mediocrity as adult life is approached."

2

Aptitude Tests for the Highly Gifted*

H. CHAUNCEY and T. L. HILTON

IT IS frequently said that even though aptitude tests may be valid for students of average ability, they are not valid for students of high ability — that is, they do not accurately separate the able, the abler, and the ablest from each other. Or it is said that intellectual skills are important up to a point, but beyond that point other qualities take over as determinants of quality of performance (1). Or it is said, especially of achievement (rather than aptitude) tests, that objective tests not only fail to distinguish but actually discriminate against the most able students, by penalizing them for their ability to see imperfections in keyed answers which average students accept without qualms as correct (2).

These criticisms do not represent the same position. Some readers would subscribe to one but not the others. But they are concerned with a common subject: the validity of aptitude tests for the more able individuals. We shall here examine a number of studies pertinent to this question. It is our conviction that aptitude tests *are* useful in detecting differences in the upper range of intellectual ability, and that both their advantages and their limitations for this purpose need to be better understood.

Our major concern will be with students, although the first studies to be summarized concern mature scientists. Most of these studies are based on groups who rank in ability in approximately the top 1% of the general population. Where the data are derived from a preselected population, as for example college students, the "high" ability sample is a larger percentage of the sub-population in question.

Since the individuals under consideration are highly able, there is one sense in which some aptitude measures, by virtue of their design, clearly may not be valid for them. When the number and difficulty of the items, or the method of timing the test or of reporting the scores, is such that all or almost all of the highly apt students receive the highest possible score, the test will be valid in the sense of discriminating the highly apt from the average or low-scoring students, but not in the sense of discriminating among those of high aptitude. Some tests simply are not designed to provide distinctions at high levels, and when they appear invalid, the fault lies in inappropriate usage rather than in any inherent limitations in objective tests.

*Science, (1965), 148, 3672, 1297–1304. Copyright 1965 by the American Association for the Advancement of Science.

When suitable aptitude tests are used, the ceiling effect is not serious. For example, accumulated data on the Scholastic Aptitude Test (SAT), which was designed for college-bound high school students, indicate that only about one candidate in 16,000 achieves the maximum score of 800 on the verbal scale, and one in 1100 achieves it on the mathematics scale. These data are based on over 2 million candidates who have taken the test since January 1958 (3). The U.S. colleges which are the most highly selective (as judged from distributions of test scores for their entering classes) typically have less than ten students who have the maximum score on either the verbal or math parts of the SAT. A similar state of affairs holds for the Graduate Record Examinations (GRE). Out of approximately 22,000 students who took the GRE aptitude tests in the spring of 1961, 14 received scores of 800 and above (the highest score interval) on the verbal part and 263 scored in the comparable interval of the quantitative tests (4).

Validity for Scientific Personnel

Turning now to the evidence in regard to validity, we will first summarize several studies of able individuals in the sciences from whom aptitude-test data were obtained earlier in their lives.

The continuing research on graduate fellowship applicants conducted by the Office of Scientific Personnel of the National Research Council includes a number of studies of the test scores of the graduate students and scientists in their samples — clearly a population of high intellectual stature. Harmon (5) examined the high school backgrounds of 2853 graduates awarded the Ph.D. in the science fields in 1958. They constituted approximately 70% of recipients of science doctorates in the U.S. that year. (The 30% not included had attended high schools outside the U.S. or high schools which could not be identified, or did not respond to the questionnaires, or did not have the required data.) Harmon converted the scores from the different intelligence tests they had taken to a common scale — that of the Army General Classification Test (AGCT) — and then counted the number of these Ph.D.'s found at each interval of the scale. Combining these data with the known distributions of intelligence scores in the general population, he arrived at an estimate of the ratio of science Ph.D.'s to the population of each level of ability. The results are shown in Table III.1. In the IQ intervals below 100, there is a total of less than one Ph.D. per 1000. In the 100–110 level the number is about one per thousand, and it increases in each successive level of intelligence until it reaches 189 per 1000 among individuals with IQs of 170 and above. For our present purposes, the important observation is that even between very high IQ levels as measured in high school, the proportion of Ph.D.'s differed considerably.

In 1959 Harmon (6) identified 355 men who had been candidates for fellowships awarded by the Atomic Energy Commission in 1948 and had taken the

TABLE III.1 *Distribution of intelligence-test scores for total doctorate popu-*
lation. Adapted from Harmon (5, p. 682)

IQ interval (AGCT units)	Approx. general population at age 32 in 1958	Observed number of Ph.D's in all fields	Number of Ph.D.'s per 1000*
170 and higher	530	46	189
160–169	2,670	101	83
150–159	12,150	337	61
140–149	39,250	530	30
130–139	108,000	826	17
120–129	218,200	806	8
110–119	361,800	520	3
100–109	457,400	298	1
Below 100	1,200,000	103	0.2

*Adjusted to include estimated number of Ph.D.'s at each level among missing cases.

GRE at that time. By means of questionnaires mailed to the supervisors of the
men, he obtained confidential ratings of their scientific achievement based on
their scientific or technical contributions and on-the-job performance. For the
136 men not awarded fellowships none of the GRE scores was significantly
related to the ratings, but for the award recipients the Quantitative Ability and
Advanced Test scores were so related. . . . The correlations were small, accounting for only about 5% of the variance in the ratings. But several factors pre-
cluded high correlations. The reliability of the ratings was limited. Eleven
years elapsed between the test-taking and the collection of the criterion data.
Additional personal and situational factors influenced performance, and many
of the recipients were preselected by means of the GRE. Many graduate schools
use it for admission decisions, and it was also used as one of the bases for awarding fellowships; as a result the range of the scores and, thereby, the observed
correlations were curtailed. Lastly, the Graduate Record Examinations were
designed to predict graduate school performance and not necessarily on-the-job
performance. In view of these factors, it is not surprising that the correlations
are not higher. The results nevertheless demonstrate that measures of quantitative aptitude and achievement obtained early in the graduate school years
can provide statistically significant predictions of the quality of work, approximately 10 years later, of a group of scientists of exceptional ability and promise.

D. W. Taylor (7) examined the relation of certain tests, including aptitude
tests, to the rated performance of research scientists. Terman's Concept Mastery
Test (Form B), which is primarily a test of verbal intelligence, was not significantly correlated with supervisors' ratings of creativity and productivity. This is
consistent with the absence of correlations between the GRE verbal-ability score
and similar ratings. A test of high-level mechanical knowledge and visualization,
the Owens-Bennett Mechanical Comprehension Test (Form CC), did, however,

have significant positive correlations with the criteria. The reliability of the ratings was limited (one estimate placed it at 0.57) and, although not reported, the range of the test scores was, no doubt, restricted.

The studies of American scientists by Anne Roe (8, 9) are well known. One (9) summarizes the test scores of 64 outstanding scientists who were selected from a sample of physical, behavioral, and social scientists nominated by panels of scientists who themselves were outstanding in the respective fields. The nominated scientists were individually given a high-level scholastic aptitude test, the Verbal-Spatial-Mathematical (VSM) test prepared by Educational Testing Service. The IQ equivalents of the scores were obtained in a separate study. These IQs are summarized in Table III.2. The study does not yield information about discrimination within the group, but it does show how the scientists stood relative to the general population. Roe's conclusion in regard to these data was:

> It is clear that the average ability of the scientists is very great. This is not surprising. On the other hand, it is surprising, and a matter of very considerable importance, that there are among the scientists a number who are not facile at the types of tasks presented by the VSM, but who have been able to make contributions of great value to society (9, p. 30).

Whether a score equivalent to an IQ of 121 is accurately interpreted as indicating the person is "not facile" is, in our opinion, subject to question. Even this score, which is the lowest reported by Roe, is well above the average of the general population. It also should be kept in mind that Roe's tests were individually administered very possibly under less than ideal conditions in some cases. Scores were not obtained for five subjects, and two subjects declined to take the spatial and math tests, which suggests the possibility that others may have been reluctant in different subjects.

TABLE III.2 *Range and median of test scores (IQ equivalents) of outstanding scientists studied by Roe (8, pp. 164–169)*

Subtest	Score			N*
	Highest	Median	Lowest	
Verbal	177	166	121	59
Spatial	164	137	123	57
Mathematical	194	154	128	39

*The scores of five of the scientists were not reported, presumably because they were not obtained. Two anthropologists declined to take the spatial and mathematical tests. Because the mathematics test was not sufficiently difficult for the physicists in the sample, Roe omitted them from the summary.

College Scores of Successful Individuals

A study by Kallop (10), which concerns success in general, was of individuals who had taken the SAT between 1926 and 1939 and who later were included in *Who's Who* or *American Men of Science* or both. The mean SAT score for 232 men and women in *Who's Who* was 564 with a standard deviation of 93; the comparable figures for 49 men in *American Men of Science* were 575 and 103. Precisely how high these scores are above present-day scores is impossible to say with any certainty, since the scales are not equated to current scales. (The practice of equating the scales from one form of the test to the next was not started until 1941, which was after Kallop's experiments.) Also, an unknown sampling bias is present, since test scores were found for only a fraction of the individuals cited in the volumes. We can, however, compare Kallop's subjects with other college students who took the SAT in an appropriate period – the years 1926–1939. When these results are analyzed by the method Harmon used, a geometric progression similar to his is obtained (11). As shown in Table III.3, the estimated proportion of the college population represented in *Who's Who* steadily progressed with increasing test scores. The percentage with scores of 696 or higher is almost four times as great in the eminent group as in the total SAT population; the percentage with scores below 450 is less than one-third that in the total SAT population.

Data for another outstanding group of individuals – the 1963 Rhodes Scholars – were recently obtained by Pearson (12). SAT scores and scores on College Entrance Examination Board (CEEB) achievement tests were found for 23 of the 32 Scholars, the missing scores being largely for those from Western states. Most of the Scholars had taken the test four to five years earlier when they had applied for admission to college. The mean verbal, math, and achievement

TABLE III.3 *Aptitude scores and proportion of eminent individuals at each level of SAT college population (10, p. 16)*

SAT score interval	% expected (E) in each interval*	% in Who's Who group (O)	O/E
696 and above	2.6	10	3.8
629–695	7.3	15	2.1
563–628	18.9	25	1.3
500–562	21.2	25	1.2
450–499	19.1	15	.8
Below 450	30.9	10	.3

*Assuming the eminent individuals were evenly distributed throughout the SAT college population and that the distribution of scores was normal.

scores of 666, 708, and 674 . . . indicate that this group, who were chosen for their "literary and scholastic attainment, . . . fondness of and success in manly outdoor sports . . . , qualities of manhood . . . and more force of character and instincts to lead" were characterized by well-above-average test performance prior to entrance to college. The approximate percentile ranks for the mean scores when compared with the CEEB scores of high school seniors in a recent year age 95 for both the verbal and math tests. Over half of the Scholars had either verbal or math scores (or both) in the 99th percentile.

In addition, the SAT scores of 10 of the 12 students who in June 1961 were selected by *Time* magazine correspondents as being among the "top graduates of the top schools" were located in the files of Educational Testing Service. Their median verbal and math scores were 681 and 680, which are at approximately the 95th percentile when compared with the reference group described in the preceding paragraph.

Follow-up of Gifted Children

The well-known studies by Terman and his associates (13–15) afford an unusual opportunity to examine whether discernible differences in intellect exist within a group of adults who as children were identified as intellectually gifted. When first given the Stanford-Binet in 1921 they stood in approximately the top 1% of all California school children of their age (an average of 9.7 years). In a follow-up of the gifted children in 1940, the Concept Mastery Test (Form A) was given to 954 of the original group, and in 1950 the Concept Mastery Test (Form T) was given to 1004 of the original group. Seven hundred and sixty-eight of the gifted subjects participated in both the 1940 and the 1950 follow-ups. The correlation between their scores on the two occasions was 0.87, even though the testing was 10 years apart and the two forms of the Concept Mastery Test (CMT) were not precisely parallel. This is evidence of remarkable reliability in the test performance of a large group of individuals of high ability.

Between the original Binet scores and the 1950 CMT scores a correlation of 0.29 was observed, despite the high curtailment of the distribution of Binet scores. The differences in mean CMT scores among subgroups grouped in accordance with their Binet IQs were highly significant as tested by the F ratio ($P<0.001$). In addition, equally significant differences were found between the mean scores for subjects grouped by educational level (Table III.4). . . .

High Test Scores and College Performance

There have been thousands of studies of academic prediction, but few that have focused on students with high aptitude. These few are summarized here.

The first is the extensive study of the National Merit Scholars conducted by

TABLE III.4 *Concept-Mastery Test scores of Terman's gifted subjects according to educational level achieved (15, p. 58)*

Educational level	N	CMT scores	
		Mean	S.D.
Ph.D.	51	159.0	19.3
M.D.	35	143.6	23.2
LL.B.	73	149.4	20.7
Master's or equivalent	151	144.3	25.4
Graduate study, 1 or more years	122	143.0	26.9
Bachelor's degree only	263	135.7	26.6
College 1–4 years	163	128.7	29.7
No college	146	118.4	28.5

Holland and his associates (16). The Merit Scholars are a group of very superior ability, having a mean Stanford-Binet IQ estimated in one study to be about 150, with a minimum of 130 (17). The range of their aptitude scores is very narrow; Holland and Astin (16) report standard deviations of approximately 52 for the SAT Verbal Test and 69 for the SAT Math Test. As far as predictive validity of the SAT scores is concerned, Holland (18) concluded that there is no relation between aptitude and academic performance for students of high ability. This conclusion was based on a correlation of only 0.09 and 0.11 between the verbal and math scores and the first-year grades of the men, and even lower correlations for the women. Subsequent studies of Merit Scholars have produced similar results.

There is, however, an alternative interpretation of these low correlations. The Scholars attended some 70 colleges and universities. For his criterion of academic performance, Holland pooled the first-year grade averages without adjusting for differences in standards of evaluation; he gave no more weight to an A at a highly selective and competitive college than to an A at any other college. Since it is likely that the more able Scholars attended the more competitive colleges and, on the average, received grades which were no higher, if not lower, than those of the less able Scholars who went to the less competitive colleges, it is not surprising that a high positive correlation was not obtained. In fact, a negative correlation might well have been obtained.

Support for this interpretation is given by the correlations reported for individual colleges, which, as shown in Table III.5 are generally higher than the correlations for the pooled sample. This is true even though the standard deviations for the individual college samples are reported by Holland (18) to be generally smaller than those for the total samples. This indicates that the standard deviations for the individual colleges are approximately 40 for the Verbal Test

TABLE III.5 *Correlation of grades of Holland's subjects with Scholastic Aptitude Test scores within colleges. Adapted from Holland (18, Table 4, p. 139)*

College	N	r SAT Verbal	SAT Math
	Boys		
California Institute of Technology	26	0.09	0.16
Harvard	81	0.15	0.07
Massachusetts Institute of Technology	73	0.22	0.49[†]
Princeton	44	0.36*	0.31[†]
Stanford	27	0.18	0.23
Yale	49	0.29*	0.14
	Girls		
Radcliffe	24	0.49*	0.31
Wellesley	24	0.40*	0.29
	Weighted average		
		0.25	0.25

*Significant at the 0.05 level.
[†]Significant at the 0.01 level.

and 60 for the Math Test, meaning that for these individual schools the Scholars represent a highly preselected group with a greatly curtailed distribution of scores.

An additional effect resulting from stringent selection concerns the relations among the predictors rather than their lack of range as such. When selection decisions are based on the sum of the applicant's scores on several measures, it is possible to select a group in which the individual measures have a negligible positive intercorrelation or, in the extreme case, a negative correlation. Assume, for example, that the admission decision of a school is based primarily on the applicant's previous academic grades and his test scores, and that if his grades are relatively low he will be admitted provided that his test scores are high, and vice versa. From the point of view of admissions, this "multiple-selector" procedure is quite sensible. It reflects the well-founded belief that diligence may compensate for limitations in intellectual aptitudes, and that high intellectual aptitudes that have not been well employed in high school may find better expression in college. But the system inevitably lowers the correlation of each of the separate measures with the criterion — college grades — and both the separate correlations and the correlation between measures are further lowered by the exclusion of students with both low test scores and low high school grades, who would have made college records closely correlated with both measures. . . .

Prediction of Performance in Graduate School

Studies of the academic performance of graduate students provide numerous examples of predictive validity, at that level, of objective measures of intellectual skill and achievement. A few of these which involve students of especially high ability will be mentioned.

In a study of the validity of the Advanced Chemistry Test of the GRE, 59 graduate students were rated on the basis of their course work and their research. Of the 14 students with scores above 790 (above the 99th percentile for college seniors) 9 were rated A, 4 were rated B, and 1 was rated C. Of those scoring between 700 and 790, none was rated A, 19 were rated B, and 4 were rated C. For those scoring below 700 the comparable frequencies were 2, 7, and 13. It is interesting that two students with scores below 700 were assigned A ratings. For our present purposes, however, the more important fact is that *in toto* there were clear differences between the groups defined in terms of the test scores (21, p. 7).

Similarly, a study of 68 graduate students in physics at the University of Chicago showed that 92% of those with Advanced Physics Test scores of 600 or above received Ph.D.'s, whereas only 53 percent of those with scores below 600 were successful (21, p. 8).

A follow-up study of 44 graduate students admitted to the English Department of Princeton University from 1950 to 1955 showed that 80% of those with GRE Verbal Ability scores of 700 or higher were rated average or above average in academic performance, whereas 38% of those with scores below 700 were so rated. Of the 17 students with scores below 690 on either the Verbal Ability Test or the Advanced Literature Test, only five received the Ph.D., and these were each rated below average on their final oral examinations. The investigator concluded that "the predictive ability of the GRE alone is about as good as a combination of all the other information regularly supplied, including academic records and letters of recommendation even after adjustment in the light of knowledge of the institution and the recommenders" (22). Significantly, the positive results were obtained only from the verbal aptitude and achievement measures not from the measure of quantitative aptitude, no doubt because of the nature of the graduate work involved, which demonstrates again the importance of having relevant aptitude measures. . . .

In a study of 119 Research Foundation Fellows in 15 different departments at Purdue University, King and Besco (24), using faculty ratings of overall performance as criteria, found a steady increase in the percentage rated above the median performance level as the verbal scores on the GRE Aptitude Test increased. Of those with a verbal score of at least 530, 59% were rated above the median; of those with at least 570, 64% were above the median, and of those with at least 640, 70% were above.

A study done for the National Research Council by Creager (25) showed that within a group of 2196 graduate students who applied for NSF Graduate Fellowship Awards — which represents a highly able group of individuals — the likelihood of completing graduate work and receiving the Ph.D. varied directly with their ability as measured by the GRE. The applicants were divided into five ability groups on the basis of the unweighted sum of the GRE Aptitude and Advanced Test scores. Thirty-five percent of the men in the lowest ability grouping eventually received the Ph.D., 56% in the next lowest, 70% of the next, 80% in the next, and 88% of those in the highest ability group.

The accumulated evidence from a number of studies in which the Miller Analogies Test (MAT) was used as a predictor of graduate school performance indicates that that instrument also has substantial validity for high-level students. In a study by Finch (26) on 112 graduate students selected for a doctoral program (and thus a curtailed sample) a biserial correlation of 0.56 for a pass–fail criterion was obtained. The median MAT score of the 59 successful students was 68 (out of a possible 100) and of the 53 unsuccessful candidates, 59. Similar results were obtained for the MAT at the University of Pittsburgh and the University of Tennessee, as well as other universities.

In their well-known study Kelly and Fiske (27) observed that MAT scores significantly predicted the rated performance of clinical psychology trainees. In addition, a preliminary follow-up showed the highest mean MAT scores for those who by that time had received the Ph.D., and then descending means for the group still in training, the group who voluntarily resigned, and the group dismissed, in that order. By the time of the first full-scale follow-up of the trainees, conducted approximately 10 years after the first data collection (28), the distinct differences in the means disappeared, possibly because of the varying standards of the many different programs from which the members of the original sample were graduated. If the average MAT scores were higher for the graduate schools with the higher standards and, in addition, with higher student-withdrawal rates, then a negative correlation between pooled MAT scores and graduate school completion could result, in the same way that Holland might have obtained negative correlations.

Perhaps the most direct effort to answer the questions raised in this article was by Angoff and Huddleston (29). In contrast to the foregoing studies they approached the question of test reliability and validity for students of high ability by determining whether a scholastic aptitude test especially tailored for such students would show greater reliability and validity than a conventional test. They devised a test with a narrow dispersion of item difficulties, the average level being high, and gave it, along with a conventional test, to 429 college students of high ability. When the results from the two tests were compared, it was found that the narrow-range test showed reliability coefficients 0.03 or 0.04 higher than the broad-range (conventional) test, and that for the prediction of academic grades the validity coefficients were 0.01 or 0.02 higher. These differences were judged to be not sufficient to justify the use of separate SAT's for students at different levels of ability.

Discussion and Conclusion

From the studies that have been summarized, it is clear that if the charge that aptitude tests do not discriminate for high-ability students is valid at all, it is valid only in some special sense.

The first possibility considered was that objective tests do not discriminate among highly able students because all such students receive the maximum score. But in fact the ceilings of the tests can be sufficiently high to provide room for all to demonstrate their ability. In principle, there is no limit to the ceiling; by including enough very difficult items in a test, the ceiling can be raised above the level of all who take it. In practice, however, this is both uneconomical and unnecessary.

The evidence is that substantial validity for high-level subjects is possible when (i) the instrument is appropriate for the sample and the predictive task at hand, (ii) a relevant criterion measure is available, and (iii) the correlation is not reduced by the effects of (a) a low ceiling on the criterion, (b) a very narrow range of ability in the group tested, or (c) what was referred to as the "multiple-selector" system. In summary, there is no evidence that aptitude tests are less valid for individuals of high ability than for individuals of average ability.

The research of Harmon, Roe, Kallop, and others showed that various aptitude measures administered early in the lives of the individuals involved significantly predicted certain aspects of their later careers. In addition, research on students of high ability demonstrated that quality of performance increases with increasing test scores even at very high levels. Holland's work (16, 18) would seem to be a demonstration to the contrary, but his negative findings can be accounted for, as Holland himself points out, by the way in which the data were pooled.

Holland's findings also illustrate in a particularly vivid fashion the problem of curtailment of range. When scholastic aptitude tests are used in two successive screenings of a group of candidates, the resulting group is unusually homogeneous in this respect and, thereby, difficult to discriminate among. It is not surprising that Holland had to turn to nonintellectual measures in order to find differences among the students in his samples.

Whether there is evidence in regard to the criticism that objective tests discriminate *against* highly able students is not answered. If there is such discrimination and it is extreme, then the studies that have been examined are irrelevant: the very students who would have provided pertinent data would have been excluded from consideration, since most of the studies reported focused on students who had scored high enough on one objective test or another to qualify for inclusion in some sample, for example, a college entering class. If the discrimination is not so extreme (which seems likely), there is still the possibility that only a small group of exceedingly able students is discriminated against and that the lack of validity for these is not detected when large samples are observed.

In none of the studies were perfect correlations reported. The possibility that some of the departures from prediction resulted from the alleged discrimination cannot be completely discounted.

Several of the studies described demonstrated that the predictor aptitude must be relevant to the academic performance in question – a truism, but one which is frequently lost sight of. A measure of verbal aptitude may not be an appropriate predictor of the quality of work in science of students high in mathematical aptitude (even though it may be a useful predictor for students with low aptitude, since whether such students have enough ability to communicate effectively may be at stake, a question which does not ordinarily exist for students high in quantitative aptitude).

A remaining question concerns how much of the variance in the intellectual performance of highly able students is explained by aptitude scores. Do the scores account for all or nearly all of the differences in performance? Although we know of few rigorous efforts to answer this question, it is clear that the answer is no. Most of the correlations reported are within a range of 0.40 to 0.70, which means that typically less than half of the variance in the criteria is accounted for by the various predictors. Also, we know that numerous studies have shown other measures to be related to intellectual performance. In the Taylor study (7) of research scientists, for example, a special test of how to plan and conduct research was more highly correlated with performance ratings than the aptitude measures were. Other studies have reported noncognitive correlates of high-level performance. Persistence, need for achievement, ego involvement, originality, high self-evaluation, intellectuality, and socialization are only a few such correlates. Unfortunately, in most of the studies there have been no attempts to control or partial out the contribution of differences in intelligence to differences in performance, but even if such steps were taken, it is highly likely that significant noncognitive effects would remain. Otherwise, the whole structure of our conception of human functioning would need drastic reformulation.

In conclusion, there is ample evidence that aptitude tests can discriminate reliably among students high in ability, and also can validly predict relevant characteristics of the performance of such individuals. This is not to say that they account for all or nearly all of the variance in high-level performance. But from the available research it appears likely that aptitude measures account for fully as much variance as do other single measures.

Notes

1. D. C. McCLELLAND, A. L. BALDWIN, U. BRONFENBRENNER and F. L. STRODT-BECK, *Talent and Society* (Van Nostrand, Princeton, NJ, 1958), p. 13.
2. B. HOFFMAN, *The Tyranny of Testing* (Crowell-Collier, New York, 1962), pp. 99–101.
3. W. E. COFFMAN, "The Scholastic Aptitude Test – a forward look, 1963," unpublished.
4. Unpublished test analysis conducted at ETS.

5. L. R. HARMON, *Science* **133**, 679 (1961).
6. L. R. HARMON, "Validation of Fellowship Selection Instruments against a Provisional Criterion of Scientific Accomplishment." *Res. Fellowship Selection Techniques, Office Sci. Personnel, Natl. Acad. Sci., Natl. Res. Council Tech. Rept. no. 15* (1959).
7. D. W. TAYLOR, "Variables related to creativity and productivity among men in two research laboratories," in *Scientific Creativity,* C. W. Taylor and F. Barron, Eds. (Wiley, New York, 1963), pp. 228–250.
8. A. ROE, *The Making of a Scientist* (Dodd, Mead, New York, 1952).
9. A. ROE, "A Psychological Study of Eminent Psychologists and Anthropologists, and a Comparison with Biological and Physical Scientists," *Psychol. Monographs: Gen. Appl.* **67**, 1–55 (1953).
10. J. W. KALLOP, "A Study of Scholastic Aptitude Test and Eminence," thesis, Princeton Univ., 1951.
11. It should be kept in mind that Harmon's results were based on the general population and Kallop's were on a selected college population. To obtain a more direct comparison of the two studies we can estimate the AGCT score which is comparable to Kallop's 75th percentile SAT score. On the basis of a table provided by C. C. Brigham [*A Study of Error* (College Entrance Examination Board, New York, 1932), p. 336] and a second table provided by the Staff, Personnel Research Section, Adjutant General's Office [*J. Ed. Psychol.* **38**, 385 (1974)], the SAT score of 629 is estimated to be comparable to an AGCT score of 150. Kallop observed that 25% of his cases fell above this score; Harmon observed 14%. In addition, by means of the same estimates, we can say that a person in the top 1% of the general population has approximately 25 times as much chance of being in *Who's Who* as has the population in general.
12. R. PEARSON, "On the Use of Multiple-Choice Tests in College Admission" (College Entrance Examination Board, New York, 1963).
13. L. M. TERMAN, and M. A. MERRILL, *Measuring Intelligence* (Houghton Mifflin, Boston, Mass., 1937).
14. L. M. TERMAN and M. H. ODEN, *The Gifted Child Grows Up* (Stanford Univ. Press, Stanford, Calif., 1947).
15. L. M. TERMAN and M. H. ODEN, "The Gifted Group at Mid-life," *Genetic Studies of Genius, V* (Stanford Univ. Press, Stanford, CA, 1959).
16. J. L. HOLLAND and A. W. ASTIN, *J. Educ. Psychol.* **53**, 132 (1962).
17. J. R. WARREN and P. A. HEIST, *Science* **132**, 330 (1960).
18. J. L. HOLLAND, *J. Educ. Psychol.* **50**, 135 (1959).
19. D. WHITLA, "PRL (Predicted Rank List) Revisions," unpublished Harvard College Study, 1962.
20. J. W. FRENCH, "The Validity of New Tests for the Performance of College Students with High-Level Aptitude," *Res. Bull.* 63–7 (Educational Testing Service, Princeton, NJ, 1963).
21. G. V. LANNHOLM, "Abstracts of Selected Studies on Relationship between Scores on the Graduate Record Examinations and Graduate School Performance," *Graduate Record Examinations Spec. Rept. 60–3* (Educational Testing Service, Princeton, NJ, 1960).
22. J. THORPE, unpublished report, Princeton University Graduate School, 1959.
23. G. V. LANNHOLM and W. B. SCHRADER, *Predicting Graduate School Success* (Educational Testing Service, Princeton, NJ, 1951).
24. D. G. KING and R. O. BESCO, "The Graduate Record Examination as a Selection Device for Purdue Research Foundation Graduate Research Fellows," unpublished report, Graduate School, Purdue University, 1960.
25. J. A. CREAGER, "A Study of Graduate Fellowship Applicants in Terms of Ph.D. Attainment," *Res. Fellowship Selection Techniques, Office Sci. Personnel, Natl. Acad. Sci., Natl. Res. Council Tech. Rept. No. 18* (1961).
26. See W. S. Miller, *Manual, Miller Analogies Test* (Psychological Corp., New York, 1952), p. 9.
27. E. L. KELLY and D. W. FISKE, *The Prediction of Performance in Clinical Psychology* (Univ. of Michigan Press, Ann Arbor, 1951).

28. E. L. KELLY and L. R. GOLDBERG, "Correlates of Later Performance and Specialization in Psychology," *Psychol. Monographs: Gen. Appl.* **73**, no. 12 (1959).

29. W. H. ANGOFF and E. M. HUDDLESTON, "The Multi-level Experiment," *Statist. Rept. 58–21* (Educational Testing Service, Princeton, NJ, 1958).

30. We are indebted to John W. French and William B. Schrader for their valuable criticisms of a draft of the manuscript.

3

What Do Tests Tell Us About Talents?*

M. A. WALLACH

QUALITY educational resources are an inevitably scarce commodity, and the decisions as to which young men and women will gain admission to highly regarded colleges and universities and receive scholarships or fellowships while they are there are difficult ones. How should these decisions be made? The relative merit of candidates is the usual criterion, but the definition of merit is problematic. Typically, "merit" is defined as scores on tests of intellectual abilities and grades in the customary types of academic course work, which themselves are usually determined by some kind of test.

Of course, test scores and grades are not indices of merit in their own right; they are thought to provide a shorthand indication of a student's competencies in the world outside testing and classroom situations. Recent research on the nature of talent indicates, however, that the premise that tests reflect the potential for achievement is false for scores across the upper part of the range on customary assessments of academic skills – precisely that part of their range in which such scores are most often used for selecting recipients of the most contested educational opportunities. The answer is not, as I and some others first thought, to replace tests aimed at assessing academic skills with tests that would reflect a person's "creativity"; rather, tests should be used only to screen out candidates who score too low. To make distinctions among the candidates who remain, we would rely not on tests but on samples of professional competencies themselves.

Disenchantment with the utility of tests in their upper ranges for predicting the sought-for competencies is not limited to the study of talent but has been increasing among most psychologists who attempt to devise ways of assessing human behavior. Traditionally, after theorizing about the relatively abstract dispositions that presumably underlie the display of the behavior, the psychologist attempts to develop tests that would signal the operation of these dispositions. Since the connection from test to criterion is mediated by complex theoretical constructions, the former need have nothing in common behaviorally with the latter. A psychologist could try to evaluate the chances that a particular therapeutic treatment would succeed with a subject by something as unrelated as the

*Current Trends in Psychology: Readings from American Scientist. Los Altos, California, William Kaufmann, (1977). Reprinted by permission.

way in which the subject completed sentence stems or interpreted ambiguous
pictures.

With enough negative evidence in hand from attempts of that sort, we now
know (see e.g. Mischel, 1972) that more reliable answers are provided by assessing
what the subject does in a sample of the treatment situation itself. The problem
is that the test responses, even if they possess a modicum of "criterion validity"
– that is, give results better than chance at predicting the behavior of direct
interest – inevitably reflect other factors as well (see Wallach, 1971a; Wallach
and Leggett, 1972). And the greater the conceptual distance between the test
and the performance to be predicted, the less reason there is to believe that the
test will tell you what you really want to know. It will tell you about the person's
response tendencies in situations that resemble the test rather than in situations
that resemble the criterion.

Academic Skills Tests

Above intermediate score levels, academic skills assessments are found to
show so little criterion validity as to be questionable bases on which to make
consequential decisions about students' futures. What the academic tests *do*
predict are the results a person will obtain on other tests of the same kind.
Some of the evidence for this statement is based on accomplishments of directly
meritorious kinds during the student years, and we shall consider it first. After
that, we will turn to accomplishments in occupational and professional roles.
The research along both lines is extensive enough that we can only sample it here
– but the sample is representative. Further amplification of this evidence and its
meaning can be found in Wallach (1971a, 1971b, 1977), Wallach and Wing
(1969) and Wing and Wallach (1971).

Most of what constitutes the usual academic course work, with its digesting
of a more or less formal curriculum which is then checked by memory-oriented
·examination questions, differs in kind from most vocational roles. The cramming
and test-taking skills needed to obtain good grades in such courses, however,
have much in common with the skills that should help earn high scores on tests
of intellectual ability, and it should not surprise us to find scores on "intelligence" tests correlating rather well with "academic achievement" indices – a
point that has been thoroughly documented (Tyler, 1965; Wallach and Kogan,
1965; Wing and Wallach, 1971). By the later high school years, however, students
are capable of producing work of intrinsic significance in a vocational sense.
Sometimes – though not always – this work is accomplished outside the school
curriculum.

In a study by Parloff, Datta, Kleman, and Handlon (1968) the novelty and
effectiveness of research projects conducted by high school students independent of course work were evaluated. Differences in quality among the projects
were substantial – but were unrelated to intellectual aptitude test scores or to

high school grades. Even course grades in *graduate* school often seem unrelated to the competencies associated with professional performance. Using a judgment scale taken from Taylor's (1958) work on the quality of research by professional scientists, Mednick (1963) asked faculty members to evaluate research projects conducted independently by psychology graduate students for the imaginativeness of the project and the degree to which it constituted a contribution to knowledge — reasonable criteria of competence for professional work. The judged quality of the projects ranged widely, but differences in quality had nothing to do with the grades received by the students in their scores on the Miller Analogies Test. Scores on this test, however, predicted the course grades.

These results typify the findings of a wide array of studies of high school, college, and graduate-level students concerned with assessing accomplishments that anticipate post-schooling achievements. Public recognition by knowledgeable evaluators is a major criterion of quality in this research — and, while admittedly imperfect, it is reasonably close to the way in which professional excellence is judged in life. Attainments in science, literature, art, music, and dramatics have all been studied, and indications of quality include, for example, publication of a scientific paper in a professional journal or of original writing in a nationally circulated periodical or a book. While sometimes direct evidence of such attainments can be obtained (e.g. Morrison, 1963, where direct judgments of competence in dramatics are made), it also has been found that student reports on these matters are sufficiently accurate to provide a usable source of data. Maxey and Ormsby (1971), for example, demonstrate high agreement between student reports on out-of-school accomplishments and information provided by the school — even when college admission is at issue for the students.

The results of these studies show that, for instance, for the more than 500 undergraduates studied by Wallach and Wing (1969), accomplishments outside the classroom in each of the seven fields explored were about as frequent among students in the lower third as among those in the upper third on the College Entrance Examination Board's Scholastic Aptitude Test (SAT). The fields chosen were intended to span a representative array of the accomplishments beyond the classroom for which school is expected to serve as a preparation. Some of these activities — work in literature and science — are close to traditional academic disciplines, while others, like music and art, though not traditionally academic fields, are still within the customary purview of most higher educational institutions. Still others — dramatics, for instance — may or may not be included in a college's curricular spectrum. For none of the areas studied — literature, science, art, music, dramatics, political leadership, and social service activities — was accomplishment related to SAT scores, either considering the sample of students as a whole or taking men and women separately. Furthermore, the extent to which students exhibited achievements in more than one of the seven areas was likewise unrelated to SAT scores. These findings hardly support the idea that the SAT in this upper range reflects brightness broadly defined. On the other hand, students with the higher SAT scores were found to have higher course grades.

Even more compelling data pointing in the same direction come from Wing and Wallach's (1971) studies of college applicants. In that work, the subject pool was broadened to include not just undergraduates but high school students who had applied for admission. Definitions of accomplishment outside the classroom were restricted to relatively rare achievements of merit – for example, publication of original writing in a regularly circulated nonschool publication or the receipt of an award for such writing; having won top prizes in state or regional science competitions or having been chosen to attend a summer science program sponsored by the National Science Foundation; having won a prize in a musical competition or having done professional work in performance or composition.

The SAT scores of the more than 4600 applicants of both sexes studied in our research on this question tell us very little about who is more likely to excel at accomplishments of these kinds. We found that if candidates are selected from the applicant population according to a hypothetical decision rule that favors applicants who scored high on SAT tests, applicants with the sorts of accomplishments just noted receive little or no differential benefit. Yet the selections actually made through the admissions process were found to be predominantly a function of the SAT score results. Similar results have been found in a study by Holland and Richards (1965), among others.

An implication of the foregoing is that score distinctions within the upper range should fail to predict the people who have demonstrated meaningful achievements in occupational and professional roles after leaving school, and this too seems to be the case. This outcome is so uncomfortable that evidence along these lines can meet with resistance. Take, for example, a careful study by Harmon (1963), in which the professional contributions of some physicists and biologists were evaluated by scientist judges on the basis of such criteria as publications and patents granted. The evaluations, by three or more experts working independently, were about as sophisticated and meaningful as such judgments could be. They were compared with college-level academic proficiency data – customary kinds of verbal mathematical aptitude test scores, the score earned on an advanced achievement test in the student's field of concentration, and grades obtained in science courses. How good a professional scientist the person became could not be predicted from any of this academic proficiency information – and indeed, for nearly half the correlations computed, the direction of the relationship was negative rather than positive. Yet Harmon's reaction to this finding is to question not the predictors but the criteria!

The same result has emerged in study after study, whether intelligence test scores or course grades are used as predictors. Helson and Crutchfield (1970) found for mathematicians, for example, that the IQ scores of those chosen by knowledgeable peers as doing particularly good research work were no different from those of controls. Chemists and mathematicians chosen by peers for the quality of their contributions were found by Bloom (1963) to score no higher than controls on a variety of intellectual ability tests. Further data on research scientists from MacKinnon (1968) yielded the same outcome, and comparable results emerge from studies of psychologists (Marston, 1971), artists (Barron, 1963), and architects (MacKinnon, 1968), as well as from a range of evidence reviewed by Hoyt (1965, 1966) on occupational activities in scientific research, engineering, medicine, and business. In Great Britain, Hudson (1960) similarly finds undergraduate academic distinctions having little relationship to subsequent occupational eminence among scientists.

Although critics like Weitzman (1972) seek to question such findings on the ground that these studies consider too narrow a range of academic skills differences, the range is broad enough to include many more individuals who *seek* superior opportunities for educational advancement than can be granted them, and the question of how, within this range, selections are to be made is a real one. The lack of predictability seems all the more striking when we consider that a self-fulfilling prophecy effect no doubt exists in some degree, leading students with superior test scores and grades to be preferred for superior occupational slots over those with less impressive academic credentials. The evidence would seem to be all the stronger, since it must be emerging in spite of a prophecy bias of that kind.

"Creativity" Tests

Extensive attempts to assess "creativity" or "originality" gained momentum in the 1960s, leading quickly to the need to make distinctions between tests that were simply assessing for intelligence once again but under a more fashionable label and tests that correlated minimally with conventional tests of intellectual skills (see Wallach and Kogan, 1965; Wallach, 1968). The tests that seemed best to meet this requirement (Wallach, 1970 provides an extensive sifting of the evidence on this question) focus on the ability to produce in response to a given task a large number of ideas that are reasonably appropriate and, at least partly because of their number, include a rather large proportion of relatively unusual responses. Surprisingly, "ideational fluency" in this sense showed, for those above an intermediate level on academic skills, little correlation with standing on intelligence tests.

The ideational fluency tests typically asked the respondent to generate possible ways in which specified pairs of objects are similar (such as a cat and a mouse), or possible uses for some ordinary object (such as a newspaper), or possible instances of a specified category (such as things that move on wheels), or possible interpretations for various presented abstract line forms (such as a triangle surrounded by three circles). Time and again it has been demonstrated that samples ranging from intermediate to high on customary intelligence indices show little or no relation to the number or unusualness of the ideational responses on tests of this kind (see e.g. Wallach and Kogan, 1965; Wallach and Wing, 1969; Wallach, 1970, 1971a). More unusual ideas tend to come later in the sequences of ideas, so that unusualness seems to ride the back, as it were, of the tendency to produce longer ideational strings, and respondents are relatively consistent in their degree of ideational fluency across different kinds of tasks.

Explanations for the observed differences in ideational fluency included varying tendencies to entertain the hypothetical (Wallach, 1967) or to pick up information from the periphery of one's attentional field (Wallach, 1970). Introspective accounts by highly talented writers, scientists, mathematicians, musicians, and artists of the importance for their creative achievements of letting ideas flow abundantly in an associative manner are also in evidence. They were far from decisive, of course, since ideational fluency could also characterize less talented contributors to the arts and sciences. All of this did serve to raise hopes that ideational fluency tests would be more helpful than academic skill tests for making prognoses about future accomplishments.

Some limited evidence can be found for the success of these tests. In Wallach and Wing's (1969) college student sample, those scoring in the highest third on ideational fluency showed more out-of-school attainments in literature and science than those scoring in the bottom third. At best, the linkages were tenuous, however, and for some kinds of talented behavior no links to ideational fluency were found at all. Another shred of positive evidence is Singer and Whiton's (1971) finding of a bit of linkage between children's ideational fluency test scores – but not their intelligence test scores – and the judged expressiveness of their drawings. In a related study, Wallbrown and Huelsman (1975) found comparable positive evidence for a clay product but not for two crayon drawings made by children. Attempts to provide criterion validation for ideational fluency tests by Cropley (1972; see also the re-analysis of Cropley's data by Jordan, 1975) and by Kogan and Pankove (1974) seem quite negative in their outcomes.

Ideational fluency tests may be minimally related to intelligence tests, but they are little if any better at predicting the achievements we care about. Subjects vary widely and systematically in their attainments – yet little if any of that systematic variation is captured by individual differences on ideational fluency tests (although the tests too show wide and consistent differences from person to person – well beyond whatever small portion of those differences may relate to significant attainments). Again, we are facing the multiply determined nature of the test responses. But the inferential gap between test responses and writing or science attainments, say, is huge. It is too easy for other factors unrelated to the attainments we want to predict to influence the test responses – perhaps overwhelmingly.

Generating larger numbers of task-appropriate responses, and reaching thereby more that are statistically infrequent, can simply reflect greater conformity to the implicit or even explicit suggestions of an authority figure – the tester – that this kind of behavior be provided. It also can reflect obsessive hair-splitting — the making of finer-grained distinctions among responses that someone else is aware of but simply ignores, as, for example, in enumerating the kinds of things a coat hanger could be used for. Thus, Bowers and van der Meulen (1970) found with college students that individual differences in ideational fluency test scores correlated positively with scores on a scale presumed to measure susceptibility to hypnosis. The finding that those who seem more suggestible in response to authority figures — the susceptibility to hynosis measure — also earn higher scores on ideational fluency tests seems to indicate that those higher in suggestibility try harder to provide what the tester seems to want on the ideational fluency tests. Yet the authors, taking ideational fluency scores as a functional equivalent for creative attainments, interpret the data to mean that creative people are more suggestible!

If academic skills tests in their upper ranges tell little about vocational competencies, "creativity" tests in this middle- to high-intelligence score range are not about to fill the gap. Even if creativity tests *had* proved to possess the hoped-for criterion validity, making them sufficiently impervious to direct coaching to be useful for practical purposes would have been difficult if not impossible.

From Tests to Attainments

We recognize talent from the display of excellence at vocational pursuits, and it is these significant accomplishments as such that offer the most legitimate basis — once certain academic skills qualifications have been met — for the judgments of merit that must accompany the allocation of educational resources. But how could this approach be implemented? My recommendation is not to abandon traditional ability tests and grades, but to limit their role to the screening out of those who score too low. In Wing and Wallach's (1971) use of direct talent assessments in college admissions, for instance, we apply cut-offs that reject candidates from further consideration if their SAT scores place them in the lower half of the distribution for high school seniors who go on to college or if their grades place them in the lowest third of their class. Choice of these particular cut-offs was based on projections indicating that those above the cut-offs should be able to do the academic work expected of students at a highly selective college. For those above the cut-offs, SAT scores and grades receive no further attention in making preferential selections for admission or scholarship support, for, as we have seen, it is within such upper ranges that test score and course grade distinctions seem to be without validity for predicting accomplishment. There is nothing absolute about the particular cut-off points: but some such thresholds should be specified and further increments above them ignored.

To select among students who fall above the academic cut-offs, we must specify the kinds of life achievements deemed meritorious in their own right;

the ones chosen may vary depending on the purposes of the selection. It will be easier to select for graduate and professional schools than for college admissions, since a more definite target of professional competence is present. For undergraduates, the best approach is to take as evidence of merit achievements in whatever pursuits a college says it prepares its students to follow, restrict consideration to achievements of high quality, and give priority to candidates with noteworthy achievements in more than one realm.

Two classes of evidence should be gathered: verifiable signs of public recognition provided by qualified judges and work samples to be evaluated by the selection committee itself. Candidates in literature would be asked to provide verified information on work they have had published in nonschool publications, on the nature of those publications, so that the kind of appraisal that went into the publication decision can be assessed, on awards they have received for written work, and on the nature of the awarding agencies, so that again an appraisal can be made of the worth of the recognition. Candidates would also be asked to provide a sample of their best written work, to be judged by appropriate faculty members on the selection committee.

For prospective scientists, signs of public recognition would include verified information on research published in scientific journals or other nonschool publications, on the nature of these publications, on research awards received in science competitions, and on the nature of the awarding agencies. Candidates would also be requested to submit reports on scientific projects they have conducted, to be evaluated by suitable selection committee faculty members. The achievements may or may not have their point of origin within a school's curriculum; for college applicants the work that qualifies is more likely to be extracurricular than for applicants for graduate school.

How are candidates to be apportioned among different fields? At the graduate level, the answer depends on each department's goals and resources. At the undergraduate level, one feasible plan would be as follows (Wing and Wallach, 1971): Define all the fields an institution wants to represent in its training. List applicants (above the academic skills cut-off) in descending order of work quality within each field, but give priority in the listing sequence to applicants doing high-quality work in more than one field. Then proceed around the fields in carousel fashion, taking the person most qualified from the first field's list, then from the next field's list, and so on, removing a candidate from any other lists in which he or she may appear as soon as the candidate has been chosen from one list. After choosing the most qualified person in each field, select the next most qualified person in each field, and continue until the available slots have been filled.

An institution can define fields as broadly or as narrowly as it wishes. It may have only two carousel positions — say, the sciences and the humanities; or it may have positions for criticism in literature and the arts, historical essays, creative writing, physics, biology, chemistry, psychology, and sociology. It may include performance in art and music or restrict itself to history and criticism in these fields. It may weight the fields in any proportion it finds appropriate, taking two people who qualify in literature and the arts, say, for every one in the sciences, or vice versa, basing the decision on its feelings about its strengths and mandate as an institution, what higher education should concern, or what the society needs. But it must make its choices clear both to itself and to its potential applicants, so that the forms of competence it undertakes to select for and nourish will be reasonably explicit and hence available for examination and critique.

The objection might be made that these proposals would be time-consuming to put into effect. But selection committees already spend large amounts of time and effort in reaching their decisions. The difference is that most of their present procedures are relatively unsystematic, and the apparent objectivity of test scores can influence them more than it should — and more than they believe it does.

It might also be objected that some students will try to develop certain competencies in order to gain admission or scholarship support at a more selective college or university. But this criticism brings home the importance of concentrating assessment efforts on inherently meritorious activities rather than on measures that take their justification from the hope that they can predict these activities. Students will always feel some pressure to do the things that will increase their educational chances. Our obligation is to make the sources of such pressure as valid as possible — to reward students for meaningful displays of competence rather than for excelling on meaningless tests.

Besides their intrinsic significance, do the accomplishments we have considered also point to what people will do in the future? Richards, Holland, and Lutz (1967) give a clearly affirmative answer to this question across the years from high school to college. In a study of nearly 4000 high school students of both sexes who were followed up after one or two years at diverse colleges, data on out-of-school achievements in literature, science, art, and music were collected for the high school and college periods, along with data on high school and college grades and scores on conventional academic skills tests taken at the end of high school. Once again, high school grades and test scores tend to intercorrelate, and both tend to predict college grades. Neither test scores nor grades, on the other hand, predict which students have excelled in nonclassroom projects in the sciences and the humanities in high school or in college, but achievements in some field while in high school tend to give a good basis for predicting that the person will continue to manifest accomplishment in that field while in college.

A recent study by Munday and Davis (1974) gives results comparable to those of Richards *et al.*, but this time comparisons were made across a longer time span — from the end of high school to six years after that, typically two years after college graduation. Academic skills test scores, high school grades, and college grades relate to one another but do not relate to out-of-school achievements during the high school years and do not predict such achievements six years later. But out-of-school achievement in a given field during high school predicts achievement in the same field six years hence. It does so, furthermore, to about the same degree as academic measures at the end of high school predict college grades — even though in the former case we are talking about a six-year span and in the latter a four-year span. And the available evidence (see MacKinnon, 1968) suggests that accomplishments outside the classroom during the student years predict who will be making substantial contributions in professional work later on — the information this time coming from what adult professionals say about their past behavior. Evidence of high-quality professional contributions at an early point in one's career, in turn, gives a good basis for predicting them later as well (see Albert, 1975) — so from high school on, competence seems to beget competence.

Would It Make a Difference?

The catalogues of the selective colleges claim to seek students who have expressed their talent outside the classroom in the ways we have been considering. To determine to what extent actual practice matches this ideology, Wing and Wallach (1971) conducted studies of actual admissions decisions which included consideration of highly selective colleges — institutions where, if anywhere, out-of-school achievements could in principle play a role in selection, since these colleges are heavily overapplied and most applicants are reasonably well qualified in terms of academic skills. The results indicated that even at these colleges selection decisions tend to be monolithically oriented toward conventional academic standards. Knowledge of as simplistic an index as an applicant's score on the verbal aptitude section of the SAT lets one predict rather accurately the likelihood of the candidate's being accepted or rejected at both selective and unselective institutions. The difference between the two kinds of colleges seems not so much whether they depend on SAT-verbal scores in making admissions decisions, but on the level of score required for acceptance.

For instance, Wing and Wallach (1971) found that, at a random sample of 45 colleges, probability of acceptance increases more than four-fold when comparing applicants with SAT-verbal scores falling within score intervals of 350–399 and 550–599 (scores can range from 200 to 800); while at a sample of 13 highly selective colleges, the same order of increase in likelihood of acceptance is found when comparing applicants whose SAT-verbal scores fall within score intervals of 500–549 and 700–749. SAT-verbal scores in the 550–599 interval put a candidate at approximately the 80th percentile of high school seniors who go on to college. Yet likelihood of acceptance at the highly selective colleges sampled is *three times as great* if the applicant's score falls in the 700–749 interval than in this already high interval of 550–599. This means that, while relatively unselective colleges use SAT-verbal scores as a basis for screening out candidates whose scores are too low for them to cope with college work, the highly selective colleges use them to discriminate among applicants who already cluster around the high end of the measure. Marginal increments in SAT-verbal scores within this upper part of the distribution determine acceptance versus rejection.

Indeed, Wing and Wallach further discovered that predicting admissions actions at a typical highly selective college in terms of combined consideration on an equal weighting basis of the candidate's verbal and mathematical scores on the SAT along with his academic achievement level in high school led to such a high degree of accuracy in accounting for acceptances and rejections as to leave little room even in principle for other factors to play a role. About 80% of all decisions, and about 80% of all acceptances as well, were correctly predicted this way — even though the possible predictive accuracy in these situations is lower than 100% because the decisions to be predicted are themselves made with less than perfect reliability. This general result was replicated across two successive recent years' applicants for admission to the freshman class, with more than 4200 applicants one year and more than 4600 the next, in spite of the fact that one year's applicants were required to provide more extensive information on out-of-school accomplishments.

Admissions practices seem to be substantially at variance, then, with the diversity of talents that highly selective institutions say they seek. Could selection be carried out instead in a way that would genuinely implement this goal? Wing and Wallach explored this question by applying a hypothetical decision rule that gave preference to candidates who had demonstrated substantial accomplishments in the fields outlined earlier. The rule also gave preference to candidates as a function of the number of fields in which such accomplishments had been demonstrated. Finally, it permitted candidates to be accepted this way only if their SAT scores and grades were high enough (SAT scores in the top half nationally for high school seniors who go on to college, and grades in the top two-thirds of the high school class). If one selects by these criteria, the hypothetical accepted class overlaps only 40–50% with the class actually accepted. (Remember, by contrast, that selecting for candidates with the highest SAT scores and grades in high school results in an accepted class that overlaps about 80% with the class actually accepted.)

What are the applicants like who are accepted by the rule that emphasizes professional accomplishments? In the Wing and Wallach results, out-of-school science achievements of high quality are found for 15.6% of the accepted males compared to 8.4% of the male applicants, and for 15.5% of the accepted females compared to 7.4% of the female applicants. Out-of-school writing achievements of high quality are found for 19.3% of the accepted males compared to 9.5% of the male applicants, and for 33.8% of the accepted females compared to 14.6% of the female applicants. The accepted group is comparably accomplished in the other fields of activity that were assessed; these achievements are represented with far higher incidences than their rates of occurrence in the applicant pool. Basing selections on conventional academic criteria, on the other hand, or considering the selections made by the actual admissions committee, yields an accepted group far less distinguished in its achievements.

One defense of the use of standardized tests like the SAT for admissions purposes is that they are nondiscriminatory as such, and perhaps less discriminatory than any alternative objective basis for selection would be. The Wing and Wallach data give us an opportunity to compare for an applicant pool the effects on nonwhite candidates of using a hypothetical decision rule based on SAT scores and one based on accomplishments once certain minimum criteria as to SAT scores and high school grades are satisfied. Use of the SAT decision rule was found to be drastically discriminatory in its consequences: almost all nonwhite candidates in the applicant pool would be excluded from the group accepted. Use of the rule based on accomplishments, by contrast, was found to lead to a quite different outcome: nonwhite candidates would be accepted in about the same proportion as their incidence in the applicant population. Thus, using accomplishments rather than test scores as the basis for selection seems, if anything, to be less discriminatory in its consequences for nonwhites.

I believe that our proposal would produce a college class qualitatively different from those selected by conventional means. Does the difference hold implications for the society? Darwin argued that *biological* characteristics prosper across generations to the degree that they are represented in the organisms that breed. Something analogous may go on in educational selection: If conventional test-taking skills more than significant competencies govern access to contested educational opportunities, these competencies will be underrepresented in the people who win more valuable educational credentials in the society. Having the credentials tends to open doors to roles of greater influence, so the attributes of the people holding such roles will be more likely to influence the overall direction of the society.

Perhaps the reason why the more selective colleges and graduate schools claim to seek students who demonstrate diverse talents, while in reality choosing the reverse, is the extent to which academic skills tests and course examinations are rather automatically construed by faculty and administrators as reflecting a person's "intelligence" or "brightness" in all the senses of the term. Obtaining the brightest students possible becomes a way of defining the quality of an institution, and when colleges and universities judge one another's national standing in terms of the average SAT scores of the incoming freshman class or the average GRE aptitude test scores of the incoming graduate students, the heavy use of such yardsticks in admissions should be no surprise. As Wing and Wallach (1971) and Campbell (1971) have pointed out, furthermore, the faculty members at such institutions have themselves been selected for educational advancement largely by the very criteria whose use we have questioned. It is natural for them to perpetuate and see virtue in the ways of defining merit that led to their own rise — even when faced with contrary evidence.

The role played by testing agencies in preserving the established ways of doing things must also be mentioned. They have, after all, a vested interest in the continued and even amplified use of the testing devices they know how to make. To justify continued emphasis on tests like the SAT and the GRE on the grounds that they predict course grades, when neither the test score nor the course grade differences in their upper ranges predict actual accomplishment, is questionable to say the least.

The irony is compounded when educational commentators like Jencks and Riesman (1968) urge even heavier use of academic aptitude test scores instead of grades in selection on the ground that the former are less subject than the latter to irrelevant sources of bias such as teachers giving higher grades to students who are more polite. For it is their correlation with grades that provides the aptitude tests with their basic justification in the first place. But to deal with real accomplishments, once certain academic ability thresholds have been crossed, is to restrict the use of tests to a much more circumscribed function than testing agencies envision. Testing agencies should perhaps devote less effort to tests and more to helping educators assess achievement in activities that we value.

References

ALBERT, R. S. (1975) Toward a behavioral definition of genius. *Am. Psychologist* **30**, 140–51.

BARRON, F. (1963) *Creativity and Psychological Health.* Princeton: Van Nostrand.

BLOOM, B. S. (1963) Report on creativity research by the examiner's office of the University of Chicago. In *Scientific Creativity: Its Recognition and Development*, ed. C. W. Taylor and F. Barron. New York: Wiley, pp. 251–64.

BOWERS, K. S. and S. J. van der MEULEN. (1970) Effect of hypnotic susceptibility on creativity test performance. *J. Personality and Social Psychology* **14**, 247–56.

CAMPBELL, D. P. (1971) Admissions policies: Side effects and their implications. *Am. Psychologist* **26**, 636–47.

CROPLEY, A. J. (1972) A five-year longitudinal study of the validity of creativity tests. *Developmental Psychology* **6**, 119–24.

HARMON, L. R. (1963) The development of a criterion of scientific competence. In *Scientific Creativity: Its Recognition and Development*, ed. C. W. Taylor and F. Barron. New York: Wiley, pp. 44–52.

HELSON, R. and R. S. CRUTCHFIELD (1970) Mathematicians: The creative researcher and the average Ph.D. *J. Consulting and Clinical Psychology* **34**, 250–57.

HOLLAND, J. L. and J. M. RICHARDS, Jr. (1965) Academic and nonacademic accomplishment: Correlated or uncorrelated? *J. Educational Psychology* **56**, 165–74.

HOYT, D. P. (1965) The relationship between college grades and adult achievement: A review of the literature. *ACT Research Report No. 7.* Iowa City: American College Testing Program.

HOYT, D. P. (1966) College grades and adult accomplishment: A review of research. *Educational Record* (Winter) 70–75.

HUDSON, L. (1960) Degree class and attainment in scientific research. *Brit. J. Psychology* **51**, 67–73.

JENCKS, C. and D. RIESMAN (1968) *The Academic Revolution.* Garden City: Doubleday.

JORDAN, L. A. (1975) Use of canonical analysis in Cropley's "A five-year longitudinal study of the validity of creativity tests." *Developmental Psychology* **11**, 1–3.

KOGAN, N. and E. PANKOVE (1974) Long-term predictive validity of divergent-thinking tests: Some negative evidence. *J. Educational Psychology* **66**, 802–10.

MacKINNON, D. W. (1968) Selecting students with creative potential. In *The Creative College Student; An Unmet Challange*, ed. P. Heist. San Francisco: Jossey-Bass, pp. 101–16.

MARSTON, A. R. (1971) It is time to reconsider the Graduate Record Examination. *Am. Psychologist* **26**, 653–55.

MAXEY, E. J., and V. J. ORMSBY (1971) The accuracy of self-report information collected on the ACT test battery: High school grades and items of nonacademic achievement. *ACT Research Report No. 45.* Iowa City: American College Testing Program.

MEDNICK, M. T. (1963) Research creativity in psychology graduate students. *J. Consulting Psychology* **27**, 265–66.

MISCHEL, W. (1972) Direct versus indirect personality assessment: Evidence and implications. *J. Consulting and Clinical Psychology* **38**, 319–24.

MORRISON, J. (1963) The comparative effectiveness of intellective and non-intellective measures in the prediction of the completion of a major in theater arts. *Educational and Psychological Measurement* **23**, 827–30.

MUNDAY, L. A. and J. C. DAVIS (1974) Varieties of accomplishment after college: Perspectives on the meaning of academic talent. *ACT Research Report No. 62.* Iowa City: American College Testing Program.

PARLOFF, M. B., L. DATTA, M. KLEMAN and J. H. HANDLON (1968) Personality characteristics which differentiate creative male adolescents and adults. *J. Personality* **36**, 528–52.

RICHARDS, J. M., Jr., J. L. HOLLAND and S. W. LUTZ (1967) Prediction of student accomplishment in college. *J. Educational Psychology* **58**, 343–55.

SINGER, D. L. and M. B. WHITON (1971) Ideational creativity and expressive aspects of human figure drawing in kindergarten-age children. *Developmental Psychology* **4**, 366–69.

TAYLOR, D. W. (1958) Variables related to creativity and productivity among men in two research laboratories. In *The Second (1957) University of Utah Research Conference on the Identification of Creative Scientific Talent*, ed. C. W. Taylor. Salt Lake City: University of Utah Press, pp. 20–54.

TYLER, L. E. (1965) *The Psychology of Human Differences.* 3rd ed. New York: Appleton-Century-Crofts.

WALLACH, M. A. (1967) Creativity and the expression of possibilities. In *Creativity and Learning*, ed. J. Kagan. Boston: Houghton, Mifflin, pp. 36–57.

WALLACH, M. A. (1968) Review of the Torrance Tests of Creative Thinking. *Am. Educational Res. J.* **5**, 272–81.

WALLACH, M. A. (1970) Creativity. In *Carmichael's Manual of Child Psychology*, 3rd ed., P. H. Mussen, ed. New York: Wiley, pp. 1211–72.

WALLACH, M. A. (1971a) *The Intelligence/Creativity Distinction.* Morristown: General Learning Press.

WALLACH, M. A. (1971b) Intelligence tests, academic achievement and creativity. *Impact of Science on Society* **21**, 333–45.

WALLACH, M. A. (1977) The psychology of talent and graduate education. In *Cognitive Styles and Creativity in Higher Education*, ed. S. Messick. San Francisco: Jossey-Bass.

WALLACH, M. A., and N. KOGAN (1965) *Modes of Thinking in Young Children: A Study of the Creativity-Intelligence Distinction.* New York: Holt, Rinehart and Winston.

WALLACH, M. A. and M. I. LEGGETT (1972) Testing the hypothesis that a person will be consistent: Stylistic consistency versus situational specificity in size of children's drawings. *J. Personality* **40**, 309–30.

WALLACH, M. A., and C. W. WING, Jr. (1969) *The Talented Student: A Validation of the Creativity-Intelligence Distinction.* New York: Holt, Rinehart and Winston.

WALLBROWN, F. H. and C. B. HUELSMAN, Jr. (1975) The validity of the Wallach-Kogan creativity operations for inner-city children in two areas of visual art. *J. Personality* **43**, 109–26.

WEITZMAN, R. A. (1972) It is time to reconsider the GRE: A reply to Marston. *Am. Psychologist* **27**, 236–38.

WING, C. W., Jr and M. A. WALLACH (1971) *College Admissions and the Psychology of Talent.* New York: Holt, Rinehart and Winston.

4

The Highly Effective Individual*

D. W. MacKINNON

IN DISCUSSING the highly effective individual I shall be focusing upon one of the least understood phenomena in the whole field of human behavior. It is, of course, understandable that for so many years study of the effective person was slighted. It was inevitable that when psychology sought to cut its affiliation with its parent discipline philosophy toward the end of the last century and attempted to become a science it turned its attention to simple problems — partial responses, simple sensory, perceptual, and motor responses, simple learning, and the like — for the study of which manageable techniques were available.

When, somewhat later, there developed a concern with the whole man rather than with his simple and isolated reactions, it was not the academic and experimental psychologist who pioneered this new field of inquiry. Instead it was the physician, the medical psychologist faced with the practical problem of alleviating the suffering of patients. Thus it was that when man as a whole came under scrutiny and investigation it was the ineffective rather than the effective person who was first probed and studied. Psychopathology is vivid; it cries out for treatment and care. So, understandably, over the years there has been a continuing emphasis upon research into the nature of human emotional and mental distress in the attempt to find some cure for them.

Still another reason why ineffective and sick persons have been more intensively studied in pscyhology than effective and healthy individuals is that they have been motivated by their distress and suffering to reveal themselves, to let the psychiatrist or medical psychologist find out as much as he could about them. But what are the motivations for a person getting along well in life to reveal himself and his innermost secrets to anyone?

The great pioneer in the investigation of the sick and disturbed individual was Sigmund Freud, founder of psychoanalysis; and it was Sigmund Freud more than anyone else who gave modern psychology its major notions about human development. The picture he painted was one in which only the direst consequences could be expected to follow marked frustrations of human needs, deprivation of individual requirements, and traumatic experiences. As a result of this, the view concerning the development of human personality which for

*Teachers' College Record, (1960), 61, 376–378. Reprinted by permission.

many years was rather uncritically accepted, and which influenced very much the preachings and preachments of the mental hygiene movement, was that the individual would have to enjoy a loving, supportive, and permissive home and life situation during the early formative years if he was to grow up to be an effectively functioning person. This view might still be very generally and un-critically held were it not for certain psychological investigations that were carried out during World War II.

During this war two major, and in many respects novel, psychological programs were developed for the selection and placement of personnel. One was conducted by the Army Air Corps, and its objective was the development of tests to pick out individuals who would have the abilities to be trained as pilots, navigators, bombardiers, etc. This program, like the earlier work of experimental pscyhologists, focused sharply upon partial responses rather than upon man as a whole. It looked for the particular, rather specialized skills and abilities, especially psychomotor skills, which enter into the complicated tasks of flying and navigating an airplane. It was not particularly concerned with the total complexly motivated individual.

Study of Man as A Whole

The other program, in contrast, was forced to focus its attention upon the whole man. This program was developed in the Office of Strategic Services. As is now well known, the Office of Strategic Services was set up to engage in irregular warfare. Its task was to recruit and train individuals to operate as spies, counterespionage agents leaders of resistance groups behind the enemy lines, creators of black propaganda designed to destroy the enemy's morale, and so forth; and it was clear that if individuals were to engage successfully in such operations they had to have rather unusual traits and abilities. Not infrequently they would be on their own in a foreign country, speaking a language which was not their native tongue. Essential in most OSS operations were an unusual degree of adaptive flexibility, a willingness to assume responsibility for rather unusual actions, loyalty to the cause and to the particular mission. A premium was placed upon independence of judgment as well as good judgment if one was to operate successfully in OSS assignments.

The group of psychologists and psychiatrists which was asked to set up a program which would assess the qualifications of individuals for the OSS type of activity was faced with the task of measuring the very complex and for the most part positive aspects of personal functioning. It seemed clear to them that no single test would serve the purpose; that it would be necessary to observe, and to measure, just as many aspects of personality as possible; and that their observations should be made in a social situation because that is where most human behavior actually does occur. The program of testing which resulted from the application of those principles was the assessment program of the OSS. Its essential feature was that the candidates to be evaluated were brought together for several days at an assessment center – a country estate outside of Washington, DC – where they lived with one another and with the assessment staff. There they were studied by a variety of means, ranging from a real-life problem situation (the total assessment situation itself) to specially contrived problem-solving experiments; from unstructured projective tests of personality to empirically derived questionnaires and tests of personality traits, attitudes, interests, and values; and from searching interviews covering the life history to formal social situations of a stressful character in which the subjects' best behavior was called for in a socially defined role.

It was in the OSS assessment program that for the first time large numbers of highly effective individuals were intensively studied by psychologists and psychiatrists who, to their surprise, discovered again and again that persons of the most extraordinary effectiveness had life histories marked by severe frustrations, deprivations, and traumatic experiences. By all generally accepted theories of personality development they should have been psychiatric casualties, but they were not.

Those of us who were members of the OSS assessment had it vividly impressed upon us how little we knew about the development of personality and how great was the need for research in this field.

Assessment Method in Personality Research

To meet this need there was established in 1949 on the Berkeley campus of the University of California through a grant from the Rockefeller Foundation, an Institute of Personality Assessment and Research. Its express purpose was to develop further the assessment method for basic research into problems of personality development and dynamics, with special focus upon the characteristics of the effectively functioning person and the life history determinants of such effectiveness.

Assessment involved both intensive and extensive study of persons who have been nominated by experts for their outstanding qualities of originality, personal soundness, creativity, or some other agreed-upon criterion. There are usually ten persons assessed at one time by a staff of roughly the same number, and since in a typical research program subjects are brought to the Institute for study over a period of three days, during which time hundreds of measures, scores, and ratings are obtained for each subject, assessment is an expensive method of personality research. Consequently there is an obligation upon assessors to record their more or less clinical impressions of each of the assessees in some quantified form which will permit them to be analyzed along with all other assessment data by various statistical operations.

Three methods of recording staff insights have been repeatedly employed in our researches. One consists of checking on an alphabetically ordered list of 300 adjectives those which best describe a given subject (1). A second method, the Q-sort method (2) requires the observer to sort into nine piles for each subject 100 statements of personal functioning, distributing them in a forced normalized distribution from those five at one end which, in the observer's judgment, are most descriptive of the subject to those five at the other end which are least applicable to him. The larger number of items, neither so clearly applicable nor so clearly nondescriptive, is sorted in the larger intermediate categories, the total distribution of the Q-items being 5-8-12-16-18-12-8-5. The third method involves rating each subject on some 20 to 30 traits of personality (3).

The checking of adjectives, the sorting of Q-items, and the rating of traits may, of course, be made on the basis of observations of the subjects' behavior in a number of assessment situations or on the basis of observations made in only one situation, for example, by the life-history interviewer, who sees the subject only during the interview.

By averaging the ratings made by all staff observers, and by compositing their adjective checks and Q-sorts, it is possible to obtain a quantitative expression of staff impressions and relate these mathematically to the more objective measures obtained in our assessments. It is thus possible to state what adjectives and what phrases as well as what objectively measured characteristics differentiate those subjects who score high from those who score low on any given variable, among them the independently rated criterion variables of effectiveness, personal soundness, and originality.

Perceptual Performance

Special attention has been given in our assessment programs to the development or relatively simple and quickly administered tests of perceptual and cognitive abilities. Preliminary work in this area suggested that such tests might turn out to be surprisingly good measures of more subtle and more complex aspects of personality. Success in this direction would be a significant extension of quantitative method to the testing of complex functions of personality.

In a test modeled after Witkin's of the perception of the vertical under the distorting influence of a tilted frame, a subject is brought blindfolded into a dark room (4, 5). When the blindfold is removed, he sees before him the illuminated outline of a square (3′ × 3′) which is tilted 28 degrees to the right from the true vertical. Centered within the area of the square is an illuminated rod. By remote control the experimenter can move independently the illuminated square and rod any desired number of degrees from the vertical. The task of the subject is to adjust the remote control so as to bring the rod into a truly vertical or truly horizontal position, overcoming the distorting influence of the only visual frame of reference in an otherwise completely dark room.

Trials are made alternately with the square tilted 28 degrees to the right and 21 degrees to the left of vertical. Under these conditions, in our investigations the mean displacement of judgments in the direction of the tilted frame may for a subject be as great as 28 degrees.

Now let us examine the correlates of this measure of an individual's tendency to be thrown off balance by a distorting visual frame of reference. We have found that those who performed better on this test also earned higher scores on several measures of intelligence. On tests of the ability to reorganize spatial materials and patterns they scored higher too, and they had more analytical interest and ability. Those who placed the rod most accurately were shown to be the more original, more complex, and more spontaneous subjects on several other tests. They gave evidence of greater ego strength and independence, while those who were most influenced by the distorting frame of reference showed a greater tendency to be involved with and oriented toward others, desiring relatedness with them.

In the test of the perception of the vertical under a distorting visual frame of reference, as in the case of all our tests, we have an opportunity to discover the way in which high and low scorers are differentially perceived by professional psychologists, by examining our adjective and Q-sort descriptions of the two groups. A survey of the Q-items which statistically differentiate (at better than the 5% level of confidence) the 20 subjects with the smallest displacements from the 20 subjects with the largest displacements confirms and extends the picture which is obtained from an examination of the test correlates of high and low scores.

Q-items More Descriptive of Those with Large Displacements

- Would become confused, disorganized, and unadaptive under stress
- Undercontrols his impulses, acts with insufficient thinking and deliberation; unable to delay gratification
- Is gregarious; prefers interpersonal and group situations to intrapersonal circumstances; seeks relatedness to others
- Is pedantic and fussy about minor things
- Emphasizes oral pleasure; self-indulgent
- Is concerned with making a good impression.

Q-items More Descriptive of Those with Small Displacements

- Is an effective leader
- Manipulates people as a means to achieving personal ends; opportunistic
- Takes an ascendant role in his relations with others
- Highly values intellectual activity
- Is masculine in his style and manner of behavior
- Is self-reliant; independent in judgment; able to think for himself
- Is cold and distant in his relationship with others

- Is concerned with philosophical problems
- Is unaware of his social stimulus value.

The patterns are clear. Subjects who are more influenced by, which is to say thrown off balance by, a distorting visual field are more likely to reveal themselves as weak, dependent, susceptible to stress, and overly concerned with others. Conversely, subjects who are little influenced by the tilted frame are more likely to appear in assessment as intelligent and analytical, capable of insightful reorganization, cognitively rather than socially oriented, spontaneous, independent, and self-contained.

From such findings as these, and from similar results with other techniques of this kind, we are encouraged to believe that we shall eventually be able to tap and to measure complex functions of personality with relatively simple tests of perceptual and cognitive processes, for it is clear that such processes, rather than being purely perceptual or cognitive in character, are vitally embedded in the total complex of personality and can be utilized to reveal significant aspects and dimensions of it.

A Technique Described

As an example of another kind of procedure with which we have worked in our assessment studies I shall describe a quasi group-interaction technique or situational test designed to study the personality correlates of cooperation.

It is necessary in such experimentation to create a group situation in which the pressures to cooperation are kept constant for all individuals so that differences in speed and degree of cooperating can be clearly related to personality variables rather than to factors in the group situation.

To this end a situational test developed by Crutchfield presents to a group of five subjects what appears to be a genuine group-interaction problem requiring the cooperation of all, but is, in fact, a situation completely controlled by the experimenter (6). . . .

This artificially created conflict situation reproduces very neatly the dynamics of real-life situations of group cooperation, which typically involve conflicting pressures on the individual.

A subjects's score in this situation corresponds to the number of times the request for a numbered counter is made before he yields. Scores range from 1 to 10, the tenth request being the last that is made. Those who have not given up the requested counter by the tenth trial are scored as "never yielded."

There are large individual differences. In one rather typical group of adult subjects, all of whom held positions of considerable responsibility, one-sixth yielded on the first request, but one-quarter never yielded within the allotted ten trials. The rest fell in between these extremes, with a piling-up of yielding on early rather than on late requests.

Our findings with this procedure have been confirmed with many groups.

Those who respond immediately to the request tend to be impulsive, hasty, social and outgoing, undercontrolled, and generally fluid in personality. Those who yield slowly, or not at all, tend to be excessively deliberate, asocial and withdrawn, overcontrolled, and generally rigid and inflexible in personality. Indeed, all of our investigations with this technique indicate that the optimal performance in this situation is to cooperate neither too quickly nor too slowly but "to strike a proper balance between the tendency to defer too readily to the demands of others and the tendency to be stubbornly resistant in the face of group requirements"(7).

Here we have found, as with many other measures, that the best performance and the most desirable traits are not associated with either the extremely high or the extremely low scores on an inventory or in a test situation, but with some range of intermediate scores. Where such curvilinearity of relationship does exist, any attempt to predict performance in a criterion situation by computing the usual product—moment correlation between test score and performance rating is bound to fail. The lack of recognition of this fact has, in my judgment, contributed to the dismal showing of so many selection and placement programs.

Dimensions of Personal Effectiveness

Turning to a consideration of some substantive findings in our assessment programs, I would first note that to ask: "What are the characteristics of the effective person?" is to raise too general a question. More specific questions must be asked: Effective in what way? Effective for what? Effective in what field or profession?

Oversimplifying what is clearly a tremendously complicated set of relationships, we have as a first approximation conceived of two variables as centrally determinative of effective functioning: (a) emotional stability or personal soundness, and (b) originality or creativity of thought and action.

Determinants of Personal Soundness

Let us look first at the factors which distinguish those high on personal soundness from those low on this dimension as summarized by Barron. Seven main findings emerge.

1. Health of the Subject during Childhood

To a striking degree the emotionally sound subjects had been healthy in childhood. Their parents were also reported as having excellent health. Subjects low in personal soundness revealed a greater frequency of childhood illnesses and accidents. Barron concludes that "to a certain extent unsoundness in adulthood seems the consequence of tragic circumstance in childhood"(9).

2. Integrity and Stability of the Home

The life histories of the Highs tended to be characterized by the continuing presence of both parents with the children in the home during the subject's childhood. The Lows more often had had homes broken by divorce, death, or illness, or by the absence of the father for long periods of time. The Highs tended to come from economically secure homes and from stable communities. The emotional, social, and physical integrity of the family in the case of the Highs appears to have provided them with "the psychological basis for the creation of the most important inner certainty: that both the world and oneself are stable and worthy of trust"(10).

3. Imagery of the Father as a Respected, Successful Person

The Highs almost always described their fathers as having been respected citizens and persons in all ways worthy of emulation. The fathers of the Lows were more often described as failures or not described at all, since they were unknown to the subjects. It appears that the Highs "had throughout their childhood the continuing presence of a model on which they could base their own conception of potent masculinity," while the Lows were "unable to take over the adult masculine role largely because no image of it existed for them to emulate"(11).

4. Affection and Close Attention from the Mother

Mothers of the Highs appear to have been loving and solicitous of their sons, closely controlling them at home when they were young. Mothers of the Lows appear, as described by them, to have been seductive, demanding, and over-protective. In the lives of the Lows the mother had been the dominant parent; in the case of the Highs the strength of the father appears to have been most determinative. In the interview the Highs often described incidents in which they had rather strikingly emerged from dependence on the mother. Lows, on the other hand, more often appeared to be still dependent to a considerable degree upon the mother.

5. Presence of Other Siblings and Positive Relations with Them

Highs tended to have more siblings and to report more friendly relationships with them that did the Lows. It would appear that, as Barron has concluded, "the family is a community in microcosm, and fullest participation in the larger community in later life should be facilitated by richness of interpersonal experience and flexibility in role-taking determined in large part by the roles available in the family circle"(12).

6. Athleticism and Competitive Play

The Highs were more inclined to be athletic and to enjoy participation in competitive sports. The Lows were less athletic and less interested in competition. In general, the Highs were more robust and vigorous, more physically courageous and characterized by greater stamina than were the Lows.

7. Sexual Expression

Both Highs and Lows among the Ph.D. candidates had come to sexual expression somewhat later than the subjects in other groups we have studied. At the time we saw them, the Highs more often than the Lows were either married or had maintained for at least a year a steady, intimate sexual relationship with one woman. "In general," Barron concludes, "the Highs were characterized either by mature, easily achieved masculinity or by a solution in which femininity was sublimated and masculine sex drives were satisfied in a stable marriage marked by close dependency on the wife; the Lows were characterized either by manneristic femininity — resulting either in homosexual relations or minimal sexual 'outlet' — or by a 'masculinity' which protested too much"(13).

These are general trends. They deserve emphasis. Yet we must not overlook the exceptions to them; and it must especially be stressed that in this study the final conclusion was that personal soundness is not an absence of problems but a way of reacting to them.

Life History of Creative Subjects

A quite different picture of the early life history appears when we examine the reports of highly original and creative persons. In one group of subjects an item analysis of the questionnaire responses of those who scored higher on a composite index of originality revealed that they tended to answer Yes to the item, "As a child, my home life was not as happy as that of most others," and to say No to the statements, "My father was a good man," "I love my mother," "As a child I was able to go to my parents with my problems," and "My home life was always happy."

A glance at the life history interview protocols for several of our samples of highly creative subjects reveals that certainly not all of them had the kind of happy family situation and favorable life circumstances so generally thought to be conducive to sound psychological development. Some endured the most brutal treatment at the hands of sadistic fathers. These, to be sure, constitute the minority, but they appear today no less creative than those whose fathers offered them quite satisfactory male figures with whom easy identification could be made. There is, however, some evidence that those who were harshly treated in childhood have not been so effective or so successful in their professions as those who were more gently treated; and there is more than a hint that these subjects have had some difficulty in assuming an aggressive professional role because, through fear of their fathers, their feminine identifications were emphasized.

It must be stressed that we are here dependent upon the self-reports of our subjects. Those of superior emotional stability tend to report happy early life circumstances, while those outstanding in originality and creativity more often describe a less harmonious and happy atmosphere within the family circle. We know nothing with certainty about the true state of affairs for either group. In reality the family situations of the two groups may have been indistinguishable. The differences may have resided only in their perceptions and memories of childhood experiences, and yet it is difficult to think that this alone explains the differences in self-report of the more emotionally stable and the more original and creative.

If, as there is some reason to believe, our more creative subjects have overcome adversities and in some instances even profited from them, what, we may ask, are some of the factors determining such favorable outcomes?

Briefcase Syndrome of Creativity

One of the most striking observations we have made is that the creative person seldom fits the layman's stereotype of him. In our experience he is not the emotionally unstable, sloppy, loose-jointed Bohemian. More often it is the unoriginal and uncreative person who appears to be artistic, clever, emotional, whereas we discover ourselves using such adjectives as deliberate, reserved, industrious, and thorough to describe truly original and creative persons. Among ourselves we have jokingly described this cluster of traits characteristic of the creative person as "the briefcase syndrome of creativity" – closer, if you will, to the notion of professional responsibility than to the Greenwich Village Bohemian or to the North Beach Beatnik.

The truly creative individual has an image of himself as a responsible person and a sense of destiny about himself as a human being. This includes a degree of resoluteness and almost inevitably a measure of egotism. But over and above these there is a belief in the foregone certainty of the worth and validity of one's creative efforts. This is not to say that our creative subjects have been spared periods of frustration and depression when blocked in their creative striving, but only that overriding these moods has been an unquestioning commitment to their creative endeavor.

Some Qualities Related to Creativity

Closely related to the above observation is our finding that although both introverts and extraverts are to be found among creative persons, they tend as individuals to be self-assertive and dominant and possessed of a high level of energy. Whether persons recognized as highly creative would show such energetic assertion and dominance in all societies we cannot say, but in mid-twentieth century in the United States they do. If such assertiveness is not a prerequisite for their creativeness, it would appear to be at least necessary if their creativity is to merit recognition and acclaim. But what is most important for their creative accomplishments is the persistent high level of energy with which they work. And this seems possible because their work is also their play. They do not need to retreat from work to be refreshed, but find refreshment and recreation for themselves in it.

Our creative subjects are in the main well above average in intelligence. Their brains have an unusual capacity to record and retain and have readily available the experiences of their life histories. The intelligent person is more discerning (more observant in a differentiated fashion), more alert (can concentrate attention readily and shift it appropriately), and more fluent in scanning thoughts and producing those which meet some problem-solving criterion. Such a person will generally have more information (in the most general sense of the term) at his command. Furthermore, items of information which he possesses may more readily enter into combinations among themselves and the number of possible combinations is increased for such a person because of the greater information and the greater fluency of combination. Since true creativity is defined by the adaptiveness of a response as well as its unusualness, it is apparent that intelligence alone will tend to produce greater creativity. The more combinations that are formed, the more likely it is that some of them will be creative.

But intelligence alone does not make for creativity, especially in the arts. Some of our most creative subjects score lower on measures of intelligence than do less creative ones. What seems to characterize the more artistically creative person is a relative absence of repression and suppression as mechanisms for the control of impulses and images. Repression operates against creativity regardless of how intelligent a person may be because it makes unavailable to the individual large aspects of his own experience, particularly the life of impulse and experience which gets assimilated to the symbols of aggression and sexuality. Dissociated items of experience cannot combine with one another; there are barriers to communication among different systems of experience. The creative person, who does not characteristically suppress or repress, but rather expresses, has his own unconscious more available to him and thus has fuller access to his own experience. Furthermore, because the unconscious operates more by symbols than by logic, the creative person is more open to the perception of complex equivalences in experience, facility in poetic mataphor being one consequence of the creative person's greater openness to his own depths.

We have discovered that our creative subjects have interests and hobbies in common with individuals in certain professions and quite unlike those of persons in other fields of endeavor (these being interests and hobbies unrelated to the field of work). For example, creative subjects in a wide range of fields share common interests with such professional people as architects, authors, journalists, and psychologists but have interests rather unlike those of office men, purchasing agents, and bankers, and understandably enough, quite unlike those of policemen and morticians.

These patterns of interests and hobbies suggest that original and creative persons are less interested in small detail, in facts as such, and more concerned with their meanings and implications, possessed of greater cognitive flexibility, and characterized by verbal skills and interests in as well as accuracy in communication with others.

Invariably we find our creative subjects entertaining both theoretical and aesthetic values, although for many people, perhaps most, there is some incompatibility and conflict between a cognitive and rational concern with truth and an emotional concern with form and beauty. When there is conflict it would appear that the creative individual has the capacity to tolerate the tension created in him by strong opposing values, and in his life and work he effects some reconciliation of them.

In the realm of sexual identifications and interests, our creative male subjects appear to give more expression to the feminine side of their nature than do less creative persons. On a number of tests of masculinity—femininity, they score relatively high on femininity, and this despite the fact that, as a group, they do not present an effeminate appearance or make frequent reference to homosexual interests or experiences in their life histories. In assessment they appear to be quite masculine, though at the same time showing an openness to their own feelings and emotions, an understanding self-awareness, and wide-ranging interests including many which in our society are thought of as feminine.

If one were to cast this into Jungian terms one would say that these creative persons are not so completely identified with their masculine *persona* roles as to blind themselves to or deny expression to the more feminine traits of the *anima*. For some, the balance between masculine and feminine traits, interests, and identifications is a precarious one, and for several it would appear that their present reconciliation of these opposites of their nature has been barely achieved and only after considerable psychic stress and turmoil.

This openness to experience, this wide perceptiveness appears, however, to be more characteristic of those with artistic creativity than of those with scientific creativity. If, grossly oversimplifying psychological functioning, one were to say that whenever a person uses his mind for any purpose he performs either an act of perception (he becomes aware of something) or an act of judging (he comes to a conclusion about something), then we might interpret our findings as follows: our artistic creative subjects are predominantly perceptive, while our scientific creative subjects tend to be more evaluative and judgmental in their orientation to life.

In his perceptions, both of the outer world and of his inner experience, a person may tend to focus upon what is presented to his senses — the facts as they are — or he may focus upon their deeper meanings and possibilities. Now there is no doubt that we would expect creative persons not to be stimulus- and object-bound in their perceptions but ever alert to the as-yet-not-realized, and that is precisely what we find to be true of all our creative groups.

The Jungian distinction between introversion and extraversion is well known: the extravert's primary interests lie in the outer world of people and things, while the introvert's primary interests lie in the inner world of concepts and ideas.

It will come as no surprise, I believe, that the majority of our creative subjects are introverts: 80% of the female mathematicians, 68% of the architects, 65% of the writers, and 60% of the research scientists whom we have tested are introverts.

Settling upon their life careers came early for some of our creative subjects, one of whom at the age of four had decided he wanted to be an architect. Others were slow in coming to a professional identity, not deciding until several years past college upon a professional career. In the case of several of these, the choice of a life profession was made the more difficult by the fact that they possessed so many skills and interests, providing them with the possibility of many quite different careers.

The independence in thought and action which all our creative subjects have tended to show is well illustrated, for example, by the architects' reports upon their college careers.

Academically they did quite well, averaging about a B. In work and courses which caught their interest they could turn in an A performance, but in courses that failed to strike their imagination, they were quite willing to do no work at all. In general, their attitude in college appears to have been one of profound skepticism. They were unwilling to accept anything on the mere say-so of their instructors. Nothing was to be accepted on faith or because it had behind it the voice of authority. Such matters might be accepted, but only after the student on his own had demonstrated to himself their validity. In a sense they were rebellious, but they did not run counter to the standards out of sheer rebellious- ness. Rather, they were spirited in their disagreement, and one gets the impres- sion that they learned most from those who were not easy with them. But clearly many of the architects as students were not easy to take. One of the most rebellious, but, as it turned out, one of the most promising, was advised by the dean of his school to quit because he had no talent, and another, failed in his design dissertation which attacked the stylism of the faculty, ended up by taking his degree in the art department.

Summary

To summarize what at this stage of our researches strikes me most forcibly

D. W. MacKinnon   **127**

about the creative persons whom we have assessed, it is their openness to experience, and the fact that they, more than most, are struggling with the opposites in their nature, striving ever for a more effective reconciliation of them, and seeking to tolerate and to bind increasingly large quantities of tension as they strive for a creative solution to ever more difficult problems which are not set for them but which they set for themselves.

Notes

1. H. G. GOUGH, (1960) The adjective checklist as a personality assessment research technique. *Psychological reports,* 6, 107–220.
2. J. BLOCK, The Q-sort method in personality assessment and psychiatric research.
3. D. G. WOODWARD and D. W. MacKINNON, (1958) *The Use of Trait Ratings in an Assessment of 100 Air Force Captains.* Lackland Air Force Base, Texas; Wright Air Development Center, Personnel Laboratory, (Technical Note WADC-TN-58-64, ASTIA Document No. AD 202 845).
4. R. S. CRUTCHFIELD, D. G. WOODWORTH and R. E. ALBRECHT (1958) *Perceptual Performance and the Effective Person.* Lackland Air Force Base, Texas; Wright Air Development Center, Personnel Laboratory, (Technical Note WADC-TN-58-60, ASTIA Document No. AD 151 039).
5. J. A. STARKWEATHER and R. S. CRUTCHFIELD, (1954) Introversion and perceptual accuracy. *American Psychologist,* 9, 560.
6. R. S. CRUTCHFIELD (1951) Assessment of persons through a quasi group-interaction technique. *Journal of Abnormal and Social Psychology* 46, 577–588.
7. R. S. CRUTCHFIELD and D. G. WOODWORTH (1954) Effective functioning of Officer Personnel in a quasi group-interaction situation. *Research Bulletin* p. 6. University of California, Berkley, Institute of Personality Assessment and Research.
8. F. BARRON, (1954) *Personal Soundness in University Graduate Students: An Experimental Study of Young men in the Sciences and Professions* (University of California Publications in Personality Assessment and Research, No. 1) University of California Press, Berkeley CA.
9. *Ibid.,* p. 23.
10. *Loc. cit.*
11. *Ibid.,* pp. 23–24.
12. *Ibid.,* p. 25.
13. *Ibid.,* p. 26.

5

The Creative Potential of Mathematically Precocious Boys*

D. P. KEATING

Abstract

The high mathematical aptitude and academic achievement of the students in the Study of Mathematically Prococious Young (SMPY) has been well documented. A further question concerns their potential for eventual productivity or creativity. A series of measures presumed to be related to and possibly predictive of later creativity were administered to 72 mathematics competition winners from 1972 and 1973. These included measures of interests, values, personality characteristics, figure preference, and biographical background. The results showed that this academically high-promise group rated moderately high on these measures also, and that several individuals rated very high on three or more. Eventual longitudinal follow-up should resolve some of the questions regarding the long-term predictive validity of various measures.

THE STUDY of Mathematically Precocious Young (SMPY) has been primarily concerned with the seeking out and facilitating of high-level mathematical reasoning ability. That the students identified by the vigorous screening procedures used by SMPY are cognitively advanced is testified to by several converging lines of evidence: their high scores on ability tests designed for students three to five years older (chapter 2 of this section); case studies (Keating and Stanley, 1972; chapter 1 of this section); and their precocity in cognitive development using Piagetian criteria (chapter 5 of this section). Further, this precocity is closely related to meaningful academic achievement criteria, such as highly successful performance in college mathematics and mathematics-related courses several years ahead of age-mates and often superior to older "classmates."

The existence of such high ability and concomitant academic achievement has thus been demonstrated, if not fully explicated. A number of intriguing questions arise following such a demonstration, one of which is examined more closely in this chapter: What is the likelihood that these abilities and academic achievements will be related to more long-term and meaningful criteria, such as productivity and creativity? Since this is a remarkably "high-promise" group, the opportunity to collect and examine potential indicators of such real-life criteria, along with the high probability of eventually observing different levels on these criteria, is rare.

*In D. P. Keating (ed.), *Intellectual Talent: Research and Development.* Baltimore: The Johns Hopkins University Press, (1976). Reprinted by permission of the publisher and author.

The next step in the process is selecting potentially useful indicators of "creativity." Several options present themselves at this point. The first is to evaluate certain cognitive processes which have been considered examples of "creative thinking." Of these, the only one that has been identified as psychometrically separate from general intelligence is associational or ideational fluency, but the validation of measures of this cognitive process against creative production has not yet been done (Wallach, 1970). The second option would be to evaluate the creative products themselves of the individuals in the sample, but given the age of these students (twelve to fourteen years old) such an endeavor is likely to be misleading by virtue of insufficient evidence. Another approach, the one employed here, is to evaluate the creative *potential* of the group and of individuals within the group by using indirect measures of creativity, i.e., measures showing some relationship to adult or adolescent creative production, but are not presumed to be in themselves measures of the construct.

Method

Subjects

The subjects in this study were junior high school students who were the top scorers in two mathematics competitions held one year apart. To be eligible for the competition the student had to be in the seventh or the eighth grade, or less than fourteen years old if in a higher grade. The top 35 scorers of 396 contestants in the first competition were invited back for further testing, as were the top 44 scorers of 953 contestants in the second competition (see chapters 2 and 3 of this section). Of the top 79 students who were invited back, 76 accepted the invitation.

Only four girls qualified for an invitation to be retested, and all accepted. The small number makes an analysis by sex impossible, however, and they have been dropped from the subject pool, leaving 72 boys for the analysis. . . .

The students were administered the various paper and pencil measures described below at several retesting sessions. Not all of the students have taken all of the measures, and thus the appropriate Ns are indicated for each measure. There were 57 of the 72 boys who did take all of the measures, and this group is used as the base group. Means on each measure for those not in the base group were calculated, and no significant differences were found between the base group and nonbase group scores. Thus the base group may be considered representative of the total group.

Measures

The Allport–Vernon–Lindzey Study of Values (SV) (Allport, Vernon, and Lindzey, 1970) has often been used in studies of creative artists and scientists.

The "classic" value structure of the creative scientist, as reported by MacKinnon (1962) is high theoretical (T), high aesthetic (A), low religious (R). Although an empirical finding, the pattern makes psychological sense in terms of the SV value structure. The T person is concerned primarily with the seeking of knowledge, a "truth" value, and the relation of this to scientific creativity is obvious. It seems intuitively that the A value is quite different from T; its basis is in an appreciation of beauty, form, and harmony. The paradox is resolved when one recalls the importance of form and harmony to the "elegant" solution in mathematics or the parsimonious scientific theory.

It has often been asserted that the best predictor of future performance is past performance. In terms of research on creativity, it does seem that the most consistently successful method of discriminating creative from less creative groups has been reported past behavior and self-ratings (Taylor and Holland, 1962). A lengthy and fairly well-normed instrument of this type is the Biographical Inventory-Creativity (BIC) (Schaefer, 1970; Schaefer and Anastasi, 1968), which yields scores on "art and writing" and "mathematics and science."

Barron and Welsh (1952) proposed that preference for certain figures may be related to a "style" factor, which may in turn have a bearing upon creativity. Creative artists tended to like more complex and asymmetrical shapes than nonartists. Although the results of extensive research with the Barron–Welsh Art Scale (BWAS) have been inconclusive (Baird, 1972), some promising possibilities are offered on its use. Helson and Crutchfield (1970) reported a significant difference on the Art Scale between creative and less creative mathematicians.

Another method that has often been used for predicting creativity is the determination of consistent personality dimensions or traits among creative people (e.g., Cattell and Drevdahl, 1955; Hall and MacKinnon, 1969). The California Psychological Inventory (CPI) (Gough, 1957, 1969) was administered to nearly all the individuals in the group. Hall and MacKinnon (1969) have published a regression equation for the prediction of creativity, using the CPI Scales.

Vocational interest inventories have also been administered to this group. Their stability over time will likely prove important in a longitudinal study. The instruments that have been used are: the Strong–Campbell Interest Inventory (SCII), which is the most recent and still experimental revision of the Strong Vocational Interest Blank (SVIB), and which unites the men's and women's forms (Campbell, personal communication); and the Holland's (1958) Vocational Preference Inventory (VPI), short form.

In addition to the above listed measures, one further evaluation of the "creative potential" of these students will be made. It rests on the idea of a "minimum IQ" level for creative attainment (e.g., Cattell and Butcher, 1968). Accordingly, scores on Raven's Advanced Progressive Matrices (APM) are analyzed to assess "sufficiency" of nonverbal reasoning ability.

Results

The "Study of Values" (SV)

The typical value pattern of creative scientists (MacKinnon, 1962) is high theoretical (T), high aesthetic (A), low religious (R). Creative mathematicians are characterized as low R (Helson and Crutchfield, 1970). This group of mathematically precocious boys clearly shows the high T scores on the SV. Table III.6 lists the values and their frequency of occurrence as highest, second highest, or lowest. Of the 72 subjects, 42, or 58%, had it as their highest values. An additional 13.5 (with ties counting 0.5), or 19%, had it as their second highest value. Thus 52.5 or 77% overall, had T as their first or second highest value, much higher than the 33% chance level. It is not surprising that these students, who participated in a mathematics competition, would show as a high value an interest in learning *per se.*

TABLE III.6 *Frequency of occurrence of the six SV[a] values as highest[b], second highest, or lowest as % of total*

	Theoretical	Political	Economic	Social	Aesthetic	Religious
1st highest	59	14	8	7	5	7
2nd highest	19	37	24	10	3	6
Lowest (6th)	0	4	12	10	30	43

[a]Allport–Vernon–Lindzey Study of Values (1970).
[b]I.e., highest, second highest, or lowest within the individual's own SV profile.

These students are not as high on A as they are on T. Only 3.5, or 5%, have it as their highest value; an additional 2% or 3%, have it as their second highest value. Thus only 6.5 students overall, or 8%, have it as their first or second highest value. The absence of an aesthetic orientation could be rationalized *post hoc* by ascribing it to the youthfulness of the group or to other causes, but it is disconcerting nonetheless. The college experience, however, which may be helpful in the development of an aesthetic orientation (Huntley, 1965), still lies ahead for this group. R is the lowest value in the sample, occurring last 43% of the time.

Vocational Interest Inventories

A modified version of Holland's (1965) Vocational Preference Inventory (VPI) contains six categories of occupations with fourteen specific occupations in each. The categories are: realistic (R); conventional (C); investigative (I); social (S); artistic (A); and enterprising (E). An individual's most preferred category is determined as the one with the most occupations checked.

As anticipated, the category most frequently checked as highest was I investigative. Most of the occupations in that category are science oriented, and typically require advanced educational degrees. Of this academically motivated, mathematics-science-oriented group, 46, or 61%, had I as their preferred category (or it was tied with another category as most often preferred). An additional 18% or 24% had it as their second value. A total of 85% of the group, therefore, had I in the top two preferred categories. Although not yet empirically related to creativity, it seems more than likely that if one is to be a creative scientist or mathematician a preference for I occupations is desirable, perhaps even necessary.

This preference for investigative occupations is borne out by an analysis of the subjects' scores on the Strong—Campbell Interest Inventory (SCII). The SCII gives scores on the six Holland categories, as well as more specific occupational preference information. On the SCII, which not all of the students have taken, 78% of those who had taken it had I as the highest score. An additional 15% had it as the second highest score. Thus, 93% overall had I as the first or second highest category. Specific scales are not included in this analysis.

The Biographical Inventory

Scores on the Biographical Inventory-Creativity (BIC—Schaefer, 1970) are separated into two scales, which for males are "Art and Writing" (AW) and "Mathematics and Science" (MS). The MS score is of more importance for this group, but the AW scores have also been analyzed. Mean scores for both BIC scales are listed in Table III.7

Some of the items on the BIC are inappropriate for this age group. Several

TABLE III.7 *Mean scores of mathematically precocious boys on five measures related to creativity*

Measure	N[a]	Mean	S.D.
BIC-AW[b]	58	100.66	8.49
BIC-MS[c]	58	106.53	4.76
CPI[d]	67	11.21	4.48
BWAS[e]	64	17.91	11.91
APM[f]	69	29.51	3.08

[a]N for total group = 71.
[b]Biographical Inventory of Creativity, Arts and Writing (Schaefer, 1970).
[c]Biographical Inventory of Creativity, Mathematics and Science (Schaefer, 1970).
[d]California Psychological Inventory, creativity regression equation from Hall and MacKinnon (1969).
[e]Barron—Welsh Art Scale (Barron and Welsh, 1952).
[f]Raven's Advanced Progressive Matrices (Raven, 1965).

questions, for example, refer to accomplishments and awards during high school, since the instrument was designed for and normed on a college population (Schaefer, 1970). Thus it is likely that the scores of these students on the BIC would increase over time.

But even in comparison with a college norm group, the mathematically precocious students fare well. On the AW scale, the mean score of this group is equivalent to about the 58th percentile of the college males. On the MS scale, their mean score falls at the 68th percentile. In terms of biographical background, then, this group appears to have considerable creative potential. The BIC administered at this age may even underestimate their creative potential.

The California Psychological Inventory

At first glance, this would appear to be a quite *un*creative group on the basis of personality inventory scores. Hall and MacKinnon (1969) developed a regression equation using CPI scales that separated more creative from less creative architects. Using that regression equation, this group appears less creative than a group of randomly selected eighth-graders, as well as a high school norm group (Weiss, Haier, and Keating, 1974 [I:7]).

But the deficiency is more apparent than real. The most heavily weighted scale in the Hall and MacKinnon (1969) equation is Achievement via Conformance (AC), which gets a *negative* weight in distinguishing between more and less creative architects. This may be inappropriate at this age, since the randomly selected groups are clearly less achievement oriented on most dimensions.

This also points up the difficulty of analyzing adolescent personality structure and comparing it to adult norms. Not only do the scale scores change considerably over time, but the personality of a creative adult may have been quite different when that adult was an adolescent (Parloff, Datta, Kleman, and Handlon, 1968).

The Barron–Welsh Art Scale (BWAS)

The BWAS has been used to discriminate between creative artists and the general population (Barron and Welsh, 1952), and in other studies of creativity (e.g., Helson and Crutchfield, 1970). Although the way in which this type of design preference develops over time is not known, some idea of the creativity of this group may be gathered from this instrument.

As a group, the mathematically precocious boys do not appear to be especially creative when compared with the general population. The mean of the male nonartist group reported by Welsh (1959) is 15.06 (of a possible 62). The mean of these students is 17.91 (see Table III.7), a nonsignificant difference. Thus, as a group these students appear to be more like the general population than artists. Their sources are closer (Helson and Crutchfield, 1970) to less creative adult mathematicians (18.5) than to the general population, but least like adult creative mathematicians (27.5).

The Advanced Progressive Matrices

MacKinnon (1962) reported that in most fields there is no correlation between intelligence and creativity, although within those areas where one can be creative there are rarely individuals of low intelligence. Among mathematicians, however, a low positive correlation between intelligence and creativity is observed.

As one can readily see from Table III.7, this group has little difficulty in meeting a "minimum intelligence" criterion. This is not surprising, given the method of selection of the group. The mean of the group, 29, is above the 95th percentile of adult norms (Raven, 1965). All but 5 of the 72 boys score at least one standard deviation above the mean for university students.

The High Creatives

From the foregoing analysis it is not clear whether as a group these mathe-matically precocious boys should be considered "potentially creative" or not. The BIC indicates that they are, but the CPI results suggest that they are not, and the BWAS characterizes them as more like the less creative mathematicians. But the proper objection is raised that it is not a group but rather an individual who is creative. The important question thus revolves around which of the individuals within this group are most likely to be creative. To discern this it is necessary to look at those individuals who score above a reasonable criterion on each of the measures, and then at those who score at or above the criterion on more than one measure. This is especially applicable since the measures are uncorrelated within this group (see Table III.8).

The criterion that was used was the mean score of the group plus one standard deviation. To check on the possibility that this might be a group with low creative potential, thus invalidating within-group comparisons, the same criterion

TABLE III.8 *Correlation matrix of five measures related to creativity for 57 mathematically precocious boys (base group)*

	BIC-AW[a]	BIC-MS	CPI	BWAS	APM
BIC-AW		0.611[b]	0.051	0.251	−0.184
BIC-MS			−0.121	0.249	0.003
CPI				−0.111	0.001
BWAS					0.064
APM					

[a]For abbreviations of measures, see Table III.7.
[b]$p < 0.01$; no other r's are significant at $p < 0.05$ level. This correlation is between two scores on the same measure, which overlap.

TABLE III.9 *Students at or above criterion,[a] within-group and norm-group comparisons*

	Measures				
	BIC-AW[b]	BIC-MS	CPI	BWAS	APM
Within group (WG) criterion	109	111	15.9	30	33
No. of students at or above WG criterion	12	10	11	12	14
Norm group[c] (NG) criterion	109	109	11.7	26	25
No. of students at or above NG criterion	12	17	28	19	64

[a]Criterion = $\bar{X} + 1\sigma$ (means plus one standard deviation).

[b]See Table III.7 for abbreviations and N's for each test.

[c]Norm groups as follows: BIC-AW and BIC-MS—college males (Schaefer, 1970).
CPI—creative architects (Hall & MacKinnon, 1969).
BWAS—nonartists (general population)—(Welsh, 1959).
APM—university students (Raven, 1965).

was applied, using relevant norm group means and standard deviations. Table III.9 gives the number of students who scored above the criterion, on both within-group and norm-group comparisons, for each instrument. If each of these instruments does measure some aspect of creative potential, then a number of individuals in this group would seem to have such potential.

Those students, however, who score above the criterion on *more* than one measure should be the ones considered to have the most creative potential. In Table III.10 are listed the numbers of individuals who scored above the criterion, for both within-group and norm-group comparison, on at least one measure, on any two or more measures, on any three or more, and on four or more. As one can readily see, the number who score above the criteria of two or more measures on norm group comparisons is still a sizeable group, and ten students,

Table III.10 *% of students at or above within-group or norm-group criteria[a] on one or more creativity-related measures (N = 57)*

	% of students at or above criterion				
	On 1 or more measures	On 2 or more measures	On 3 or more measures	On 4 or more measures	On 5 measures
Within group comparison	56	26	7	2	0
Norm group comparison	96	77	32	10	2

[a]For measures and criteria, see Table III.9.

or nearly 14% of the total group, meet the criteria on three or more measures. Thus if each of these tests do indeed measure some aspect related to creative potential, the outlook for a good minority of the group is quite bright.

Discussion

From the use, with this group of mathematically precocious boys, of several different types of measures which have been held to relate to some dimension of creativity, it appears that the creative potential of this group is high. Although as a group they do not stand out from the norm groups on any measures except the APM, where they are much above the mean for university students, and on BIC-MS, where they are slightly above the mean for college students, a number of individuals within this group are far above the mean on three or four of the five measures used (see Table III.10).

There is a strong theoretical—investigative orientation of the group, and to the extent that this is important for creativity in mathematics and science, there is little difficulty for anyone in the group. If, however, the aesthetic orientation is important, a large segment of the group may have some difficulty. This is mitigated somewhat by the expectation that this aesthetic orientation will grow during the college experience. The low religious scores reflect those of creative mathematicians and scientists.

Some of the students, who at this time using these measures do not appear to be particularly creative, may in the future come up to the criteria that were used in this investigation. Developmental data on the BWAS is scant, but it seems reasonable that the scores of these students on the BIC and the CPI creativity regression equation will increase over time.

There are at least two possible explanations for the lack of agreement of creativity-related measures in this group. First, one or more of the measures used may not bear any deep relationship to creativity. The second possibility is that there is a problem of restriction of range within this group. Since they are homogeneous to a large extent on cognitive measures (although not as much as one might expect — see Keating, 1974 [I:2]), the possibility of too little variation on measures that are even slightly correlated with the selection measure is acute.

A third possibility is more intriguing. It may be that each of the measures does bear some relationship to creativity, and that each of them is measuring a different aspect of creative potential (i.e., interests, values, family background). If they are valid measures in this sense, the fact that they are uncorrelated would strongly suggest such a possibility. Creativity, as used to describe highly creative production, would have to be viewed not as a unitary construct, but rather as a situation toward which a great many factors must contribute. A longitudinal follow-up of this large group of mathematically talented youngsters, which is planned, should provide some answers to these questions.

In conclusion, the third possibility discussed above suggests a multifactor theory of creativity. Many factors and influences contribute to the development of the highly creative individual, and all or nearly all of them must contribute positively for the individual to be truly creative. If but a few of the factors are negative or even neutral, the individual may be routinely productive or erratically unproductive, but not truly creative. Such an explanation would account not only for the lack of correlation among measures of creativity but also for the observed rarity of truly creative individuals.

References

ALLPORT, G., VERNON, P. E., and LINDZEY, G. (1970) *Manual for the Study of Values* (3rd ed.). Boston: Houghton Mifflin.
ASTIN, H. S. (1974) Sex differences in mathematical and scientific precocity. In J. C. STANLEY, D. P. KEATING, and L. H. FOX (eds), *Mathematical talent: Discovery, description, and development.* Baltimore: The Johns Hopkins University Press, chapter 4.
BAIRD, L. L. (1972) A review of the Barron–Welsh Art Scale. In O. K. Buros (ed.), *The seventh mental measurements yearbook.* Highland Park: The Gryphon Press, pp. 81–83.
BARRON, F. and WELSH, G. S. (1952) Artistic perception as a possible factor in personality style: Its measurement by a figure preference test. *Journal of Psychology* 33, 199–203.
CATTELL, R. B. and BUTCHER, H. S. (1968) *The prediction of achievement and creativity.* New York: Bobbs-Merrill.
CATTELL, R. B. and DREVDAHL, J. E. (1955) A comparison of the personality profile of eminent researchers with that of eminent teachers and administrators and of the general population. *British Journal of Psychology* 46, 248–61.
GOUGH, H. G. (1957, 1969) *Manual for the California Psychological Inventory.* Palo Alto: Consulting Psychologists Press.
HALL, W. F. and MacKINNON, D. W. (1969) *Journal of Applied Psychology* 53(4), 322–26.
HELSON, R. and CRUTCHFIELD, R. S. (1970) Mathematicians: The creative researcher and the average Ph.D. *Journal of Consulting and Clinical Psychology* 34(2), 250–57.
HOLLAND, J. L. (1965) *Manual for the Vocational Preference Inventory.* Palo Alto: Consulting Psychologists Press.
HUNTLEY, C. W. (1965) Changes in Study of Values scores during the four years of college. *Genetic Psychology Monographs* 71, 349–83.
KEATING, D. P. (1974) The study of mathematically precocious youth. In J. C. STANLEY, D. P. KEATING, and L. H. FOX (eds), *Mathematical talent: Discovery, description, and development.* Baltimore: The Johns Hopkins University Press, chapter 2.
KEATING, D. P. and STANLEY, J. C. (1972) Extreme measures for the exceptionally gifted in mathematics and science. *Educational Research* 1(9), 3–7.
LESSINGER, L. M., and MARTINSON, R. A. (1961) The Use of the CPI with gifted pupils. *Personnel and Guidance Journal* 39, 572–75.
MacKINNON, D. W. (1962) The nature and nurture of creative talent. *American Psychologist* 17, 484–95.
PARLOFF, M. B., DATTA, L., KLEMAN, M., and HANDLON, J. H. (1968) Personality characteristics which differentiate creative male adolescents and adults. *Journal of Personality* 36, 528–52.
RAVEN, J. C. (1965) *Advanced progressive matrices.* London: H. K. Lewis and Co.
SCHAEFER, C. E. (1970) *Manual for the Biographical Inventory–Creativity.* San Diego: Educational and Industrial Testing Service.
SCHAEFER, C. E. and ANASTASI, A. (1968) A biographical inventory for identifying creativity in adolescent boys. *Journal of Applied Psychology* 52(1), 42–48.

TAYLOR, C. W. and HOLLAND, J. L. (1962) Development and application of tests of creativity. *Review of Educational Research* **32**(1), 91–102.

WALLACH, M. A. (1970) Creativity. In P. H. MUSSEN (ed.), *Carmichael's Manual of Child Psychology*. New York: Wiley, chapter 17.

WEISS, D. S., HAIER, R. J. and KEATING, D. P. (1974) Personality characteristics of mathematically precocious boys. In J. C. STANLEY, D. P. KEATING, and L. H. FOX (eds), *Mathematical talent: Discovery, description, and development*. Baltimore: The Johns Hopkins University Press, chapter 7.

WELSH, G. S. (1959) *Preliminary manual for the Welsh Figure Preference Test*. Palo Alto: Consulting Psychologists Press.

IV

Parental Influences on Creative Behavior and Exceptional Achievement

AT THIS point the papers become more specific. Having blocked out the major parameters in the preceding sections we now examine many of the critical factors and experiences underlying creative behavior and exceptional achievement. Over the years there have been three basic ideas offered to explain exceptional achievement — exceptional intelligence (or some talents), unusual and often unpleasant early family experiences, and fate. We have looked at the influence of intellectual giftedness in chapters II and III; now we turn our attention to the family — more specifically parental influences. To the extent that parents are themselves creative, there is evidence for believing that they enhance the likelihood of one or more of their offspring's own creativeness. Also, because parents pass on some of their genes, they are biological contributors to their children's make-up and potential in terms of cognitive abilities and talents. Moreover evidence has been found for a weak but significant positive association among biologically related persons' career interests. And yet, when all the evidence is assayed, if there are little or no innate gifts, regardless of the parents' own wishes and efforts, they will likely not be able to educate their child to be either talented or exceptionally achieving. Such are the limits on parental influence. It is important to keep in mind that we have joined creative behavior and exceptional achievement although several writers question whether or not creative behavior inevitably leads to exceptional achievement or that exceptional achievement requires what we usually believe is creative ability.

No group has been held more responsible for high achievement as much as parents since Galton pointed out the family networks among eminent persons and Freud stipulated the great dynamics and training within families. Families are the most complex human organization and do much of their work on levels that we only rarely glimpse. Thus, to say that families "cause" eminence is to a large extent to explain one unknown with another. This section is an effort to conceptualize how families are linked to the achievement to eminence and to isolate those specific aspects of the family (e.g., birth order) that are involved.

In the first paper Albert (IV-1) describes several basic cognitive transformations that are necessary before early giftedness can become exceptional achievement. Some of the underlying family history and dynamics are described. Of special interest are the high achieving persons' tendency to have been a "special" child (especially sons) and the extremely high rate of early parental loss among them. Both experiences are common to high achievers in various fields. Together they make up the special early family experience often influential in later achievement. The reader might wish to follow this article with Berrington's detailed and sympathetic discussion (VII-3) of the more subtle personal and professional consequences that early parental loss can have in career choice and attainment. Next comes McCurdy's paper (IV-2). It is a classic in the sense of being both early in its appearance and an inspiration of subsequent work in the area by others. The readers' attention is directed to the influence of available family libraries and adult conversations in the early intellectual development of youth who became recognized geniuses. The critical role of early cognitive stimulation through parental cultural interest, conversations, education, and readings that both McCurdy and Oden (IV-5) point to is now an established fact.

No book on eminence would be complete without presenting Roe's basic research (IV-3) on eminent scientists from several fields. Her work, among the earliest of its kind, pioneered first-hand observations and measurement of living eminent persons, and helped break the impasse in coming to grips with living evidence as opposed to more speculative methods of study. Eiduson's comprehensive paper (IV-4) shows where Roe's earlier work led and fills out our knowledge about the many intricacies of career choices and fulfillment. Those readers interested in scientists may wish to move to the articles by Zuckerman (V-3) and Merton (V-4) for more detailed analyses of exceptional scientific achievement.

So important is its evidence that we have already referred several times to Oden's (IV-5) report on the 1960 follow-up of Terman's gifted youth. Oden tells us how two groups of his subject — 100 of the more successful men (the A group) and 100 of the least successful men (the C group) — differed in their early family and educational experiences and values. These two groups, both of extremely high and not significantly different IQs, received quite distinctly different amounts and types of parental encouragement and ambitions, which affected their later education and careers. Not only is the A group more success-ful than their group C counterparts (and similar to MacKinnon's effective individuals) in their vocations but there are other positive consequences of their early family experiences in their health and in their later satisfactions.

1

Family Positions and the Attainment
of Eminence*

R. S. ALBERT

THERE are two basic transformations in the achievement of eminence. The first is that of intellectual giftedness to creative giftedness (Albert, 1978); the second, even more important, is the transformation of this intelligent creativeness into a combination of talent, drive, and values that "succeed." The transformation of early giftedness into adult eminence is one of the most enthralling and secretive processes of human development. Because its occurrence is relatively difficult to predict, it does not mean one should appeal to shopworn explanations such as "luck," "breaks," "knowing the right people," "genius," or other cliché. The attainment of eminence, although difficult to predict, is not without rational, developmental aspects (Albert, 1975). In this paper I wish to show how the family position of gifted children can put them in alignment with selected family experiences, socialization, and motivations that help prepare them for particular careers; secondly, I wish to show that often an unanticipated event such as the death of older siblings and/or a parent is not necessarily an impediment to this growth but can be an opportunity and a challenge to healthy ego development. The means and the direction in which these traumatic experiences influence a gifted child's development is determined by the family's prior preparation and values and the fit between the family's aspirations and the child's particular gift.

Like all behavior, the achievement of adult eminence is overdetermined, depending upon the push and pull of many persons, motives, values, and facilitation experiences, most of which occur unexpectedly. Yet we also know that as a child such a person often shows that he is somewhat different from his contemporaries in significant ways (Albert, 1971, 1975, 1978, 1980; Cox, 1926; Roe, 1952; Terman, 1954). Most studies of eminent persons indicate that as children they are cognitively gifted and often the first or only sons of better-than-average educated and socioeconomically placed families with particular interests and motivations of their own. Another determinant often pointed to is birth-order, itself an overdetermined influence upon a child's development.

For many years studies have shown weak but consistent relationships between birth-order and various developmental outcomes. As a focus, birth-order is an

*Gifted Child Quarterly, (1980), 24, 87–95 (edited). Reprinted by permission.

important family variable. A child's birth-order in his family is both a structural and a processional variable. As structure, it is organizational, giving order and focus to crucial family relationships, determining which family member is most likely to take an active interest in the child. As process, birth-order involves quality and tone of essential developmental functions, determining to some extent which family dynamics, interests, and values will be directed toward the child, for how long, and at what levels of intensity. In the development of a child families are *not* neutral, but encourage behaviors and developments in specific areas deemed important to them. Thus, it is clear that birth-order functions constantly as a selective factor, orienting the child and other family members to one another. A child's birth-order is a powerful determinant of psychological role in the family, although it is one among other important determinants such as sex, age spacing, and number of siblings, as well as family-significant gifts and talents.

By being in a family, the occupant of any birth-order is selectively influenced by the family's place in the parent culture and history, for every family operates and is aligned to some degree with a larger culture and its historical events. As culture and historical events vary, so will the influence of specific birth-orders.

This paper focuses on birth-order as a family position in hopes of elucidating how many eminent persons appear to be mainly from a few ordinal positions and from families of higher than average socioeconomic status. Such families, viewed through autobiographies, biographies, or empirical studies (Cox, 1926; Galton, 1869, 1874; McCurdy, 1957; Roe, 1952; Terman, 1954) show that many eminence-producing families themselves differ significantly from surrounding families (Albert, 1978). Usually they are highly stimulating for the child, singularly value-oriented, with a continuous sense of postsocial emphases and priorities not only evident in the family for several generations but quite evident in the treatment of their children. These emphases help define members' intrafamilial commitments, and the family's relationships to the wider culture. These are families rarely unaware of both the opportunities possible to their members or the possible family member(s) who might be best suited to these opportunities.

Along with the general assumption that there must be a high degree of congruence and interaction among talents, motivations, values, and the opportunities and achievement values of the culture for an individual to achieve within any field, five specific assumptions regarding the family are proposed. First, the family is intergenerational: important, extensive (often special) interactions go on between persons of two and more generations. Secondly, it is transactional: information (often special) is exchanged between family members. Although each member knows in broad outline what every other family member knows and can adequately participate with them, different combinations of family members have distinctive patterns of understanding and interactions. Thirdly, the family is, along with being a cultural and psychological unit, a historical one.

Not only do family members usually have a keen sense of their own linkage to past members and early, key family experiences, but a person's family position places him in a distinct relationship to these values, resources, and memories; e.g., Alex Haley, author of *Roots*, for whom his grandmother's recounted memories of early family history *were* extremely significant. Another fact of history which has great, albeit unpredictable, impact on the development of family members is the unexpected deaths, separations, or diminution of saliency of important members. As we will see, this historical event often brings a formerly lesser member into more direct alignment with the family's educational and career emphases and achievement socialization processes. The fourth assumption is that socialization and identification processes are the same processes, viewed respectively from the perspective of teacher and learner. They are never distinctly one or the other, nor is a person involved in one process only at any given time. Fifth and last, the family's historical orientation and ongoing socialization are selectively focused upon its children according to what their differences, aegrees of talents, and uniquenesses are perceived to be. Thus, a child's family position and capacities interact as *organizers* in family interactions.

It is not only the "special" child who is subjected to a family's socialization. Where a child's giftedness and/or specialness fit (or appear to fit) with the family's interests and values, they combine with birth-order to especially accentuate the child; he becomes the child who gets an intense socialization in those family traditions and interests. For example, Oliver Cromwell, upon going to Parliament, was met by six cousins already members (Hill, 1970); the daughter of 1903 Nobel winners Pierre and Marie Curie, Irene, and her husband Frederic Joliot were 1935 Nobel Laureates; Hitler (Stierlin, 1976), Nixon (Mazlish, 1972), John Kennedy, and Lyndon Johnson (Kearns, 1976) are examples from recent political history. Such intense socialization may occur in any area of behavior to which a family and its culture attach importance and have adult roles (careers) available for lifetime implementation.

Therefore, functioning as it does, a family operates as a selective experience-producing, experience-selecting agent motivated towards achieving specific developmental outcomes for its members. Looking closely at various developmental outcomes, healthy and unhealthy, one notices that in many cases there are highly selective matches, usually between one but sometimes between both parents and child, e.g., Philby the spy (Page, Leitch, and Knightley, 1968).

It is important to recognize that a child's "special" position need not always correspond to traditional birth-orders of high saliency. One finds a number of eminent persons who were labelled "special" as children because of unusual circumstances of birth, e.g., Freud (Jones, 1953). The unexpected may also bestow specialness, e.g., the death at birth of a twin brother for singer Elvis Presley who thereafter was raised as an only child, with recognizable talents. It is possible for traumatic family events to place a child in a special position. Unpredictable as they are, they stimulate and help shape the development of motivations, values, and talents in ways which often lead to exceptional developmental outcomes.

Method

The above observations are worked out in more detail with data in two distinct fields of adult eminence – politics and science. I use archival and biographical data on American presidents and vice presidents (Kane, 1974), British prime ministers (Pike, 1968), and Zuckerman's (1977) interviews with 39 American Nobel Laureates. Roe's (1952) and Eiduson's (1962) data on American scientists are referred to as well as findings from a variety of samples of noneminent special groups and census material for comparison. These sources were supplemented by various encyclopedias and fact books, especially the *Encyclopedia Britannica*, the *Dictionary of National Biography*, and the *New York Times*.

One would expect that the birth-order of eminent persons is a well-documented fact. Next to parentage, it is an essential piece of information, but birth-order is not always known or reported, or what is thought to be known may differ for two or more investigations. For example, both Stierlin (1976) and Bullock (1961) give Hitler's birth-order but do not agree on it. According to Stierlin, Hitler was the fourth-born of his mother, the first three children dying in quick succession. He does not report the other children's sex or specific spacing. Bullock is quite specific. He gives dates, sex, and spacing of births. Moreover, according to Bullock, Hitler is the third-born of his mother, preceded first by a brother and then a sister, each of whom died in their infancy. An additional family fact reported by Bullock is that Hitler was followed five years later by a brother who lived only six years (died when Hitler was 11) and a sister, Paula, who survived Hitler. The point is clear: nothing can be assumed established knowledge in a person's history, famous or not. I could not ascertain the birth-order for 8 of the 39 Nobel Laureates interviewed by Zuckerman.

Along with their high visibility and intrinsic interest, presidents and prime ministers were selected for several other reasons: (1) they clearly constitute groups of eminent politicians; (2) the two offices began at approximately the same time and for some of the same social and political reasons; (3) both offices have drawn their candidates from similar socioeconomic backgrounds – presidents from middle- and upper-middle-class families and prime ministers initially from the gentry and aristocracy and now also from upper-middle-class family backgrounds and; (4) the number of office holders – 39 presidents, 48 ministers – is similar.

The eminence of Nobel winners is also perfectly clear; the eminence of Roe's scientists is at a lower level of attainment (or was when she studied them), but her information regarding them is useful in understanding the early family background of eminent scientists.

The comparison groups of noneminent persons come from either the United States or Great Britain and were studied within this century.

Results

Special Family Position

Table IV.1 shows that being an only child or only son is not the proper path or best preparation for becoming an American president since only 1 of 39 was an only son (Coolidge). Being born the eldest son or becoming an oldest surviving son, however, does seem to prepare one for the presidency (72%). If, however, one is neither an only, eldest, or oldest surviving son, then being the "last son— last child" of one's family helps toward the presidency. The helping factor, however, is not clear. All four such placed presidents had also lost a parent early in their development.

The middle position is not the disadvantage it is usually described to be. That often undistinguished family position was occupied by 6 presidents (15%) and 11 prime ministers (23%). Again a special family event — early parental death — occurred to give specialness to two of the middle-born presidents and two of the prime ministers. In the case of eminent scientists, 8 Nobel Laureates (26%) and 13 of Roe's eminent scientists (21%) were middle positioned.

The number of presidents who were in a special family position, either through their birth or the unpredictable death of an older brother or a parent by age 16 is 35 or 39 (90%). An interesting subgroup among the presidents is the nine vice presidents who succeeded to the presidency through the death or resignation of a president. Eight of the nine (89%) were first sons; and Andrew Johnson, the only one not a first son among this group, became the oldest surviving son through the death of two older brothers before Johnson was born.

Although the birth-orders of the groups are approximate, more British prime ministers than American presidents were only children or only sons (7:1). However, the proportions of oldest sons are close (35%:49%) as are the proportions of prime ministers and presidents who were only surviving sons (10%: 18%). Each political office appears to recruit its holders from slightly different positioned candidates. Nonetheless, almost all of the successful candidates held special family positions either through their birth or the death of other family members. When the birth-orders of only child, only son, eldest son, only surviving son, and last son-last child are tallied, the proportion of presidents' and prime ministers' special family positions are quite high and close to one another — 85%:77%.

Regarding Nobel Laureates, more of them (36%) were either an only child (10%) or only son (26%) than either group of eminent politicians (3%, 14%), indicating that there are not only differing talents but differing early family experiences operating in the development of eminent persons of distinctly

TABLE IV.1 *Percentage (rounded) of Eminent Persons in Various Birth-orders and Special Family Positions*

Group	N	Both Parents' Only Child	Only Son	Oldest Son	Last Child and Last Son	Middle Child	One Parent's Oldest Son	Became the Oldest Surviving Son in Childhood (O.S.S.)
American Presidents, Vice Presidents	39	1 (3%)		19a (49%)	4d (10%)	6e (15%)	2ab (5%)	7c (18%)
(who became presidents)	9			8 (89%)				1 (11%)
British Prime Ministers	48	3 (6%)	4 (8%)	17a (35%)	8d (17%)	11e (23%)		5 (10%)
Nobel Laureates	31g	3 (10%)	8 (26%)	6 (19%)	5 (16%)	8 (26%)		1 (3%)
Eminent Scientists (Roe, 1952)	62g	15 (23%)	5 (8%)	24 (38%)	3 (5%)	13 (20%)		2 (3%)
Competent Researchers (Eiduson, 1962)	40	5 (13%)	5 (13%)	19f (47%)	9 (23%)	7 (17%)		

aFive presidents (Washington, Jefferson, Monroe, Lincoln, and Coolidge) lost a parent by age 16; eight prime ministers lost a parent by age 11.

bWashington and Franklin D. Roosevelt were mothers' first sons.

cThis includes J. F. Kennedy and Nixon who became O.S.S. after adolescence but before their careers were decided.

dAll four (Jackson, Johnson, Hayes, and Garfield) were last sons—last children and lost a parent by age 15. Jackson lost both. Two prime ministers lost parents by age 11 years.

eTwo of the six presidents (Taylor and Hoover) lost a parent (Hoover both parents) by age 15. Two prime ministers lost a parent by age 11.

fSeven of 19 competent researchers had very large age differences between siblings; no close relationships were established between them.

gSufficient data for 62 of 64 original subjects; 31 of 39 Nobel Laureates.

different careers. Nonetheless, 74% of the Nobel winners came from special family positions. Roe's (1952) group of eminent scientists were similarly placed in their families. Of the 62 for whom there is appropriate information, 76% were "specials" of one kind or another.

Parental Deaths

In comparing eminent scientists and eminent politicians one finds somewhat different sets of special family positions (and backgrounds) for each group. More eminent scientists were only children or only sons (33%) than were eminent politicians (9%). On the other hand, death plays a larger role in the early family positioning of eminent politicians.

Eminent politicians appear to experience more early family deaths than do eminent scientists. The death of either a parent or an older brother was experienced in childhood by 51% of the presidents and 45% of the prime ministers. This occurred to 22% of the Nobel Laureates and 41% of Roe's sample of eminent scientists (data found in Tables IV.1 and 2). We find that, although eminent politicians experience more early family deaths than eminent scientists, when one compares both groups' proportions of early parental deaths with other groups having unusual developmental outcomes, i.e., antisocial or psychological problems, as children eminent persons are neither the only group to experience a significantly greater proportion than the general population nor have they a significantly greater proportion of such early experiences than persons with other exceptional developments. Another feature to the data is that there is an increased proportion of early parental deaths among the samples, as we move from the usual to unusual developmental outcomes, i.e., the general population to gifted youth, competent but undistinguished scientists and delinquent boys to those groups of clearly exceptional and problematic developments. This is an area worth close examination for it suggests that this unpredictable family event may have potentially adaptive as well as maladaptive influences. Which early parental death becomes is clearly a function of other factors besides parental loss.

It is not only eminent persons who have a significantly high frequency of such experiences. Compared to the average of 8% general population experiencing early parental deaths, the percentages for adult criminals, adult psychiatric patients (especially depressives), and eminent adults are high and quite close to one another (32%, 27%, 28%). These figures are unusual in comparison with younger, exceptional subjects — juvenile delinquents, Terman's gifted children (Burks, Jensen, and Terman, 1930), or college students (20%, 16%, 6%) — most of whom do not attain noticeable levels of eminence. At the least such an experience as early parental death appears to give drive and focus to many a child's giftedness and family emphases. . . .

TABLE IV.2 *Percentage (rounded) of Children Experiencing Family Disruption through Early Parent Death or Separation-Divorce*

		Pro-social Outcomes					
		Parental Death by Age 16			Parental Loss through Causes other than Death		
Group	N	Father	Mother	Total %	Father	Mother	Total %
American Presidents	39	21%	13%	34%			
British Prime Ministers	48	27%	8%	35%			
Cox's Historical Geniuses	135*	19%	11%	30%			
Eminent Scientists (Roe, 1952)	64	16%	10%	26%			6%
Competent Scientists (Eiduson, 1962)	40	15%	5%	20%			
Eminent French and English Poets (Martindale)†	33	24%	Regarding mothers' deaths: it is writer's impression "that this is less frequent"				
Eminent English Poets and Writers (Brown, 1968)	57			55%			
College Students (Gregory, 1965)	1,696	4%	2%	6%			Not living with both parents = 2.4%
Able Misfits (IQ = 130) (Pringle-Kellmer, 1970)	103						18%
Terman Gifted (Burks, Jensen and Terman, 1930)	1,000	11%	5%	16%			11%
Adolescence, General Population (Hathaway and Monachesi, 1963)	11,329	6%	2%	8%			6%
General British Population (Ferri, 1976)	17,000	4%	5%	9%	8%	2%	9%

*Cox reports on 301 subjects; the data varies considerably in detail. The present sample consists of subjects for which data was sufficient to make a judgment regarding parental loss.
†Martindale, C. Personal communication to the author, October 4, 1971.

Psychological Problems	
Parental Death by Age 16	Parental Loss through Causes other than Death

Group	N	Father	Mother	Total %	Father	Mother	Total %
(...,...,and ...,196?)	100	7%	3%	12.0%*			
Adolescent Lesbians with severe school problems (Krammer and Rifkin, 1969)	25						
Out Patient Depressives	216	8%	21%	49.0%	64%	28%	
Controls (Out Patients of G.P.)	267	28%	7%	21.0%			
1921 Census (Brown, 1968)		14%	8%	21.0%			
Hospitalized Psychiatric Patients	549	13%	15%				
Controls (Brown, 1968)			5%				
Hospitalized Adult Psychiatric Patients	748	9%	8%	17.0%			7%
Matched Non-psychiatric Controls (Pitts, Myer, Brooks, and Winokus, 1965)	250	12%	6%	18.0%			7%

*As reported.

Anti-social Outcomes

Group	N	Parental Death by Age 16			Parental Loss through Divorce or Separation		
		Father	Mother	Total %	Father	Mother	Total %
Male Prisoners (Brown, 1968)	168	13%	9%	22%			
Female Prisoners (Brown, 1968)	546	18%	13%	31%			
Short-term Male Prisoners (Andry, 1963)	21* 100**	28% 21%	12% 14%	40% 35%			
Habitual Male Criminals (Morris, 1951)	196				"almost 70% come from broken homes"		70%
Delinquent Boys	100			24%			40%
Non-delinquent Boys (Cortes and Gatti, 1972)	100			9%			5%
Juvenile Offenders (Ferdinand, 1964)	1,292M 318F	7% 12%	3% 1%	10% 12%			
Delinquent Women	500C	18%	19%	37%			20% childhood families separated or divorced
(Glueck and Glueck, 1934)	500A	10%	6%	17%			2% adolescence families separated or divorced

*= recidivists   M = males   C = childhood
**= nonrecidivists   F = females   A = adolescence

General Discussion and Conclusions

Any discussion of the achievement of eminence must begin with Galton (1869) and Freud (1959). Together they set the basic parameters for understanding the major determinants of eminence, or the failure to do so, when giftedness and talent are not in question. Family position was a concern of both Galton and Freud. Galton mapped out the hereditary family paths that eminence may take; Freud the early emotional and social learning which motivate it. There has been no clearer statement than Freud's of how powerful a child's early favored family position can be upon his future self-regard and potential for achievement: "A man who has been the indisputable favorite of his mother keeps for life the feeling of conqueror, that confidence of success which often induces success" (Jones, 1953, p. 5). There are dangers inherent in this favored position, especially for politicians, e.g., Hitler, Nixon, and L. B. Johnson. Because of the intense intrafamily (Oedipal) competitions, such favoritism often leaves the child prone to guilt and unconscious self-defeating behaviors. Again Freud (1959) anticipated such dangers when he spoke of men who were "destroyed" by their success, part of their success being to out-achieve their less than adequate (in the mother's eyes), unsuccessful fathers. It was the dilemma of talent and family loyalty that Freud wrote, spoke, and dreamed of extensively throughout his long career. (What is the story of Oedipus but of fathers, mothers, and sons, all in battle for supremacy and ultimate success?) As for birth-order being specifically a critical variable in a person's success, Galton's *English Men of Science* (1874) is the first major empirical statement. After Freud and Galton, matters regarding personal history and achievement became a focus of many social scientists. And yet it seems at times as if the issues are confused, too complex, the methodological problems too difficult for us to get much past the lines drawn earlier by Freud and Galton. The main impediment appears to be that we do not know scientifically what transpires within families that might facilitate or inhibit the conversion of early giftedness into eminent careers. The present study attempts to fill this gap by focusing on the child in conjunction with its family.

"Birth-order" appears too vague a term to use without specific qualifications. "Special family position" is better because it accents a characteristic that is rampant in accounts of many high achieving careers — that the high achiever was perceived and treated as "special" in the family early in his development. Also, this "specialness" may often be the result of events over which no one has control but which offer opportunities for child and family to develop different relationships. In time these alter the child's skills, competencies, and career goals. Three world-famous examples (other than John Stuart Mill) are Mozart, an only son whose older, talented sister was quickly shelved by their musician father as soon as he became aware of his very young son's exceptional talents; Malthus, a second son whose gifts so attracted his father's attention that he was given special tutors; and lastly, William Pitt the younger, a second son who so clearly outshone his older brother that the older brother was enlisted by the family in the Army to make way for the younger, much more talented son. In all three cases, precociousness was the signal to elevate the child into a more special, closer relationship with the father and the family's interests and values. "Special" in these cases covers two conditions: the position of the child in regard to his psychological role and treatment, and position in regard to the place of the family in society and its prevailing commitment to achievement.

"Special family position" points us in the right direction. As we look closely into the birth-order of successful politicians and scientists, we find that its impact is often conditioned by events that are out of the family's control but which distinctly influence their relationships to past and present family members. Participants in both fields show that high achievers almost invariably held special family positions, although the proportions in any particular position were not identical for the two fields. The early family life of eminent politicians and scientists do not read alike yet each group's families appeared to provide a "facilitating environment" (Winnicott, 1957) for the child in question. These environments are "facilitating" because they identify relatively early and capitalize on the particular talents of the child. This paper stresses that it is the child's early observed giftedness that helps to orient a family toward him in a special way. Giftedness is an organizer, as are values and goals. They pull together diverse personal and interpersonal factors to make a more coherent organization of a child and family's transactions.

What is also often found in the development of many eminent men and women is that the special training given them is often in the areas of a parent's, usually their father's, own special interests and aptitudes (McCurdy, 1957; Roe, 1952). The three eminents mentioned above, Malthus, Mozart, and Pitt, each clearly followed in their families' traditions, as did Churchill, John and Robert Kennedy, the Adams, the Tafts, the Roosevelts, and Irene Joliot-Curie. They were all "selected" by their families. It is important, however, to know that such selection and socialization processes can occur in many fields. The College Basketball Player of 1976, Marquis Johnson, is the only son among six children. At his birth, the doctor predicted to his basketball playing-coaching father that the baby would grow to be 6'6". From his second year on, his father constantly taught him basketball, until the father could no longer keep up with the son (*Los Angeles Times*, 1977).

There is one set of data on middle children that is in line with developmental assumptions. Although the birth-order of adult criminals is not well documented, it does appear (Andry, 1963; Glueck and Glueck, 1934; Morris, 1951) that the middle and the last birth-orders are over-represented among a variety of antisocial samples. This seems to hold for college populations as well. As to the nature of the motivations that are involved, Sears, Maccoby, and Levin (1957) show that middle-class fathers, according to mothers' reports, involved themselves more with only and older children, leaving the middle either alone or with the mother.

Middles also receive less praise for carrying out more expected household responsibilities and often are allowed less expression of aggression than only or oldest children toward their parents and other children. The combination of less father attention, less praise, more family chores, and fewer outlets for frustrations could put great strain on a young child's ego processes, stimulating the denial and repression of aggressive impulses. These two psychological defenses are the most antagonistic defenses to emotional maturity and creative behavior.

The higher than average rate of early parent loss for eminent persons shows in terms of family experiences and cognitive development that the frequency of such early parental death is not unusually high when compared to other groups with different types of exceptional developmental outcomes, and early parental death does not necessarily constitute a debilitating experience for the survivors. Although samples of eminent persons do have inordinately high rates of early sibling death, the rates of parental death were not higher than those for samples of noneminent persons who had problematic developmental outcomes. In an important paper, Zajonc (1976) stated that "a one-parent home constitutes an inferior intellectual environment and should result in intellectual deficits. . . ." He concluded that the early loss of a parent should produce greater deficits, that "in comparison with other causes of loss of parent, death may have an especially depressing effect on intellectual performance" (p. 230). Our results suggest that the issue is not so clear. If any type of parental loss appears in the literature as developmental debilitation, it is parental loss through separation, divorce, or extreme passivity (e.g., Santrock, 1972). Early parental death by itself is not cognitively damaging. Two major determinants of whether or not this loss leads to fuller development and even eminence rather than psychological sickness or criminality are the presence of giftedness, special talents, high aptitudes (indices of what often is spoken of as ego strength), and recognition and opportunities for appropriate, stimulating education by a parent or an interested third party (Albert, 1978).

How early parent death works in the development of a child is not clearly understood. However, one clue lies in the results of a nationwide survey (Veroff, Atkinson, Feld, and Gurin, 1960) which showed that males who experienced a parental death by age 16, when compared with matched males from intact homes, had significant reductions in their affiliation and achievement motivations and a significant increase in their power motivation. (Females reacted to early parental death in opposite directions than males.) We can see where part of eminent men's and criminals' motivation to succeed may come from, although toward whom or what it is directed and how it is expressed is a matter of their own talents and aptitudes, their early family positions, and their families' values and type of child rearing.

One last point emerges from these data. Darwin, whose mother died when he was 8, and Galton and Golda Meir (1975), whose parents lived full and busy lives, were all raised by older sisters. Other siblings often have a large share of childrearing, frequently without close parental supervision or to the detriment of the younger child. (We might note that American presidents come from families averaging 6.4 children.)

We know little about this phenomenon but perhaps the influences of older, involved siblings in the achievement of eminence are too commonly credited to parents and need to be examined in their own right. This phenomenon, and the fact that early parental deaths do not necessarily debilitate the gifted child's cognitive development and achievement motivation, suggest that in order for us to understand what occurs in the early development of any child, gifted or not, we need to look closely and continually at what occurs *within* families. Anything less appears to leave us at the mercy of our assumptions.

References

ALBERT, R. S. (1971) Cognitive development and parental loss among the gifted, the exceptionally gifted, and the creative. *Psychological Reports*, 29, 14–26.

ALBERT, R. S. (1975) Toward a behavioral definition of genius. *American Psychologist*, 30, 140–151.

ALBERT, R. S. (1978) Observations and suggestions regarding giftedness, familial influence and the achievement of eminence. *The Gifted Child Quarterly*, 22, 201–211.

ALBERT, R. S. (1980) Genius. In R. H. Woody (Ed.), *Encyclopedia of clinical assessment*. San Francisco: Jossey-Bass.

ANDRY, R. G. (1963) *The short-term prisoner*. London: Stevens and Sons.

BARBER, J. D. (1972) *The presidential character: Predicting performance in the White House*. Englewood Cliffs: Prentice-Hall.

BECK, A. T., SETHI, B. B. and TUTHILL, R. W. (1963) Childhood bereavement and adult depression. *Archives of General Psychiatry*, 9, 295–302.

BROWN, F. (1968) Bereavement and lack of a parent in childhood. In E. Miller (Ed.), *Foundations of child psychiatry*. Oxford: Pergamon Press.

BULLOCK, A. (1961) *Hitler: A study in tyranny*. New York: Bantam Books.

BURKS, B. S., JENSEN, D. W and TERMAN, L. M. (1930) *The promise of youth: Follow-up studies of a 1000 gifted children*. (Vol. 3 of *Genetic studies of genius*, (Ed.) L. M. Terman). Stanford: Stanford University Press.

CORTES, J. B. and GATTI, F. M. (1972) *Delinquency and crime: A biopsychosocial approach*. New York: Seminar Press.

COX, L. M. (1926) *The early mental traits of 300 geniuses*. (Vol. 2 of *Genetic studies of genius*, (Ed.) L. M. Terman), Stanford: Stanford University Press.

EIDUSON, B. (1962) *Scientists: Their psychological world*. New York: Basic Books.

FERDINAND, T. N. (1964) The offense patterns and family structure of urban, village and rural delinquents. *Journal of Criminal Law, Criminology, and Police Science*, 55, 86–93.

FERRI, E. (1976) *Growing up in a one-parent family*. Slough: NFER Publishing Co., Ltd.

FREUD, S. (1915) Some character types met in psychoanalytic work. In *Collected Papers*.

GALTON, F. (1869) *Hereditary genius*. New York: Macmillan.

GALTON, F. (1874) *English men of science: Their nature and nurture*. London: Macmillan.

GLUECK, S. and GLUECK, E. T. (1934) *Five hundred delinquent women*. New York: Alfred Knopf.

GREGORY, J. (1965) Anterospective data following childhood loss of a parent. *Archives of General Psychiatry*, 13, 99–120.

HATHAWAY, S. R. and MANACHESI, E. G. (1963) *Adolescent personality and behavior*. Minneapolis: University of Minnesota Press.

HILL, C. (1970) *God's Englishman: Oliver Cromwell and the English Revolution*. London: Weidenfeld and Nicolson.

JONES, E. (1953) *The life and work of Sigmund Freud*, Vol. 1. New York: Basic Books.
KANE, J. N. (1974) *Facts about the presidents* (3rd ed.). New York: H. W. Wilson.
KEARNS, D. (1976) *Lyndon Johnson and the American dream.* New York: Harper-Row.
KRAMMER, M. W. and RIFKIN, A. H. (1969) The early development of homosexuality: A study of adolescent Lesbians. *American Journal of Psychiatry*, 126, 91–96.
Los Angeles Times (1977) A father's dream comes true. March 1, 1977, (Part III), pp. 1, 10.
MAZLISH, B. (1972) *In search of Nixon: A psychohistorical inquiry.* Baltimore: Penguin Books.
McCURDY, H. G. (1957) The childhood pattern of genius. *Journal of Elisha Mitchell Science Society*, 73, 448–462.
MEIR, G. (1975) *My life.* New York: G. P. Putnam's Sons.
MORRIS, N. (1951) *The habitual criminal.* Cambridge: Harvard University Press.
PAGE, B., LEITCH, D. and KNIGHTLEY, P. (1968) *The Philby conspiracy.* New York: Signet Books.
PIKE, E. R. (1968) *Britain's Prime Ministers.* Feltham, England: Odhams Books.
PITTS, F. N., MEYER, J., BROOKS, M. and WINOKUR, G. (1965) Adult psychiatric illness assessed for childhood parental loss and psychiatric illness in family members – a study of 748 patients and 250 controls. *American Journal of Psychiatry*, 121, June supplement, i–x.
PRINGLE-KELLMER, M. L. (1970) *Able misfits: The educational and behavior difficulties of intelligent children.* London: Longman.
ROE, A. (1952) *The making of a scientist.* New York: Dodd, Mead.
SANTROCK, J. W. (1972) Relation of type and onset of father absence to cognitive development. *Child Development*, 43, 455–469.
SEARS, R. R., MACCOBY, E. E. and LEVIN, H. (1957) *Patterns of child rearing.* Evanston: Row, Peterson.
STIERLIN, H. (1976) Hitler as the bound delegate of his mother. *History of Childhood Quarterly: Journal of Psychohistory*, 3, 463–499.
TERMAN, L. M. (1954) The discovery and encouragement of exceptional talent. *American Psychologist*, 9, 221–230.
VEROFF, J., ATKINSON, J. W., FELD, S. C. and GURIN, G. (1960) The use of thematic apperception to assess motivation in a nationwide interview study. *Psychological Monographs*, 74, (Whole no. 499), 1–32.
WINNICOTT, D. W. (1957) The only child. In *The child and the family.* London: Tavistock Publications.
ZAJONC, R. B. (1976) Family configuration and intelligence. *Science*, 192, 227–236.
ZUCKERMAN, H. (1977) *Scientific elite.* New York: The Free Press.

2

The Childhood Pattern of Genius *

H. G. McCURDY

GENIUS by any definition is rare. If, following Galton, we make lasting fame one of the requirements, it is very rare indeed, and we are reduced to studying it at a distance through biography. Now, biographies have their limitations; as Havelock Ellis noted, one may search through them in vain for the most ordinary vital statistics. Above all, they cannot be expected to yield information on those details of early life, such as nursing and weaning and toilet training, to which psychoanalysis has attached so much importance. When, therefore, one proposes as I do here to explore the question whether there is some pattern of environmental influences operating on children of genius which might help to account for their later achievement, it should be self-evident that the question is necessarily adjusted to something less than microscopic precision. Not only so, but, because the factor of heredity cannot be controlled, any answer whatsoever must be regarded as partial and tentative and ambiguous. Nevertheless, there may be some profit in asking the question, and insofar as it is directed simply toward the discovery of uniformity of environmental pattern there is no inherent reason why it should not be answerable, provided we do not insist on minute detail.

Table IV.3 presents the twenty geniuses into whose childhood this paper will inquire. The selection was partly deliberate, on theoretical grounds, and partly random, as will be explained. In Cox's monumental study of great geniuses (7) the main sample consists of 282 men drawn from the list of 1000 which was compiled by J. McKeen Cattell on the principle that the amount of space allotted to them in biographical dictionaries could be taken as an objective measure of their true eminence. Though one may certainly quarrel with some of Cattell's results, the sifting process applied by Cox was admirable. She arrived at her smaller list by requiring: one, that the attained eminence should clearly depend upon notable personal achievement; and two, that the biographical material available should be sufficient to permit a reliable estimate of early mental ability. Men born before 1450 were eliminated. The chief task of Cox's investigation was to estimate the intelligence level displayed by these rigorously selected geniuses during childhood and youth. For this purpose the appropriate information was extracted from biographical sources and submitted to the judgment of three

*Journal of Elisha Mitchell Science Society, (1957), 73, 448–462. Reprinted by permission of the author.

TABLE IV.3

	Estimated IQ in Childhood	Fame (rank in 282)	Birth Order	Age at Marriage
J. S. Mill (1806–1873)	190	103	1 in 9	45
Leibniz (1646–1717)	185	19	Only	–
Grotius (1583–1645)	185	72	1 in 5	25
Goethe (1749–1832)	185	4	1 in 6	39
Pascal (1623–1662)	180	35	2 in 3	–
Macaulay (1800–1859)	180	53	1 in 9	–
Bentham (1748–1832)	180	181	1 in 2	–
Coleridge (1772–1834)	175	157	10 in 10	23
Voltaire (1694–1778)	170	2	5 in 5	–
Leopardi (1798–1837)	170	280	1 in 5	–
Chatterton (1752–1770)	170	163	3 in 3	–
Niebuhr (1776–1831)	165	135	2 in 2	24
Mirabeau (1749–1791)	165	30	9 (?) in 11	22
J. Q. Adams (1767–1848)	165	274	2 in 5	30
Wieland (1733–1813)	160	152	1 in ?	32
Tasso (1544–1595)	160	48	3 in 3	–
Pope (1688–1744)	160	50	Only	–
Pitt (1759–1806)	160	9	2 in 5	–
Musset (1810–1857)	160	261	2 in 2	–
Melanchthon (1497–1560)	160	77	1 in 5	23

raters thoroughly experienced in the use of intelligence tests and the valuation of IQ from behavior. Their three independent ratings, expressed as IQs, were combined. Separate estimates were made for two periods of life: from birth to age 17, and from age 17 to age 26. As might be expected, the reliabilities of the estimates increased in proportion to the amount of biographical information, and, in general, the IQs based on the more adequate material were higher. Consequently, one in search of illumination on the early environment of genius would naturally turn most hopefully to the geniuses in Cox's list who had been assigned the highest childhood IQs. This I did. From her list I chose as my preliminary sample the 27 men whose IQs in childhood had been estimated at 160 or higher. The final sample of 20, as given in Table IV.3 was reached by dropping out those individuals for whom the biographical material in the University of North Carolina Library appeared to be inadequate. As will be observed, the order of listing in the table is from the highest childhood IQ downwards. The reputation of each man is indicated in the column headed "Fame" by his rank number in Cox's sample, as based on Cattell. With respect to fame the sample appears to be a fair cross-section of Cox's larger group; with respect to IQ, as explained, it is highly selected. One sees at a glance that here are individuals who did extraordinary work in science, law, literature, or politics, and who fully deserve to be called geniuses. Their biographies should be relevant to the proposed question.

It should be understood from the outset that Cox did not neglect the problem of environment. Her biographical sketches furnish some very pertinent information, and she states as an important conclusion that, on the whole, youths who achieve eminence have superior advantages in their early days. Though she notes exceptions, she says: "The average opportunity of our young geniuses for superior education and for elevating and inspiring social contacts was unusually high." . . . The extraordinary training for leadership received by Pitt the younger, John Quincy Adams, Niebuhr, and the Humboldt brothers; the specialized instruction of Mozart, Weber, and Michelangelo undoubtedly contributed to the rapid progress of these great men among the great" (7, p. 216). The object of the present study is to push forward in the same direction of inquiry, but with more pointed attention to the social relations and their repercussions.

In Table IV.3 one column briefly summarizes facts concerning order of birth. Considerable theoretical importance is sometimes attached to the chronological position of a child in the family. In particular, Galton, who was not prone to overemphasize environment, thought enough of order of birth to pay some heed to it in his investigation of British scientists; and he comments that "the elder sons have, on the whole, decided advantages of nurture over the younger sons. They are more likely to become possessed of independent means, and therefore able to follow the pursuits that have most attraction to their tastes; they are treated more as companions by their parents, and have earlier responsibility, both of which would develop independence of character; probably, also, the first-born child of families not well-to-do in the world would generally have more attention in his infancy, more breathing-space, and better nourishment, than his younger brothers and sisters in their several turns" (13, p. 26). There is an intuitive appeal in the argument, but Galton does not support it by any precise analysis of his data. What may be said about the present sample? First, it must be admitted that there are several ways of stating the facts, depending on whether one includes or excludes half-siblings and siblings who died at an early age. The figures given in the table stand for full siblings and include all births. The half-siblings excluded in the three cases involved (Leibniz, Coleridge, Pope) were children by previous wives of their fathers. The impression produced by inspection is that there may be an excess of only and first children among these twenty geniuses. But an analysis of the probabilities does not favor this view very strongly. The average likelihood of being born in first place in the twenty families works out to about one-third, and the observed frequencies deviate from the theoretically expected only enough to yield a chi square of 2 in support of the hypothesis; since this corresponds to a confidence level of between 0.2 and 0.1 for the one degree of freedom, one is left in doubt. Pascal, Niebuhr, and Adams were first sons. If we estimate in terms of first sons, a total of 13, and adjust the probabilities to the expectation that about half the children in multiple birth would be girls, the chi square is 1.8, again too small to support the hypothesis firmly.

Though the figures do not support a birth order hypothesis, there may never-theless be something about position in the family which is significant. Let us look at the seven who do not rank as first-born children or first-born sons. Coleridge was born in his father's old age and was his "Benjamin"; Voltaire was so sickly during the first year of his life that there was daily concern over his survival, and his mother, an invalid, was incapable of having any more children; Chatterton was a posthumous child, and the previous boy in the family had died in infancy; Mirabeau was the first son to survive after the death of the first and a succession of girls; Tasso was the only surviving son, his older brother having died before he was born; Pitt was in the interesting position of being able to follow his father in a parliamentary career in the House of Commons, as his older brother could not do because of the inherited title; and Musset, the second of two sons, was younger than the first by a significant span of six years. When we weigh these additional facts, the general notion of some sort of positional effect begins to reassert itself.

One way in which position in the family might favor the development of a child would be by giving it higher attentional value for the parents. Close examination of the biographical data leads to the conclusion that these twenty men of genius, whether because of their position in the family or not, did as children receive a high degree of attention from their parents, as well as from others. In several cases it is clear that the attention exceeded that accorded to their brothers and sisters. Both very decided and very positive parental interest was displayed toward Mill, Leibniz, Grotius, Goethe, Pascal, Macaulay, Bentham, Coleridge, Niebuhr, Adams, Wieland, Pope, Pitt, and Melanchthon. Voltaire and Musset were far from neglected, but the attention bestowed upon them may have lacked some of the intensity of focus notable in the preceding cases. If any of the children suffered comparative neglect or abuse, they would be Leopardi, Chatterton, and Mirabeau. Chatterton had no father from the time of his birth, and the fathers of Leopardi and Mirabeau were lacking in sympathy or worse. On the other hand, Chatterton's mother and sister helped him to learn to read, saw that he went to school, and were good enough to him that the promise he made them when a child to reward them with all kinds of finery when he grew up was fulfilled in the last year of his short life; Leopardi was provided with tutors and had access to his father's rich library; and Mirabeau, cuffed and persecuted as he finally was by his erratic father, was received into the world with an outburst of joy and was always provided for educationally, even though the arrangement may have been savagely disciplinary.

Favorable parental attention may take the two forms of displays of affection and intellectual stimulation. There is strong evidence for both in most of the cases in our list. Remarkable indeed are the educational programs followed by Mill, Goethe, Pascal, Bentham, Niebuhr, Adams, Wieland, Tasso, and Pitt, under the encouragement, guidance, and powerful insistence of their fathers. Yet it is not the educational program itself which requires our notice so much as it is the intimate and constant association with adults which it entails. Not only were these boys often in the company of adults, as genuine companions; they were to a significant extent cut off from the society of other children. The same statement can be made, on the whole, for others in the list whose educations proceeded less directly, or less strenuously under the guidance of fathers.

Warm attachments to children outside the family circle seem to have been rare, and there are several cases of isolation within the family, too. Yet it is within the family that most of the recorded intimacies between these geniuses and other children developed. Goethe, Pascal, Niebuhr, Macaulay, Voltaire, and Mirabeau experienced some intensity of affection for sisters; Musset for his older brother; Macaulay and Voltaire remained attached to their favorite sisters throughout their lives, becoming devoted uncles to their sisters' children; Goethe's and Pascal's affection for their younger sisters approached passion; and Mirabeau speaks of incestuous relations with his.

The reality and nature of the pattern to which I am pointing – the very great dominance of adults in the lives of these children, and their isolation from contemporaries outside the family and, sometimes, within – can be adequately appreciated only through a more detailed statement about each individual.

Mill, under his father's personal and unremitting tutelage, began hard intellectual work before he was three. From very early he was given the responsibility of acting as tutor to his brothers and sisters. This did not increase his affection for them. In fact, he came to share some of his father's own antipathy toward them and toward his mother. He explicitly states in his autobiography that his father kept him apart from other boys. "He was earnestly bent upon my escaping not only the ordinary corrupting influence which boys exercise over boys, but the contagion of vulgar modes of thought and feeling; and for this he was willing that I should pay the price of inferiority in the accomplishments which schoolboys in all countries chiefly cultivate" (21, pp. 24f.). And again: "as I had no boy companions, and the animal need of physical activity was satisfied by walking, my amusements, which were mostly solitary, were in general of a quiet, if not a bookish turn, and gave little stimulus to any other kind even of mental activity than that which was already called forth by my studies" (p. 25).

Leibniz, his mother's only child, lost his father, a prominent university professor, when he was six. He retained two vivid memories of him, both of them expressive of the high esteem in which his father held him. His mother, who died when he was eighteen, devoted the remainder of her life to caring for him. He lived at home, free from "the doubtful liberties, the numerous temptations, the barbarous follies of student life" (18, p. 12). Before he was ten his father's carefully guarded library was opened to him, and he plunged into its treasures eagerly. It was conceivably no small thing to Leibniz that his father had regarded his christening as marked by a symbolic movement which seemed to promise that his son, as he wrote in his domestic chronicle, would continue in a spiritual and burning love for God all his life and do wonderful deeds in honor of the Highest (15, p. 4).

Grotius was close to his father. He signed his early poems Hugeianus, thus joining his own name Hugo with his father's name Janus or Joannes. At eight he reacted to the death of a brother by writing his father consolatory Latin verses. He had competent teachers at home, and entered the University of Leiden at eleven; there he dwelt with a devoutly religious man who impressed him deeply. He was famous in the literary world very early, and received high praise from distinguished men. He sought his father's advice when he chose a wife. One would infer from the limited evidence that his association from early childhood was primarily with adults.

Goethe throughout his childhood was carefully and energetically supervised in his varied studies by his father. He associated frequently with numerous skilled and learned and eminent men in Frankfurt, among whom was his grand-father Textor. He enjoyed considerable freedom of movement through the city, in the intervals of his studies, and struck up several acquaintances outside the home among boys and girls; but these were certainly far outweighed by his adult contacts, and by his intimacy with his sister, who had much less freedom than he and who became increasingly embittered by the educational discipline of their father. In his autobiography he notes that he was not on friendly terms with a brother, three years younger, who died in childhood, and scarcely retained any memory of the three subsequent children who also died young. How close he and his sister were may be gauged by these words regarding the after-effects of his love-affair with Gretchen, at about fourteen: "my sister consoled me the more earnestly, because she secretly felt the satisfaction of having gotten rid of a rival; and I, too, could not but feel a quiet, half-delicious pleasure, when she did me the justice to assure me that I was the only one who truly loved, under-stood, and esteemed her" (14, p. 192).

Pascal was so precious in the eyes of his father, after his mother's death when he was three, that, as the older sister tells us, the father could not bear the thought of leaving his education to others, and accordingly became and remained his only teacher. At eighteen Pascal's health broke down from ceaseless applica-tion. He was frequently in the company of the learned men surrounding his father. His primary emotional attachment was to his younger sister, Jacqueline; her religious retirement strongly influenced his own religious development.

Macaulay early became absorbed in books, but his studies were more unobtru-sively guided by his father and mother and other relatives than in the cases preceding. He was especially attached to his mother in early childhood, and at home among his brothers and sisters was overflowingly happy and playful. A sister writes: "He hated strangers, and his notion of perfect happiness was to see us all working round him while he read aloud a novel, and then to walk all together on the Common" (30, p. 67). He was reluctant to leave home for school for even a single day, and he was acutely homesick when placed in a boarding school at about twelve; there, though tolerated and even admired by his fellow pupils, he had little to do with them, living almost exclusively among books. The children at home passionately loved him. It should not be overlooked that his father was a deeply religious man of great force of character, energetic in religious and political reform movements of considerable scope.

Bentham's father, ambitious to make ,a practical lawyer of his first and for nine years his only child, kept him to a rigorous schedule of instruction in everything from dancing and military drill to Greek from a very early age. From seven to twelve he spent the winters at a boarding school, which he did not enjoy; in the vacations at home his schooling, under private tutors, was much more intensive. He was happiest on visits to grandparents in the country, where he could talk to an old gardener or climb up in a tree and read a novel. Too small and weak to win the admiration of his fellows, "he tried to be industrious and honest and noble and dutiful, finding that such a course brought praise from his elders" (10, pp. 20f.). When the death of his warmhearted mother desolated his father and himself, Jeremy "was just turned twelve, and was ready for Oxford, if a frail and undersized boy of twelve could be said to be ready for anything" (10, p. 22).

Coleridge's father, though unambitious in general and not very attentive to the education of his numerous other children, took special pride in him and endeavored from the beginning to prepare him for the Church. Coleridge was the last of fourteen children (ten by his mother), and the extreme fondness of his parents aroused the hostility of the older boys toward him. They drove him from play and tormented him. On one occasion, when he was eight, he ran away from home after a ferocious combat with the brother whom he had displaced as baby of the family; he was found only after a prolonged search, and he remembered all his life the tears of joy on his father's face and his mother's ecstasy when he was recovered. Death of the father, when he was nine, deprived him of his most valued companion. Shortly afterwards he was sent to a charity school in London. Here he made a few friends, notably Lamb, but he lived a great deal in books and in his own imagination.

Voltaire was born five years after the death in infancy of the next preceding child, and his own life was despaired of daily for the first year. His mother was an invalid; his father was a busy lawyer and does not seem to have concentrated any particular attention on him, beyond desiring that the boy should himself be prepared for the law. His education at home proceeded under the guidance of three distinguished and learned men, particularly the Abbé Chateauneuf, his godfather. The two other surviving children were considerably older than he; the brother he disliked, but he was fond of his seven-years-older sister, and, after his mother's death when he was seven, it was she to whom he was chiefly attached in the family. At ten he was quartered in the best Jesuit school in France by his ambitious and wealthy father; here he made the warmest and most lasting friendships in his life, but they were with the teachers rather than with the boys.

Leopardi, the oldest of five children, remained until he was twenty-four, practically immured, in the house of his father, the Count, in a town which he despised. In Leopardi's own words: "Had no teachers except for the first rudiments, which he learned under tutors kept expressly in the house of his father. But had the use of a rich library collected by his father, a great lover of literature. In this library passed the chief portion of his life, while and as much as permitted by his health, ruined by these studies; which he began independently of teachers, at ten years of age, and continued thenceforth without intermission, making them his sole occupation" (29, p. 2). His closest companion was his brother Carlo, a year younger; but he was reticent even with him. With the other children he liked to produce plays in which the tyrant (his father) was worsted by the hero (himself). At a later age he regarded his home as a prison from which he had to break out.

Chatterton, born three months after his talented father's death, was the second surviving child of his very young mother, who had borne her daughter four or five years earlier before her marriage was legalized. Under their instruction, he learned the alphabet from an old illuminated music manuscript of his father's, which his mother had been about to throw away, and learned how to read from an old blackletter Testament. He had been dismissed from his first school as a dullard. Later, he went to the uninspiring charity school which had been attended by his father. A note on his relations with playmates before he was five speaks of him as "presiding over his playmates as their master and they as his hired servants" (20, p. 22). Already at five he was greedy for fame, and asked that a cup which had been presented to him by a relative should have on it "an angel with a trumpet, *'to blow his name about,'* as he said" (20, p. 23). He did form friendships at school, one in particular; and the death of this boy plunged him into melancholy. But with none of these, or with his sister, was he intimate enough to share the secret of his Rowley poems, those impressive forgeries which seem to have been written under the inspiration and tutelage of the beautiful church of St. Mary Redcliffe rather than any human preceptor.

Niebuhr's father, who had been a military engineer and explorer, took up residence after his marriage at forty in a retired little town and devoted himself to his wife and family of two children. He liked to entertain his own and other children with stories, games, and music; but he concentrated particularly on the instruction of his son, for whom he also provided tutors from about four or five. A cultured neighbor, Boje, who was editor of a literary periodical, took much interest in the boy; and Boje's wife began his instruction in French. Her death when he was ten overwhelmed him with grief and inclined him even more seriously to his studies. Between fourteen and eighteen he spent most of the day in hard work and general reading. When he was sixteen his father, thinking that his attachment to home was excessive and that he was studying too much alone, sent him off to a school in Hamburg in the hope that he would become more sociable; but he was unhappy, and insisted on coming back. From an early age ill health and his mother's anxiety contributed their share to his inclination to solitude.

Mirabeau, the first surviving son of a family of the nobility, was in the beginning his father's pride. Later, after disfigurement by smallpox at three and displacement from the position of only son by the birth of a brother when he was five, he became increasingly the object of his erratic father's dislike. Intense marital discord made him the more hateful because he resembled his mother's side of the house. He was unfavorably compared with the other children, and repeatedly put under severe disciplinarians as tutors. Eventually his father had him imprisoned more than once. In the face of this persecution, helped partly by the affectionate interest of an uncle, Mirabeau succeeded nevertheless in developing an extraordinarily winning manner in speech and personal contacts, even charming his jailers into relaxing their punishments. Whether or not he was inclined to solitude, it was forced on him by his father; much of his learning and literary production took place in prisons or their equivalents. He was highly erotic, and may have had sexual relations with his younger sister; for so he asserts.

Adams regarded even his name, John Quincy, which was his great-grandfather's, as a perpetual admonition to live nobly. The Revolutionary War and the battle of Bunker Hill, which he witnessed, confirmed a serious habit of mind from early childhood. As his father was absent from home a great deal, he was already as a small boy depended upon by his mother as if he were a man. His education commenced at home under a tutor, and continued in Europe in the company of his father and other men notable in the governmental service. It was not until he entered Harvard that he attended a regular school for any length of time. Both his mother and his father tried to keep him from the corrupting influence of other boys, and it is evident from the nature of his life that his chief contacts were with grown men of serious and intellectual character. He read a great deal under the guidance of his father, whom in his earliest letters he obviously wished to please.

Wieland was educated at home under the eyes of his father, a pastor, in somewhat the same severe manner as was Goethe. He studied hard from three years of age. He says of his childhood: "I was deeply in love with solitude and passed whole days and summer nights in the garden, observing and imitating the beauties of nature" (26, p. 19). He was much more attached to books than to people. Prior to age seventeen, says his biographer, "We encounter not a single friend of his own age, only books and those who helped with them!" (26, p. 24). He was sensitive and unsociable when away at school, and when he returned home he lived alone or associated only with older men. His biographer makes no mention of his relations with his several siblings.

Tasso, whose old father was often compelled to be away from home, lived with his young mother and his sister until he was separated from them forever at ten, to join his father at the court of his patron prince. Even while he remained at home he was being strictly educated, first by an old priest, and then in a Jesuit school, which he loved. His mother, of whom he was passionately fond, died two years after he went to join his father. Of his childhood, Boulting says: "The prolonged absences of his father, the tears of his mother, the straitened circumstances and this sudden death were not healthy influences for a sensitive lad, and there was a great deal too much educational pressure put upon him. Bernardo was proud of Torquato's talents and ambitious as to his future. He forced him on and took scudi from a slender purse to pay for special lessons in Greek. But a cousin came to Rome from Bergamo to share in Torquato's studies. No bookworm was this lad, but full of fun and a thorough boy. Nothing could have been luckier" (3, p. 31). A little later he had as his companion in the study of the graces (horsemanship, jousting, etc.) a boy of eight, son of Duke Guidobaldo. Otherwise he seems to have associated primarily with men, often men of great dignity and learning.

Pope, the only child of his mother (there was a half-sister more than nine years older), was from the earliest period a domestic idol, as Stephen says. His father and mother, both forty-six at his birth, and a nurse, concentrated their affection upon him, which must have been all the more intense because he was sickly, and humpbacked like his father. "The religion of the family made their seclusion from the world the more rigid, and by consequence must have strengthened their mutual adhesiveness. Catholics were then harassed by a legislation which would have been condemned by any modern standard as intolerably tyrannical" (28, p. 2). Most of his education was accomplished at home, with some help from a family priest and his father, who corrected his early rhymes. From twelve he threw himself into his studies so passionately that his frail constitution threatened to break down.

Pitt was born at the high peak of his father's career as Prime Minister of England. When the title of Earl of Chatham was conferred on him, this second son, then seven, exclaimed, "I am glad that I am not the eldest son. I want to speak in the House of Commons like papa." Partly because of his feeble health, the boy was brought up at home under the instruction of his father and a tutor. His father concentrated upon developing his oratorical powers. At fourteen he was sent to Cambridge, where he was placed in the care of a sound scholar, who remained his inseparable companion, and practically his only one, for more than two years. He had no social life there. He read with facility such books as Newton's *Principia* and the obscurest of the Greek poets. "Through his whole boyhood, the House of Commons was never out of his thoughts, or out of the thoughts of his instructors" (17, p. 129).

Musset was the second son in a family devoted to literature, "an infant prodigy on whom the intelligence of his brother, six years his elder, did not fail to exercise a stimulating effect. Alfred developed his mind in the constant companionship of Paul much more rapidly than he would have in the company of children his own age" (5, p. 12). He was notable from early childhood for his sensitivity, charm, emotional ardor, dramatic power, and susceptibility to feminine beauty. At a very tender age he was already disappointed in love. He went to school for a short time with his brother, but sickness and the hostility of the other children toward these Bonapartists soon led to their being tutored at home, by a young man who knew how to combine pleasure with instruction.

Melanchthon always remembered the dying injunction of his father: "I have seen many and great changes in the world, but greater ones are yet to follow, in which may God lead and guide you. Fear God, and do right" (25, p. 6). Before this time (his father died when he was eleven) he was, by his father's express wishes, strictly educated, for a while in a local school, and then by a tutor, a conscientious teacher and stern disciplinarian. Afterwards, he came more directly under the influence of the celebrated scholar Reuchlin, who was his relative. It was Reuchlin, impressed by the scholarship of the little boy, who changed his name from Schwartzerd to its Greek equivalent Melanchthon. Of his earlier childhood it is related that he often gathered his schoolfellows around him to discuss what they had been reading and learning; and his grandfather delighted to engage him in learned disputes with traveling scholars, whom he usually confounded.

The brief sketches preceding tend to confirm the rule, I believe, that children of genius are exposed to significantly great amounts of intellectual stimulation by adults and experience very restricted contacts with other children of their age. Nor should we overlook the fact that books themselves, to which these children are so much attached, are representatives of the adult world. This is true in the superficial sense that they are provided by adults and, more significantly, may be drawn from a father's sacred library (one thinks of Leibniz, Leopardi, even Chatterton); it is true in the profounder sense that they are written by adults, and, in the case of most of the reading done by these children, *for* adults. Books extend the boundaries of the adult empire.

There is an effect of this constant intercourse with the adult world which may be especially important in the development of genius. Not only is there an increase of knowledge, which is the usual aim of the instructors; there is also, in many cases, a profound excitement of imagination. Even John Stuart Mill confesses that he did not perfectly understand such grave works as the more difficult dialogues of Plato when he read them in Greek at seven. What, then, happens to such adult material pouring into the child's mind? Mill does not elucidate his own case; but there is evidence in a number of the biographies before me that the dynamic processes of phantasy go to work on it and richly transform both what is understood and what is not.

Much of Goethe's association with other children was simply an occasion for expressing his vivid phantasy life; he entranced them with stories of imaginary adventures. Musset, also, reveled in a world of make-believe based upon the Arabian Nights and similar literature, and bewitched his enemies by the magic power of imagination. These were to become poets. But Bentham, who was no poet, imagined himself growing up as a hero like Fénelon's Telemachus and was stirred to moral fervor by sentimental novels. And two of the practical politicians in the list, Pitt and Niebuhr, may give us some insight into the process. When Pitt was around thirteen or fourteen he had written a tragedy, of which Macaulay has this to say: "This piece is still preserved at Chevening, and is in some respects highly curious. There is no love. The whole plot is political; and it is remarkable that the interest, such as it is, turns on a contest about a regency. On one side is a faithful servant of the Crown, on the other an ambitious and unprincipled conspirator. At length the King, who had been missing, reappears, resumes his power, and rewards the faithful defender of his rights. A reader who should judge only by the internal evidence, would have no hesitation in pronouncing that the play was written by some Pittite poetaster at the time of the rejoicings for the recovery of George the Third in 1789" (17, pp. 68f.). Out of his learning Pitt had constructed a dream prescient of his own future career. And who can say that the actions of a Prime Minister are not as much the expression of a private drama as they are the realistic application of the sciences and the laws? Niebuhr, who became a practical man of business and politics as well as the historian of Rome, writes explicitly about his own childhood experience, in a letter to Jacobi in 1811: "Our great seclusion from the world, in a quiet little provincial town, the prohibition, from our earliest years, to pass beyond the house and garden, accustomed me to gather the materials for the insatiable requirements of my childish fancy, not from life and nature, but from books, engravings, and conversation. Thus, my imagination laid no hold on the realities around me, but absorbed into her dominions all that I read – and I read without limit and without aim – while the actual world was impenetrable to my gaze; so that I became almost incapable of apprehending anything which had not already been apprehended by another – of forming a mental picture of anything which had not before been shaped into a distinct conception by another. It is true that, in this second-hand world, I was very learned, and could even, at a very early age, pronounce opinions like a grown-up person; but the truth in me and around me was veiled from my eyes – the genuine truth of objective reason. Even when I grew older, and studied antiquity with intense interest, the chief use I made of my knowledge, for a long time, was to give fresh variety and brilliancy to my world of dreams" (4, p. 354).

My point is that phantasy is probably an important aspect of the development of genius, not only in those cases where the chief avenue to fame is through the production of works of imagination in the ordinary sense, but also in those where the adult accomplishment is of a different sort. Instead of becoming proficient in taking and giving the hard knocks of social relations with his contemporaries, the child of genius is thrown back on the resources of his imagination, and through it becomes aware of his own depth, self-conscious in the fullest sense, and essentially independent. There is danger, however, in the intense cultivation of phantasy. If it does not flow over into the ordinary social relations by some channel, if it has to be dammed up as something socially useless, then it threatens life itself. An expression of what I am referring to is given in that powerful scene in the first part of Goethe's *Faust* where the physician–magician, tampering with incantations, raises a spirit of overwhelming presence and quails before him. Something nearer to an outright demonstration is furnished by the life of Chatterton and his suicide.

Before he was eighteen Chatterton was dead by his own hand. If we examine his life, we see that it breaks apart into two distinct regions: an outer shell of schoolboy, apprentice, pretended antiquarian, and writer of brittle satire; and a core — the serious and deeply emotional 15th century poet Rowley, whose connection with himself he never publicly acknowledged. One must not forget that Chatterton's phantasy existence as Rowley has points of contact with his father, the musician schoolteacher who died before his son was born, but who, in a sense, presided over the boy's education through the music manuscript from which he learned his letters and the blackletter Testament in which he learned to read, and who, by his connection and the connection of his family with the magnificent church of St. Mary Redcliffe, which overshadowed the place of Chatterton's birth and was his favorite resort from the brutalities of Bristol, might surely continue to hold converse with the imaginative boy. The Rowley poems furthermore are related to Chatterton's search for a pedigree. In short, through Rowley, Chatterton established relations with the world of the dead; and since he could not admit that he himself was the author of the Rowley poems, but had to pretend to have found them in his role as antiquary, and was thus rejected as an impostor by Walpole, he could not through Rowley establish contact with the world of the living. The surface which he was able to present to the world was hard, brittle, violent, unreal. Yet even in his relations with the world he appeared to be doing the same thing he was doing through the Rowley phantasies, namely, seeking a father to love and protect him. He evidently placed great hopes in Walpole; but he had also tried and been disappointed in the patronage of men of lower caliber in Bristol. Eventually he came to a dead end in London, where he had no friends even of the quality of Bristol's Catcott. Just before he committed suicide he was Rowley once again in the most beautiful of his poems, the *Balade of Charitie*, which sums up his experience of the world and his yearning for a loving father. If it was Rowley who enabled Chatterton to live, it was also Rowley who opened the door of death for him and ushered him out of a world of constant bitter disappointment into a world of kindly and Christian spirits.

Chatterton is a supreme example of the dangers and costs of genius. Having no father or other appreciative adult to link him to the world, he was swallowed up by his imagination. But it is too often overlooked in the textbooks that genius in less tragic cases is generally a costly gift. Superficially an enviable piece of luck, it is actually a fatality which exacts tribute from the possessor. Extreme absorption in very hard work is one of the penalties, and sometimes broken health. Isolation from contemporaries, often increasing with the years, is another. Whether we should include heterosexual difficulties as another, I an not sure, but I have indicated some of the facts in the last column of Table IV.3 and wish to consider the matter briefly. Fifty-five percent of our sample did not marry at all. There may be no special significance in this, since according to statistics for the United States (11) the marriage rate for the total population of males above fifteen is only about 60% and may have been lower in earlier times. On the other hand, this group, with the exception of Chatterton, ranges in age from 39 to 84 and should be compared with the higher age groups. According to the 1930 census in the United States marriage had been entered into by 86% of men in the age range from 35 to 44, and by age 60, which is about the median for our group of geniuses, it had been entered into by about 90%. I will only note further that some delay or reluctance or dissatisfaction attend the marriages of Mill, Goethe, Coleridge, Mirabeau, Wieland, and perhaps Melanchthon, but it would not be desirable here to go into greater detail because of the impossibility of making appropriate comparisons. It may be that for marriages both freely contracted and happily sustained a rate of 3 in 20 is not out of the ordinary, though I should be inclined to say that here too we have an expression of the costliness of genius.

In summary, the present survey of biographical information on a sample of twenty men of genius suggests that the typical developmental pattern includes as important aspects: (1) a high degree of attention focused upon the child by parents and other adults, expressed in intensive educational measures and, usually, abundant love; (2) isolation from other children, especially outside the family; and (3) a rich efflorescence of phantasy, as a reaction of the two preceding conditions. In stating these conclusions I by no means wish to imply that original endowment is an insignificant variable. On the contrary, Galton's strong arguments on behalf of heredity appear to me to be well-founded; and in this particular sample the early promise of these very distinguished men cannot be dissociated from the unusual intellectual qualities evident in their parents and transmitted, one would suppose, genetically as well as socially to their offspring. It is upon a groundwork of inherited ability that I see the pattern operating. Whether the environmental phase of it summarized under (1) and (2) is actually causally important, and to what extent the environmental factors are related to the blossoming out of phantasy, are questions which could be examined experimentally, though obviously any thorough experiment would require both a great deal of money and a certain degree of audacity. It might be remarked that the mass education of our public school system is, in its way, a vast experiment on the effect of reducing all three of the above factors to minimal values, and should accordingly tend to suppress the occurrence of genius.

Notes

1. ADAMS, C. F. *Memoirs of John Quincy Adams*. Vol. I. Philadelphia: Lippincott. 1874.
2. BIELSCHOWSKY, A. *The Life of Goethe*. Vol. I. New York: Putnam. 1905.
3. BOULTING, W. *Tasso and his Times*. London: Methuen. 1907.

4. BUNSEN, C. C. J., BRANDIS, J. and LOEBELL, J. W. *The Life and Letters of Barthold George Niebuhr*. Vol. I. London: Chapman & Hall. 1852.
5. CHARPENTIER, J. *La Vie Meurtrie de Alfred de Musset*. Paris: Piazza. 1928.
6. COURTNEY, W. L. *Life of John Stuart Mill*. London: Walter Scott. 1888.
7. COX, C. M. *The Early Mental Traits of Three Hundred Geniuses*. Stanford University Press. 1926.
8. ELLIOT, H. S. R. *The Letters of John Stuart Mill*. Vol. I. London: Longmans 1910.
9. ELLIS, H. *A Study of British Genius*. Boston: Houghton Mifflin. 1926.
10. EVERETT, C. W. *The Education of Jeremy Bentham*. New York: Columbia University Press. 1931.
11. FOLSOM, J. K. *The Family and Democratic Society*. New York: Wiley. 1943.
12. GALTON, F. *Hereditary Genius*. New York: Appleton. 1871.
13. GALTON, F. *English Men of Science*. New York: Appleton. 1875.
14. GOETHE, J. W. von. (The Auto-Biography of Goethe.) *Truth and Poetry: from my own Life*. London: Bohn. 1848.
15. GUHRAUER, G. E. *Gottfried Wilhelm Freiherr von Leibnitz, eine Biographie*. Vol. I. Breslau: Hirt. 1842 (?).
16. HANSON, L. *The Life of S. T. Coleridge: the Early Years*. New York: Oxford University Press. 1939.
17. MACAULAY, T. B. *Life of Pitt*. New York: Delisser & Procter. 1859.
18. MERZ, J. T. *Leibniz*. New York: Hacker. 1948.
19. MESNARD, J. *Pascal, l'Homme et l'Oeuvre*. Paris: Boivin. 1951.
20. MEYERSTEIN, E. H. W. *A Life of Thomas Chatterton*. London: Ingpen & Grant. 1930.
21. MILL, J. S. *Autobiography of John Stuart Mill*. New York: Columbia University Press. 1948.
22. MONTIGNY, L. *Memoirs of Mirabeau*. London: Edward Churton. 1835.
23. PARTON, J. *Life of Voltaire*. Vol. I. Boston: Houghton Mifflin. 1881.
24. PÉRIER, Mme. "Vie de B. Pascal." In *Pensées de B. Pascal*. Paris: Didot. 1854.
25. RICHARD, J. W. *Philip Melanchthon, the Protestant Preceptor of Germany, 1497–1560*. New York: Putnam. 1902.
26. SENGLE, F. *Wieland*. Stuttgart: Metzler. 1949.
27. STANHOPE, Earl. *Life of the Right Honourable William Pitt*. Vol. I. London: Murray. 1861.
28. STEPHEN, L. *Alexander Pope*. New York: Harper. N.d.
29. THOMSON, J. *Essays, Dialogues and Thoughts of Giacomo Leopardi*. London: Routledge. N.d.
30. TREVELYAN, G. O. *The Life and Letters of Lord Macaulay*. Vol. I. New York: Harper. 1876.
31. VALLENTIN, A. *Mirabeau*. New York: Viking. 1948.
32. VREELAND, H. *Hugo Grotius, the Father of the Modern Science of International Law*. New York: Oxford University Press. 1917.
33. WILLERT, P. F. *Mirabeau*. London: Macmillan. 1931.

3

Early Background of Eminent Scientists*

A. ROE

THIS monograph has presented the life history and test data of 14 eminent psychologists and 8 eminent anthropologists, and compared them with the biologists and physicists previously studied. This summary will omit the comparative material.

Selection was by peer ratings of men presently doing research. Average age is 46.7 for the psychologists, 49.4 for the anthropologists. The majority of both groups came from lower to upper middle-class backgrounds. The economic level was generally higher for the anthropologists. The fathers of half of the psychologists and of three of the anthropologists were professional men.

All of the subjects are married and most of them have children. Average age at marriage was 26.5 for psychologists and 26.1 for the anthropologists. Five of the psychologists and four of the anthropologists have been divorced at least once.

They received their B.A.'s at an average age of 21.4 for psychologists, 22.1 for anthropologists; their Ph.D.'s at an average age of 25.8 for psychologists, 28.6 for anthropologists.

Early interests in literature and the classics was common among both groups, and there were a few with early natural history interests. The psychologists were relatively late in determining upon a profession, largely because psychology was not taught in high school or early college.

Among both groups, particularly the anthropologists, early feelings of personal or family superiority on a social or intellectual basis were common. Patterns involving overprotection and firm, if not overt, control were frequent, and strong rebelliousness was usual. A number of the subjects still show resentment over family discipline or interference.

All but two of the men came from Protestant homes, none from Catholic homes, and most had some religious training. Only two are now interested in church.

Average raw scores on the verbal test were 57.7 for psychologists, 61.1 for anthropologists. On the spatial test they were 11.3 and 8.2 respectively, and on the mathematical 15.6 and 9.2.

On the Thematic Apperception Test both groups gave relatively long stories,

*Psychological Monographs, (1953), 67 (2, No. 352), pp. 27–30, 46–54. Reprinted by permission.

and manifested generally a similar picture. A common theme is of general helplessness in the face of severe problems. There is considerable dependence on parent figures, and a number of stories of unhappiness and guilt with regard to this relation. The group is strongly concerned with interpersonal relations, fairly free in discussing heterosexual ones, and not particularly conventional.

On the Rorschach the social scientists are remarkably productive, rather uncritical, and somewhat haphazard in their use of rational controls. They are very sensitive, intensively concerned with persons, rather freely aggressive, and often troubled with conflicts over dominance and authority.

The group Rorschach records of 129 other psychologists and anthropologists have a much lower average number of responses and a significantly better adjustment score. The eminent group . . . were both more original and less controlled, produced a wider range of responses, including more anatomy and sex responses, and more concept-dominated series of responses, and tended to proportionately more color than movement. . . .

How Smart are these Scientists? The Verbal-Spatial-Mathematical Test

This test (VSM) was compiled for the study by the Educational Testing Service. The verbal test contains 79 items in two sections, in each the task being the selection of antonyms. Time limit was 15 minutes for the two sections. The spatial test comprised 24 items, with a time limit of 20 minutes. The task was to select from four stimuli, the two views of the same figure. The mathematical test comprised 39 items, of mathematical reasoning. Time limit was 30 minutes. . . .

The difference in means between psychologists and anthropologists is not significant for the verbal test, but t for the difference between means for the spatial test is 6.88 and $p < 0.01$; for the mathematical test, t is 6.68 and $p < 0.01$.

All but one of the experimental psychologists has a higher sigma score for either spatial or mathematical than for verbal. Two of the others have their highest scores on the spatial test and two on the verbal, the difference in one instance being very slight. No tendencies are evident among the anthropologists.

The intercorrelations for the social scientists on this test are: verbal–spatial +0.18; verbal–mathematical +0.27; spatial–mathematical +0.36. None is significant.

Comparison with Other Scientists

Table IV.4 presents the material for comparison with the other groups studied. The mathematical test was not difficult enough for the physicists. Differences between the means of the different groups are small and not significant. It should be noted that there is a large difference between the subgroups of

TABLE IV.4 *Comparison with Other
Scientists on the Verbal-Spatial-
Mathematical Test*

Test	Biologists (N = 19)	Physicists (N = 18)	Social Scientists (N = 22)
Verbal			
N right, range	28–73	8–75	23–73
Mean	56.6 ± 2.8	57.3 ± 4.1	59.0 ± 4.2
Spatial			
N right, range	3–20	3–22	3–19
Mean	9.4 ± 1.0	13.0 ± 1.2	10.4 ± 0.9*
Mathematical			
N right, range	6–27		4–27
Mean	16.8 ± 1.4		13.7 ± 1.5*

*N = 20

physicists on the verbal test, the experimentalists averaging 46.6 and the theorists 64.2. On the spatial test, their averages are 11.7 and 13.8 respectively. . . .

Correlation with age is significant only for the spatial test, with a $p < 0.01$. Of test intercorrelations, only the verbal–spatial reaches this level. It is clear from descriptions by the subjects that the spatial test can be done in various ways, and in part by verbal reasoning. . . .

Transformation of scores on the VSM to Scholastic Aptitude Test scores is given in Table IV.5. The SAT equivalents of various percentile scores are given for each subtest. The normal mean and standard deviations for this test for applicants to college as undergraduates are 500 and 100. For doctoral candidates at Teachers College these figures are 570 and 130. . . . VSM equivalents for this average SAT score are 32 on the verbal test, 11 on the spatial test, and 8 on the mathematical. Five of the scientists are below the mean on the verbal, 29 on the spatial (but it must be remembered that this test correlates – 0.40 with age) and 3 on the mathematical.

It is clear that the average ability of the scientists is very great. This is not surprising. On the other hand, it is surprising, and a matter of very considerable importance, that there are among the scientists a number who are not facile at

TABLE IV.5 *Scholastic Aptitude Test Equivalents for
VSM Raw Scores*

Percentile	Verbal I and II	SAT Equivalent	Spatial	SAT Equivalent	Math.	SAT Equivalent
100	75	892	22	784	27	1042
75	67	833	15	651	22	918
50	61	788	10	556	13	694
25	52	722	7	499	10	619
0	8	395	3	423	4	470

the types of tasks presented by the VSM, but who have been able to make contributions of great value to society. . . .

Discussion

The direct study of eminent men raises numerous and very difficult problems. One clearly does not have the complete freedom of a biographer writing centuries after the lifetime of the subject. But these difficulties are more than compensated for by the value of direct clinical and test data. In the first study of such a nature, much time must be spent in exploratory work and the first monograph pointed out that at this stage, "All that one can hope for in such work is to get some idea of the nature of the relationships, the points at which a direct attack can be made and the sort of tools to use" (21, p. 1). I feel that this has been accomplished. Before explicit discussion is presented, however, something should be said about the limitations of the study.

In the first place the sample is small in absolute numbers although relatively very large. The subjects are the best research men in each field and they comprise a high percentage of the men who could be so designated. The conclusions drawn, however, apply directly only to the first-rate scientist, and only indirectly, and with some qualifications, to scientists generally. The group Rorschachs have offered useful confirmation, however.

We lack comparable groups in nonscientific vocations. A more serious limitation is the lack of any control group of relatively unsuccessful scientists, men who had the training and appeared to have the promise, but who have produced little or not at all in research. This is the next most important step and a prerequisite to the satisfactory development of hypotheses about choice of science as a vocation and success in it. One cannot always be certain whether the situations noted in this study refer to choice of vocation or to success, or to what extent they are affected by high frequency of a middle-class socioeconomic background. . . .

It is evident that the family backgrounds of the 64 scientists studied are by no means randomly selected with respect to the population at large. According to census reports for 1910, only 3% of the gainfully employed men in the country were professional men. In this group, however, 53% of the fathers of the subjects were professional men. One-eighth of the group came from farm homes; and the fathers of 31% were in business, many of them owning their own. Only two fathers were skilled laborers. None of the scientists came from homes in which the father was an unskilled laborer and none came from families of very great wealth. Cattell and Brimhall (5) in 1921 found a 51% incidence of professional fathers for the 66 leading scientists they studied.

What seems to be the operative factor here is that in practically all of these homes, whatever the occupation of the father, learning was valued for its own sake. Its concomitants in terms of possible better income or social position were not scorned, but it was rare for these to be the most important. This certainly was a major factor in the facilitation of intellectualization of interests. In my opinion this, rather than the probable associated intellectual levels, is the important aspect here. "Overintellectualization" may be a middle-class characteristic and it may interfere with libidinal development in other spheres, as some psychoanalytic writers have pointed out. Yet it seems to me doubtful whether one can develop the sort of intense personal involvement which is characteristic of these scientists without some degree of this, if a channeling of energy in one direction means a lessening of it in others. There is a serious problem here. Unquestionably overintellectualization is frequently a technique for escaping emotional problems, especially those bound up in interpersonal relationships, but it is not necessarily so. I believe it is possible to concentrate upon intellectual activities without having a relatively sterile life emotionally, but we certainly have not developed educational techniques which foster this.

I have reported a greater than chance incidence of first-born among these eminent men. The problem of birth order is an extremely tricky matter statistically and I would not be inclined to pay much attention to this finding in a group of 64 were it not that Cattell and Brimhall reported the same finding in a group of 855 scientists. It could be argued that the point here also is that intelligence levels are higher in the first-born, for which there is some evidence, but it seems much more probable that both of these facts are results of the same cause, whatever that is.

Certain aspects of the data offer evidence on the basic importance of the need to achieve, or to keep independence, which is so well met by a career in research. There are no Catholics in the group. The Protestant churches to which all but five of the scientists' families belonged have varying degrees of insistence on the authority of the church over its members' interpretations of life, but all but three of these subjects have dismissed organized religion as a guide and usually had done so by late adolescence. In this respect, also, they have achieved independence. The dearth of Catholics in research science is corroborated in other studies (11, 29) and the Wesleyan survey found that production of scientists from Catholic institutions is uniformly low (10).

In the life histories of many of these men there are factors which indicate a feeling of apartness from others which takes different forms and seems to have a number of different causes. Ten of these men suffered the death of a parent before they were 10 years old, 7 others in their teens. Among most of those whose loss occurred early, this was apparently a factor in the acceptance of isolation. For several of these men, this early loss appears to have had an indirect effect upon vocational choice. There may have resulted an intensified problem over the acceptance of the inevitability of death. Study of life processes and study of ancient civilizations (reassuring in the continuity of mankind if not of a man) may be a technique, and an effective one, for coping with this. But not every biologist has strong death fears, nor is every archeologist concerned with survival problems.

Among the theoretical physicists, there was a very high incidence of severe childhood illnesses which certainly contributed to isolation. It was only among the social scientists that this feeling of apartness characteristically carried a tone of superiority. With the other groups it appears to be sometimes inferior, but characteristically neither. It is a related fact that the social scientists do not show the type of psychosocial development characteristic of the other groups – that is, a pattern of general avoidance of intimate personal contacts, a considerably later than usual development of heterosexual interests, or at least of their expression, and even at the present time, a decided preference for a very limited social life.

The biologists and physicists show a considerable present independence of parental relations, and without guilt for the most part. This has also been noted in business executives (8). The social scientists, on the other hand, are much less free of parental ties, in the sense that a number of them still harbor resentment and rebellion, even though they have achieved an outward independence. It is more than possible that this difference is a major factor in the choice of vocation. An unresolved conflict over parental relations could as easily be displaced to a concern with personal relations generally, as an unresolved conflict over death could lead to study of living processes.

More of these men than not, as boys, pursued rather independent paths – playing with one or a few close friends, instead of with a gang, following their own particular interests (shifting or not) with somewhat more than the usual intensity. There are some to whom this does not apply, but it is fairly characteristic, and such interests were more often intellectual than not, except among the experimental physicists and biochemists. It is, of course, true that their high level of intelligence would, in itself, have some of these effects.

There is no one general pattern by which they approached science as a career. The modal age at which the decision was made was during the last two undergraduate years, but in some cases it was made in early childhood or as late as the second year of graduate work. The introduction may have been through natural history interests, through gadgeteering, through interests in laboratory sciences as found in high school courses, or, for the social scientists, through dissatisfaction with literature as a means of studying the behavior of people, or through a service motivation. When the decisive point can be determined it was usually the discovery of the possibility of doing research, of finding out things for oneself. For some this was understood very early – as with those experimental physicists who spent much of their childhood playing with erector sets, radios, and all the other sorts of equipment that permit manipulation and construction. For others, it came as a revelation of unique moment. Once it was fully understood that *personal* research was possible, once some research had actually been accomplished, there was never any question. This was it. The educational implications are obvious enough. There has been no question since. From then on, absorption in the vocation was so complete as seriously to limit all other activity. In the case of the social scientists, at least for those for whom people themselves provide the data, this did not limit social participation; for the others it intensified an already present disinterest. Although a few of them have cut down somewhat on their hours of work as they have grown older, it is still the common pattern for them to work nights, Sundays, holidays, as they always have. Most of them are happiest when they are working – some only when they are working. In all these instances, other aspects – economic return, social and professional status – are of secondary importance.

Being curious plays a major role – a trait which many aspects of our educational practice tend to discourage. It is of crucial importance that these men set their own problems and investigate what interests them. No one tells them what to think about, or when, or how. Here they have almost perfect freedom. Their limitations are only those of equipment and time, and the limitations of their own understanding. (It is certainly true that the free flow of their work can be inhibited by emotional problems, but I believe that this could be dealt with directly. It would be worth while to try.) Certainly this is one vocation in which man can most nearly approach what he can be, and one that satisfies both autonomous and homonymous drives (1).

That the need for this sort of independence is one with deep roots can be seen in situations remote from that of research science. . . .

The position these men have reached has not been reached easily, and one must ask why this particular group has made so great an effort. It must be noted that this effort has usually been directed quite specifically toward the immediate problem rather than to a long-term goal of eminence. There is some evidence that a basic insecurity of perhaps more than the usual proportions is present in many, if not most, of this group, but the causes for this insecurity appear varied. (This would tend to support the hypothesis that the need for independence in this group is generally compensatory.) That intellectual channels were sought to alleviate it must be in large part because of the family background, but there is no question that the research aspect is of more importance than the general intellectualization.

The question also arises as to why one subject chose one field of science and others chose other fields. Apart from the often overlooked matter of necessary contact with the field, there is some further evidence from the study. The problem of coping with early affectional loss has been mentioned. It would also appear that there are some, particularly among the experimental physicists, who seem early to have formed direct relationships with objects rather than people, not compensatorily. In others, a generalized anxiety, of unknown cause, and possibly only an exacerbation of normal anxiety, is alleviated by concentration on a particular field. For example, I know biochemists who seem to me to live in a very dangerous world – they are always conscious of the presence about them of dangerous micro-organisms. They tolerate this in part because they are able to manipulate these organisms to some extent professionally. I am sure, however, that to them psychologists live in an equally dangerous world, surrounded by irrational emotional people, a situation which they would find quite intolerable.

The social scientists stand apart as having been more concerned at an earlier age, about personal relations (or as being willing to tolerate this concern as such, without translation). This may reflect an unconscious uncertainty over the consciously felt superiority that characterized half of the psychologists and most of the anthropologists. It is also certainly related to their difficulties in freeing themselves from their parents. The other groups seem to have been able, fairly early, to work out an adaptation not nearly so dependent upon personal relations, but rather strikingly independent of them. Certainly psychology to some extent, particularly social psychology, and anthropology to a large extent, particularly cultural anthropology, offer an ideal vocation to the person whose conviction of personal superiority is not accompanied by asocial characteristics; they permit a somewhat Jovian survey of their own society as well as others, and maintain the social scientist in a state of superiority just because he is able to make the survey. . . . The experimental psychologists are generally less concerned with people as people, although this is by no means true of all of them. The further observations that a conflict over dominance and authority is common in the group, and that in a number of their homes the mother was dominant indicate the possibility of difficulties in achieving masculine identification.

In this respect it would seem very probable that the physicists, particularly the experimentalists, were able to identify more easily with their fathers than the other groups and hence to follow comfortably a science which has rather more of a "masculine" tinge in our culture than the others do.

It must be pointed out that it is likely that the kind of person who has gone into social science may have had a biasing effect on the theories produced by social scientists, particularly with regard to the desirable or the mature personality. Practically all current psychological theory of development stresses strongly the central importance in any life of the richness of personal relations as a basis for "adjustment." But the data of this study demonstrate, and it seems to me quite conclusively, that a more than adequate personal and social adjustment in the larger sense of an adjustment which permits a socially extremely useful life and one which is personally deeply satisfying, is not only possible, but probably quite common, with little of the sort of personal relations which psychologists consider essential. Many of the biological and physical scientists are very little concerned with personal relations, and this is not only entirely satisfactory to them, but it cannot be shown always to be a compensatory mechanism. . . . It can also apparently be satisfactory to others who are closely associated with them. That divorces are so much commoner among the social scientists is of interest in this connection. Problems with masculinity and dominance must be important here;

but also, where much more attention and emotion are invested, demands are certain to be greater and more specific, and hence failure commoner.

Another finding of considerable importance is the differences of imagery which are associated with the different fields of science, and which accord with and perhaps explain some of the test data. Briefly, the biologists and experimental physicists tend strongly to dependence upon visual imagery in their thinking; the theoretical physicists and the social scientists, to dependence upon verbalization or similar symbolization in theirs. Nothing is known about the development of these modes of thinking, but it seems probable that they were developed early (they are associated with father's occupation) and played a part in the choice of a science. Further, it was shown that those scientists whose preferred mode of thinking differed from that characteristic for their science also differed in some aspects of their early history, and in the things they did or the ways they went about their work. (This is good reason for not using such a factor selectively — their contributions have a special place.) The domination of the formal qualities of the blots in the biologists' Rorschachs, which the others do not show, is in accord with this, as is the generally much more fluid verbalization of the social scientists.

Doubtless, also, some intellectual factors enter. So far as the test used is a measure of these, it is clear that the theoretical physicists surpass all other groups on both verbal and spatial tests. The experimental physicists are high on the spatial and relatively very low on the verbal test. Psychologists are at about the mean for this total group on all three. Anthropologists are high on the verbal and lowest on both spatial and mathematical. These patternings are probably of importance in selection of vocation — particularly the relatively low nonverbal abilities of the anthropologists and the relatively low verbal ability of the experimental physicists.

I suspect that the verbalization so characteristic of the social scientist has also exerted some bias on his activities. This is probably most obvious in the field of testing where the emphasis still remains on verbal tests, although other tests have come into general use. But psychologists, and educators who are probably much like them in this respect, are in a position which makes possible the operation of this bias to keep out of college many adolescents who are verbally inept but have other capacities of equal value to society, and for whom college could be important. This bias may have affected the development of techniques of teaching and of therapy. The effect in the first is obvious. In therapy it may well be a factor in the common insistence on verbalization of insights as essential to therapy.

That verbalization and intense interest in persons are related has long been noted peripherally. This relation is accompanied by some cultural sex differentiation. Girls test higher verbally than boys; the M–F (or masculinity–femininity indexes) for certain occupations which have culturally a strongly feminine tinge are very different from those with a culturally strongly masculine tinge, and these are also associated with verbalization. . . .

The range of test intelligence in this group is also of importance. All of the evidence confirms Cox's remark: ". . . high, but not the highest intelligence, combined with the greatest degree of persistence, will achieve greater eminence than the highest degree of intelligence with somewhat less persistence" (6, p. 187). Portenier noted that "It would seem then that while there is a positive correlation between psychological test ratings and honor awards, the honor recipients are not limited to students with high psychological tests scores, and many students who make high test scores fail to win honors" (14, p. 499). Clearly a certain degree of intelligence is a necessary condition for a career in research science, but it is not a sufficient one.

The strength of the achievement drive which these men have shown is rarely reflected in the TAT in any direct way, and there are a number of Rorschachs which give no indication that the subject is capable of great accomplishment. Indeed there are a number of subjects for whom none of the test material would give the slightest clue that the subject was a scientist of renown.

There are Rorschach protocols which would occasion no surprise in a clinic for the maladjusted. It is certainly true that those who work only with persons whose lives show considerable disruption seem to have no idea of the extra-ordinary range of tolerance of difficulty which "normals" show. A number of these men are particularly good examples. It should also be pointed out that for many of these subjects, the career itself has served as a technique for handling the personal problems. In some instances the basic problem has been in a sense, extrapolated into a more general one, and the subject has then settled down to working on the general problem. This is a very neat and effective method. In other instances, absorption in the career has made possible the encapsulation of the difficulty in such a manner that it can be almost ignored by the subject. The price he may pay for this is another matter. There is nothing in these data to suggest that any measure from these or other projective techniques, or from intelligence tests, would be nearly so adequate in predicting their success as the fact that they worked long hours in graduate school, many more than the course requirements, and that they preferred to work on their own. (But I do not know how many less successful scientists have worked hard and preferred independence.)

Nevertheless the tests have contributed materially to our understanding of what sort of men these scientists are, and have also offered essential clues as to how and why they have become what they are. These now can be followed up in more direct fashion. . . .

Most of these subjects were fortunate enough somewhere along the line to have found a teacher who induced them to find things out for themselves, or who let them do so, or who insisted that they do so because he did not want to be bothered. Once intellectual independence was really tasted, nothing else mattered much pedagogically; bad teaching then was only an irritation. But how many are there who have never learned to rely upon themselves, to find how valid their own thinking may be? Certainty of this own worth is any man's greatest need. Though some of them may find it only there, scientists do find this certainty in science.

Notes

1. ANGYAL, A. *Foundations for a science of personality.* New York: The Commonwealth Fund, 1941.
2. BAAS, M. L. Kuder Interest patterns of psychologists. *J. appl. Psychol.*, (1950), 34, 115–117.
3. BECK, S. J., RABIN, A. I., THIESEN, W. G., MOLISH, H. and THETFORD, W. N. The normal personality as projected in the Rorschach test. *J. Psychol.*, (1950), 30, 241–298.
4. BORING, E. G. Great men and scientific progress. *Proc. Amer. phil. Soc.*, (1950), 94, 339–351.
5. CATTELL, J. M. and BRIMHALL, D. R. *American men of science.* (3rd Ed.) Garrison: Science Press, 1921.
6. COX, C. S. *Genetic studies of genius.* Vol. II. *Early mental traits of three hundred geniuses.* Stanford: Stanford University Press, 1926.
7. GUILFORD, J. P. Creativity. *Amer. Psychologist*, (1950), 5, 444–454.
8. HENRY, W. The business executive: the psychodynamics of a social role. *Amer. J. Sociol.*, (1949), 54, 287–291.
9. KLOPFER, B. and KELLEY, D. M. *The Rorschach technique.* Yonkers, New York: World Book Co., 1942.
10. KNAPP, R. H. and GOODRICH, H. B. The origins of American scientists. *Science*, (1951), 113, 543–545.
11. LEHMAN, H. C. and WITTY, P. A. Scientific eminence and church membership. *Sci. Mon.*, (1931), 33, 544–549.
12. MORGAN, C. D. and MURRAY, H. A. A method for investigating phantasies: the Thematic Apperception Test. *Arch. Neurol. Psychiat., Chicago*, (1935), 34, 298–306.
13. MUNROE, RUTH. Prediction of adjustment and academic performance of college students. *Appl. Psychol. Monogr.* (1945), No. 7.
14. PORTENIER, L. G. Mental ability ratings of honor students. *J. educ. Psychol.*, (1950), 41, 493–499.
15. RAPAPORT, D. *Diagnostic psychological testing.* Chicago: Year Book Publishers, 1945.
16. ROE, ANNE. Analysis of group Rorschachs of biologists. *J. proj. Tech.*, (1949), 13, 25–43.
17. ROE, ANNE. Psychological examinations of eminent biologists. *J. consult. Psychol.*, (1949), 13, 225–246.
18. ROE, ANNE. Analysis of group Rorschachs of physical scientists. *J. proj. Tech.*, (1950), 14, 385–398.
19. ROE, ANNE. A study of imagery in research scientists. *J. Pers.*, (1951), 19, 459–470.
20. ROE, ANNE. Psychological tests of research scientists. *J. consult. Psychol.*, (1951), 15, 492–495.
21. ROE, ANNE. A psychological study of eminent biologists. *Psychol. Monogr.*, (1951), 64, No. 14 (Whole No. 331).
22. ROE, ANNE. A psychological study of eminent physical scientists. *Genet. Psychol. Monogr.*, (1951), 43, 121–239.
23. ROE, ANNE. Analysis of group Rorschachs of psychologists and anthropologists. *J. proj. Tech.*, (1952), 16, 212–224.
24. ROE, ANNE. Group Rorschachs of university faculties. *J. consult. Psychol.* (1952), 16, 18–22.
25. ROGERS, C. R. *Client-centered therapy.* Boston: Houghton Mifflin, 1951.
26. TERMAN, L. M., *et al. Genetic studies of genius.* Vols. I through IV. Stanford: Stanford University Press, 1925–1947.

27. STRONG, E. K. *Vocational interests of men and women.* Stanford: Stanford University Press, 1948.
28. SURVEY RESEARCH CENTER, UNIVERSITY OF MICHIGAN. Productivity, supervision and employee morale. *Human Relations Series*, 1948, I, Report 1.
29. VISHER, S. S. Starring in *American men of science. Science*, (1947), 106, 359–361.
30. WYATT, F. The scoring and analysis of the Thematic Apperception Test. *J. Psychol.*, (1947), 24, 319–330.

4

Early Influences on Research Scientists*

B. T. EIDUSON

Introduction

IF THE last two decades were the decades of the physical sciences, the next two will be the decades of social and behavioral sciences. It is generally agreed that current social problems loom so large, and impinge so ponderously on the lives of all of us, that only massive and concerted efforts to understand and eradicate the problems will make tomorrow's world a viable one. With this in mind, social scientists and planners have begun to confront the weighty problems involved in mobilizing the resources, expertise, and sophistication essential to social science research enterprises. . . .

Such concerns seem analogous to those confronting the physical sciences in the period prior to Sputnik. At that time, Sputnik stimulated an ambitious and wide-ranging effort to identify, recruit, and train promising scientists to work on the new problems of space. Needs, motivations, and requisites for performance in the physical sciences were evaluated, so that potential talent could be fostered, and the conditions of work under which such talent flourishes, could be provided. Considering the enormous flow of talent into the physical and natural science professions, and the undeniable creativity of their performance, this was a highly successful effort, and one in which guidelines for a mobilization of talent in the social sciences surely reside.

But to what extent can a body of work generated mainly through studies of the natural and physical sciences contribute to the identification and recruitment problems in social and behavioral sciences? Can information gained on "hard" scientists be generalized to researchers in "softer" areas? Of course the social and behavioral scientist is not completely unknown. Some descriptive survey data have been accumulated on current geographical concentrations of psychologists, sociologists, anthropologists, their subspecialties, and their origins by birthplace or university degree (Carpenter, 1954; Clark, 1957; Harmon, 1961; Knapp, 1963; Wispé, 1969). A few detailed developmental and clinical studies have produced fragmentary insights into the psychology of some social scientists: psychologists, for example, have been described as unconventional, bohemian, and imaginative

*From "Science as a Career Choice: Theoretical and Empirical Studies," edited by Bernice T. Eiduson and Linda Beckman (ca.) 1973, by Russell Sage Foundation. By permission of Russell Sage Foundation.

in personality, and thus distinguished from chemists (Chambers, 1964) or teachers and administrators (Cattell and Drevdahl, 1955). They have also been shown to demonstrate little affection toward their parents, and a preference, if any, for the mother over the father in childhood (Galinsky, 1962). Psychologists have been described as relatively isolated in childhood (Chambers, 1964) and rebellious toward authority during adolescence (Galinsky, 1962).

In terms of career selection, work choice for social scientists seems at least in part reflective of childhood interests (Strauss, 1965). The average social scientist elects his career at the undergraduate level, in contrast to the physical scientist who chooses his work at an earlier stage, primarily in high school (Clark, 1957). Social scientists achieve their Ph.D.'s at a later age than do physical scientists and, perhaps not unrelatedly, make their most important contributions at a later age, i.e., 35–39, in contrast to 30–34 for natural scientists (Dennis and Gruden, 1954; Lehman, 1966; Pressey, 1960).

One of the predictors of choice of work in the social sciences seems to be the significantly lower high school grades in mathematics and science subjects, in contrast to generally high scholastic performances (Harmon, 1961). In line with this finding, favorite subjects of social scientists are foreign languages, English, and social studies (Chambers, 1964).

A prominently voiced motivation of the psychological career is an early interest in behavior; however, many psychologists have been unsuccessful medical school aspirants, or have flirted with teaching and business as possible careers (Clark, 1957). Since social scientists have an urban rather than a rural background, heightened sensitivity to social problems has also been regarded as a motivating factor for professional work choice (Glenn and Weiner, 1969). Psychologists who choose a career in research report being motivated by desires for eminence and by strong feelings of professional commitment; they have outstanding conceptual ability, and in contrast to nonresearchers, are not altruistic (Wispé, 1963). Some psychologists appear to have drifted into their careers, but those who have achieved eminence have been very much advantaged by their upper middle-class origins (Wispé, 1963). In contrast to their noneminent colleagues, eminent psychologists have had a significantly higher proportion of eminent psychologists as fathers. The less eminent have worked their way through school since their parents placed a low value on an education.

These findings, while provocative, suggest the sparse and unsystematic data base that exists on the psychology of the social and behavioral scientist. Also, it is apparent that in many of these studies, comparative analyses with physical and natural scientists were thought to be the logical way to proceed. Such a strategy has presupposed that the same background, personality, and motivational variables will be found in both social and physical scientists, and that they will have the same meaning. This may or may not be the case. Some variables may be characteristic of researchers in general, regardless of field, but others may be discipline-dependent. The demand characteristics of the behavioral fields in general or of specific behavioral fields may be sufficiently different from those of the physical sciences so that they possibly may call out quite different psychological characteristics in persons who work in them. Only systematic comparative studies or a tightly formulated and well-supported conceptual framework will provide compelling evidence on this problem.

A rather comprehensive overview of investigations on scientists done to date suggests that certain issues directed the development of the main body of work:

(*1*) What conditions, background features, or early milieu encourage selection of a scientific career?

(*2*) What personal resources are requisite, and how are these resources shaped by experiences and life events?

(*3*) By what processes or mechanisms are salient experiences, attitudes, and interests focused and internalized that they finally lead to a research career?

(*4*) Are there certain conditions or stimuli that precipitate the decision to become a scientist?

(*5*) How does an individual become professionalized and gain the identity, values, and goals that he shares with his colleagues?

(*6*) As a scientist, what options are available in terms of behaviors, activities, or roles?

(*7*) Are these choices which are predictable from his own background, preference, and previous experience?

(*8*) Could the level of performance achieved be predicted from earlier events or behaviors?

(*9*) What is the course of the scientific career, and the influences on such a course?

(*10*) What are some of the psychological components of being a scientist — i.e., the conflicts, attitudes, emotional satisfactions, and frustrations? How are these related to the perceptions of the scientific life?

Obviously these questions grow out of a long view of the scientific career, one which presumes notable precursors or antecedents and identifiable consequents. This is the case whether a personality or a socialization approach is used. Most of the empirical data on the process by which decisions related to careers are reached has developed within a personality model, which has given particular attention to aptitudes, talents, resources, and early environmental factors which have encouraged specific interests and experiences at the expense of others. The encouraged and rewarded activities, relationships, and motivations tend to direct an individual increasingly along avenues felicitous to the demands of a scientific career. Thus the decisions about work that are formulated at some specific point reflect skills, motivations, relationships, and activities that have been most satisfying in earlier life as they have matured and become refined, as well as the anticipation that adult work in science will provide more of the kinds of experiences and challenges that have been most rewarding.

This developmental perspective also characterizes a socialization theory orientation. Early social roles set the stage for the kinds of later experiences which are sought in one's adult socialization patterns. The social reward systems that proved most potent and durable in early relationships become modified, elaborated, and changed over time so that new knowledge, ability, and motivations are available to meet the demands of new learning and the revised goals and expectations of others. However, early learning often sets limits for future socialization patterns. In the case of taking on an adult role as scientist, precursory behaviors, knowledge, and skills that were developed earlier and perceived as useful, become recombined and refined so that they meet the levels of proficiency and sophistication required by the professional scientific context. At the same time conscious and unconscious aspects of personality which also were developed in earlier learning situations become restructured so that adult behaviors and values meet what is valued and required in a professional scientific role. Thus, continuity between precursory experiences which have shaped early roles and the later adult work roles is established.

The questions also reflect the organismic view of development, a perspective which puts the study of growth and change into the foreground, and the total individual into focus. This viewpoint seems consonant with the theoretical and empirical work on vocations, occupations, and professions – although the data bank here is so limited that prominent conceptual underpinnings are obscured (Becker and Carper, 1956; Moore, 1969; Osipow, 1968). It also shares a common base with the work on normal adults, their development and vagaries (Erikson, 1968; Grinker, Grinker, and Timberlake, 1962; Hughes, 1965). Thus far, psychological data on adults appear strikingly discontinuous and even discordant, showing little evidence of the anticipated smooth and consistent course (Goulet and Baltes, 1970) and, to a large extent, this is the case with the work on scientists, too.

In this company, the investigator on the psychology of scientists is forced to think about such problems as how behaviors move steadily toward decisions favoring science as adult work; what behaviors, activities, interests, attitudes, roles show visible change and maturity in the direction of scientific skills and preferences; what subgoals encapsulate the final goals of a professional career; what role preceptives make the idea of becoming a scientist syntonic to the personality. The developmental perspective is also evident in the two main strategies used to study scientists: the mature person functioning at the professional level, and the fledgling, the potential scientist.

Scientist Populations

Scientific populations have generally been classified into two groups:

1. *Professionals:* Those mature, actively functioning, and, on occasion, retired scientists who have already achieved professional training leading to a Ph.D., or

in some cases to a master's degree, who are employed in research settings, and used un research capacities.

2. *Preprofessionals:* Fledgling or would-be scientists who are in preprofessional stages, or those who are enrolled as science majors or adolescents in high school programs.

The latter have often been identified as having exceptional promise in science through the Westinghouse Science Talent programs, or the National Merit Scholarship winners, or Project Talent, which utilize extensive assessment measures to spot young people with interests and aptitudes commensurate with a scientific career. It generally has been assumed that data from these two populations would feed into each other, i.e., that studies of established scientists would provide clues as to what to look for in embryonic scientists and, in turn, that data on emerging scientists would anticipate and show in developmental or even transitory form, characteristics of more established men. However, this is an assumption that has thus far been given only preliminary test (Datta and Parloff, 1965; Taylor and Ellison, 1967). The studies on very young children who seem scientifically inclined or creative, and therefore apt to consider scientific careers, have not been part of the scientific literature. The chronological distance of such children from the phases of maturity at which they choose careers often makes an apparent correlation more spurious than real.

Some studies have analyzed scientists with nonscientist adults as controls. However, an equivalent number of studies have attempted to distinguish more creative from less creative individuals within scientific populations. In this framework, some criterion of creativity has served as predictor. The predictor variables have ranged from more objective measures such as scores on tests or originality or from measurements of outside validity drawn from findings on the individual's scientific contributions, number of patents, number of publications, or citations, to subjective estimates of the individual's creativity by peers, colleagues, and supervisors. In a few instances self-reports and self-judgments of creativity have been used. Measures of creativity have often been interchanged with measures of success. However, for the later some additional criteria have proved useful, as honors, distinguished awards, and other indications of meritorius service.

A number of disciplines have been included under the title of research scientist. The natural or physical sciences category includes the biological scientist, sometimes called the life scientist, as well as chemist and physicists. Social and behavioral scientists include characteristically psychology, sociology, and anthropology as well as history, economics, and political science; but studies of persons in the latter three areas are rare. Mathematicians, who are not easily encompassed under the rubric of social and behavioral scientist, or natural scientist, have been studied as creative persons. Those in the fields of the arts have sometimes been used as control groups in studies of creative persons. Although arts or humanities are usually not considered to be research fields. Nor are persons in psychology or sociology who are clinical practitioners or social service workers, or persons who primarily teach considered research scientists.

Scientists have also been studied in a number of research environments such as industrial, academic, and governmental laboratories. Investigations of these organizations and of the various roles scientists assume in each, show that in some respects the milieu places unique demands on the scientist's function. In some studies these differences are highlighted; in others they are ignored, on the assumption that the differences are not significant for the question under study.

In similar vein, studies have been conducted mainly on the American scientist. However, studies of scientists in other countries as France, Germany, and India, are present though infrequent (Chandra, 1970; Raychaudhuri, 1966; Grubel and Scott, 1967; Wilson, personal communications, 1969). In these studies the influence of findings on American populations is generally acknowledged, and may be responsible for similarities in data across national boundaries.

Predictor Variables

The variables predisposing an individual to science have generally been selected from the following areas:

(*1*) Family background, life style, practices, and attitudes, variables that provide a picture of the milieu into which the scientist is born and grows up.

(*2*) Events in childhood, particularly relating to school and academic background.

(*3*) Variables which describe the intellectual and emotional resources of the subject, as endowment that has been shaped through interaction with environment.

The rationale determining selection of variables has grown out of the literature on personality development and on the requisites for performance in the scientific environment. In the personality literature, special attention has been paid to the data on bright, high-achieving individuals and to individuals who show promise of unusual intellectual development. The studies on the research environment have elucidated the kind of resources, skills, aptitudes, behaviors, and patterns that mark successful performance in research, on feedback denote variables of personality, cognition, and motivation that might be profitably studied. Analysis of still other variables that have been scrutinized for their predictive capacity suggests that they have been chosen out of methodologically opportunistic considerations. They are accessible, easy to isolate from context and to manipulate statistically, so that the fact that they are difficult to embrace conceptually is ignored.

Family Background and Environmental Variables

Among the demographic and cultural variables that have been examined in the search for background variables that predispose an individual toward a scientific career, are the father's occupation and educational level, socioeconomic status of the family, geographical and regional origins, religion, race, and political background. These variables embrace the intellectual, and socioeconomic status of the family and, thus, presumably provide referents to the opportunities, exposure, and value systems available to the scientist during his childhood.

The notion of "occupational inheritance" has been tested in numerous studies on scientists. In one, which used a sample of over 80,000 college freshmen, Werts (1968) found that the students tended to gravitate toward their father's career, if the latter were a professional. However, parental occupations of scientists range over many levels of skill (Visher, 1948). In the case of creative scientists, however, more fathers are professionals than would be expected by chance, as Chambers (1964) found for chemists, and Knapp (1963) for social as compared to natural scientists. Creative adolescents who have shown strong potential for science (Parloff, Datta, Kleman, and Handlon, 1968) also disproportionately come from homes in which fathers are professional. Evidence, however, has not been supported in Roe's highly selective sample of natural scientists (1953). Attitudes of parents toward work are more difficult to establish when looking at their influence on sons. Yet West (1961) found no differences when the motivations toward education were studied in fathers who were blue-collar workers, as compared with those in white-collar jobs.

Astin (1963) noted that fathers who were engaged in physical activities, science, or social service chose colleges for their sons that were high producers of scientists, as contrasted to fathers who were engaged in sales businesses, law, or persuasive vocations. In quite another vein, Roe (1951) found that among highly selected scientists, those who scored highest on verbal imagery indices, came from families in which fathers were in law, clergy, or in college teaching. Thus, the role of the father's vocational level and attitudes for scientific career remains of interest, though for not very conclusive reasons.

In a closely related area, educational background of the parents, Clark (1957) found that 48% of eminent psychologists had professional fathers. Six to ten percent of the fathers had a Ph.D. degree, while only 10–20% of the fathers and mothers had less than high school training. Parents of adolescents who were sufficiently distinguished in scientific aptitudes to have become part of the Westinghouse Science sample, were also found to be educationally privileged, with 25% of the mothers having some college, 29% of the fathers having a B.A. degree, and 22% of the latter achieving an advanced degree. Educational status of the parents has been shown to be a good indication for the kind of intellectual interests encouraged in the child (Getzels and Jackson, 1961; Schaefer, 1967) and for the pull toward intellectual stimulation. More specifically, West (1961) has been able to show that the parents' level of academic performance is pirmarily an index of whether the child wili go on to the Ph.D. level.

Evidence on class status of scientists' families supports a cluster of variables pointing to the generally middle-class background of scientists who have been studied in the past (Glenn and Weiner, 1969; Roe, 1953; Werts, 1968). Social scientists seem to be more upper class than natural scientists (Knapp, 1963). Class status seems to make some difference in the choice of a social science versus a natural science discipline when sex is also taken into consideration (Werts, 1968). Class membership is not a relevant factor in determining whether the college chosen by the subject is recognized as a high or low producer of scientists (Holland, 1957).

When psychologists have been separated into clinicians and experimentalists, it has been found that clinicians tend to come from larger cities and are more urbanized than are experimental psychologists. Since sociologists also have urban origins, awareness of urban problems has been considered a prominent factor in motivating interest in social science areas (Carpenter, 1954; Glenn and Weiner, 1969).

Such demographic features at best offer faint clues to support the association between educational and urbane sophistication of parents and scientific careers of their children. A related stimulus, however, may be their attitude and acceptance of vocational goals which demand intensive training, preparation, and financial support.

As study has turned toward parental attitudes and behaviors toward children, early interests and accomplishments, a sizable number of family-related variables have been studied, such as place in family, discipline, relations with mothers, fathers, and siblings, and sources of intellectual satisfaction. Only a few of these turn out to be of more than passing importance. By and large, families of scientists are smaller than expected in the general population; at least this was the case in the late fifties (West, 1960). In line with the rather abundant data which has established the consistent relationship between eminent persons and their first-born status in the family (Altus, 1965; Apperly, 1939; Jones, 1931; Sutton-Smith and Rosenberg, 1970), Roe (1953) found that the eminent scientists in her study were predominantly firstborns or only children. However, in the Westinghouse sample of adolescents interested in science, these trends were not supported. Datta's (1968) analysis of the Westinghouse sample suggested that the favorable effects of ordinal position noted were attenuated when such factors as sex, size of family, and number of siblings were considered.

Schachter's (1963) hypothesis that actual or psychological "onliness" may be of greater psychological import than ordinal position is supported by the consistent finding of periods of isolation in the early life of scientists. These isolation times usually occur during preadolescence or latency, from 8 to 11 years, and make for real and imagined distance from peers and siblings (Eiduson, 1962; Roe, 1953; Super and Bachrach, 1957; West, 1960). Isolation or separation was at times stimulated by physical illness, psychological problems, or mobility of the family. However, the stimulus was not considered as significant as was the response generated in the subject by the fact of isolation — the need to develop his own personal resources, a tolerance for being alone, and for finding ways to amuse himself during these periods (Bush, 1969; Eiduson, 1962). Closely allied to periods of isolation are a number of other relationships contributing to the feeling of "onliness," as (1) significant incidents of father-absence through death, divorce or vocational circumstances during formative years (Barron, 1969; Eiduson, 1962; Roe, 1960); and (2) the lack of strong positive ties in relationships with families (Eiduson, 1962; Roe, 1957; Terman, 1954). Comparing psychological to natural scientists (physicists and chemists, specifically), conflictual and stormy relationships were the more prevalent milieu during early childhood years. The tenuous relationships have not invariably been found in scientists or would-be scientists (Strauss and Brechbill, 1959; Weisberg and Springer, 1961) but they do appear with sufficient regularity to suggest a less than warm or intimate involvement with parent figures.

The affective and emotional tone of the home has received considerable attention, especially since parental orientation and attitudes toward the child have been singled out as critical dimensions in the kinds of occupations to which the subject then turns (Roe, 1963). For scientists, the home has generally appeared to be rejecting, although this does not deny considerable interest in the child who becomes a scientist (Strauss and Brechbill, 1959). Empirical data do not bear out the postulated significance of the parent–child relationship for choice of field (Brunkan, 1965; Hagen, 1960). The notion seems too simplistic, or imprecise, based as it is on retrospective data that tend to be overdetermined by events in intervening years. Rejection by parents also may be too global a notion, for family values, aspirations, attitudes, beliefs, and ways of thinking, can be incorporated despite negative relationships.

A less than completely gratifying emotional environment has been also perceived as a condition encouraging the initiative desired in science. Autonomy and independence seem to have been encouraged by the child's physical and/or emotional distance from father, by ordinal position, by being an only child or a psychological "only," or by the rewards and gratifications given for showing initiative. Scientists often come from homes which are individualistic and nonconformist (Strauss and Brechbill, 1959), democratic in orientation (Myer and Penfold, 1961), and where discipline is not authoritarian or overly domineering (Nichols, 1964; Weisberg and Springer, 1961). According to their own reports, creative scientists have often experienced less discipline than have noncreative scientists (Stein, 1963) and a much less strict upbringing (Dauw, 1966). Social scientists report less harmonious homes and more inconsistent discipline than do natural scientists; as adults they feel more rebellious in their feelings toward parents (Galinsky, 1962; Roe, 1957). The low levels of authoritarianism found in the studies of high achievers is also found in scientists (Rosen, Crockett, and Nunn, 1969).

Identification with the mother as achiever is an equivocal finding. In the Eiduson (1962) sample, mothers of scientists were identified more with achievement than were fathers, who were absent from the home to such an extent that more than half the subjects could be rated as "fatherless" by the age of 12. The lack of fathering is more prevalent than the lack of adequate mothering (Bush, 1969; Taylor, 1963). Family relations are notably lacking in warmth or closeness, and remain tenuous through life. Mothers are perceived to be insecure, frustrating, preoccupied, and not too warm or protective, and fathers, though distant, are viewed with more respect (Bush, 1969; Eiduson, 1962; Roe, 1957).

These data conform with the greater autonomy permitted scientists as children, especially those who show signs of creativity (Datta and Parloff, 1967; West, 1960). The need to experience independence, curiosity, and the need to pursue their own way have been recognized as important formative experiences by parents of alert and bright scientists (Nichols, 1964). However, some sex differences are noted here: Dauw (1966) has found that fathers, but not mothers, encourage independence in girls. And retrospectively, adult women who are scientists report that only their fathers have been strong sources of encouragement (Rossi, 1965).

Some of the same distance and aloofness characterizing relationships with authority are noted in peer relationships. Physical scientists generally show less personal interaction than do social scientists (Cattell and Drevdahl, 1962; Galinsky, 1962; Roe, 1953). Psychosexual development of the scientists altogether appears retarded in the early and adolescent phases of his life, as Terman (1954) has found in his more intensive, longitudinal studies of gifted children who have turned to science as an adult career. When relationships are not intense, as in the case of physicists as compared to clinical psychologists (Galinsky, 1962), they of course have less of the stormy and conflictful characters that psychologists report.

Despite the generally lukewarm family relationships, substantive intellectual stimulation is provided in the family setting (Eiduson, 1962; McClelland, 1962; Super and Bachrach, 1957). Thus, the childhood environment of the scientist is far from the closely knit, warm milieu that is often idealized as the soil for fostering curiosity, independence, and maturity. Perhaps it is the very absence of nurturant and security-giving family background that fosters the initiative and resourcefulness that scientists show.

Childhood Interests as Predictors of Career

In line with the importance attributed to intellectual growth and development, the development of scientific and intellectual interests has been followed rather closely. Eiduson (1962), McClelland (1962), and Schaefer (1967) have found that satisfaction from intellectual activities appears early, becomes overdetermined, and can generally be traced to parents. Reading scientific material and mechanics are early preoccupations (Walberg, 1969). In fact, scientific interests seem to be crystallized in boys by the time they are in the eighth grade, with the 10- to 14-year-old period most important for this development, few interests in natural science being stimulated for the first time beyond that age period (Tyler, 1964).

Since scientific interests are found in boys who are more masculine, these interests are thought to grow possibly out of a masculine matrix. The girls tend to develop scientific interests at a later period in their development, during high school years, and those who turn to science tend, also, to be outstanding in both personality and achievement.

The adult social scientist shows some definitive interest patterns which point to possible childhood precursors (Goldschmid, 1967, Rossman, Lips, and Campbell, 1967), yet none have been traced back to childhood as yet. Campbell and Soliman (1968) show that interest patterns of female psychologists remain stable over the extended period of their adult professional life, so it is quite likely that these interests had some identifiable determinants in childhood hobbies and activities.

Academic Performance

In line with general scientific interests, Myer and Penfold (1961) note that future scientists show an interest in physical science courses in their early school years. This specificity does not appear in many studies; more characteristic is the good ability which scientists show in grade school and high school (Roe, 1957; Strauss and Brechbill, 1959; Visher, 1948). By the seventh grade, skills predictive of creativity in the twelfth grade can be identified in scientists (Chambers, 1964). In addition, the motivation for good attainment in school is present.

Pressey (1960) has found that college at an early age is a favorable index to career performance. By the college years, when vocational decisions have been made, undergraduate grades in science appear to be a good index of later performance (Platz, McClintock, and Katz, 1959). This is the case for eminent psychologists, too, who range in the top 5% of their classes (Clark, 1957). Taylor and Ellison (1967) find, however, that grades are only good predictors if the course work itself is very directly related to the areas in which later performance is accomplished, a finding aligned with studies on assessment and prediction of performance in professional psychology and psychiatry (Holt and Luborsky, 1958; Kelly and Fiske, 1951; Kelly and Goldberg, 1959).

Interestingly, only natural scientists have chosen their major areas of professional interest by college. Less than half of the Ph.D. sociologists in the American Sociological Association (ASA), surveyed by Glenn and Weiner (1969), were undergraduates in sociology although they had studied social science and psychology. Subject majors for eminent psychologists, too, were often in the area of humanities, as opposed to the "hard" sciences. This finding suggests that interests and aptitudes go together, for social scientists score lower in high school math and science as compared with physical science majors (Harmon, 1961, 1966). These scores are not reflective of differences in endowment, for in intelligence quotient as well as in grade-point average, social science majors rank second only to physicists, and are superior to biologists and chemists.

This trend of findings has raised the question of the ways in which university and preprofessional training institutions reinforce the interests and good aptitudes that scientists show in earlier years. Do good scientific institutions select or attract the good students, or do promising science candidates initiate the choice of schools, teachers, and opportunities that will be conducive to a fruitful career? Knapp, Greenbaum, and Wertheimer (1953), Holland (1957), and Astin (1963), find that good students and good science programs do get together; yet it is not easy to unconfound the factors that bring about this integration. Evidence suggests that students first select the most productive institutions; and then that institutions rise to the caliber of their students. Teachers who are masterful, warm, and intellectually eminent make the most impression on science students (Knapp, 1963).

Intellectual Resources and Capabilities

What intellectual aptitudes does the child bring to academic experiences? Does he show a superior basic endowment which in turn encourages problem-solving activities and attitudes, or do problem-solving activities and intellectual interests encourage talents which might otherwise remain latent?

In the early stages of work on the requisites of scientific performance, superior intelligence was thought to be a minimal requirement. However, often mature and very capable scientists, with outstanding creative abilities, were shown to display a fairly wide range of ability extending from high-average levels into genius categories on standard intelligence tests (Barron, 1969; MacKinnon and Hall, 1971). Although standard tests are known to be poorly refined at high levels with insufficient top for groups clustered at the high end, MacKinnon and Hall (1971) were able recently to report reliable Wechsler-Bellevue Intelligence Test scores on a group of more than forty industrial research scientists studied initially some years earlier. Their findings run from lows in the high average range (118) to very superior, and correlation between the Wechsler scores with a test of intellectual ability emphasizing abstract thinking (California Concept Mastery Test or CCMT) were low but positive.

The CCMT, and the Miller Analogies Test (MAT) have been used with some effectiveness to show that conceptual ability does vary within scientific populations. This is also the case in regard to tests of originality and creative thinking which developed in response to Guilford's theoretical and empirical work elaborating the structure of intellectual abilities. Results on the Guilford tests which measure such dimensions as fluidity, flexibility, and reasoning are not consistent for scientific samples (Barron, 1969; Drevdahl, 1956). Scientists were not included in the populations on which these tests were standardized, although other groups showing creative abilities were utilized.

Prior to the more systematically developed theses of Guilford regarding the structure of the intellect, investigators approached the dimensions of ability and aptitude involved in science in various ways. For example, analysis of perceptual styles, preferences for complexity and disorder, which frequently were formulated in response to tachistiscopically presented stimuli, imagery modes, and associative facilities, supplemented the assessment of more traditional verbal—mathematical—spatial skills (Barron, 1963; Mednick, 1962; Roe, 1963; Stein, 1963). In these endeavors, motivational elements in intellectual performance came under scrutiny, and in recent work these have become an even more prominent focus (Eiduson, 1962; Holt, 1970). Thus, the scientist's orientation toward intellectual stimuli, his attention to novel, unusual, nonhackneyed percepts, his desire to restructure reality once obvious recognition occurs, his interest in fantasy, and attention to sensuous and unusual sensory impressions, have been noted. It is within this framework which enhances both conceptual and perceptual factors that the role of unconscious elements and primary-process thinking in the more rational secondary-process thinking of science has been explored. In science the structure of acceptable thought process is so formalized that signs of individuality in conventional, logical, rational thinking and personalized elaboration stand out (Bush, 1969; Holt, 1970; Pine, 1959).

Enjoyment of fantasy (Eiduson, 1962), access to early recall (Weisberg and Springer, 1961), application of analytic thinking to thinking about early childhood (McClelland, 1962), tolerance for ambiguity (Frenkel-Brunswick, 1948; Bruner, 1962) are characteristic of scientists' thinking, along with verbal facility, fluidity, flexibility, and capacity for abstract and symbolic thinking (Mednick, 1962; Andrews, 1965; Drevdahl, 1956; Garwood, 1964). The loosening of intellectual controls or regression without too much anxiety or disorganization (Kris, 1951) are among the most provocative descriptors attributed to the cognitive processes that scientists display. These permit the "paranoid leaps," Kierkegaard's felicitous phrase for the original and revolutionary thinking which takes reality as its point of departure.

There is some evidence that the orientation which adult scientists display is observable during adolescence (Taylor and Ellison, 1967), and leads to unusual dedication and commitment to intellectual activities at the expense of other pursuits (Bush, 1969; Cattell and Drevdahl, 1955; Eiduson, 1962; Roe, 1957; Taylor and Ellison, 1967).

Personality and Emotional Resources

By describing scientists as adventurers, risk-takers, independent and self-sufficient producers who are autonomous in activities, enthusiastic in regard to work, dominant, and sensitive (Cattell and Drevdahl, 1955; Eiduson, 1962; McClelland, 1962; Parloff et al., 1968; Van Zelst and Kerr, 1954), investigators point to characteristics which enhance intellectual as well as emotional behaviors. There is a remarkable consistency in findings across studies, techniques of investigation and populations. Scientists exhibit an interest in things rather than in people or personal relationships, somewhat loose controls in behavior, an acceptance of challenge, unusual drive and commitment to task, high aspirations, confidence and self-esteem. Less consensus is found among studies in regard to the scientist's level of adjustment, his anxieties, impulsiveness, and modes of reacting to aggressive and sexual drives. The latter are variables that are perhaps more difficult to assess, and are more open to interpretation. This may account for the ambiguity of data in these areas. However it is equally tenable that scientists as a group show more variance in these characteristics (Eiduson, 1962).

It is apparent, too, that the stereotypes the public tends to hold about the personality of scientists (see section on "Sequential Characteristics of Mechanisms Involved in Scientific Career: Continuities and Discontinuities") relate to the better confirmed personality characteristics. Scientists are perceived as being withdrawn, introverted, preferring distance from interpersonal involvements. These features also come out in tests (Cattell and Drevdahl, 1955; Chambers, 1964; Drevdahl, 1956; McClelland, 1962).

There has been some interesting speculation about the value to science of such personality characteristics. It has been suggested that they permit intense persistence, reduce the tendency for distractability, and provide a kind of defensiveness or paranoid thinking that resists too easy acceptance of the obvious. Less clear are the values of the impulsiveness or instability that some tests show (Cattell and Drevdahl, 1955).

Are the characteristics found in mature scientists also found in embryonic scientists? Parloff *et al.* (1968) have found that more creative adolescents are like more creative adults, and differentiated from less creative adolescents and adults, in many characteristics, such as assertiveness, self-confidence, and autonomy. However, there is not continuity in all personality characteristics between creative adolescents and creative adults. For example, in this study the creative adolescent showed self-discipline, was reasonably circumspect in his dealings with others without detriment to his capacity to be independent in thinking and to integrate his ideas in novel ways. This characteristic was less notable in the creative adult. Although the significance of this finding for creative performance is ambiguous, the caution against assuming that the same traits will identify and characterize creative persons as they develop chronologically is clear: those characteristics which differentiate more and less creative adult groups cannot be applied indiscriminately for the purpose of identifying the potentially creative adolescent.

Data are equivocal regarding the expression of aggression and sexual drives: Knapp (1963) found physical scientists less aggressive than the general population while McClelland (1962), reviewing results of many investigations, concluded that scientists are more disturbed by aggression, especially in the interpersonal areas, and thus turn away to "safer" things and objects. The jealousy, competitiveness, hostility, and intracommunity feuds suggest that a great deal of aggression is expressed toward colleagues (Eiduson, 1962; Hagstrom, 1965; Merton, 1957,

1969). Undoubtedly the constraints provided by the rules and regulations of science encourage this open expression. For some men, the ethos of science merges and becomes one with their superegos; for other men, personal and professional conflicts are more discomforting.

Obviously certain personality and emotional characteristics are more advantageous for scientists than are others. On the basis of data to date it is extremely difficult to determine whether more adaptive resources have emerged slowly through the events and experiences of the scientist's life so that they have become characteristics which the work situation capitalizes upon or exploits; or whether the demands of scientific environment stress certain characteristics which among many others are part of the scientist's emotional make-up. The methodological difficulties of trying to chart the development of traits over time has been pointed out very perceptively by Kagan (1968), Goulet and Baltes (1970), and Kagan and Moss (1962). Some traits of personality are notoriously vagarious over a person's lifespan. Certain features can be identified early and reliably charted so that individual base lines can be established; other features, however, are notably unpredictable. They may not be manifest in every developmental phase, may be transitory, or may appear in phenotypes which are unrecognizable. Our ability to trace tendencies or characteristics of scientists to earlier manifestations may have to await a more sophisticated understanding of the stability and consistency of personality and intellectual traits over time.

Mechanisms or Processes Leading to a Scientific Career

By what processes or mechanisms are the important variables that predispose an individual to science integrated along the developmental course so that choice of a scientific career results? Thus far, understanding of a scientific work choice has been mainly dependent on the theoretical understanding of vocational choice in general. Uniquely professional, or science-specific aspects have emerged to some small degree.

Two theorists have moved science into the broader concept of occupational choice: Roe (1963) representing a need-theory approach and Holland (1966) in a factor-theory framework. Roe has given primacy in her system to early child-rearing modes, the responses to childhood needs which in turn lead to preferences for certain satisfactions. The range of vocations from which an individual chooses his adult work depends on his general orientation toward providing service to others, a derivative of attitudes derived from parental relationships; the level of work he chooses depends on genetic structure and endowments. Vocational occupations are divided into six groups, from which prediction is made, once the child-rearing attitudes of the home are known. The lack of success of this model in early empirical tests (Brunkan, 1965; Hagen, 1960) led Roe to a more elaborate formulation in which childhood interests, aptitudes, personality, and special environmental events were also contributing factors. Theoretically, the extent to which each of these factors moves the individual toward a selection of science as a career can be mathematically expressed, but this has not as yet been undertaken (Roe, 1968).

Holland (1966) has worked within a factor-trait approach. He organizes individuals into six personality types – realistic, intellectual, social, conventional, scientific, and artistic. Also, six model environments are formulated. Careers and behaviors are postulated through sets of axioms, laws, and hypotheses that predict the interaction of different types of persons in different environments. The internal relations of the theory rely also on a few constructs, such as homogeneity, consistency, and congruency. From this theory a comprehensive classificatory system of environments and personalities emerge, which permits organization of individuals along career lines and other dimensions of their lives.

The development of a personality type, in Holland's schema, involves the preference for certain activities which in turn encourages the development of competencies in those areas. In the case of the scientist or investigative personality type, the special heredity and experience of the investigative person lead to a preference for activities that entail the observational, symbolic, systematic, creative investigation of physical, biological, and cultural phenomena; and to an aversion to social, repetitive, and persuasive activities. These behavioral tendencies lead in turn to an acquisition of scientific competencies and to a deficit in persuasive competencies.

This pattern of preferences and competencies creates a scientific personality type which is predisposed to exhibit the following behaviors: achievements have an investigative quality; perceives self as scholarly, intellectually self-confident, having mathematical and scientific ability, and lacking in leadership ability; perceives the world in complex, abstract, independent, original terms with ability to integrate diverse stimuli; values science; susceptible to abstract, theoretical, and analytic influences, and least sensitive to materialistic and social influences; prefers occupations and occupational roles that facilitate his preferred activities and competencies and that minimize his aversions and incompetencies. Therefore, a scientific personality prefers investigative occupations and the role of the researcher or investigator. He avoids enterprising occupations and persuasive roles; copes with others in intellectual, analytic, indirect ways; and is characterized as analytical, rational, independent, radical, introverted, curious, and critical.

This theoretical position may be conceived as describing a way of organizing information about oneself, and focusing on the cognitive aspects of decisions involved in work choice. Other theorists have also seen choice as an information-processing task. Its developmental aspects, for example, are evident in the early work of Ginzberg, Ginsburg, Herma, and Axelrad (1951), who stated that choice becomes more settled as fantasies are increasingly restructured in the direction of reality. Super (1953), in a very comprehensive model of the occupational choice, saw that the family directly influenced the child through the direct information and attitudes it provided, and indirectly influenced the child through its vocational models. In addition to the tangible resources and opportunities it provided, the family also opened up to the potential scientist supportive information. Some of the system-analytic approaches also attempt to work toward a comprehensive theory of information input: Rogers (1959), e.g., notes that the inputs of the family, society, and genetic endowment are each important cognitive sources. Ellis and Tyler (1967) see the work situation contributing input about such realities as the rewards, feasibility of accomplishments, scope of activities.

This focus on the cognitive and decision-making aspects of choice represents a shift from the more classic developmental framework in which vocational roles were seen either as representing an expression of personality and motivational needs or as crystallization of specific aspects of identification (Darley and Hagenah, 1958; Forer, 1953; Golann, 1963). The latter was the rationale for studies of the similarities between the occupational choices of father and son. While father's occupation has in the past shown itself to be an anchoring point for the son (Caplow, 1958), as have class membership and economic opportunity, this may be in the process of becoming an outdated phenomenon. Even in science, change seems to be occurring so rapidly that "psychological inheritance" is no longer tenable; neither opportunities, professional structures, nor conditions of work are sufficiently similar to those of the past to be relevant (Dubos, 1961).

In the psychoanalytic framework, identification has been only one of the mechanisms by which remnants of earlier psychosexual relationship and conflicts become expressed. Interestingly, psychoanalysis itself has not given particular attention to work behaviors, assuming that any one of a number of behaviors could encapsulate aspects of identity; work was implicated only if occupational choice was an apt reflector of psychosexual development. Bordin, Nachmann and Segal (1963) have attempted to demonstrate that various impulse–defense configurations and the superego manifestations, different for distinct personality types, predispose to certain professional choices. So far the only scientifically relevant professional studied by this group in line with this hypothesis is the social worker, who is service rather than research oriented, and therefore probably quite different from the scientist.

No conceptual model for the development of a professional career has as yet grown out of the empirical work on scientists. However, the studies of salient variables suggest that once intellectual requisites are assured, rewarded, and reinforced in early experiences, interests, personality and motivational factors become important. Further, as children move chronologically into experiences which provide exposure to scientific research or toward suitable counterparts, the number of situations which can serve as valid predictors increases.

References

ALTUS, W. D. (1965) Birth order and academic primogeniture. *J. Personality and Social Psychology*, 2, 872–876.

ANDREWS, F. M. (1965) Factors affecting the manifestation of creative ability by scientists. *J. Personality*, 33, 140–152.

APPERLY, F. L. (1939) A study of American Rhodes scholars. *J. Heredity*, 30, 493–495.

ASTIN, A. W. (1963) Undergraduate institutions and the production of scientists. In Eiduson and Beckman (Eds), 1973.

BARRON, F. (1963) The needs for order and for disorder as motives in creative activity. In C. W. Taylor and F. Barron (Eds), *Scientific Creativity: Its Recognition and Development*, pp; 153–160, New York: Wiley.

BARRON, F. (1969) *Creative Persons and Creative Process.* New York: Holt, Rinehart & Winston.

BECKER, H. S. and CARPER, J. W. (1956) The development of identification with an occupation. *Am. J. Sociology*, 61, 289–298.

BORDIN, E. S., NACHMAN, B. and SEGAL, S. J. (1963) An articulated framework for vocational development. In Eiduson and Beckman, 1973.

BRUNER, J. S. (1962) The conditions of creativity. In H. E. Gruber, G. Terrell and M. Wertheimer (Eds), *Comtemporary Approaches to Creative Thinking*, pp. 1–30. New York: Atherton.

BRUNKAN, R. J. (1965) Perceived parental attitudes and parental identification in relation to Field of vocational choice. In Eiduson and Beckman (Eds), 1973).

BUSH, M. (1969) Regression in the service of ego. In Eiduson and Beckman (Eds), 1973.

CAMPBELL, D. P. and SOLIMON, A. (1968) The vocational interests of women in psychology. *Am. Psychologist*, 23, 158–163.

CAPLOW, T. (1958) *The Academic Marketplace.* New York: Basic Books.

CARPENTER, B. (1954) Birthplaces and schools of experimental and clinical psychologists. *Am. Psychologists*, 9, 637–639.

CATTELL, R. B. and DREVDAHL, J. E. (1955) A comparison of the personality profile of eminent researchers with that of eminent teachers and administrators, and of the general population. In Eiduson and Beckman, (Eds), 1973.

CHAMBERS, J. A. (1964) Relating personality and biographical factors to scientific creativity. In Eiduson and Beckman, (Eds), 1973.

CHANDRA, S. (1970) *Scientists: A Social-Psychological Study.* New Delhi: Oxford & IBH Publishing Co.

CLARK, K. E. (1957) Background and early training of psychologists. In Eiduson and Beckman, (Eds), 1973.

DARLEY, J. G. and HAGENAH, T. (1955) *Vocational Interest Measurement: Theory and Practice.* Minneapolis: University of Minnesota Press.

DATTA, L.-E. (1968) Birth order and potential scientific creativity. In Eiduson and Beckman, (Eds), 1973.

DATTA, L.-E. and PARLOFF, M. B. (1967) On the relevance of autonomy: Parent–child relationships and early scientific creativity. *Proc. 75 Ann. Convention of Am. Psychological Assn.* Washington DC, pp. 149–150.

DAUW, D. B. (1966) Life experiences of original thinkers and good elaborators. *Exceptional Children*, 32, 433–440.

DENNIS, W. and GRUDEN, E. (1954) Current scientific activities of psychologists as a function of age. *J. Gerontology*, 9, 175–178.

DREVDAHL, K. E. (1956) Factors of importance for creativity. In Eiduson and Beckman, (Eds), 1973.

DUBOS, R. (1961) Problems of biological adaptations of children to modern society. Paper presented at the Presidential Session of the meeting of the Am. Orthopsychiatric Assn., New York, March, 1961.

EIDUSON, B. T. (1962) The beginnings of scientists. In *Scientists, Their Psychological World.* New York: Basic Books, pp. 21–67.

EIDUSON, B. T. and BECKMAN, L. (Eds), (1973) *Science as a Career Choice: Theoretical and Empirical Studies.* New York: Russell Sage Foundation.

ELLIS, R. A. and TYLER, L. (1967) Planned and unplanned aspects of occupational choices by youth, toward a morphology of occupational choices. (Mimeo.) December 1967; University of Oregon, Contract No. OE5-86-026, US Office of Education.

ERIKSON, E. H. (1968) *Identity: Youth and Crisis*. New York: Norton.

FORER, B. R. (1953) Personality factors in occupational choice. *Education Psychological Measurement*, 13, 361–366.

FRENKEL-BRUNSWICK, E. (1948) Intolerance of ambiguity as an emotional and perceptual personality variable. *J. Personality*, 18, 108–143.

GALINSKY, M. D. (1942) Personality development and vocational choice of clinical psychologist and physicists. In Eiduson and Beckman, (Eds), 1973).

GARWOOD, D. S. (1964) Personality factors related to creativity in young scientists. In Eiduson and Beckman, (Eds), 1973.

GETZELS, J. and JACKSON, P. (1961) Family environment and cognitive style: A study of the sources of highly intelligent and of highly creative adolescents. *Am. Sociological Review*, 26, 351–359.

GINZBERG, E., GINSBURG, S. W., HERMA, J. L. and AXELRAD, S. (1951) *Occupational Choice*. New York: Columbia University Press.

GLENN, N. D. and WEINER, D. (1969) Some trends in the social origins of American sociologists. In Eiduson and Beckman, (Eds), 1973.

GOLANN, S. E. (1963) Psychological study of creativity. *Psychological Bulletin*, 60, 548–565.

GOLDSCHMID, M. L. (1967) Prediction of college majors by personality tests. In Eiduson and Beckman, (Eds), 1973.

GOULET, L. R. and BALTES, P. B. (1970) *Life-span Developmental Psychology*. New York: Academic Press.

GRINKER, R. R., GRINKER, R. R. Jr. and TIMBERLAKE, J. (1962) "Mentally Healthy" young males: A study, *Archives of General Psychiatry*, 6, 405–453.

GRUBEL, H. G. and SCOTT, A. D. (1967) The characteristics of foreigners in the US economics profession. *Am. Economic Review*, 57, 131–145.

HAGEN, D. (1960) Careers and family atmospheres: An empirical test of Roe's theory. *J. Counseling Psychology*, 7, 251–256.

HAGSTROM, W. O. (1965) Social control in Science. In Eiduson and Beckman, (Eds), 1973.

HARMON, L. R. (1961) High school backgrounds of science doctorates. *Science*, 133, 679–688.

HARMON, L. R. (1966) *Profiles of Ph.D's in the Sciences*. Washington, DC: National Academy of Sciences, National Research Council.

HOLLAND, J. L. (1957) Undergraduate origins of American Scientists. In Eiduson and Beckman, (Eds), 1973.

HOLT, R. R. (1970) Artistic creativity and Rorschach measures of adaptive regression. In B. Klopfer, M. M. Meyer and F. Brawer (Eds), *Developments in the Rorschach technique*. Volume 3. New York: Harcourt Brace Jovanovich, pp. 263–320.

HOLT, R. R. and LUBORSKY, L. (1958) *Personality patterns of psychiatrists*. New York: Basic Books.

HUGHES, E. C. (1965) Professions. In K. S. Lynn and Eds. of *Daedalus* (Eds), *The professions in America*. Boston: Houghton Mifflin, pp. 1–14.

HUGHES, E. C. (1958) *Men and their work*. Glencoe: Free Press.

JONES, H. E. (1931) Order of birth in relation to the development of the child. In C. Murchison (Ed.), *Handbook of child psychology*. Worcester: Clark University Press, pp. 607–608.

KAGAN, J. (1968) The three faces of continuity in human development. In D. A. Goslin (Ed.), *Handbook of socialization theory and research*. Chicago: Rand McNally & Co., pp. 983–1002.

KAGAN, J. and MOSS, H. A. (1962) *Birth to maturity: A study in psychological development*. New York: Wiley.

KELLY, E. L. and FISKE, D. W. (1952) *The prediction of performance in clinical psychology*. Ann Arbor: University of Michigan Press.

KELLY, E. L. and GOLDBERG, L. R. (1959) Correlates of later performance and specialization in psychology. *Psychological Monographs*, 73, 1–32. (Whole No. 482).

KERSTER, M. and HIRSCH, W. (1958) Scientists in popular magazine fiction. Unpublished manuscript, Purdue University.

KNAPP, R. H. (1963) Demographic, cultural and personality attributes of scientists. In C. W. Taylor and F. Barron (Eds), *Scientific creativity: Its recognition and development*. New York: Wiley, pp. 205–216.

KNAPP, R. H., GREENBAUM, J. J. and WERTHEIMER, M. (1953) Recent undergraduate origins of scholars in the behavioral sciences. *American Psychologist,* 8, 479–483.

KRIS, E. (1951) On preconscious mental processes. In D. Rapaport, *Organization and pathology of thought*. New York: Columbia University Press, pp. 488–491.

LEHMAN, H. C. (1966) The psychologist's most creative years. In Eiduson and Beckman, (Eds), 1973.

MACKINNON, D. W. and HALL, W. B. (1971) Intelligence and creativity. In Eiduson and Beckman, (Eds), 1973.

McCLELLAND, D. C. (1962) On the psychodynamics of the creative physical scientists. In Eiduson and Beckman, (Eds), 1973.

MEDNICK, S. (1962) The associative basis of the creative process. *Psychological Review,* 69, 220–232.

MERTON, R. K. (1957) *Social Theory and Social Structure*. Glencoe: Free Press.

MERTON, E. K. (1969) Behavior patterns of scientists. In Eiduson and Beckman, (Eds), 1973.

MOORE, W. E. (1969) Occupational socialization. In D. Goslin (Ed.), *Handbook of Socialization Theory and Research*. Chicago: Rand McNally, pp. 861–883.

MYER, G. R. and PENFOLD, D. M. (1961) Factors associated with interest in science. *Br. J. Educational Psychology,* 31, 33–37.

NICHOLS, R. C. (1964) Parental attitudes of mothers of intelligent adolescents and creativity of their children. In Eiduson and Beckman, (Eds), 1973.

OSIPOW, S. H. (1968) *Theories of Career Development*. New York: Appleton-Century-Crofts.

PARLOFF, M. B., DATTA, L.-E., KLEMAN, M. and HANDLON, J. H. (1968) Personality characteristics which differentiate creative male adolescents and adults. In Eiduson and Beckman, (Eds), 1973.

PINE, F. (1959) Thematic drive content and creativity. *J. Personality,* 27, 136–151.

PLATZ, A., McCLINTOCK, C. and KATZ, D. (1959) Undergraduate grades and the Miller Analogies Test as predictors of graduate success. *Am. Psychologist,* 14, 285–289.

PRESSEY, S. L. (1960) Toward earlier creativity in psychology. In Eiduson and Beckman, (Eds), 1973.

RAYCHAUDHURI, M. (1966) Creativity and personality: A review of psychological researches. *Indian Psychological Review,* 2, 91–102.

ROE, E. (1951) A study of Imagery in Research Scientists. In Eiduson and Beckman, (Eds), 1973.

ROE, A. (1953) Early determinants of vocational choice. In Eiduson and Beckman, (Eds), 1973.

ROE, A. (1957) A psychological study of eminent psychologists and anthropologists, and a comparison with biological and physical scientists. In Eiduson and Beckman, (Eds), 1973.

ROE, A. (1960) Crucial life experiences in the development of scientists. In E. P. Torrance (Ed.), *Talent and Education*. Minneapolis: University of Minnesota, pp. 66–77.

ROE, A. (1963) Personal problems and science. In C. W. Taylor and F. Barron (Eds), *Scientific Creativity: Its Recognition and Development*. New York: Wiley, pp. 132–138.

ROE, A. (1968) Perspectives on Vocational Development. Paper presented at the Symposium on Vocational Development. Washington University. July, 1968.

ROGERS, C. R. (1959) Towards a theory of creativity. In H. H. Anderson (Ed.), *Creativity and its Cultivation*. New York: Harper, pp. 69–82.

ROSEN, B. C., CROCKETT, H. N. and NUNN, C. E. (Eds) (1969) *Achievement in American Society*. Cambridge, MA: Scheukman.

ROSSI, A. S. (1965) Barriers to the career choice of engineering, medicine or science among American women. In J. A. Mattfeld and C. G. Van Aken (Eds), *Women and the Scientific Professions*. Cambridge, MA: M. I. T. Press, pp. 51–213.

ROSSMAN, J. E., LIPS, O. and CAMPBELL, D. P. (1967) Vocational Interests of sociologists. In Eiduson and Beckman, (Eds), 1973.

SCHACHTER, S. (1963) Birth order, eminence and higher education. *Am. Sociological Review,* 28, 757–767.

SCHAEFER, C. E. (1967) Biographical inventory correlates of scientific and artistic creativity in adolescents. *Dissertation Abstracts,* 1173B–1174B.

STEIN, M. I. (1963) Explorations in typology. In Eiduson and Beckman, (Eds), 1973.

STRAUSS, S. (1965) Career choices of scholars. *Personnel and Guidance Journal,* 44, 153–159.

STRAUSS, S. and BRECHBILL, H. (1959) Traits of Scientists. *Science Education,* 43, 35–41.

SUPER, D. E. (1953) A theory of vocational development. In Eiduson and Beckman, (Eds), 1973.

SUPER, D. E. and BACHRACH, P. B. (1957) *Scientific Careers and Voccational Development Theory.* New York: Teachers College, Columbia University.

SUTTON-SMITH, B. and ROSENBERG, B. G. (1970) *The Sibling.* New York: Holt, Rinehart & Winston.

TAYLOR, D. W. (1963) Variables related to creativity and productivity among men in two research laboratories. In C. W. Taylor and F. Barron (Eds), *Scientific Creativity: Its Recognition and Development.* New York: Wiley, pp. 228–250.

TAYLOR, C. W. and ELLISON, R. L. (1967) Biographical predictors of scientific performance. In Eiduson and Beckman, (Eds), 1973.

TERMAN, L. M. (1954) Scientists and non-scientists in a group of 800 gifted men. In Eiduson and Beckman, (Eds), 1973.

TYLER, L. E. (1964) Development of scientist patterns of interest in boys. In Eiduson and Beckman, (Eds), 1973.

VAN ZELST, R. H. and KERR, W. A. (1954) Personality self-assessment of scientific and technical personnel. *J. Applied Psychology,* 38, 145–147.

VISHER, S. S. (1948) Environmental backgrounds of leading American scientists. *Am. Sociological Review,* 13, 65–72.

WALBERG, H. (1969) A portrait of the artist and scientist as young men. *Exceptional Children,* 36, 5–11.

WEISBERG, P. S. and SPRINGER, K. (1961) Environmental factors in creative function. *Archives of General Psychiatry,* 5, 554–564.

WERTS, C. E. (1968) Paternal influence on career choice. *J. Counseling Psychology,* 15, 48–52.

WEST, S. S. (1960) Class origin of scientists. In Eiduson and Beckman, (Eds), 1973.

WEST, S. S. (1961) Sibling configurations of scientists. In Eiduson and Beckman, (Eds), 1973.

WILSON (1969) Personal Communication.

WISPÉ, L. (1963) Traits of eminent American Psychologists. In Eiduson and Beckman, (Eds), 1973.

WISPÉ, L. (1969) The bigger, the better: Productivity, size and turnover in a sample of psychology departments. *Am. Psychologist,* 24, 662–668.

5

A 40-year Follow-up of Giftedness: Fulfillment and Unfulfillment*

M. ODEN

THERE is no evidence that vocational success among these gifted men is related to such factors as birthplace of parents (however, the parents of 75% of both A's and C's† were American born), age of either parent at birth of subject, mother's health during pregnancy, length of breast feeding, birth order, or number of siblings. The proportion of first-born children was 52% for both the A and C groups (including one A man who was a twin). Third-born or later children included 20% of A's and 17% of C's. More C's than A's had no siblings; the "onlies" comprised 21% of C's as compared with 13% of A's. Forty-eight per cent of A's and 46% of C's had two or more siblings, while the proportion with three or more siblings was 19% for A's and 21% for C's. None of these differences is significant.

A relationship to A–C status, however, was found among such home background factors as education of parents, occupation and marital status of parents, interests, activities, and honors of father, and size of home library. Of interest also in the family background is the fact that more than twice as many A's as C's are from Jewish parentage; 17% of A's and 8% of C's. The total Jewish representation in the Terman group is slightly over 10%.

Education of Parents

The parents, both fathers and mothers, of the A group had a greater amount of schooling than did those of the C group, but the differences are significant only for the fathers. The figures on parental education . . . show that 47% of A fathers and only 25% of C fathers were college graduates. Less than 30% of A fathers and more than one-half of C fathers did not complete high school. On the maternal side, college graduation was reported for 20% of A group mothers and 12% of C group mothers. Information on the education of grandparents was available for 78 A's and 71 C's and here also the differences are in the direction

*Genetic Psychology Monographs, (1968), 77, 71–74, 78–86 (Edited). Reprinted by permission.
†'A' group consists of men selected as most successful in 1940; 'C' group consists of men selected as least successful in 1940. A's IQ ≃ 157.3; C's IQ ≃ 150 (Editor).

of greater schooling among the grandparents of the A men than those of the C men. College attendance of one or more years was reported for 38% of the paternal grandfathers of A men and 18% of those of C men (p = <0.01). The maternal grandfathers of the A men also had more schooling than those of the C men, but the difference is not significant. A larger proportion of A than of C grandmothers, both paternal and maternal, had a high school or better education, but again the differences are not reliable.

Occupational Status of Fathers

As would be expected from their superior educational attainments, the A fathers rank higher in occupational status than do C fathers. The occupations of the fathers were classified according to the Minnesota Occupational Scale, the same as that used in classifying the occupations of the male subjects of the Terman group . . . as of 1922, the approximate date at which the subjects were originally selected for study. Significantly more A than C fathers were employed at the professional level; 41% of A's and 20% of C's (p = <0.01). The representation in the higher business and semiprofessional occupations (Group II) was about the same for the A's and C's, but the C fathers greatly outnumbered those of the A group in occupational Groups III to V.

Information on the occupations of fathers was also obtained in 1928 when the subjects were chiefly in high school or entering college and in 1940 when they had reached adulthood. The differences in occupational status continued to be in the same direction and of about the same magnitude as in 1922, but with smaller representation from each group because of death or retirement among the fathers.

Incidence of Death and Divorce in Parental Background

The C's are more likely than the A's to come from homes broken either by the death of a parent or by divorce. When the group was first selected for study in 1922, more than twice as many C as A parents had been divorced and the difference in divorce rate was even greater in 1928 and 1940. There was also a higher death rate among C parents than among A parents, but the difference in mortality did not become marked until 1940; by that date 31 A fathers and 11 A mothers had died as against 43 C fathers and 19 C mothers. To what extent the greater mortality of C parents was due to age is not clear. The information on age of the parents at birth of the subjects shows that the C parents were only slightly older than the A parents and the A and C men themselves average approximately the same age. Thus it appears that the age difference between the two sets of parents was not great enough to account fully for the much higher death rate among C parents. . . .

Other Aspects of Home Background

Ratings made in 1922 on the Whittier Scale for Grading Home Conditions were available for 38 A's and 34 C's and showed no difference; close to 92% of both A and C homes were rated above average to very superior. On the other hand, there was a reliable difference in size of home library; according to the parents' 1922 reports, 38% of A homes and 19% of C homes had 500 or more books ($p = 0.01$). Information on hobbies and interests and on positions of honor, trust, and recognition to 1922 was furnished for approximately 90% of fathers of each group. The A fathers, as compared to C fathers, showed a reliably greater breadth of interests and had received more recognition as shown in positions of honor and trust (social, civic, political, professional or business, school, or church); 51% of A fathers and 31% of C fathers had received one or more such honors ($p = <0.01$). The A and C mothers did not differ reliably in number and breadth of interests or in positions of trust and recognition; what differences there were, however, favored the A's. The parents' report in 1922 on the amount of home instruction received by the gifted subject in childhood, including reading and telling stories to the child as well as instruction along particular lines, showed no difference between the A's and C's. . . .

Interests, Abilities, and Personality Characteristics in Childhood and Youth

Neither the age at learning to read, the amount of reading, nor reading interests in childhood showed any difference between the groups. In their feeling about school, the groups differed considerably according to the parents. A "strong liking for school" was reported for 57% of A's as compared with 42% of C's ($p = 0.04$). Information from parents on indications of special ability in music, mathematics, science, art, or dramatics did not differ reliably, although the presence of one or more special ability was more often noted for the A's than for the C's. The subjects themselves as well as their parents reported on the number and size of their collections. The A's were more often collectors than were the C's; four or more collections of significant size were reported for 35% of A's and 18% of C's ($p = 0.01$).

The C parents (according to their 1922 report) more often punished the child and more often listed faults, such as disobedience and impudence, but the differences were small and not reliable. The parents' 1928 reports when the subjects were adolescent showed a significant difference in attitude toward discipline; those rated "rather" to "very headstrong" included 38% of C's as against 13% of A's ($p = 0.001$). There were no differences of consequence in either parents' or teachers' opinions on the occupation for which these young people were best suited, nor was there any difference in the subjects' own occupational preferences for the future.

Nervous Tendencies and Social Adjustment in Childhood and Youth

Information on tendencies toward nervousness obtained from parents, teachers, and (in 1922 only) the medical examiner showed no difference between the A's and C's in either 1922 or 1928. Those rated "little or none" on nervous tendencies included approximately 90% of each group. The composite parent and teacher ratings on social adjustment were classified as follows: "satisfactory," "some maladjustment," "serious maladjustment." The ratings favored the A's at both dates; in 1922 the proportion rated "satisfactory" included 96% of A's and 86% of C's ($p = 0.02$) and in 1928 "satisfactory" ratings were given to 95% of A's and 83% of C's ($p = 0.02$). The A–C differences in childhood and youth in social adjustment became increasingly marked as the subjects grew older. . . .

Autobiographical Report of 1950

An information schedule called "Supplementary Biographical Data" was one of the questionnaires filled out by the subjects in the 1950–52 follow-up. It was an eight-page blank designed "to obtain certain kinds of information that will throw light on your personality development and on factors that may have helped or hindered you in achieving your life goals." The biographical data called for were supplied by 85% of the A and 70% of the C men.

Parent–Child Relationships

Seven aspects of parent–child relationships were listed, each followed by a five-point rating bar ranging from "extremely" to "not at all." The respondents checked the point on the scale that best described their relationship with their parents in childhood and youth. Fathers and mothers were rated separately on each trait. The only variable that showed a reliable A–C difference was the extent to which parents had encouraged initiative and independence, with the A's more often than the C's reporting encouragement toward independence from both their fathers and their mothers. The difference, however, was somewhat more marked for the fathers than for the mothers. Little difference appeared in such other aspects of child–parent relationships as admiration for parents, rebelliousness toward parents, resistance by parents to subject's attempt to achieve independence, feelings of rejection by parents, affection and under-standing between subject and parents, and tendencies to over-protectiveness and solicitude on the part of parents. Table IV.6 compares the opinions of the A and C men regarding their relationships with their parents.

Other Parental Traits

The subjects were asked to rate their parents on five traits of personality

TABLE IV.6 *Report of A and C Men on Early Parent–Child Relationships. (From biographical report of 1950–52)*

Variable	A Group N	A Group %	C Group N	C Group %	CR
a. Extent admired and wanted to emulate parents					
Father:	82		63		
A good deal to extremely		51.2		39.7	1.4
Moderately		28.0		31.8	
Slightly or not at all		20.7		28.6	
Mother:	82		69		
A good deal to extremely		40.3		39.1	
Moderately		43.9		34.8	
Slightly or not at all		15.9		26.0	1.4
b. Extent felt rebellious toward parents					
Father:	81		62		
A good deal to extremely		12.4		16.1	
Moderately		24.7		29.0	
Slightly or not at all		63.0		54.8	1.0
Mother:	82		69		
A good deal to extremely		20.7		15.9	0.8
Moderately		24.4		29.0	
Slightly or not at all		54.9		55.0	
c. Extent parents encouraged initiative and independence					
Father:	80		62		
A good deal to extremely		62.5		41.9	2.4
Moderately		25.0		22.6	
Slightly or not at all		12.5		35.5	3.3
Mother:	83		69		
A good deal to extremely		60.2		44.9	1.9
Moderately		25.3		23.2	
Slightly or not at all		14.4		31.8	2.6
d. Extent parents resisted efforts to achieve normal independence					
Father:	78		61		
A good deal to extremely		5.1		6.5 ⎫	1.1
Moderately		6.4		11.5 ⎭	
Slightly or not at all		88.4		82.0	
Mother:	83		69		
A good deal to extremely		19.2		26.0	1.0
Moderately		12.0		17.4	
Slightly or not at all		68.7		56.5	1.6
e. Extent felt rejected by parents					
Father:	80		62		
A good deal to extremely		8.8		9.7	
Moderately		11.3		12.9	
Slightly or not at all		80.0		77.4	

TABLE IV.6 (*continued*)

Variable	A Group N	A Group %	C Group N	C Group %	CR
Mother:	81		69		
A good deal to extremely		2.4		5.8	
Moderately		3.7		5.8	
Slightly or not at all		93.8		88.4	1.2
f. Extent of affection and understanding between subject and parents					
Father:	79		64		
A good deal to extremely		36.8		28.1	
Moderately		34.2		32.8	
Slightly or not at all		29.1		39.1	1.3
Mother:	83		70		
A good deal to extremely		57.9		48.6	1.1
Moderately		28.9		34.3	
Slightly or not at all		13.2		17.1	
g. How solicitous were parents (anxious affection, over-protection, etc.)					
Father:	77		62		
A good deal to extremely		6.5		11.3	1.0
Moderately		26.0		24.2	
Slightly or not at all		67.6		64.5	
Mother:	82		69		
A good deal to extremely		37.8		39.1	
Moderately		21.9		34.8	
Slightly or not at all		40.3		26.0	1.8

"entirely apart from their relationship toward you or their other children." The traits were: *how self-confident, how helpful, how domineering, how friendly, how intelligent.* The only one of these traits for which the A–C difference approached reliability was intelligence of the fathers: 28% of A's as opposed to 15% of C's rated their fathers as "extremely intelligent" ($p = 0.05$).

Family Relationships and Socioeconomic Factors in Childhood and Youth

There were no clear-cut trends or reliable differences in the reports on sibling attachment or rivalry, serious friction among family members, or such socio-economic factors as financial situation, social position of parents, or subject's opinion of the vocational success of his father.

Religious Influences and Attitudes

A somewhat smaller proportion of A than of C men said that they had had "considerable" to "very strict" religious training in childhood and youth, but the difference (54% of A's as compared to 61% of C's) was not significant. There was also little difference in the reports of religious inclination as an adult; however, slightly more A than C men expressed a moderate to strong religious inclination (38% of A's and 30% of C's).

Physical Factors

Although a somewhat larger proportion of A's than of C's rated their health "good" or "very good" both in childhood and in adolescence, the differences were slight. Nor did the groups differ in their feeling about the effects on the personality (favorable or unfavorable) of such physical factors as size, appearance, ability at sports or games, or serious and extended illness or accidents. There was, however, a fairly reliable difference in the ratings on "amount of physical energy in recent years." Rating themselves as more energetic than average to extremely energetic were 62% of A's and 45% of C's ($p = 0.04$). Only 9% of A's but 25% of C's considered themselves below average in amount of energy.

Emotional and Social Factors

This section of the biographical data blank is in four parts. The first asked the subjects to rate themselves on the extent of their interest as compared to their friends in succeeding at five variables at age 12–20 and since age 20. The variables listed were *Being a leader, Having friends, Making money, Being a social success*, and *School work*. Except for interest in school success (reliably more A's than C's were interested), the two groups did not differ significantly in the 12–20 period, but there were marked differences in the period since age 20. The A's more often than the C's expressed a good deal to extreme interest in succeeding at all the variables after 20. The differences were highly reliable for *being a leader, having friends*, and *succeeding at school work*. Interest in *making money* did not differ markedly for the two groups; 48% of A's and 44% of C's expressed a good deal to extreme interest. This variable, however, ranked in first place in amount of interest with the C's but in fourth place with the A's. Both groups agreed in ranking interest in *being a social success* since age 20 at the bottom of the list. . . .

The second and third parts of this section asked for information on whether in childhood or youth the subject had felt "different" from his classmates and whether it had been difficult for him to enter social and other activities of his classmates. Neither question yielded very reliable differences between the A's and C's. The A's more often said that they felt "different" from their classmates than did the C's (63% of A's and 48% of C's, $p = 0.05$). About 31% of A's and 25% of C's had felt intellectually superior and 32% of A's and 22% of C's had felt inferior or at a disadvantage either physically or socially with their classmates.

According to their own reports, the A's had more difficulty than the C's in entering into social activities and making friends in their youth. Thirty-nine per cent of A's and 25% of C's reported such difficulty ($p = 0.06$).

The last question in this section asked if there had been either in childhood or later any major problems or marked difficulties related to sex. Approximately three-fourths of both A and C men indicated none, or only minor problems. The difficulties mentioned were varied and there were no significant differences between the two groups.

Factors Related to Education and Vocational Choice

Some of the most striking A–C differences came out in this section of the autobiographical report. The subjects' remembrance of their parents' attitude toward their schooling indicates greater pressure for scholastic achievement on the part of the A than of the C parents. The A's were significantly more often encouraged to forge ahead in school, to get better grades, and to go to college. Table IV.7 compares the responses of the A and C men regarding three aspects of parental attitude toward their education.

In reply to the question, *Did you have as much schooling as you wanted?*

TABLE IV.7 *Report of A and C Men on Parental Attitudes Toward Education. (From biographical report of 1950–52)*

Variable	A Group ($N = 86$) %	C Group ($N = 71$) %	CR
a. Attitude of parents toward school progress			
Encouraged to forge ahead	59.3	39.3	2.4
Allowed to go own pace	39.5	60.7	
Held back	1.2		
b. Attitude of parents toward school work			
Demanded high marks	15.1	5.7	
Encouraged high marks	73.3	52.9	4.3
Took high marks for granted	11.6	34.3	
Showed little concern		7.1	
c. Did parents encourage college attendance?			
Yes	96.5	62.3	5.4
One encouraged, other opposed	2.4	1.5	
No, because of financial circumstances		17.4	
No, because of youth, delicate health, etc.		2.9	
No, not considered or were indifferent	1.2	15.9	

91% of A's and only 49% of C's said "Yes" (p = <0.001). The most frequent explanation given by 28% of the C's was "lacked money" or "parents not willing to finance."

Another question asked the subjects what occupation their parents had thought they should plan for. A comparison of the replies to this question with the subject's actual occupation in 1950 shows that 28% of A's and 14% of C's followed their parents' choice; the difference, however, was not very reliable (p = 0.05). Fifty-seven per cent of A's and 48% of C's said their parents did not indicate a choice. In response to a question on other circumstances that influenced vocational choice, 68% of A's and only 23% of C's mentioned aptitude or marked interest (p = <0.001). The most frequent influence in the vocational choice of the C's was financial necessity, reported by 44% of C men but by only 17% of A men (p = <0.001). Chance factors, such as job opportunity or personal contacts, were mentioned by more C than A men; 34% as compared to 16% (p = 0.01). Asked at what age they had first seriously thought about their life work, significantly more A's than C's were considering the matter before age 18; included here were 76% of A's and 44% of C's (p = <0.001). The A–C difference in those who first seriously considered their life work before age 16 was also significant; 48% of A's and 25% of C's (p = <0.01). Those who did not decide on their life work until after age 21 included only 5% of A's but 28% of C's.

In reply to a question on how they felt about their present vocation, 78% of A's as compared to 22% of C's expressed deep satisfaction and interest (p = <0.001). Only 2% of A's reported discontent to strong dislike of their work, while 17% of C's said they were dissatisfied with their vocation. Another indication of the lack of fulfillment on the part of the C's appeared in responses to the question, "Does your life offer satisfactory outlets for your mental capabilities?" The reply was "Yes" or "Fairly well" for 94% of A's but for only 56% of C's. A "No" or a qualified negative reply was given by 6% of A's and 45% of C's (p = <0.001).

Self-appraisals and Evaluations

The last section of the Supplementary Biographical Data blank of 1950 called for an overview of their lives including appraisal of their accomplishments, opinion on factors related to achievement, self-rating on 14 traits of personality, feeling about the most important sources of satisfaction in life, and opinion on what constitutes success.

In appraising the extent to which they have lived up to their intellectual abilities, the A's far more often than the C's respond with "fully" or "reasonably well." Those who consider that they have lived up to their abilities (1950 report) include 83% of A's and only 27% of C's (p = <0.001). No A men but 32% of C men thought that they had "fallen far short" or that their lives were "largely a failure" from the standpoint of realization of their abilities. . . .

A list of 10 factors from which the respondents were asked to check those that had contributed to their life accomplishment yielded marked A–C differences. . . . The factor most frequently checked by the A men was *Adequate education*, with mention by 90%, and the factor most frequently checked by the C's was *Good mental stability* (56%), followed closely by *Adequate education* (55%). The most striking difference between the A and C men was in the proportion who checked *Persistence in working toward a goal* as a contributing factor in their life accomplishment. All of the items in the list of helpful factors were more often checked by A's than by C's, and the differences were all significant except for *Excellent health*. Seven per cent of the C's did not check any item as having been helpful.

The same 10 factors were stated in reverse (*Inadequate education* for *Adequate education*, etc.) in a second list in which the subjects were asked to check those which had hindered life accomplishment. More than twice as large a proportion of A's than of C's did not check any of the hindering factors (44% vs. 20%). The two factors most frequently checked by the A's, each by about one-fifth of the group, were *Poor work habits* and *Poor social adjustment*. Interestingly, a somewhat smaller proportion of C's than of A's checked *Poor work habits*. The greatest obstacle to achievement for the C's was *Lack of persistence*, just as *Persistence* had been the least mentioned helpful factor. The A–C differences were significant for only two of the hindering factors: *Lack of persistence* and *Inadequate education*. The relatively small proportion of A's (about 56%) who checked any hindering factor probably accounts for the decreased magnitude of the differences between the two groups.

Self-ratings on a group of 12 personality traits were called for in the biographical data blank of 1950 as well as in the personality inventory of 1940. . . . The traits that discriminated the most between the A's and C's were self-confidence, perseverance, and integration toward goals, with the A's possessing all of these characteristics to a reliably greater degree than the C's. . . .

A question asking the subjects to check in a list of nine aspects of life from which they derived the greatest satisfaction also brought out a number of clearcut differences between the two groups. The greatest differences was in "work itself" as a source of satisfaction, checked by 91% of A's as compared to 46% of C's ($p = <0.001$). "Recognition for you accomplishments" also was more often mentioned by A's than by C's; 74% of the former and 27% of the latter ($p = <0.001$). Though less than half of the A's (44%) checked income as a source of great satisfaction, the proportion was reliably greater than the 19% of C's who mentioned this aspect of life ($p = <0.01$). "Marriage" and "children" each ranked high with the A's (just below "work itself"), but the figures cannot be fairly compared with the C's, since 18% of the C's are single and of those who married a larger proportion are divorced. . . .

Finally, the 1950 biographical report asked, *From your point of view, what constitutes success in life?* There was a wide range of replies, often overlapping, and frequently a respondent gave more than one definition. The most striking difference between the two groups was in greater emphasis given by the A's to vocational satisfaction and achievement and the realization of potentialities. The groups also differed significantly in their opinion of the fulfillment of social responsibility as a definition of success, with the A's much more oriented in this direction than the C's. Income did not rate very high with either A's or C's as a hallmark of success, though it was mentioned more often by C's than by A's.

V

Social and Educational Influences on Creative Behavior and Exceptional Achievement

NO FAMILY is an island, to paraphrase John Donne, and all families operate within wider social networks. This is a truism but one that has been extremely difficult to flesh out. Each of the papers in this chapter take a particular aspect of this wider environment and show how it influences early giftedness either by channeling or sustaining it. Without these more general but nevertheless profound social and educational influences, even the highest degree of early giftedness is likely to abort within the family. As this chapter shows these are the influences which pull such abilities out of the narrow confines of family and broaden their reach.

Lynn's paper (V-1) is a gem, presenting a nexus of social factors one usually does not consider in accounting for the attainment of eminence. This paper clearly shows why it is difficult to argue that eminence is strictly a personal or family matter. Lynn is followed by an equally comprehensive article. Paper V-2 is a synopsis of Simonton's large body of research on the historical events and resources contributing to the somewhat episodic appearance of geniuses. His research, using the most sophisticated statistics, is archival research at its best. But it is much more than its methodology that recommends Simonton's work. Using his methods, he has thrown new, compelling light on subtle historical factors at work in the attainment of eminence and has shown a subtle interweave of history and personal ability.

No single group of eminent persons exists more clearly in the public's mind than Nobel Laureates. Zuckerman's findings (V-3) regarding the recruitment, highly mutual and deliberate, of Laureates and Laureates-to-be tells one that there is probably no group of gifted youth as scrutinized, recruited, and channelled as the mathematically and scientifically gifted. And with such results! If ever there was an argument against believing in the overly simple idea that "Genius will out" without assistance on the basis of chance or its mere presence, Zuckerman's research is that argument. The following article by Merton (V-4) is an astute blend of sociological detail, psychological insight, and historical perspective. Starting with the early reactions to Watson's autobiographical *The Double Helix,*

Merton quickly disabuses us of our short-sightedness regarding the indifference and altruistic sense of mission many persons ascribe to scientists. As Merton shows, they have been like us and bled like us for centuries. What distinguishes their careers from that of some other careers are the tightly organized institutions of scientific education and pursuit and the dual institutionalized imperatives to be the first *and* the best. This paper describes the powerful social psychological demands upon scientists, none more explicit than the requirement to be original. It is this demand that often triggers ambition and feeds an individual's attempt of the extraordinary in his work. If the scientific community is as well organized and involved in the excellence of its members as Zuckerman and Merton demonstrate, their work comprises convincing evidence of how and why both ambition and achievement are not solely the individual's in their origin or fulfillment.

1

The Social Ecology of Intelligence and Achievement*

R. LYNN

Abstract

Data are presented to show that there are differences in mean population IQ in different regions of the British Isles. Mean population IQ is highest in London and South-East England and tends to drop with distance from this region. Mean population IQs are highly correlated with measures of intellectual achievement, *per capita* income, unemployment, infant mortality and urbanization. The regional differences in mean population IQ appear to be due to historical differences which are measured back to 1751 and to selective migration from the provinces into the London area.

THE SOCIAL ecology of intelligence is concerned with the relationship between the mean IQ of populations and their social, economic, demographic and epidemiological characteristics. The subject has received relatively little attention. The classical work in the field is Thorndike's (1939) *Your City* and its development in Thorndike and Woodyard (1942), which took American cities as population units and demonstrated associations between mean population IQs and a number of indices of *per capita* income, literacy, health and crime. In Britain the first notable study was that of Burt (1937) on the populations of London boroughs which showed relationships between several social, economic and psychological variables including educational attainment but not intelligence. The only other significant study is that of Wiseman (1964) which was essentially a replication of Burt's prewar investigation but included measures of intelligence and used as its populations the boroughs of Manchester.

The present paper endeavours to extend this area of inquiry in two directions. In the first place, it presents a study of the social ecology of intelligence for the whole of the British Isles, taking different regions as the population units and examining the relationship between the mean IQs in different regions and a variety of social and economic phenomena. Secondly, it introduces historical data into the analysis and attempts to explain the contemporary associations between mean population IQ and various social and economic phenomena in terms of historical processes going back to the middle of the eighteenth century.

British Journal of Social and Clinical Psychology, (1979), 18, 1–12. Reprinted by permission.

The paper falls into three parts. First, mean population IQs are estimated for 13 subpopulations in the British Isles. Secondly, data are given for a number of social and economic phenomena and the relationships between these and mean population IQs are demonstrated and discussed. Thirdly, indices are presented of historical differences in mean population IQs and of migration between the regions and the effects of these on contemporary mean population IQs are analysed.

The Distribution of Intelligence in the British Isles

There have been three major studies of the distribution of intelligence in the regions of Great Britain. The first was carried out by Vernon (1947) from the results of the administration of Raven's Progressive Matrices to approximately 90,000 candidates for the Royal Navy during the Second World War. From these data Vernon calculated mean scores for nine geographical regions of Great Britain. The resulting mean IQs have been transformed by the writer into IQs based on an overall mean of 100 and SD of 15, and range from 102.1 for Eastern England to 97.3 for Scotland with other regions of England and Wales scoring between these two figures.

One of the problems in work on social ecology is to obtain populations for which there is a variety of economic and social data. The best populations in England and Wales from this point of view are those of the Registrar General, who divides the country into a number of "standard regions" for which considerable social data of various kinds are collected. These standard regions were altered in 1965. The regions used in the present study are the pre-1965 regions, at which time the population of England and Wales was divided by the Registrar General into 10 standard regions.

The intelligence test data reported by Vernon (1947) do not in all cases correspond precisely with the Registrar General's standard regions but consist of mean IQs for groups of counties. To transform Vernon's data to the Registrar General's regions each county was given the mean IQ of its group, and the counties were then recombined into the Registrar General's regions. For each county the mean IQ has been weighted by the population in the 1961 census to give a mean IQ for each standard region. The results of these calculations are shown in Table V.1.

The second major study of regional differences in intelligence in Britain was also carried out by Vernon (1951) and was based on the test results of approximately 9000 conscripts into the army in 1947. On this occasion the country was divided into 12 regions and the highest mean IQ was obtained by the conscripts from South-East England and the lowest by the Scots. The data have again beeen transformed into mean IQs for the Registrar General's standard regions in the same way as the Royal Navy sample, as described above, and the results are shown in Table V.1.

TABLE V.1 *Population IQs derived from three studies, overall mean IQs, and similar data derived from Davie et al. (1972)*

Region	Vernon Navy	Vernon Army	Douglas	Overall mean	Davie et al.
London–South Eastern	101.9	103.0	101.5	102.1	7.34
Eastern	102.1	101.7	101.4	101.7	7.35
East–West Ridings	101.6	101.2	100.6	101.1	7.14
Southern	100.0	101.5	101.2	100.9	7.38
North Midland	100.6	101.5	100.3	100.8	6.99
North Western	101.2	98.1	101.5	100.3	7.12
Northern	99.8	99.6	99.7	99.7	7.11
South Western	98.2	101.4	99.1	99.6	7.12
Wales	98.5	97.9	98.8	98.4	7.24
Midland	98.6	97.2	98.4	98.1	6.91
Scotland	97.3	96.6	98.1	97.3	6.73

The third study of regional differences in mean population IQ in Britain is that of Douglas (1977). This investigation took as its subjects all children born in Great Britain in the first week of March, 1946. The children have been followed up and samples tested at the ages of 8, 11 and 15. The total number of children in this investigation was approximately 5000. Two intelligence tests were given at each age, and also tests of English and arithmetic. The intelligence test means are calculated as t scores and these have been transformed into a mean IQ for each region based on an overall mean of 100 (SD 15) for the total population. The data are based on the Registrar General's regions and so no transformations are necessary. The London–South-East region and the North West obtain the highest means and Scotland the lowest. The data are shown in Table V.1.

A comparison of the data in the two Vernon studies and the Douglas study will show that the mean IQs of the regions in all three investigations are broadly consistent. There are two regions which normally obtain above-average mean IQs, namely the London–South East and the East. The remaining eight regions of England and Wales have mean IQs around 100, while in all three studies the Scottish score is the lowest. Since any particular study of population IQs is subject to sampling errors the most reliable method of obtaining an accurate measure for the regions is to take the mean of the three readings. These means are shown in Table V.1 and are proposed as the best estimates currently available of mean population IQs in the regions of Great Britain.

The reliability of the three studies of mean population IQs can be tested by intercorrelation. The correlation coefficients are as follows: Navy × Army, $r = +0.66$; Navy × Douglas, $r = +0.92$; Army × Douglas, $r = +0.68$. All three correlations are statistically significant at the 1% level.

In addition to these three studies there is one other investigation which deserves mention. This is a survey by the National Children's Bureau published by Davie, Butler and Goldstein (1972). This investigation has been concerned with all the babies born in Great Britain during the week 3–8 March, 1958 and the sample has been examined, followed up and tested over the years of childhood. At the age of 7 the children were given a copying designs test similar to the subtest in the Stanford–Binet and results are presented for the standard regions of England, Wales and Scotland. The data are not given in terms of mean˙ IQs or scores but in percentages of children falling into different score bands. It is possible to calculate approximate means from these data and these are also shown in Table V.1. As will be seen, children from the London–South East and East regions obtained high mean scores, although in this study the highest mean was obtained by the children in the Southern region of England, and the lowest score was obtained by children in Scotland. It is not possible to convert these scores into IQs because the standard deviation is not given, so they cannot be combined with the other regional data. Nevertheless, there is a correlation of 0.74, statistically significant at the 1% level, betweeen these figures and the mean IQs derived from the first three studies. Thus the National Children's Bureau results lend further confirmation to the three other investigations and the high degree of general agreement between all four studies suggests that real differences in mean IQ are present between the 11 subpopulations in Great Britain.

In order to increase coverage, sample size and general interest· it seemed desirable to extend the study to Ireland. It is convenient to divide Ireland into two populations, namely Northern Ireland and the Republic of Ireland. In Northern Ireland there have been several studies of reasonably representative samples of children and all have found lower mean IQs than in children in mainland Britain. Forbes carried out two surveys and obtained mean IQs of 91.4 and 96.9 (Forbes, 1945, 1955). Fee (1964) obtained a mean IQ of 97.4.

These three studies were all made on samples from particular geographical areas. The only investigation covering the province as a whole was made in 1969 and has been reported by Wilson (1973). The sampling procedure was to stratify all primary schools in the province by size, location and religion and from this a 10% stratified sample of children was derived. The children tested were aged 7 and 10, the numbers involved being something over 2000 for each group. The 7-year-olds were given a Moray House Picture Intelligence Test, and the 10-year-olds were given tests of verbal and non-verbal intelligence standardized by the British National Foundation for Educational Research. The mean IQs for these three tests were respectively 96.2, 100.0 and 94.0, giving an overall mean of 96.7.

Thus all the surveys of intelligence in Northern Ireland have found that the mean IQ is a little lower than in the mainland of Great Britain. Since the Wilson study is the most thorough in terms of sampling it is proposed that its result of 96.7 is adopted as the most reliable reading of the mean IQ in Northern Ireland.

In the Republic of Ireland the first major survey of intelligence was carried out in 1961 by MacNamara (1966). His sample of 928 English speaking children obtained a mean IQ of 75 on a British non-verbal intelligence test.

A second study was carried out by Hart and O'Sullivan (1970) in which the sample was 167 male adults in Dublin tested with Cattell's Culture Fair Test. The sample is a small one but it was well drawn and stratified to make the age and occupational distribution representative of the population of Dublin. The mean IQ of this sample was 88. The third major study of intelligence in the Irish Republic has been carried out by Byrt and Gill (1973, 1975). This involved the standardization of Raven's Standard Progressive Matrices on 3466 Irish children aged 6–13 drawn as a representative sample of the population from the whole of the country. The means were transformed into IQs based on British means of 100, and in all age groups the Irish children scored a little below the British. The overall mean difference is reported as approximately three IQ points, yielding a mean Irish IQ of 97. The difference between this and the British mean is statistically significant although comparatively small. Examination of the data reveals a small source of error, namely that the Irish samples were approximately 2 months older than the British standardization samples. This has led to a slight overestimation of the mean Irish IQ. Correction of the result for this error reduces the mean Irish IQ by approximately one point, giving a mean IQ of approximately 96.

The discrepancies in the three results from the Republic of Ireland are far from satisfactory. Nevertheless, we are not concerned particularly with this problem in this paper. For our own purposes it seems clear that measured intelligence in the Republic of Ireland is a little lower than in Britain. The most conservative reading of the results is to take the corrected Byrt and Gill figure of 96 as our working estimate of mean IQ in the Republic of Ireland. . . .

The Relation of Mean Population IQ to Social and Economic Variables

The mean population IQs in the 13 regions are now considered in relation to a number of social and economic phenomena. These phenomena consist of measures of intellectual achievement, *per capita* income, unemployment, infant mortality, crime and urbanization. For all these variables there is reasonably strong evidence of a relationship with intelligence at the individual level, i.e. individual intelligence is related positively to intellectual achievement, income and urbanization and negatively to infant mortality and crime. It would take considerable space to review this evidence fully but it is sufficiently well known for this to be unnecessary. The point is made to indicate that the investigation is predictive in the sense that it predicts that the known relationship of intelligence to various social and economic phenomena at the individual level will also be found at the group level. This set of predictions is reductionist in so far as it treats populations as simply aggregates of individuals.

The data are described below and are shown in Table V.2. Where possible data are taken for the year 1961, the reason for this being that 1961 was a census year for which exact population figures are available.

1. *Intellectual achievement: (a) first-class honours degrees.* All first-class honours graduates of the year 1973 were taken from all the universities in the British Isles (with the exception of graduates of Birkbeck College, a London College for mature and part-time students whose inclusion would bias the results in favour of London). Each graduate was allocated to the region where he lived between the ages of 11 and 18. This information was derived from the location of the graduate's school. Most of the data were obtained from *The Times*, which publishes annually lists of students obtaining first-class degrees and the schools they attended. Students who had been to boarding schools were written to requesting information on their home residence. Information from the Republic of Ireland universities was obtained from the college records. The total number of students obtaining first-class honours degrees was 3477, and information was obtained on place of residence for 3340 of these, representing 96.06% of the total.

There are various ways of calculating the proportions of first-class honours graduates produced by each region. Probably the most satisfactory is to express the numbers of firsts in each region per 1000 of the total age cohorts recorded in the census of 1961. In this year the cohorts were approximately 9 years old. The reason for going back to 1961 for a population base is that the criterion taken for residence is the school attended and the 1961 figures reduce the distorting effects of subsequent migration between the regions. However, the numbers in the regions have not changed appreciably during this period, so that it does not matter greatly which year is taken for picking up the total numbers of young people in the regions aged approximately 21 in 1973. (An alternative method of calculating the regional output of firsts is to express the output as a percentage of those attending university. This method yields similar figures.)

2. *Intellectual achievement: (b) Fellowships of the Royal Society.* A second measure of intellectual achievement taken for the regions is Fellowships of the Royal Society. These are well-known distinctions for scientific work in the British Isles and are open equally to citizens of both the United Kingdom and the Republic of Ireland. The population consists of all Fellows of the Royal Society elected during the period 1931–71 who were born after the year 1911. The number of individuals in this population is 321 and it proved possible to ascertain the place of birth of 98% of these. The Fellows were allocated to the region in which they were born and the numbers of Fellows born in each region were then calculated per million of the total population of the region recorded in the census of 1911. These are the data shown in Table V.2. The year 1911 was taken as the population base because the majority of the sample was born between the years 1911–20, so that the populations in 1911 represent approximately the numbers in the regions around the time most of the Fellows were

TABLE V.2 *Regional data for social and economic phenomena*

Region	Mean IQ	Fellows of the Royal Society	First class honours degrees 1973	Per capita income (£)	Unemployment	Infant mortality	Crime	Urbanization
London—South Eastern	102.1	8.7	5.32	351.1	1.0	20	21.7	91.8
Eastern	101.7	6.2	4.58	242.7	1.1	18	14.4	65.7
East—West Ridings	101.1	7.3	3.29	274.0	1.0	24	17.2	86.2
Southern	100.9	6.5	5.00	274.5	1.1	19	14.4	65.2
North Midland	100.8	5.7	3.55	271.6	1.0	20	13.8	65.8
North Western	100.3	5.7	3.83	271.9	1.6	25	18.2	91.6
Northern	99.7	5.0	2.73	240.9	2.5	23	17.7	77.2
South Western	99.6	5.2	4.39	222.9	1.4	18	13.4	61.0
Wales	98.4	4.1	3.34	232.1	2.6	24	17.0	69.1
Midland	98.1	5.2	3.11	302.2	1.4	22	17.2	83.1
Scotland	97.3	2.5	3.92	242.2	3.2	26	21.0	70.4
Northern Ireland	96.7	1.6	3.89	177.1	7.5	27	7.0	54.0
Republic of Ireland	96.0	0.6	2.18	127.1	5.7	31	5.3	37.3

born. (The populations of the regions relative to one another do not change greatly over the period, so that it does not make much difference to the results which census year is taken for the population base.)

3. Per capita *income*. Figures for *per capita* incomes for the regions of the United Kingdom are collected by the United Kingdom Inland Revenue. These have been analysed by McCrone (1965) for the standard regions of the UK for the year 1959/60. These results have been used and a figure for the Republic of Ireland calculated from the United Nations Statistical Yearbook.

4. *Unemployment*. The data are the percentages of the labour force unemployed in the regions for the year 1961 (Statistical Abstracts of the UK and of Ireland).

5. *Infant mortality*. The data are the numbers of deaths during the first year of life expressed per 1000 live births for the year 1961 (Registrar General's Reports).

6. *Crime*. The data are offences known to the police for 1961 and expressed per 1000 population (Statistical Abstracts of the UK and of Ireland).

7. *Urbanization*. The data are the percentages of the population living in county boroughs, municipal boroughs and urban districts in 1961 (Census).

These seven social and economic variables together with the figures for the mean population IQs were intercorrelated and the correlation matrix is shown in Table V.3. It will be noted that all the variables are correlated in the expected direction with the exception of the crime rates which show a positive correlation with mean population IQ. An explanation for this result is suggested below and in the meantime crime rates are excluded from consideration. Another variable whose causal relation with the rest is unclear is urbanization and this is also set aside for later consideration. The remaining six variables were factored by principal components analysis and the results are shown in Table V.4.

It is apparent that a strong first factor is present, accounting for 77% of the variance. It is suggested that the first factor should be interpreted as intelligence. This interpretation rests partly on the high loading of intelligence on the factor and partly on the considerable weight of existing evidence indicating that intelligence is a determinant of these social and economic variables. This interpretation implies that the mean population IQs should be regarded as the cause

TABLE V.3 *Product moment correlations between mean population IQ and social and economic variables. Significance levels: 0.55 > 5%, 0.68 > 1%*

1. Population IQ							
2. Fellows of the Royal Society	94						
3. First-class honours degrees	60	57					
4. *Per capita* income	73	87	54				
5. Unemployment	−82	−87	−39	−78			
6. Infant mortality	−78	−76	−68	−62	77		
7. Crime	51	64	35	82	−68	−39	
8. Urbanization	60	75	29	87	−65	−34	86

TABLE   V.4   *Principal   components
analysis*

	Factor 1
Population IQ	94
Fellows of the Royal Society	96
First-class honours degrees	70
Per capita income	87
Unemployment	−89
Infant mortality	−87
Eigenvalue (%)	76.99

of the other variables. When causal relationships between the variables are considered, it is obvious that some of the variables are dependent on others. For instance, people do not become intelligent as a consequence of getting a first-class honours degree. Rather, they get firsts because they are intelligent. The most plausible alternative causal variable, apart from IQ, is *per capita* income, since the remaining four are clearly dependent variables. The arguments against positing *per capita* incomes as the primary cause among this set of variables are twofold. First, among individuals it is doubtful whether there is any good evidence that differences in income in affluent nations are a major cause of differences in intelligence. This was the conclusion reached by Burt (1943) in a discussion of this problem. On the other hand, even Jencks (1972) admits that IQ is a determinant of income. Secondly, the very substantial increases in *per capita* incomes that have taken place in advanced Western nations since 1945 do not seem to have been accompanied by any significant increases in mean population IQ. In Britain the longest time series is that of Burt (1969) on London schoolchildren from 1913 to 1965 which showed that the mean IQ has remained approximately constant. Similarly in the United States the mean IQ of large national samples tested by two subtests from the WISC has remained virtually the same over a 16-year-period from the early 1950s to the mid-1960s (Roberts, 1971). These findings make it doubtful whether the relatively small differences in *per capita* incomes between the regions of the British Isles can be responsible for the mean IQ differences. It seems more probable that the major causal sequence is from the IQ differences to the income differences although it may be that there is also some less important reciprocal effect of incomes on IQ. This is a problem which could do with further analysis.

One point in this set of data which deserves some consideration concerns the magnitude of the regional differences in first-class honours degrees and Fellowships of the Royal Society (FsRS). On both these criteria of intellectual distinction the London–South East region scores about double the average for the regions as a whole and the two Irish regions about half, and the range between the two extremes is of the order of 400%. It may be questioned whether differences of this magnitude can be reasonably explained in terms of population differences in mean IQ of two or three points or even the 6.1 IQ points which differentiate the two extreme cases of London–South East and the Republic of Ireland. The answer to this point is that apparently trivial differences in the mean IQ of populations entail substantial differences in the proportions at the extremes of the distribution. For example, a difference of three IQ points between two populations in mean IQ entails difference of approximately 100% in the proportions of the populations falling in the IQ ranges over 130 and below 70, e.g. a population with a mean IQ of 103 has about twice as many individuals with IQs of 130+ and about half as many with IQs of less than 70 (compared with a population with a mean IQ of 100). It seems reasonable to suppose that first-class honours graduates and Fellows of the Royal Society are drawn from those with IQs over 130. If this is granted it is evident that the six IQ point disparity between London–South East and the Republic of Ireland would entail a disparity of around 400% in the proportions of the population achieving first-class honours degrees and FsRS. Thus the regional differences in intellectual achievements are broadly of the magnitude that would be expected from the differences in mean population IQ.

Causes of the Regional Differences in Mean Population IQ

We turn now to a consideration of the causes of the differences in mean population IQ in the different regions of the British Isles. These causes are not considered from the point of view of the contribution of heredity or environment and this problem is left as an open question. The causes considered here are historical. There are two hypotheses which are suggested as plausible. The first is that the contemporary mean population IQ differences are reflections of historical differences perhaps going back some considerable time and transmitted down the generations. The second hypothesis is that the contemporary mean IQ differences have arisen from the selective migration of more intelligent individuals out of some regions and into others. Since it is the London region that has the highest mean IQ it does not seem improbable that over the course of centuries intelligent individuals have migrated to London and raised the mean IQ there, while at the same time depressing the mean IQ in their own regions.

In order to test these two hypotheses it is necessary to obtain indices of mean population IQs for the regions for historical periods and also of migration. As far as population IQ is concerned it is not possible to obtain direct measures for historical periods. However, it is proposed that this problem can be overcome by taking the proportion of the population attaining some criterion of intellectual distinction as an index of the mean population IQ. It has already been shown that in the contemporary period the proportion of the population obtaining Fellowships of the Royal Society is highly correlated with the mean population IQs ($r = 0.94$) and this supports the contention that one can be taken as an approximate index of the other.

The measures obtained are termed achievement quotients because this is the most accurate description of what they are. The methods used for calculating these achievement quotients are now described. Data for the variables are shown in Table V.5.

1. *Achievement quotients, 1901.* Fellowship of the Royal Society was used as the criterion of intellectual achievement. The sample consists of all fellows born between 1891–1910. The total number is 486. Information on place of birth was obtained for 98% of the subjects. Fellows born outside the British Isles were excluded from the analysis. Achievement quotients were calculated by expressing the numbers of fellows born in each region per million of the populations recorded in the census of 1901.

2. *Achievement quotients, 1851.* For the year 1851 Fellowship of the Royal Society is no longer a usable criterion because of inadequacy of information on places of birth. An alternative criterion is entries in the Dictionary of National Biography. This is a collection of biographies of all persons of distinction born in the British Isles. The great majority of entries are people who have attained distinction by intellectual efforts and are mainly scientists, writers, artists and musicians, scholars and people in public life such as statesmen and military men. The procedure was to take all entries born in the decade 1851–60 and allocate them to the regions where they were born. There are 757 entries in total, of which 88 were born abroad and were eliminated. There were only three subjects whose place of birth could not be ascertained. This leaves a sample of 666 who were allocated to their regions of birth. Achievement quotients were calculated by expressing the number of subjects from each region per 100,000 of the populations recorded in the census of 1851.

3. *Achievement quotients, 1801.* The same method was used as for 1851. The DNB has 1586 entries born in the decade 1801–10, of whom place of birth was ascertained for 1365 representing 86% of the total. Regional populations were taken from the 1801 census for Great Britain and from Connell (1950) for Ireland (the first census in Ireland was not carried out until 1821). DNB entries were expressed as proportions of the 1801 populations for the different regions.

4. *Achievement quotients, 1751.* These were calculated as for 1801 and 1851. The DNB has 931 entries born in the decade 1751–60, of whom place of birth was ascertained for 756 representing 81% of the total. Populations were taken from Mitchell and Deane (1962) and Connell (1950). Regional achievement quotients were calculated by expressing DNB entries as proportions of the 1751 populations.

5. *Migration.* A measure of migration between the regions was obtained from the growth of population. The data are the average annual percentage increases in population from 1751 to 1951. It is assumed that rates of natural increase have been approximately constant between the regions and hence that differences in population growth are largely reflexions of net emigration or immigration. It

TABLE V.5 Achievement quotients for four historical periods and migration 1751–1951

	Achievement quotients 1751	Achievement quotients 1801	Achievement quotients 1851	Achievement quotients 1901	Migration 1751–1951
London–South Eastern	16.73	23.18	6.63	15.5	1.21
Eastern	7.16	8.48	1.95	14.2	0.68
East–West Ridings	8.75	7.42	1.45	10.5	1.20
Southern	8.18	8.99	2.39	6.8	0.96
North Midland	4.87	5.33	2.15	8.1	0.91
North Western	6.35	8.36	1.42	8.3	1.37
Northern	10.73	7.57	1.03	6.3	0.93
South Western	7.12	9.93	2.44	14.1	0.50
Wales	8.57	7.50	1.81	11.3	0.91
Midland	6.10	8.31	1.70	8.3	1.04
Scotland	10.36	16.04	3.83	8.4	0.71
Northern Ireland	2.57	2.64	0.83	2.4	0.38
Republic of Ireland	2.57	2.64	0.90	1.4	0.08

is not possible to demonstrate directly that migrations have been selective for intelligence, but evidence considered below suggests that this has been the case.

To summarize, it is assumed that historical regional differences in the achievement quotients for the years 1751, 1801, 1851 and 1901 provide indices of differences in mean population IQs and that population growth over the period 1751–1951 provides an index of migration. It is now possible to examine how far these historical variables have determined contemporary mean population IQs and also urbanization and crime rates which were left over from the analysis in the earlier part of the paper.

The relationships between the entire set of variables are best analysed by path analysis, a method of analysis which sets out a series of variables in causal sequence (Duncan, 1966). The proposed path diagram is shown in Fig. V.1. The relationship between independent and dependent variables is shown by the path coefficients. Where the variables are arranged in a simple causal chain linking one independent variable to one dependent variable, the path coefficient is the same as the product moment correlation. All the product moment correlations shown in the path diagram are statistically significant (5%: 0.55; 1%: 0.68). Where two independent variables determine one dependent variable the path coefficients are the beta coefficients determined from regression analysis. In the present path diagram there is only one case of this kind, namely the dependence of contemporary mean IQ on the achievement quotients for 1901 and migration 1751–1951. Here the multiple regression of achievement quotients for 1901 and migration 1751–1951 on contemporary IQ is 0.81 and is statistically significant at the 1% level. This indicates that 65% of the variance in contemporary regional mean IQ is determined by these two antecedent variables.

The path diagram shown in Fig. V.1 should be largely self explanatory. The important points in the diagram are as follows:

1. The achievement quotients for 1751, 1801, 1851 and 1901 are envisaged as a simple causal chain, that is to say regional achievement quotients at any point in time are significantly and substantially determined by regional achievement quotients 50 years earlier. It is suggested that the chief mechanism in this chain lies in the transmission of phenotypic intelligence from one generation to

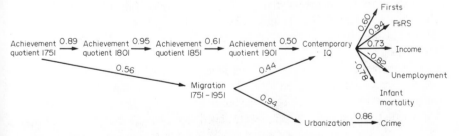

FIG. V.1 Path analysis showing hypothesized causal sequence.

the next. This transmission may take place through either environmental or genetic factors or some mixture of the two.

2. Contemporary regional mean population IQs are envisaged as being determined partly by the achievement quotients for 1901 (themselves envisaged as an index of IQs in 1901) and partly by the effects of migration over the period 1751–1951. The values of the two path coefficients linking achievement quotients for 1901 to IQ (0.50) and migration to IQ (0.44) are approximately equal, indicating that the two antecedent variables have had about the same effect on contemporary mean population IQs.

The explanation of the apparent effect of migration on contemporary mean population IQs is probably that the migration has been to some degree selective for intelligence. This explanation is supported by several studies indicating that migrants tend to have above average intelligence (e.g. Douglas, 1964; Maxwell, 1969).

3. The path linking achievement quotients for 1751 to migration 1751–1951 suggests that historical differences in mean population IQ and associated *per capita* income were causal to subsequent migrations, i.e. people have tended to migrate out of the poorer regions and into the more affluent ones. The relationship between migration and mean population IQ would therefore seem to be one of positive feedback, each variable tending to augment the other.

4. Our major concerns is with general associations between mean population IQ and social variables among this set of populations. However, the cases of Scotland and Ireland considered as individual entities may be sufficiently interesting to deserve some comment. Scotland is remarkable in so far as her relative position has deteriorated from second place in the achievement quotients for 1801 and 1851, to sixth place in 1901 and 11th place in contemporary mean IQ. This apparent decline suggests exceptionally severe selective migration of the more able. There is reasonably strong evidence that selective migration has indeed taken place since the 18th century (e.g. Clement and Robertson, 1961). In contemporary times the effect of selective migration from Scotland can be quantified from Maxwell's (1969) follow-up study on the 1000 sample tested as part of the 1947 Scottish survey of 11-year-olds. In this sample 17.2% emigrated and their mean IQ was 108.1. These figures imply a fall in the mean Scottish IQ of 1.7 points for that generation and around four IQ points over the course of a century. The apparent effect of selective migration in producing a decline in intelligence in Scotland has been discussed more fully in a separate publication (Lynn, 1977).

5. The two Irish regions show considerable regularity in coming in the last two places among the regions from 1751 to the present day. To preserve the simplicity of the model it has been assumed that this has been a consistent expression of lower mean IQ. However, the critic may argue that the low position of the Irish regions in historical times can be more reasonably explained in terms of the discrimination against the population and relative lack of educational

opportunities, rather than in terms of lower phenotypic intelligence and *per capita* income. It is difficult to see how a test could be devised to distinguish between these two hypotheses. Until such a test is made both possibilities should perhaps be left open. Either could have been responsible for the extensive emigration which has taken place from Ireland since 1846 and in which a selective element may have been present.

6. Urbanization in the regions is envisaged as a function of historical migration out of rural areas and into urban areas. Although urbanization is associated with mean population IQ it is not suggested that this is a direct causal relationship. There seems no particular reason why an urban environment should raise intelligence and it seems more parsimonious to explain the association between urbanization and mean population IQ as largely a result of migration in which there has been a selective element.

7. Crime rates are envisaged as solely a function of urbanization. The positive correlation between crime rates and mean population IQ ($r = +0.51$) is surprising in view of the many findings of a negative relation among individuals. The discrepancy may arise because the results for individuals are based on apprehended criminals and these are probably biased samples with overrepresentation of the less intelligent. On the other hand our own data are all crimes known to the police and are a more accurate measure of crime rates. When urbanization is partialled out the correlation between crime rates and mean population IQ drops to zero. Perhaps this is the true relationship between crime and intelligence.

Acknowledgements

The author is indebted to the Esmée Fairbairn Foundation for financial support for the work reported in this paper and to Dr J. W. B. Douglas for making available his intelligence test results.

References

BURT, C. (1937) *The Backward Child.* London: University Press.
BURT, C. (1943) Ability and income. *British Journal of Educational Psychology*, **13**, 83–98.
BURT, C. (1969) Intelligence and heredity: Some common misconceptions. *Irish Journal of Education*, **3**, 75–94.
BYRT, E. and GILL, P. (1973) Unpublished MA thesis, University College, Cork.
BYRT, E. and GILL, P. (1975) Article, *Irish Times*, March 20, p. 13.
CLEMENT, A. G. and ROBERTSON, R. H. S. (1961) *Scotland's Scientific Heritage.* Edinburgh: Oliver & Boyd.
CONNELL, K. H. (1950) *The Population of Ireland, 1750–1845.* Oxford: Clarendon Press.
DAVIE, R., BUTLER, N. and GOLDSTEIN, H. (1972) *From Birth to Seven.* London: Longman.
DOUGLAS, J. W. B. (1964) *The Home and the School.* London: MacGibbon & Kee.
DOUGLAS, J. W. B. (1977) Unpublished data.

DUNCAN, O. D. (1966) Path analysis: Sociological examples. *American Journal of Sociology*, 72, 1–16.

FEE, F. (1964) A survey of the intelligence and attainments of County Antrim children at the beginning of the secondary stage. Unpublished report.

FORBES, J. K. (1945) The distribution of intelligence among elementary school children in Northern Ireland. *British Journal of Educational Psychology*, 15, 39–45.

FORBES, J. K. (1955) A comparison between the qualifying examination papers in English and Arithmetic and standardised tests. In *Selection of Pupils for Secondary Schools*, Advisory Council for Education in Northern Ireland. Belfast: HMSO.

HART, I. and O'SULLIVAN, B. (1970) Inter-generational social mobility and individual differences among Dubliners. *Economic and Social Review*, 2, 1–18.

JENCKS, C. (1972) *Inequality*. New York: Basic Books.

LYNN, R. (1977) Selective emigration and the decline of intelligence in Scotland. *Social Biology*, 24, 173–182.

MacKAY, D. I. (1969) *Geographical Mobility and the Brain Drain*. London: Allen & Unwin.

MacNAMARA, J. (1966) *Billingualism and Primary Education*, Edinburgh: Edinburgh University Press.

McCRONE, G. (1965) *Scotland's Economic Progress 1951–1960*. London: Allen & Unwin.

MAXWELL, J. (1969) *The Level and Trend of National Intelligence*. London: London University Press.

MITCHELL, B. R. and DEANE, P. (1962) *Abstract of British Historical Statistics*. Cambridge: Cambridge University Press.

ROBERTS, J. (1971) Intellectual development of children as measured by the Wechsler Intelligence Scale. Washington, DC: Department of Health, Education and Welfare.

THORNDIKE, E. L. (1939) *Your City*. New York: Harcourt, Brace.

THORNDIKE, E.L. and WOODYARD, E. (1942) Differences within and between communities in the intelligence of the children. *Journal of Educational Psychology*, 33, 641–656.

VERNON, P. E. (1947) The variations of intelligence within occupation, age and locality. *British Journal of Statistical Psychology*, 1, 52–63.

VERNON, P. E. (1951) Recent investigations of intelligence and its measurement. *Eugenics Review*, 43, 125–137.

WILSON, J. A. (1973) Pupil achievement in Northern Ireland primary schools. *Irish Journal of Education*, 8, 102–116.

WISEMAN, S. (1964) *Education and Environment*. Manchester: Manchester University Press.

2

History and the Eminent Person*

D. K. SIMONTON

Abstract

Why do creative geniuses appear in some periods of history but not in others? A review of recent research suggests that various external events — including formal education, role-model availability, zeitgeist, political fragmentation, war, civil disturbances, and political instability — tend to have a critical impact on the development of creative potential in the young genius. Once that potential is established, however, and the genius enters adulthood, creative productivity tends to proceed with little interference from outside events.

WHY IS it that some periods in history are veritable "Golden Ages" replete with creative giants whereas other historical periods yield a dearth of first-rate minds? Concretely put, what are the historical circumstances responsible for the emergence of a Shakespeare, Michelangelo, Beethoven, or Aristotle? Although a number of classical and recent studies have attempted to address this question (e.g., Gray, 1958, 1966; Kroeber, 1944; Naroll, Benjamin, Fohl, Fried, Hildreth and Schaefer, 1971; Schaefer, Babu, and Rao, Note 1; Sorokin, 1937–1941), these investigations ignore what I consider to be a very critical distinction between two phases of a creator's life. On the one hand, sociocultural events may influence the productive period of a creator's life. For example, warfare may have an adverse impact on a person's creative output at a particular point in his or her career. On the other hand, sociocultural events may affect the developmental period of a creator's life, a possibility having more rich implications for understanding the foundation of creativity. Perhaps a special set of political, cultural, and social conditions is more conducive to the development of creative potential in a youthful genius. In adulthood, that creative potential then becomes fully actualized in the form of prolific and significant creative productivity. Thus, it is quite conceivable that the creative genius is either made or broken during childhood, adolescence, and early adulthood. So complete knowledge of the historical forces behind a creative genius requires that productive and developmental period influences be carefully segregated.

In a series of recent investigations I have attempted to discern the consequences of this distinction. One of the most significant findings is that developmental period influences are far more important than productive period influences.

*Gifted Child Quarterly, (1978), 22, 187–195. Reprinted by permission.

In other words, the development of creative potential is often critically affected by external events, whereas creative productivity is virtually immune from such influences. To support this generalization, let me first mention the few productive period influences which have been found, and then turn to the numerous and significant developmental period influences.

Adulthood creativity fails to be affected by a diverse array of possible influences, including personal problems or life changes (Simonton, 1977a), social honors and rewards (Simonton, 1977a), contemporary revolts or rebellions (Simonton, 1975c, 1977a), and cultural persecution (Simonton, 1975c). Moreover, of the three variables which do operate during the productive period, two are not all that surprising. Thus it is hardly astonishing that creative productivity is adversely affected by physical illness (Simonton, 1977a), nor is it utterly novel to show that creative productivity is a curvilinear inverted backwards-J function of the creator's age (Simonton, 1975a, 1977b). The remaining causal factor is war. Although a series of earlier inquiries found no relationship between war and creativity (Naroll *et al.*, 1971; Simonton, 1975c, 1976b, 1976d, 1976e, 1977b), these studies failed to distinguish several kinds of war. When such a distinction is implemented, as I have done very recently, a curious result obtains: Although balance-of-power wars fought close to the creative individual tend to discourage productivity, balance-of-power wars fought far away tend to encourage productivity (Simonton, Note 2). Whatever the substantive interpretation of this difference, the fact remains that war is the only sociocultural event which affects creativity during the productive period.

Influences on Creative Development

Nonetheless, when we survey the relationship between external events and creative development, a diversified list of influences has been found. The following seven are probably the most important:

1. Formal Education

In a multivariate analysis of the 301 eminent geniuses studied by Cox (1926), I found that achieved eminence is partly a function of the amount of formal education (Simonton, 1976a). Significantly, the precise form of this function depends on whether eminence was achieved as a creator (scientist, philosopher, writer, artist, or musician) or as a leader (soldier, statesman, revolutionary, or religious leader). For creators, eminence is a curvilinear inverted-U function of formal education. Thus formal education tends to increase creativity up to a certain point, after which it has a negative effect. Clearly some formal education greatly aids the development of creative potential, but excessive amounts may inhibit creative development by enforcing an overcommitment to traditional perspectives. This finding fits nicely with some previous research on creative development in contemporary children (e.g., Torrance, 1962). Curiously, for leadership the functional relation between eminence and formal education is strictly negative: The ultimate achievement of politicians, soldiers, and religious leaders is inhibited by the kind of training offered by colleges and universities. Incidentally, it is worth pointing out that the positive correlation which Cox (1926) found between IQ and eminence is spurious. Even though her 301 geniuses are much brighter than average – more than four standard deviations above the mean – the correlation between IQ and eminence within the sample vanishes when a time-wise sampling bias is controlled (see Simonton, 1976a). Naturally, this finding fits in better with contemporary research suggesting that above an IQ of around 120, intelligence bears little relationship with creativity.

2. Role-model Availability

Recent studies have shown that the number of eminent creators in one generation is largely a function of the number of eminent creators in the previous generation (Simonton, 1974, 1975c). In other words, the more creative individuals available for emulation when a genius is in his or her developmental period, the greater the increase in creative potential. Subsequent research has indicated that the availability of role models increases creativity largely through a single intervening variable, namely, creative precociousness (Simonton, 1977b). The greater the number of adult creators around for possible imitation, the sooner the youthful genius begins producing creative works. This creative precociousness then leads to enhanced creative productivity and creative longevity, which in turn raise the eventual level of achieved eminence. Although role-model availability tends to increase creative eminence, two additional research findings indicate the complexity of its impact. In the first place, and most obviously, the effectiveness of role models depends on the discipline. Certainly a precocious musical genius is going to be more influenced by those geniuses in the preceding generation whose achievements are also musical rather than scientific or literary. Interestingly, when creativity in one discipline does influence creative development in another discipline, the impact is not always beneficial. For instance, there is evidence that the number of religious leaders in one generation has a negative effect on the number of philosophers to emerge in the next generation (Simonton, Note 3). Thus religious activity is not conducive to creative development in philosophy, probably because religious leaders provide "negative role models" of philosophical thinking (cf. Simonton, 1975b, 1976d). The second complication in the relation between role-model availability and creativity is that the former variable can have certain adverse effects as well. For example, even though philosophical creativity is increased if a genius has many philosophers as role models during his or her developmental phase, attainment of the highest ranks as a thinker may be hindered by an excess of role models (Simonton, 1976e). What seems to happen is that a potential genius may make a premature commitment to a particular school of thought, that is, the youth may become a disciple rather than break completely new ground (also see Simonton, 1977b). Hence, even though role-model availability has a generally positive effect on creative development, its impact can be reversed when we consider those creators in the highest of all ranks.

3. Zeitgeist

In one study I attempted to determine the relationship between the fame of a given thinker and the prevailing zeitgeist (Simonton, 1976e). Is it the case that the major minds in the history of ideas tend to be ahead of their time? Or is it the case that the major figures in intellectual history tend to be highly representative of their contemporary zeitgeist? A multivariate analysis of 2012 famous thinkers in Western history revealed a surprising result. The answer to both of these questions is "no"! Rather than epitomize the prevailing beliefs and mores of their generation, and rather than be precursors of the subsequent generation's zeitgeist, the most eminent philosophers tend to be *behind* their times. Unlike the lesser thinker, the major thinker seems to be most influenced by the zeitgeist which dominated the intellectual scene during his or her developmental period. What seems to be happening is that the most famous thinkers are synthesizers who take the accomplishments of the preceding generation and consolidate them into a single, unified philosophical system. Because the most eminent intellects are thus preoccupied with elaborating the ideas to which they were exposed during their developmental period, these thinkers tend to be least representative of their contemporary zeitgeist and of future intellectual trends.

4. Political Fragmentation

In a pioneer cross-historical investigation, Naroll *et al.* (1971) tried to discover what political and economic circumstances are most favorable to creativity in four civilizations. The one variable found to have a consistent effect was political fragmentation, or the number of independent states into which a civilization is divided in any given century. Unfortunately, Naroll *et al.* used rather large time-wise units, and therefore they could not determine whether political fragmentation acts on creative productivity or on creative development. Nonetheless, I have argued that political fragmentation indicates a large amount of cultural diversity and that cultural diversity tends to nurture the development of creativity (Simonton, 1974, 1975c). Such cultural diversity tends to encourage the capacity for divergent thinking, remote association, breadth of perspective, and related cognitive attributes required for a fully developed creative potential. Although the evidence is not unambiguous (Simonton, 1976c, 1976e), one transhistorical study of 5000 creators from Western civilization has shown that political fragmentation may indeed more significantly affect creative development than creative productivity (Simonton, 1975c): If the number of sovereign political units increases, the number of eminent creators tends to increase after about a 20-year lag. But political fragmentation apparently does a lot more than encourage creative development, since the philosophical beliefs of eminent thinkers may be influenced by the amount of political fragmentation prevailing in their youth. In a cross-lagged correlation analysis I found that thinkers who grow up in times of political fragmentation are more likely as adult creators, to espouse empiricism, skepticism, materialism, temporalism (e.g., evolutionary change), nominalism, singularism (viz., individualism) and the ethics of happiness (e.g., hedonism or utilitarianism) (Simonton, 1976f). So not only does political fragmentation tend to heighten creative development, but additionally it tends to shape the content of the creator's intellectual base.

5. War

The ideology of the mature thinker is also influenced by the occurrence of warfare during the stage of creative development. In fact, the impact of war on the youthful genius is virtually the opposite from that of political fragmentation. Thinkers whose early years were characterized by constant warfare tend to be *less* likely to advocate empiricism, skepticism, materialism, temporalism, nominalism, singularism, and the ethics of happiness (Simonton, 1976f). Thus while political fragmentation tends to encourage the development of a mind open to experience, change, individualism, and material welfare, war tends to discourage such intellectual qualities.

6. Civil Disturbances

Yet a third political variable tends to affect the ideology of the adult creator by influencing the course of creative development. Thinkers whose youth was surrounded by popular revolts, rebellions, and revolutions tend to adopt highly polarized philosophical positions as adults (Simonton, 1976f). On the one hand, some thinkers exposed to civil turmoil may become extremely committed to the ideas of empiricism, skepticism, materialism, temporalism, nominalism, singularism, determinism, and the ethics of happiness. On the other hand, some thinkers exposed to the same events may become strongly devoted to the ideas of rationalism or mysticism, idealism, eternalism (i.e., unchanging reality), realism (in the medieval sense), universalism (e.g., collectivism or socialism), indeterminism (viz., free will), and the ethics of principles. Even though civil disturbances thus polarize the forthcoming generation in quite contrary directions, the intriguing fact remains that such political events have a truly potent effect on creative development. The exposure to political conflict seems to instill the need to take extreme stances on philosophical issues as well. Given this finding, it is perhaps not surprising that civil disorder also encourages general creative development, as one empirical study has shown (Simonton, 1975c). That is, eminent creators in Western history tend to be most likely to grow up in times of revolts, rebellions, and revolutions, especially those directed against large empire states. Such disturbances seem to heighten cultural diversity in a given civilization (Simonton, 1975c; cf. Simonton, 1976c).

7. Political Instability

So far we have not mentioned any political events which might hinder the development of creative potential in the youthful genius. But imagine, if you will, a political milieu where violent conflict among the ruling elite is the natural order of things, where a coup d'etat by some military figure is commonplace, where political assassinations are the norm, or where strife among rival claimants to the throne is chronic. Such political instability might well prove detrimental to the development of creative potential. And two recent studies have actually shown that political instability, while having no appreciable impact on creative productivity, does damage the prospects for creativity in the forthcoming generation. The first study examined 5000 eminent creators in Western civilization and discovered that such creators were less likely to grow up in times of political instability (Simonton, 1975c). The second study focused on 2012 thinkers and revealed that the most famous intellects in Western history tend not to grow up in times of political instability (Simonton, 1976e). Thus, coups d'etat, military revolts, dynastic conflicts, political assassinations, and like internecine struggles among the powers-that-be tend to decrease both the number of creators and the quality of those creators who survive the adverse circumstances. Why? It seems that to be creative requires the belief that the world is somewhat predictable and controllable, and accordingly that personal efforts will eventually prove fruitful, even if only in the long run. In terms of Rotter's (1966) External–Internal dimension, creative individuals probably must feel they have internal locus of control. When a young genius is exposed to political anarchy, this internalistic disposition may fail to develop. Hence, the ultimate impact of political instability is to destroy the development of creative potential, and thereby undermine the prospects for achievement in adulthood.

Conclusion

It must be stressed that research on the sociocultural context of creative development is a relatively recent enterprise. So future research may add many more influences, including economic and demographic factors. Still, the evidence gathered to date allows us to conclude that sociocultural conditions play a significant part in the development of creative potential in the youthful genius. The following three socio-psychological processes are especially central to creative development:

1. The potential genius must have access to numerous role models very early in life. Without such models, the genius may have a lower probability of being precocious, and such precociousness is apparently essential to creative productivity and longevity in adulthood.

2. Exposure to cultural diversity also seems to nourish the precocious youth. Thus, on the one hand, political fragmentation and civil disturbances tend to increase creative potential by injecting an awareness of diverse perspectives, whereas excessive formal education can harm creative potential by placing too much emphasis on a restricted range of solutions to creative problems.

3. The young genius adapts to the political environment by generating a set of philosophical beliefs. Should the genius grow up to become a thinker, these intellectual adaptations will influence his or her philosophical leanings. Even more importantly, certain political events may produce an ideological disposition which proves antithetical to adulthood creativity. This latter possibility may be illustrated by the manner in which political instability inhibits creative development by producing a fatalistic *Weltanschauung* in the would-be genius.

So, to offer a partial response to the question posed at this paper's outset, the Golden Ages of history may have given the young genius the necessary role models, the cultural diversity, and the philosophical commitment essential to the development of creative potential. This potential was then merely actualized in adulthood without much hinderance or help from external events.

Notes

1. SCHAEFER, J. M., BABU, M. C. and RAO, N. S. (1977) *Sociopolitical causes of creativity in India 500 BC–1800 AD: A regional time-lagged study.* Paper presented at the meeting of the International Studies Association, St. Louis, March.
2. SIMONTON, D. K. (1977) *Techno-scientific activity and war: A yearly time-series analysis.* Manuscript submitted for publication.
3. SIMONTON, D. K. (1974) *International networks among creative disciplines: a cross-lagged correlation analysis.* Unpublished manuscript, University of Arkansas, November.

References

COX, C. (1926) *The early mental traits of three hundred geniuses.* Stanford: Stanford University Press.
GRAY, C. E. (1958) An analysis of Graeco-Roman development: The epicyclical evolution of Graeco-Roman civilization. *American Anthropologist,* 60, 13–31.
GRAY, C. E. (1966) A measurement of creativity in Western civilization. *American Anthropologist,* 68, 1384–1417.
KROEBER, A. L. (1944) *Configurations of culture growth.* Berkeley: University of California Press.

NAROLL, R., BENJAMIN, E. C., FOHL, F. K., FRIED, M. J., HILDRETH, R. E. and SCHAEFER, J. M. (1971) Creativity: A cross-historical pilot survey. *Journal of Cross-Cultural Psychology*, 2, 181–188.

ROTTER, J. B. (1966) Generalized expectancies for internal versus external control of reinforcement. *Psychological Monographs*, 80, (1, Whole No. 609).

SIMONTON, D. K. (1974) *The social psychology of creativity: An archival data analysis.* Unpublished doctoral dissertation, Harvard University.

SIMONTON, D. K. (1975a) Age and literary creativity: A cross-cultural and trans-historical survey. *Journal of Cross-Cultural Psychology*, 6, 259–277.

SIMONTON, D. K. (1975b) Interdisciplinary creativity over historical time: A correlational analysis of generational fluctuations. *Social Behavior and Personality*, 3, 181–188.

SIMONTON, D. K. (1975c) Sociocultural context of individual creativity: A transhistorical time-series analysis. *Journal of Personality and Social Psychology*, 32, 1119–1133.

SIMONTON, D. K. (1976a) Biographical determinants of achieved eminence: A multivariate approach to the Cox data. *Journal of Personality and Social Psychology*, 33, 218–226.

SIMONTON, D. K. (1976b) The casual relation between war and scientific discovery: An exploratory cross-national analysis. *Journal of Cross-Cultural Psychology*, 7, 133–144.

SIMONTON, D. K. (1976c) Ideological diversity and creativity: A re-evaluation of a hypothesis. *Social Behavior and Personality*, 4, 203–207.

SIMONTON, D. K. (1976d) Interdisciplinary and military determinants of scientific productivity: A cross-lagged correlation analysis. *Journal of Vocational Behavior*, 9, 53–62.

SIMONTON, D. K. (1976e) Philosophical eminence, beliefs, and zeitgeist: An individual-generational analysis. *Journal of Personality and Social Psychology*, 34, 630–640.

SIMONTON, D. K. (1976f) The sociopolitical context of philosophical beliefs. A trans-historical casual analysis. *Social Forces*, 54, 513–523.

SIMONTON, D. K. (1977a) Creative productivity, age, and stress: A biographical time-series of 10 classical composers. *Journal of Personality and Social Psychology*, 35, 791–804.

SIMONTON, D. K. (1977b) Eminence, creativity, and geographic marginality: A recursive structural equation model. *Journal of Personality and Social Psychology*, 35, 805–816.

SOROKIN, P. A. (1937–1941) *Social and cultural dynamics* (4 vols.). New York: American Book.

TORRANCE, E. P. (1962) *Guiding creative talent.* Englewood Cliffs: Prentice-Hall.

3

The Scientific Elite:
Nobel Laureates' Mutual Influences*

H. ZUCKERMAN

. . . LAUREATES, like other members of the scientific elite, studied in a comparatively small number of colleges and universities. This concentration resulted from the jointly operating processes of self-selection by the future scientists and selective recruitment by the academic institutions. Though sometimes subject to socioeconomic constraints that limited their range of choice, the eventual laureates tended first to seek out the institutions of reputation for undergraduate study and then turned, in even greater proportions, to the outstanding departments in their field for graduate study. Postdoctoral study involved a third phase in this joint process of self-selection and selective recruitment, which contributed even more to the observed pattern of apprenticeship of the laureates-to-be to older laureates.

The filiation of laureates can thus be thought of as the result of mutual search by young scientists of promise and by their prospective masters. Both apprentices and masters were engaged in a motivated search to find and then to work with scientists of talent.

The most striking fact in the process of self-selection is that future members of the ultra-elite were clearly tuned in to the scientific network early in their careers. The laureates' reports on their own early experiences indicate how much this was the case. A laureate in physics contrasted the basis for his own choice of a potential master with that of his less knowledgeable classmates: "Many of the students were just silly about the way they choose professors. They just didn't know the professors of real quality. They were very innocent. I was far from innocent and made my own judgment of quality." Along the same lines, another physicist laureate reported: "I was attracted by his name. I knew enough about physics to appreciate him and to appreciate his style of work." (It happens that both were referring to Enrico Fermi who, it will be remembered, had no fewer than six graduate students and junior collaborators go on to become Nobel laureates. They did not come to him by chance.)

The laureates, in their comparative youth, sometimes went to great lengths to make sure that they would be working with those they considered the best in

*Reprinted by permission of the author, Harriet Zuckerman, The Free Press (1979).

their field. The case of the physicist C. N. Yang is a bit extreme, but it illustrates the deeply motivated search for the particular master rather than only for the outstanding graduate department or university ambience.

At the age of 23, a student at the Southwest Associated University in Kunmiṅg, a provincial city in southwest China, Yang resolved to continue his graduate studies with Fermi and Eugene Wigner. Arriving in New York late in 1945, Yang went directly to Columbia University, in the belief that Fermi was still there. In fact, Fermi had during the war years been engaged in research on the atomic bomb at the University of Chicago and Los Alamos. That research beïng top secret, no one at Columbia could tell Yang of Fermi's doings or even of his whereabouts. Yang went on to Princeton University, only to discover that Wigner, a member of Princeton's department of physics, was also away (as it happens, also at work on the Manhattan project, first at Chicago and then at Oak Ridge). At Princeton, Yang heard the "rumor" that Fermi would head up a new institute at the University of Chicago. Continuing his quest, Yang finally found himself sitting in Fermi's class in January 1946. He got to see a good deal of Fermi, who explained that he could not supervise Yang's thesis work since he himself was still occupied with "highly classified research." Fermi then directed Yang to Edward Teller, another physicist in the network of talented scientists at Chicago, who helped turn Yang's attention from experimental physics, at which he was plainly not his best, to theoretical physics, where he was plainly better than most (Bernstein, 1962, p. 49ff.).

This episode brings out a major aspect of the search for an appropriate master. Clearly, Yang knew what he was about, having been socialized perhaps in the ways of science by his mathematician father. By the time Yang began his search, Fermi had been a laureate for seven years and so had acquired a heightened visibility that extended to bright young students of physics even in remote China. It is therefore not surprising that Yang knew of Fermi's distinctive contributions to the field and, further, that he elected to work with so conspicuous a star. What is perhaps more revealing is that he also wanted to work with Wigner who, though he had by then gone far with his ultimately prizewinning work on nuclear structure, was visible only among physicists and was not to receive his Nobel for another twenty years (ironically, a dozen years after Yang received *his* prize).

Thus the case of Yang illustrates a general pattern. The young scientists who would later receive Nobel prizes were tuned in early to the major channels of communication about new developments in their fields. They knew the most significant work that was being done, where it was being done, and by whom. . . . In fully 69% of all cases of apprenticeship with laureates, the young laureates-to-be had chosen their masters *before* the masters' important work was conspicuously "validated" and made fully visible by the award of a Nobel prize. The fact that as many as thirty of the forty-eight Americans who had laureate masters did so as postdoctorates rather than as graduate students suggests that even they needed a little time to learn precisely who was working on what they wanted to study. . . .

The eventual laureates, in their youth, had a discriminating eye for the masters of their craft as well as for the major universities and departments doing work at the frontiers of the field. . . . Early in their careers, the laureates-to-be searched out scientists who, as we now know, were destined to move into the Nobel elect. But at the time the majority had not yet done so. In this respect, these informed young scientists, at the time of their apprenticeships, were able to identify scientific talent of Nobel caliber. It is less clear whether their fellow students made the same choices. Especially at great universities, many students seek out scientific stars with whom they hope to work, and many are turned away. Thus self-selection is only one component in the process of linking masters and apprentices.

For various reasons, the choices of masters by would-be apprentices were not always reciprocated. We have already seen, for example, how Yang almost missed out on working with Fermi and actually did miss out on working with Wigner. In this case, the constraints that kept his preferred choices from being realized were external to the masters themselves. But in other cases, the potential masters themselves refused to accept as apprentices many of those who wanted to work with them, even those of obvious talent. For example, it was evident even to tyros that, long before he was awarded the prize, Percy Bridgman had "occupied the field of the physics of high pressure all by himself," as the laureate-to-be Edward Purcell put it. But Bridgman's solitary style of scientific work was such that neither Purcell, had he been so minded when he studied at Harvard, nor other young scientists of talent had much prospect of becoming his apprentice. As the *Dictionary of Scientific Biography* notes:

> The desire for full personal involvement in the experiment probably also accounted for Bridgman's reluctance to do joint research or to take on thesis students. He rarely had more than two at a time; the record shows fourteen doctoral theses on high-pressure topics, in addition to several on other subjects that he supervised. He was usually most pleased when least consulted [Kemble, Birch, and Holton, 1970, v. II, p. 459].

Such nonreciprocation of choices means that the selection of *future* laureate masters would have been even higher . . . had the would-be apprentices had their way. The pattern of young talent identifying older talent is thus even more marked than the surface figures indicate.

Correlatively, some of the future laureate masters of future laureates contributed to the observed pattern by actively searching for youngsters of talent. If his lonely style of work helps to explain why Bridgman had "only" one future laureate as an apprentice — John Bardeen — then Fermi's style of work helps to explain why he had as many as six. For, as Segrè has observed, Fermi actively sought out younger co-workers of ability: "Fermi . . . decided that he needed some pupils — what we call graduate students. He decided also that they had to be seriously interested in physics and of reasonable ability so that his time would not be wasted. Given the right quality, he would see to it that they were taught" (Segrè, n.d., p. 2).

In other words, just as the younger laureates-to-be were able to assess the achievements of the older laureates-to-be, so the older ones were able to assess the potentialities of the younger ones. In some cases, the master served as scientific talent scouts or "truffle dogs" (Merton, 1960, pp. 308–309). The story told about I. I. Rabi's encounter with the young Julian Schwinger is a case in point. In 1936 the 18-year-old Schwinger, then an undergraduate at the City College of New York, chanced to accompany a friend to Columbia who wanted to transfer to the department of physics there. Rabi, still eight years away from his Nobel prize, talked to the young men and soon turned his attention chiefly to Schwinger rather than to his friend, who had initiated the interview. Rabi found Schwinger knowledgeable in physics far beyond his years. More important, he noted Schwinger's capacity to think mathematically and his ingenuity in mathematical formulation. Rabi soon arranged for Schwinger to enter Columbia College and eventually to earn his doctorate at the University. By the time Schwinger was a graduate student, his gifts were evident to anyone who cared to look. As his fellow student Mitchell Wilson (1969) wrote in retrospect, Schwinger "was at once so obviously in a class by himself that no one bothered to envy him. One thing, each of us assured the others: eventually, he would earn a Nobel Prize." With his record of having identified many distinguished physicists, including the laureates Kusch and Schwinger, Rabi must be counted among the more successful scientific truffle dogs. Even so, the question remains open of how clear the signals of scientific promise actually are. The existence of ample numbers of "comers" who never made the grade and of smaller numbers of "late bloomers" suggests that there is considerable noise in the evaluation system and that judgments of scientific promise by the elite are far from perfect.

The joint processes of self-selection and social selection making for entry into the scientific ultra-elite did not always proceed smoothly. Error in early evaluation of scientific talent involved its own kind of vicissitudes. Thus James D. Watson, widely known as the co-discoverer of the structure of DNA, reports that in 1947 he had applied for admission to graduate school both at Cal Tech, whose "Biology Division was loaded with good geneticists," and at Harvard, where he had applied "without considering what he might find." He was refused admission to both. In retrospect, Watson found Harvard's rejection of him fortunate. For had he gone there, he "would have found no one excited by the gene and so might have been tempted to go back into natural history." Guided by his mentor at the University of Chicago, the human geneticist Herluf Strandskov, Watson applied to Indiana University, where he was to find the renowned geneticist H. J. Muller and two first-rate young geneticists, Salvador Luria and Tracey Sonneborn.

This episode has a particular interest for us in tracing the processes underlying the striking statistic that 68% of apprenticeships involved master scientists who had not yet gotten their prize. Having missed out on working with one laureate-to-be, Beadle at Cal Tech (who was not to receive his prize for another eleven years), it now appeared that Watson would be working with an actual laureate, Muller at Indiana (who had gotten a prize just the year before). Watson would then have slipped out of the category of those young laureates-to-be who recognized talent of a high order that had not yet been "validated" by a Nobel. But soon after he arrived at Indiana, Watson decided that although it first "seemed natural that I should work with Muller . . . I soon saw that Drosophila's better days were over and that many of the best younger geneticists, among them Sonneborn and Luria, worked with micro-organisms." We can continue to trace, in Watson's own words, the way in which his own judgment of comparative opportunities for training led to his ultimate choice of a master at Indiana:

> The choice among the various research groups was not obvious at first, since the graduate-student gossip reflected unqualified praise, if not worship, of Sonneborn. In contrast, many students were afraid of Luria who had the reputation of being arrogant toward people who were wrong. Almost from Luria's first lecture, however, I found myself much more interested in his phages than in the Paramecia of Sonneborn. Also, as the fall term wore on I saw no evidence of the rumored inconsiderateness toward dimwits. Thus with no real reservations (except for occasional fear that I was not bright enough to move in his circle) I asked Luria whether I could do research under his direction in the spring term. He promptly said yes and gave me the task of looking to see whether phages inactivated by X-rays gave any multiplicity reactivation [1966, pp. 239–40].

Watson's experiences thus delineate the kind of informed search that led many eventual laureates to be apprenticed to already arrived or prospective laureates. Had Watson been admitted to his first choice of Cal Tech, he would probably have studied with the laureate-to-be George Beadle and would thus have appeared as another case making up the dominant pattern. . . . Rejected at Cal Tech, Watson might have persisted in his trial choice of the laureate Muller at Indiana, thus contributing to the minor pattern. . . . But appraising the kinds of work that held most promise for fundamental advances in biology, Watson made the (reciprocated) choice of working under the yet-to-be-laureate, Luria. (This placed him definitely in the dominant pattern of laureate masters and apprentices.) Finally, through the sponsorship of Luria, Watson spent summers at the famous summer phage course instituted at Cold Spring Harbor by Max Delbrück (who later shared a Nobel prize with Luria). Thus Watson ends up as another laureate who had studied with laureates-to-be.

Watson's case is instructive in still another respect. Some laureates believe that luck played an important role in their having found congenial mentors and congenial places to work. And so it must seem in individual cases. Watson himself has not embraced the "luck" hypothesis, but his case perhaps may illustrate why that hypothesis is often unsound. Watson did not know about Sonneborn or Luria while he was still at Chicago and therefore could not have chosen Indiana to study with them. But the fact that a Sonneborn or a Luria happened to be there is not altogether accidental. As we have seen, excellent scientists tend to converge on a small number of places where the other excellent scientists, such as H. J. Muller, are at work. And this was so even though Sonneborn and Luria may already have been convinced that they would be post-Mullerian geneticists rather than traditional *Drosophila* specialists. (It also turns out that Renato Dulbecco, laureate in medicine in 1975, was working in Luria's laboratory that year.) So the fact that Watson found a mentor at Indiana worthy of his mettle was probably not the result of luck but rather of the joint processes of self-selection and selective recruitment that we have repeatedly noted.

From such processes of self-selection and selective recruitment there results the observed pattern of more than half of the American laureates having been apprenticed to laureates, 69% of these apprenticeships before the masters had yet won the prize. These patterns of apprenticeship in turn link up with the careers of laureates-to-be. . . .

Socialization for the Scientific Elite

The importance that these members of the scientific elite attach to their apprenticeships is perhaps better indicated by their behavior at the time than by what they said about them in our interviews much later. As we have seen, they often exerted great effort to find their way to masters at the forefront of their fields, typically masters who were already in the aristocracy of science or would become members of it before long. We now turn to the evidence provided in our detailed interviews to find out what actually went on in the interaction between masters and apprentices, what this meant for the quality of scientific work the apprentices went on to do, and how it contributed to their mobility into the elite.

Education, Training, and Socialization

. . . One point on which the laureates are largely agreed is that the least important aspect of their apprenticeship was the acquiring of substantive knowledge from their master. Some even reported that in the limited sense of information and knowledge of the scientific literature, apprentices, focused on one or another problem, sometimes "knew more" than their masters. A laureate in chemistry speaks for many of them:

> It's the contact: seeing how they operate, how they think, how they go about things. [Not the specific knowledge?] Not at all. It's learning a style of thinking, I guess. Certainly not the specific knowledge; at least not in the case of Lawrence. There were always people around who knew more than he did. It wasn't that. It was a method of work that really got things done.

A physicist sums up the difference between the learning of specifics and the learning of a style of qualitatively distinctive thought as a difference between the techniques and the traditions of major scientific work:

> I knew the techniques of research. I knew a lot of physics. I had the words, the libretto, but not quite the music. In other words, I have not been in contact with men who were deeply imbedded in the tradition of physics; men of high quality. This was my first real contact with first-rate creative minds at the high point of their power.

Thus the laureates testify that for them the principal benefit of apprenticeship was a wider orientation that included standards of work and modes of thought. They report, in effect, that the apprenticeship was a time of what social scientists call socialization. Socialization includes more than is ordinarily understood by education or by training: it involves acquiring the norms and standards, the values and attitudes, as well as the knowledge, skills, and behavior patterns associated with particular statuses and roles. It is, in short, the process through which people are inducted into a culture or subculture.

Like other scientists, then, the future laureates were continuing their socialization in the culture of science. But, unlike most other scientists, they were also being prepared to take a distinctive place in the forefront of science. In terms of social stratification, they were being socialized for a position in the aristocracy of science. Seldom explicit, this was often tacitly understood. Although it was far from evident, of course, during the time of their apprenticeship that they would become Nobel laureates, it was largely understood that, with few exceptions, they would become very good rather than run-of-the-mill scientists. For, by the time they got to their masters, they had already given evidence of uncommon scientific ability. . . .

Standards of Performance

Even before they found their way to the masters with whom they studied and worked most closely, these young scientists had acquired fairly demanding standards for judging scientific work. Still, with few exceptions, the future laureates report that their standards for assessing performance, their own as well as others', became considerably more exacting in the course of their advanced socialization. The biochemist Hans Krebs reflects:

> If I ask myself how it came about that one day I found myself in Stockholm, I have not the slightest doubt that I owe this good fortune to the circumstance that I had an oustanding teacher at the critical stage in my scientific career. . . . Otto Warburg set an example in the methods and quality of first-rate research. Without him I am sure I would never have reached those standards which are prerequisites for being considered by the Nobel committees [1967, p. 1244].

From the interviews with laureates, it appears that the acquiring of these elevated standards came about in three mutually reinforcing ways: the masters' own performance provided a model to be emulated; the masters evoked excellence from the apprentices working with them, and they were severe critics of scientific work.

To begin with, the masters generally served as role models, teaching less by precept than by example. By themselves adhering to demanding standards of work, they sustained the moral authority to pass severe judgments on work that failed to meet comparable standards. As one physicist remembered his teacher: "You tried to live up to him. It was wonderful to watch him at work. Sometimes I eventually did things the way he did."

The authority of masters gained or reinforced through their own exemplary behavior enabled them to serve as "evokers of excellence": bringing out the best in others and, by their own report, eliciting better performance than ordinarily occurs (Merton, 1960, p. 341ff.).

The evoking of excellence by these elite masters had its own dynamics. As role models for the younger scientists, the masters sometimes led them to levels of accomplishment they could not ordinarily imagine for themselves. A physicist laureate and apprentice to Enrico Fermi described the experience in this way:

> If you worked with him, it was as if you were a mediocre tennis player and you were playing with a champion. You would do shots that you had never dreamt of. He got quite a few suggestions of important things from his collaborators but there people were just – I don't know, the solution developed in ten minutes with him, you see.

In part, the elite masters evoked superior performance by conveying through their own behavior a sense of how much could be achieved in scientific inquiry and what it was like to do scientific work of importance. In part, they did so by inducing a feeling of obligation, a sense of reciprocity requiring the apprentice to justify through the quality of his work the master's decision to invest time and effort in training him. The need to reciprocate in this way was reinforced by periodic signals from masters, not least through their comments on other students, that they had little interest in continuing to work with apprentices who were satisfied with routine performance.

A laureate in medicine described his reinforced motivation to live up to the exceedingly high standards of performance set by H. H. Dale and L. J. Henderson:

> Both were men of great intellectual and personal stature. Each one was so tremendous an individual that you could not help but be impressed. You worked much harder because you felt it was the only thing that was fair to them.

. . . To summarize, the elite apprentices of elite scientists internalized exacting standards of work through several related processes. They emulated the masters whose own work exemplified those standards; they were led to see things they did not know they knew and to have ideas of a kind they had not had before through the evocative behavior of the masters; and they experienced these elevated standards in practice by having their own work severely evaluated. In the process, they acquired scientific taste, another mark of the scientists being prepared for their roles at the frontiers of scientific development.

Scientific Taste and Styles of Work

Like other departments of culture, science has its own esthetic. Among the elite scientists, the prime criteria of scientific taste are a sense for the "important problem" and an appreciation of stylish solutions. For them, deep problems and elegant solutions distinguish excellent science from the merely competent or commonplace.

Looking back on their apprenticeships, the laureates typically emphasize that they were able to acquire a better sense of the significant problem. This occurred through the same processes of socialization we have been examining. For example, here is a laureate in physics referring to a role model:

> A great scientist is someone who is working on the right thing and the important thing. Millikan was an outstanding example of this, a man who could pick out the important things. He opened up what later turned out to be large and very important fields in physics. He had a knack for finding what was important to look into.

It is one thing to observe this "knack," another to acquire it oneself. Again, it appears that this is not a matter of didactic instruction but, rather, one of intuition. For this set of creative scientists, learning to identify good problems occasionally involved a growing awareness of the importance of timing and feasibility in selecting significant questions for investigation. . . .

In the scientific genealogies of the laureates, we noted the numerous sequences of elite masters and apprentices extending over several generations. We now see that aspects of scientific taste are transmitted along chains of masters and apprentices, aided by the apprentices' strong identification with their teachers (sometimes involving what is, for them, a thorough hero worship). Thus, the German laureate in medicine (1931) Otto Warburg reminisces about his master:

> The most important event in the life of a young scientist is personal contact with the great scientists of his time. Such an event happened in my life when Emil Fischer, the second scientist to be awarded the Nobel prize in chemistry, 1902, accepted me in 1903 as a co-worker in protein chemistry, which at that time was at the height of its development. During the following three years, I met Emil Fischer almost daily. . . . I learned that a scientist must have the courage to attack the great unsolved problems of his time, and that solutions usually have to be forced by carrying out innumerable experiments without much critical hesitation [1965, p. 531].

What the laureate-to-be Warburg reports having learned from his master, the laureate Fischer, is in turn largely reiterated by Warburg's own apprentice, the British laureate in medicine (1953) Hans Krebs:

> If I try to summarize what I learned in particular from Warburg I would say he was to me an example of asking the right question, of forging new tools for tackling the chosen problems, of being ruthless in self-criticism and of taking pains in verifying facts, of expressing results and ideas clearly and concisely and of altogether focusing his life on true values [1967, pp. 1245–1246].

Identifying a good problem takes these scientists some distance toward making an important contribution but, as they testify, not the whole way. They must also have a sense of how good solutions look. An excess of concern with precision can easily be mistaken for experimental elegance. As a laureate student of the chemist G. N. Lewis reported: "He led me to look wherever possible for important things rather than to work on endless detail or to do work just to improve accuracy.". . .

In composite, the interviews with the American laureates indicate the ways in which association with elite masters form scientific taste. A sense for "the right kind of question" and for the character of its solution develops during the interaction between masters and apprentices and among the apprentices themselves as they pass judgment on the quality of scientific work, new and old, their own and that of others. It develops also as they speculate about the direction their field "should take," identify gaps in basic knowledge, and argue about which problems are "ripe" for solution at the time and which are not. These matters are of evident and prime interest to scientists who intend to help shape the fields in which they work: they might be of less interest to scientists who see themselves playing a more modest role. The substantive aspect of the process of socialization, involving a concern with such basic issues and problems, is congruent with the self-images of the future laureates as scientists located actually or potentially on the advancing frontiers of their special fields.

Thus, the elite masters shape their apprentices and prepare them for elite status by inculcating and reinforcing in them not only cognitive substance and skills but the values, norms, self-images, and expectations that they take to be appropriate for this stratum in science.

Socialization and Self-Confidence

The laureates who have lived through the process of stringent socialization with elite masters typically emerge as scientists even more confident of their own abilities than before. Without much self-consciousness, they declare that they almost always know a good problem when they come upon it, that they can cope with failure and on occasion transform it into success, and that they are not deeply disturbed by periods of scientific infertility, which they tend to see as fallow times before a new harvest.

Their self-confidence, the laureates typically report, was increased through study with master scientists. In part, it is a result of early success, as these young scientists discover that they are really quite good at their job. As apprentices to scientists for whom good research is commonplace and exceptional research not unusual, these future laureates have often had the opportunity to take part in important work. One of them put it this way: "I learned that it was just as difficult to do an unimportant experiment, sometimes more difficult, than an important one." And the experience of success, validated by the judgments of demanding masters as well as of peers, heightens confidence in their own capabilities as it reinforces their commitment to science.

Their confidence is also reinforced in the course of a demanding apprenticeship, by comparing themselves, as young scientists, to "the best" in the field and finding that they measure up reasonably well. Along these lines, a laureate in physics remarked on his association with two older Nobelists: "I'm quite sure that I would have been greatly handicapped if I had not developed that kind of confidence which one gets by being able to talk to and measure oneself against the leaders in the field."

Such reference group behavior, in which people assess themselves by comparison with selected others, can of course be devastating rather than reassuring (see Hyman and Singer, 1968; Merton, 1960). But in the special case of the future laureates, who were beneficiaries rather than victims of the process, this leads to their accepting the idea that they need not be *primus inter pares,* considering that their equals are themselves first class. They make the comparisons without damage to their self-esteem. Thus, a physicist laureate who had watched Enrico Fermi at work reported:

> Knowing what Fermi could do did not make me humble. You just realize that some people are smarter than you are, that's all. You can't run as fast as some people or do mathematics as fast as Fermi. You can't do everything.

This matter-of-fact acceptance of difference is almost echoed in a published observation by Paul Samuelson, laureate in economics:

> When one heard the late John von Neumann lecture spontaneously at breakneck speed, one's transcendental wonder was reduced to mere admiration upon realizing that his mind was grinding out the conclusions at rates only twice as fast as what could be done by his average listener. Is it so remarkable that a few leading scholars will again and again lead the pack in the conquering of new territory? If you think of a marathon race in which, for whatever reason, one clique gets ahead, then you will realize that they need subsequently run no faster than the pack in order to cross each milestone first [1972a, p. 157].

For young scientists as talented as these destined laureates, great advantages accrue from being apprenticed to elite masters. Once internalized, standards of performance and scientific taste, unlike material facilities, do not generally depreciate with use. Combined with the special access to resources that often comes from being sponsored by eminent scientists, these basic orientations and the skills and knowledge that go with them contribute greatly to the process by which advantage accumulates for young scientists moving into the elite. . . .

References

BERNSTEIN, J. (1962) Profiles: A question of parity, *New Yorker,* **38**, 490.
HYMAN, H. H. and SINGER, E. (Eds.) (1968) *Readings in Reference Group Theory and Research,* New York: Free Press.
KEMBLE, E. C., BIRCH, F. and HOLTON, G. (1970) Percy Williams Bridgman, *Dictionary of Scientific Biography,* **2**, 457–610.
KREBS, H. (1967) The making of a scientist, *Nature,* **215**, 1441–1445.
MERTON, R. K. (1960) Recognition and excellence. Instructive ambiguities. In A.

Yarmolinsky, (Ed.), *Recognition and Excellence: Working Papers.* pp. 297–328, Glencoe: Free Press.

MERTON, R. K. and ROSSI, A. S. (1965) Contributions to the theory of reference group behavior. In *Social Theory and Social Structure,* pp. 279–334, New York: Free Press.

SAMUELSON, P. A. (1972a) Economics in a golden age: A personal memoir. In G. Holton (Ed.), *The Twentieth Century Sciences: Studies in the Biography of Ideas,* pp. 155–70, New York: W. W. Norton.

SEGRÈ, E. (undated) From Atoms to Antiprotons. 47th Ann. Faculty Research Lecture, Berkeley: University of California (Mimeo).

WARBURG, O. (1965) Experiments in biochemistry. In *The Excitement and Fascination of Science,* pp. 531–544, Palo Alto: Annual Review.

WATSON, J. D. (1966) Growing up in the phage group. In J. Cairns, G. S. Stent and J. D. Watson, (Eds.), *Phage and the Origins of Molecular Biology,* pp. 239–245, Cold Spring Harbor, NY: Cold Spring Harbor Laboratory of Quantitative Biology.

WILSON, M. (1969) How Nobel prizewinners get that way. *Atlantic Monthly,* **224,** 69–74.

4

Behavior Patterns of Scientists*

R. K. MERTON

THE HISTORY of science indelibly records 1953 as the year in which the structure of the DNA molecule was discovered. But it is 1968 that will probably emerge as the year of the double helix in the history that treats the behavior of scientists, for James Watson's deeply personal account of that discovery has clearly seized the public imagination. To judge from the great variety of reviews of *The Double Helix,* the essential message of the book is that "scientists are human, after all".

What, then, are the stories Watson tells about the social and intellectual interactions that entered into the discovery, stories eliciting the popular response that scientists are all too human? Above all else, he tells of the race for priority; a close awareness of the champion rival who must be defeated in this contest of minds; a driving insistence on getting needed data from sometimes reluctant, sometimes inadvertent collaborators; a competition for specific discoveries over the years between the Cavendish and Cal Tech; an allegedly English sense of private domains for scientific investigation that bear no-poaching signs; an express ambition for that ultimate symbol of accomplishment, the Nobel. . . . He tells, too, about alternating periods of intense thought and almost calculated idleness (while the gestation of ideas pursues its course); about false starts and errors of inference.

. . . An intuitive and stubbornly maintained imagery of the nature of its solution, together with the implications as these were expressed in that master-stroke of calculated understatement wrought by Francis Crick: "It has not escaped our notice that the pairing we have postulated immediately suggests a possible copying mechanism for the genetic material."

The stories detailed in *The Double Helix* have evidently gone forth to dispel a popular mythology about the complex behavior of scientists. . . . Embodying as they do some of the prime values of world civilization, scientists have long been placed on pedestals where they may have no wish to be perched — not, at least, the more thoughtful among them. This is not the result of a conspiracy, not even a conspiracy of goodwill. It is only that men and women of science have long been pictured, through collective acts of piety, as though they were

*Reprinted with the permission of the author, Robert K. Merton, *The Sociology of Science,* University of Chicago Press (1973).

more than human, being like gods in their creativity, and also as less than human, being deprived in their work of the passions, attitudes and social ties given to ordinary men and women. As a result, scientists have been dehumanized in the public mind of being idealized and, on occasion, idolized. Contributing greatly to this centuries-long process of distortion are the pious biographers who, in sapless prose, convert indubitably great men of science into what Augustus de Morgan once described as "monsters of perfection".

In part, too, the imagery of scientists moving coolly, methodically and un-erringly to the results they report may stem from the etiquette that governs the writing of scientific papers. This etiquette, as we know, requires them to be works of vast expurgation, stripping the complex events and behaviors that cul-minated in the report of everything except their cognitive substance. Compare only the lean, taut, almost laconic, nine-hundred-word article that appeared in *Nature* that momentous April in 1953 with the tangled web of events reported in Watson's forty-thousand-word account of the same discovery. . . .

The sense of popular revelation upon learning that scientists are actually human testifies, then, to the prevalence of an earlier *belief* to the contrary. Ironically enough, that older mythology now threatens to be replaced by a new variant expressed in responses to the Watson memoir by scientists and humanists alike. The patterns of motives and behavior set out in Watson's irreverent, naturalistic narrative are held to be distinctive of the newest era of science, staffed by "a new kind of scientist and one that could hardly have been thought of before science became a mass occupation.". . .

As another scientist—reviewer sees it, part of what Watson reports is an expression of "no more than the general opportunism that is the hallmark of modern competitive science" — a statement in which the governing phrase is "modern competitive science." And in still another version, this one the response of a humanist to *The Double Helix,* it is suggested, with unconcealed reluctance, that "a keenness of early recognition may even be, these days, as essential to discovery as intelligence. Science, like all other activities *now"* — again, I accent the temporal qualifier — "is crowded and accelerated. There is no sitting alone *anymore* and letting apples fall down."

There is a certain plausibility to this view that the mores of science and the behavior of scientists must surely have changed in the recent past. For plainly, all the basic demographic, social, economic, political and organizational para-meters of science have acquired dramatically new values. The size of the popu-lation of working scientists has increased exponentially from the scattered hundreds three centuries ago to the hundred or more myriads today. The time of the amateur is long since past; scientists are now professionals all, their work providing them with a livelihood and, for some, a not altogether impoverished one. The social organization of scientific inquiry has greatly changed, with collaboration and research teams the order of the day. . . .

As science has become more institutionalized, it has also become more intimately interrelated with the other institutions of society. Science-based technologies and the partial diffusion of a scientific outlook have become great social forces that move our history and greatly affect the relations obtaining between the nations of the world. Scientists do not, of course, make the major political decisions, but they now affect them significantly (e.g., The Bomb).

There must also be a new ethos of science abroad, a new set of values and institutionally patterned motives. . . . The psychiatrist Lawrence Kubie notes that young scientists, unwarned that "their future success may be determined by forces which are outside their own creative capacity or their willingness to work hard" may suffer "a new psychosocial ailment . . . which may not be wholly unrelated to the gangster tradition of dead-end kids." And he goes on to ask: "Are we witnessing the development of a generation of hardened, cynical, amoral, embittered, disillusioned young scientists?". . . . It was just thirty years ago that I suggested in a footnote tucked away in a monograph on science in seventeenth-century England that the race for priority might constitute a strategic subject for study and might provide clues to ways in which the institution of science shapes the motives, passions and social relations of scientists. So far as I can tell, the youthful author of that footnote on early competition in science proved to be its only reader. . . .

Although it may have surprised the outsider, Watson's unabashed report on the race for priority scarcely came as news to his fellow-scientists. They know from hard-won experience that multiple independent discoveries at about the same time constitute one of their occupational hazards. They not only know it, but often act on it. That the consequent rush to achieve priority is common in our time hardly needs documentation. . . . A few years before Watson reached his much wider audience, Arthur Schawlow casually noted in the public prints that Charles Townes and he had been "in a hurry, of course. We feared that it might only be a matter of time before others would come up with the same idea. So we decided to publish before building a working model . . . Subsequently, Theodore Maiman won the frantic race . . . to build the first laser." Townes had ample biographical reason to be in a hurry. After all, in the early 1950s, he had been involved in that fivefold independent discovery of the laser.

The contemporary annals of science are peppered with cases of scientists spurred on to more intense effort by the knowledge that others were on much the same track. Harriet Zuckerman's interviews with Nobel laureates in her book *Scientific Elite* find many of them testifying, in the words of one of them, that "it was bound to happen soon, had I not done it.". . . Warren Hagstrom found that two-thirds of a sample of some 1400 scientists had been anticipated by others in their own contributions, a good number of these on more than one occasion. . . .

The fact is a commonplace. But does the fact warrant the inference, drawn in the emerging mythology, that intense competition for discovery is in a significant sense distinctive of the new era of science. . . . I think not. . . . For the plain fact is, of course, that the race for priority has been frequent throughout the entire era of modern science. Moving back only a generation or so, we observe the good-natured race between Hahn and Boltwood, for example, to discover the "parent of radium" which Boltwood was able to find first, just as, when Hahn discovered mesothorium, Boltwood acknowledged his having been outdistanced, saying only, "I was almost there myself . . .". There is Ramsay telegraphing Berthelot in Paris "at once" about his isolation of helium; writing Rayleigh to the same effect and sending a note to the Royal Society to establish priority, just as he and Travers were to announce having nosed out Dewar in the discovery of neon. There is the forthright account by Norbert Wiener of the race between Bouligand and himself in potential theory, making Wiener "aware that he must hurry," but having it end in a "dead heat" since Bouligand has submitted his "results to the French Academy in a sealed envelope," just a day before. . . .

We can scarcely forget the race run by the technologist Robert Goddard, the American father of the rocket, to achieve "primacy in outer space," spurred on by the "jouranlistic claims to priority then made by the German partisans of Hermann Oberth . . . to redouble his efforts" and to launch his first liquid-propellant rocket only three years later. . . .

The fact is that almost all of those firmly placed in the pantheon of science — Newton, Descartes, Leibniz, Pascal and Huyghens, Lister, Faraday, Laplace and Davy — were caught up in passionate efforts to achieve priority and to have it publicly registered. . . . Newton and Watson were both in their golden years, decidedly young men. Just as Jim Watson took up the problem he made his own in his twenty-third year, so we will remember, from Newton's own account, the *annus mirabilis* when at twenty-three or twenty-four he discovered the binomial theorem, started work toward invention of the calculus, took his first steps toward establishing the law of universal gravitation, and began his experiments on optics.

Long after . . . Newton was still busily engaged in ensuring the luster and fame owing him. He was not merely concerned with establishing his priority but was periodically obsessed by it. . . . Newton's voluminous manuscripts contain at least twelve versions of a defense of his priority, as against Leibniz, in the invention of the calculus. . . . As I shall presently suggest,this was not so much because Newton was weak as because the newly institutionalized value set upon originality in science was so great that he found himself driven to these lengths. . . .

Here, then, is one pattern that repeats itself through the centuries of modern science. Two or more scientists quietly announce a discovery. Since it is often the case that these are truly independent contributions, with each scientist having exhibited originality of mind, the process is sometimes stabilized at that point. But as the behavior of Newton, Leibniz, Hooke and an indefinitely large number of other scientists testifies, this peaceful acceptance of the fact of independent discovery does not always occur. Since the situation is often ambiguous, with the role of each scientist not easy to identify, and since each one *knows* that he had himself arrived at the discovery, . . . and since the institutionalized stakes of reputation are high and the joy of acknowledged discovery immense, this militates against mutual acknowledgement of a parallel contribution. One or another of the discoverers − or, often, his colleagues or fellow nationals − suggests that he rather than the rival was really first, and that the independence of his rival is at least unproved. Then begins the familiar deterioration of standards governing conflictful interaction. . . .

Among the multitude of multiple discoveries in the history of science, Elinor Barber and I have examined a sample of 264 in detail and have found, among other things, that there is a secular decline in the frequency with which multiples are an occasion for intense priority-conflicts. Of the thirty-six multiples before 1700 that we have examined, 92% were strenuously contested; the figure drops to 72% in the eighteenth century; remains at about the same level in the first half of the nineteenth century and declines to 59% in the second half, reaching the lowest level of 33% in the first half of this century. Perhaps the culture of science today is not so pathogenic as it once was.

The absence of historical perspective marks another component of the new mythology of science. This one holds that quick, if not premature, publication to ensure priority is peculiar to our new breed of scientists, as witness the manuscript that went off to the editors of *Nature* that fateful April 2nd 1953. . . . Today as yesterday, Scientists are caught up in one of the many ambivalent precepts contained in the institution of science. This one requires that scientists must be ready to make their newfound knowledge available to their peers as soon as possible *but* must also avoid an undue tendency to rush into print. (Compare Faraday's motto "Work, Finish, Publish" with Erlich's "Viel arbeiten, wenig publizieren!")

From its very beginning, the journal of science introduced the institutional device of quick publication to motivate men of science to replace the value set upon secrecy with the value placed upon the open disclosure of the knowledge they had created (a value that, in our own time, has often acquired, through the displacement of goals, a spurious emphasis on publication for its own sake, almost irrespective of the merit of what is published). . . . The concern with getting into print fast is scarcely confined to contemporary science. Watson fluttered the dovecotes of academia, to say nothing of the wider reading public, by telling us of having joined with Crick in an enthusiastic toast "to the Pauling failure. . . . Though the odds still appeared against us, Linus had not yet won his Nobel." Once again, Watson had violated the mores. . . . Yet seen in historical perspective, how mild and restrained is this episode by comparison with judgments on contemporaries set out in public by great scientists of the heroic past. There is Galileo becoming a seasoned campaigner as he flays one Grassi who "tried to diminish whatever praise that may be in this [invention of the telescope] which belongs to me.". . .

The seventeenth-century Edmond Halley was forthrightly described by the first Astronomer Royal, John Flamsteed, as a "lazy and malicious thief.". . . And Flamsteed asserts that he found Newton "always insidious, ambitious, and excessively covetous of praise.". . .

This introduces an instructive paradox. These, indeed, are changing times in the ethos of sciences. But Watson's brash memoir does not testify to a breakdown of once-prevailing norms that call for discreet and soft-spoken comment on scientific contemporaries. A memoir such as his would have been regarded as a benign model of disciplined restraint by the turbulent scientific community of the seventeenth century. . . .

Within such a context, the behavior of scientists involved in races for priority or in priority-disputes tends to be condemned rather than analyzed. It is morally judged, not systematically investigated. The disputes are described as "unfortunate" with the moral judgment being substitute for the effort to understand what they imply for the psychology of scientists and the sociology of science. At least since Goethe, we note references to "all those foolish quarrels about earlier and later discovery, plagiary, and quasi-purloinings." We are free, of course, to find this behavior unpleasant or foolish or comic or sad. But these affective responses to the behavior of our ancestors-in-science or our brothers-and-sisters-in-science have usurped the place that might be given to analysis of the behavior and its implications for the ways in which science develops. It is as though the biomedical scientists were to respond only judgmentally to disease, describe it as unfortunate or painful, and consider the job done, or as though the psychiatrist were to describe the behavior of schizophrenics as absurd and substitute this sentiment for the effort to discover what brings that behavior about. The undisciplined tendency to respond in terms of sentiments has generated resistance to recognizing the central place of competition throughout the modern era of science.

This resistance is expressed in various ways: by seeking to trivialize the fact, by regarding concern with priority as rare or aberrant (when it is in truth frequent and typical), by motivated misperceptions of the facts or by a hiatus in recall and reporting. Such resistance often leads to those wish-fulfilling beliefs, false memories and mythologies that we describe as illusions. And of such expressions of resistance the annals of science are uncommonly full. So much so, that I have arrived at a rule of thumb that seems to work fairly well. The rule is this: whenever the biography or autobiography of a scientist announces that he had little or no concern with priority, there is a reasonably good chance that, not many pages later in the book, we shall find him deeply embroiled in one or another episode where priority is at issue. A few cases must stand for many.

The authoritative biography of that great psychiatrist of the Salpêtrière, Charcot, states that, despite his many discoveries, he "never thought for a moment to claim priority or reward." Our rule of thumb leads us to expect what we find: some thirty pages later, there is a detailed account of Charcot insisting on having been first in recognizing exophthalmic goiter and, a little later, emphatically affirming that he "would like to claim priority" (the language is his) for the idea of isolating patients suffering from hysteria. . . .

But perhaps the most apt case of the myth taking precedence over an accessible reality is provided by Ernest Jones, writing in his comprehensive biography that "Although Freud was never interested in questions of priority, which he found merely boring, he was fond of exploring the source of what appeared to be original ideas, particularly his own. . .". This is an extraordinarily illuminating statement by a scholar who had devoted his own life to plumbing the depths of the human soul. For, of course, no one could have known better than Jones – "known" in the narrowly cognitive sense – how very often Freud turned to matters of priority: in his own work, in the work of his colleagues (both friends and enemies) and in the history of psychology altogether. In point of fact, Freud expressed an interest in this matter on more than 150 occasions (I make no estimate of the unrecorded ones). With characteristic self-awareness, he reports that he even dreamed about priority and the due allocation of credit for accomplishments in science. . . .

At other times, he reluctantly or insistently acknowledges anticipations of others; he "implores" his disciple Lou Andreas-Salomé to finish an essay in order "not to give me precedence in time"; he admonishes Adler for what he describes as his "uncontrolled craving for priority"; . . . over a span of forty years, he repeatedly reassesses the distinctive roles of Breuer and himself in establishing psychoanalysis; he returns time and again to his priority-conflict with Janet; he writes nostalgically about the days of "my splendid isolation" when "there was nothing to hustle me.". . .

That Freud was ambivalent toward matters of priority, true; that he was pained by conflicts over priority, indisputable; that he was concerned to establish the priority of others as well as himself, beyond doubt and significant. But to describe him as "never interested" in priority and "bored" by it, as Jones does, is a massive example of *resistance* to a rejected reality.

Not only the historians and biographers of science but scientists themselves often manifest ambivalence toward the facts of priority-oriented behavior. Darwin registers his mixed feelings, writing Lyell: "My good friend, forgive me. This is a trumpery letter, influenced by trumpery feelings." In a postscript, he assures Lyell that "I will never trouble you or Hooker on the subject again." The next day, he writes Lyell: "It seems hard on me that I should lose my priority of many years' standing. . . . Fifty years after the joint Darwin–Wallace paper was presented to the Linnean Society, Wallace was still insisting upon the contrast between his own hurried work, written within a week after the great idea came to him, and Darwin's work, based on twenty years of collecting evidence. "*I* was then (as often since) the 'young man in a hurry,' " said the reminiscing Wallace, "*he*, the painstaking and patient student seeking ever the full demonstration of the truth he had discovered, rather than to achieve immediate personal fame.". . .

All of this brings us finally to the question touched off by the responses of many scientists and laymen to the Watson memoir. We are perhaps ready to see now that those responses related to the long-standing denial that through the centuries, scientists, and often the greatest among them, have been concerned with achieving and safeguarding their priority. The question is, of course: what leads to this uneasiness about acknowledging the drive for priority in science? Why the curious notion that a thirst for significant originality . . . accredited . . . is depraved?

There is, nevertheless, a germ of psychological truth in the suspicion enveloping the drive for recognition in science. Any extrinsic reward — fame, money, position — is morally ambiguous and potentially subversive of culturally esteemed values. For as rewards are meted out, they can displace the original motive; concern with recognition can displace concern with advancing knowledge. An excess of incentives can produce distracting conflict. But when the institution of science works effectively (and, like other social institutions, it does not always do so), recognition and esteem accrue to those scientists who have best fulfilled their roles, to those who have made the fundamental contributions to the common stock of knowledge. Then are found those happy circumstances in which moral obligation and self-interest coincide and fuse. The ambivalence of scientists toward their own interest in having their priority recognized — an ambivalence we have seen registered even by that most astute of psychologists, Freud — shows them to assume that such an ancillary motive somehow tarnishes the purity of their interest in scientific inquiry. . . .

In another aspect, the ambivalence toward priority means that scientists reflect in themselves the ambivalence built into the social institution of science itself. On one side, the institutional norms of science exert pressure upon scientists to assert their claims. . . . On every side, scientists are reminded that it is their role to advance knowledge and their happiest fulfillment of that role, to advance knowledge greatly. This is only to say, of course, that in the institution of science originality is at a premium. . . . Yet the same institution of science emphasizes selfless dedication to the advancement of knowledge. . . .

In still another aspect, ambivalence toward concern with priority derives from the mistaken belief that it must express naked self-interest, that it is altogether self-serving. On the surface, the hunger for recognition appears as mere personal vanity, generated from within and craving satisfaction from without. But when we reach deeper into the institutional complex that gives added edge to that hunger, it turns out to be anything but personal, repeated as it is with slight variation by one scientist after another. Vanity, so-called, is then seen as the outer face of the inner need for assurance that one's work really matters, that one has measured up to the hard standards maintained by at least some members of the community of scientists. . . . Only after the originality and consequence of their work have been attested by significant others can scientists feel reasonably confident about it. Deeply felt praise for work well done, moreover, exalts donor and recipient alike; it joins them both in symbolizing the common enterprise. . . . The function of reassurance by recognition has a dependable basis in the social aspects of knowledge. Few scientists have great certainty about the worth of their work.

Thus, Darwin writing Huxley about the *Origin of Species* "with awful misgivings," thought that "perhaps I had deluded myself like so many have done, and I then fixed in my mind three judges, on whose decision I determined mentally to abide. The judges were Lyell, Hooker, and yourself.". . . In almost the same language, Schrodinger writes Einstein that "your approval and Planck's mean more to me than that of half the world." And a Leo Szilard or a Max Delbrück, widely known as exceedingly tough-minded and demanding judges who, all uncompromising, will not relax their standards of judgment even to provide momentary comfort in their associates, are reference figures whose plaudits for work accomplished have a multiplier effect, influencing in turn the judgments of many another scientist. . . .

The drive for priority is in part an effort to reassure onself of a capacity for original thought. Thus, rather than being mutually exclusive, as the new mythology of science would have it, joy in discovering and the quest for recognition by scientific peers are stamped out of the same psychological coin.

VI

Personality Correlates to Creative Behavior and Exceptional Achievement

IF GIFTEDNESS and parents have been highlighted as the prime early influences to genius and exceptional achievement, then the product of the two, the personality of the individual, must be viewed as the single most powerful, non-intellectual factor involved in achievement. Twentieth-century thinking is that the family focuses upon the raw material of youth and creates a very distinct set of personality traits which mediate great ability and talents and exceptional achievement. Quite often efforts to disentangle personality traits and development are too convincing. One turns from them knowing that life is more complex and less linear than what we are often asked to believe. When done as masterfully as a Freud or as Bates in his biography of Samuel Johnson, the product is a revelation. Unfortunately, such masterful presentations are rare. Paradoxically, if there is any one area in which efforts have abounded while understanding has remained a bit soft, it is in the area of personality and achievement.

The papers of this chapter discuss what is known about the personality characteristics of creative people, of men and women who have distinguished themselves in architecture, writing, mathematics, and psychology. Although the articles pay attention to both the differences and similarities of personality observed among creative persons in these fields, it is the similarities (regardless of sex) that are most striking and most influential in their achievements. Nicholls (VI-1) discusses in great detail the unfortunate enshrinement of "creativity" that has occurred in contemporary western societies, especially the United States. He points to the confusions involved in such thinking and how research into creativity does not always involve creative *behavior*. He is especially acute in indicating how the creativity that is often discussed and measured is less likely to lead to or be similar to that which contributes to the attainment of eminence. Some readers may find what Nicholls says therapeutic. His article is followed by an excerpt from a chapter in Cattell's book, *Abilities: Their Structure, Growth, and Action* (VI-2). It summarizes a lifetime's work by one of the most influential contemporary psychologists. Although his theoretical system differs from others working on questions of creativity and achievement, it would be short-sighted not to present Cattell's work. His extensive findings regarding the personality similarities (and differences) among persons eminent in a variety of fields complements and extends Cox's earlier work, while putting the relationship between personality and achievement on very solid ground. MacKinnon's article (VI-3) is based upon his well-known research with architects. In it he describes the important professional values and self-images associated with various degrees of creativity and eminence. One of the highlights of this report is that it vividly shows how persons of different levels of eminence within the *same* profession work from and conform to very different sets of values and images of themselves, i.e., differences of identity. Barron's article (VI-4) points up the personality differences among eminent writers and their less achieving controls. Especially striking is what Barron writes about high artistic achievement and signs of psychopathology. Because of the prevalent belief that to be a genius or highly original is to flirt with insanity if not to be "insane," readers may compare Barron's work with Woody and Claridge (VII-1).

The last two articles in this chapter broaden our considerations. They are each concerned with creative women in the fields of mathematics (Helson, VI-5) and Psychology (Bachtold and Werner, VI-6). Each paper represents a particular tradition: Helson works with the same methodology and tests as Barron and MacKinnon; Bachtold and Werner use Cattell's tests and personality model in their project.

Helson's recent comprehensive paper summarized the results of her many years of research comparing the early backgrounds, performances, and personalities of creative women mathematicians with those of creative male mathematicians, creative male and female writers, as well as less creative women mathematicians. Her results were elaborate and engrossing, pointing to important similarities among creative men and women that apparently go beyond occupational differences, both groups overcoming the broad, powerful, cultural pressures that often contribute to sex differences. Bachtold and Werner (VI-6) report the results of their study of 124 women psychologists, most of whom were in their sixties and at their professional peak. Their results also have to do with comparison. In this case it is the comparison of these successful women with the "general" female population, female college students, successful academic men, and of creative and less creative female and male psychologists as determined by their scientific productivity. Bachtold and Werner present us once again with evidence for significant differences in the personalities and values-interests of successful, gifted academic female psychologists when compared to their less successful control group. Like Helson, these authors describe basic comparisons between creative men and women in their personalities that are laced with some very interesting group differences in intelligence, conscience development, and capacity to be unconventional.

1

Creativity in the Person Who Will Never Produce Anything Original or Useful*

J. G. NICHOLLS

THE TERM creativity is used with something approaching gay abandon by both psychologists (Yamamoto, 1965) and people in general (Bruner, 1962; Morreale, 1969), but is most appropriately applied where there is evidence of achievements that are original and make a meaningful contribution to culture. Writers on creativity would surely agree that if the term is to be applied to people who in the strict sense are not creative, the links between these and eminent creators must be established clearly. However, these links have not been clarified adequately, and when they are, one popular approach to creativity will rest on uncertain foundations.

Creativity research can be categorized in a number of ways (e.g., Golann, 1963). This article suggests that there are two major approaches to creativity in normal populations. In one, products are rated on a continuum of creativity, and the personal and social factors associated with creative achievement are examined. In the other, the central concern of this article, it is assumed that there is a trait (or traits) of creativity – the psychological significance of the trait and its contribution to creative production are examined.

The first approach has been used in the study of eminent or high-level creators (e.g., Helson and Crutchfield, 1970a; MacKinnon, 1965; Taylor and Ellison, 1967) and with less outstanding subjects (e.g., Csikszentmihalyi and Getzels, 1970; Holland, 1961). If this approach to creativity in normal populations is adopted, the continuity between eminent and everyday creativity resides in the criteria for judging the creativity of products. It is not necessary to assume a normally distributed trait (or traits) of creativity. In MacKinnon's (1964, 1965) studies of architects, creative subjects are characterized as high or low on a number of psychological dimensions, none of which are called traits of creativity, but which provide a coherent picture of the creative individual suggesting how and why he is creative. These dimensions are of interest in their own right and relevant to many topics in addition to creativity. Though evidence on eminent creators is a likely source of hypotheses about creativity in normal populations (Dellas and Gaier, 1970), it need not be assumed that the same personal

*American Psychologist, (1972), 27, 717–727. Copyright 1972 by the American Psychological Association. Reprinted by permission of the publisher and author.

characteristics will be associated with product-defined creativity in eminent creators and ordinary people. Rating less-than-eminent achievements for creativity can be difficult, but Jackson and Messick (1965) have outlined a useful taxonomy, with originality as a minimum requirement.

A large proportion of the large volume of creativity research with children and adolescents has followed the second approach and implicitly or explicitly assumed a normally distributed trait of creativity (Ausubel, 1964; Day, 1968; Zimmerman, 1964). Divergent thinking tests remain the most popular measures of creativity (Wallach, 1970). Validation studies typically involve examination of the relations of these measures with other traits, supposedly typical of eminent creators, or with achievements rated for creativity. In some cases, studies in this second category differ from those in the first, primarily in that they assume a trait of creativity. If we consider parsimony important, we might also consider this difference important and abandon the concept of a trait of creativity in favor of the product-based approach to the topic. However, not only is the assumption of a normally distributed trait of creativity unnecessary, it is, as will be shown below, difficult to sustain. Further, the use of divergent thinking tests as measures of creativity has, by leading to research on divergent thinking which is conceived and interpreted in the context of creativity, impaired our understanding of this process.

Concept of a Trait of Creativity

To ensure that a trait of creativity has essentially the same meaning for normal subjects and eminent creators, we must isolate the distinctive characteristics of eminent creators and show that these are related positively in unselected samples.

We neither can assume that any personal characteristic has the same psychological significance in eminent and ordinary men nor arbitrarily select one of the distinguishing characteristics of eminent creatives as the index of creativity in all men. This point can be made clear by considering commitment to or involvement in tasks, which is a salient characteristic of eminent creators. No one has identified task commitment as an index of creativity in normal subjects, presumably because it is so obvious that the characteristic can have widely different meanings in outstanding creators and people in general. For some reason, this possibility with regard to divergent thinking creativity tests does not appear to have unsettled many psychologists.

Two steps are needed to validate the concept of a normally-distributed trait of creativity. First, the salient characteristics of high-level or eminent creators, which contribute to their ability to create, must be isolated. Second, these characteristics must be measured in normal populations and, if the concept is to be accepted, found positively related. In the absence of convergence between the different dimensions, continuity of meaning from eminent to average people cannot be assumed, and it is unjustifiable to label any one of the dimensions creativity. Even if one such dimension related consistently to product criteria of creativity in average populations, there would be limited justification for calling it creativity unless, perhaps, it related more consistently to criteria of creativity than to others not integrally related to creativity (e.g., preference for arts versus science).

The next step, then, is the isolation of the essential characteristics of individuals who have made original and useful contributions to culture. Both theory and research evidence on high-level or eminent creativity are examined. It should be clear that the following discussion does not convey the complexity and diversity of creative persons or the processes by which they create. In part, this diversity reflects the range of areas of creative endeavor (Helson and Crutchfield, 1970b; McNemar, 1964; Roe, 1952; Vernon, 1967), but considerable diversity is also found within disciplines (Fox, 1963; Helson and Crutchfield, 1970a). The differences between Einstein and Rutherford illustrate the latter point (Snow, 1966, see especially p. 106). The picture is complicated further by the possibility that different qualities may be called for at different points in a discipline's development.

Inevitably, the concept of a trait of creativity will not include that which is peculiar to one field of creativity or to atypical workers who may be singularly creative (Roe, 1952) in any one field. It can only embody an emasculated version of what we recognize as eminent creativity. Though some might wish to abandon the concept at this point, there are sufficient similarities across creators in different fields to justify proceeding, provided the limitations of the exercise are remembered.

Characteristics of Creative Persons

The characteristics selected, with some reservations and omissions, as typical of eminent creators are divergent thinking, intelligence, intrinsic task involvement, and preference for complexity.

Divergent Thinking

Though Guilford (1964, 1967), in his discussions of abilities involved in creative production, does not deal exclusively with divergent thinking abilities, these abilities have been widely called creative. There are some grounds for holding that ideational productivity is an essential aspect of creativity.

Wallach and Kogan (1965) adopt Mednick's (1962) associational concept of creativity, which stresses availability of remote associates, and present examples suggesting the importance of availability of associations. Campbell's (1960) blind-variation-and-selective-retention model of creative thinking also suggests the importance of ideational fluency. Availability of associations could also be regarded as an indication of accessibility of unconscious material that might be the basis of creativity (Kris, 1952). It does not follow from these positions that ideational productivity is sufficient to ensure creativity. Other processes in Guilford's scheme, such as evaluation and sensitivity to problems and the selection and retention processes in Campbell's model, cannot be ignored. In both these models, processes traditionally included in the concept of intelligence are important.

Though there is some theoretical support fot the notion that ideational productivity is important for creative achievement, the research evidence for the predictive validity of divergent thinking tests is far from impressive (Dellas and Gaier, 1970; Golann, 1963; McNemar, 1964; Vernon, 1967). In the cases where the tests do relate to criteria of creativity with adults (Dellas and Gaier, 1970; Guilford, 1967), the forms of creativity are generally far from qualifying as eminent.

Shapiro's (1968) study of research scientists is an apparent exception to the trend of failure to validate divergent thinking tests against criteria of creativity. Correlations of predictors with four criterion measures ranged from 0.08 to 0.52 with a mean of 0.29. However, the criteria did not deal with quality of scientific achievement, but were ratings by subjects and their supervisors, on two scales designed to discriminate creative from noncreative scientists on the basis of personal characteristics and work habits. . . .

This part of Shapiro's study can be interpreted as evidence that there is some degree of convergent validity across performance measures, self-report, and supervisor ratings of ideational productivity and originality.

Though similar comment could be made of the personality schedule also used as a criterion measure, a large number of these items do not fit this interpretation. However, scientists scoring high on the divergent thinking tests were rated high, by selves and supervisors, on items that Hudson's (1966) divergers would probably score high on. (Divergers were typically biased toward arts rather than science.) Hudson suggested that while scientists may be relatively low scorers on divergent thinking tests, those scoring high within the group range might prove more creative than low scorers (p. 110). Further evidence from Shapiro's study offers limited support for this hypothesis.

Shapiro made three ratings of the creativity of his subjects' achievements. Two ratings involved relatively sophisticated and analytic evaluations. Neither of these significantly discriminated high and low divergent thinking scorers, while the third, a global rating of quality of work, did. As the global rating is likely to reflect quantity rather than quality of production (Harmon, 1958; Taylor, 1958), Shapiro's study achieves only marginal validation of divergent thinking tests as measures of creativity.

The lack of association between high-level creative achievement and divergent thinking tests could reflect inadequacies of test form and content. This may also be because these tests measure only one portion of the creative process. The way the variety of relevant skills are deployed could be more critical than the separately measured level of any one skill (Covington, 1967).

Intelligence

As noted above, both Guilford and Campbell implicate conventionally defined intelligence, or aspects of it, in creativity. It is generally acknowledged that a fairly high, though perhaps not exceptional level of intelligence is necessary for creative achievement (Barron, 1969; McNemar, 1964; Vernon, 1967). The extent to which capacity for creative achievement is limited by intelligence, as normally measured, would vary with area of achievement (McNemar, 1964), but presumably no one would suggest that individuals with IQs of 70 are generally as likely to make significant creative achievements as individuals with IQs of 130.

Much attention has focused on the question of whether divergent thinking measures define a coherent dimension with some independence of intelligence. Under gamelike conditions of divergent thinking measurement, intelligence and divergent thinking are unrelated (Boersma and O'Bryan, 1968; Nicholls, 1971; Wallach and Kogan, 1965). It has been argued that gamelike conditions are the most appropriate for creativity assessment (Wallach, 1970; Wallach and Kogan, 1965). However, if creativity measures are unrelated to intelligence, this suggests that the capacity for original, culturally meaningful achievement is unrelated to intelligence. (The alternative is that creativity has no connection with the capacity for original, meaningful achievement.) While traits that contribute to eminent creativity may well be unrelated to intelligence in normal populations, considerable confusion results if such traits are called creativity.

Motives and Creativity

As Ghiselin (1955) has pointed out, the reshaping or extension of human achievement in any field requires a high level of mastery of the field; this is not attained lightly. Barron (1969) observed "hard work and dedicated practice are the almost invariable precursors of original and distinctive achievement [p. 3]." Maddi (1965) also emphasized the active striving and intensity of involvement that is typical of eminent creatives but overlooked in much of the creativity literature. According to Campbell's model, motivation can play a major part in the generation of thought trials.

> The number of trials necessary to arrive at a new construction is commonly so great that without something of a fascination for the subject one grows weary of the task. This is the emotional condition of originality of mind in any department [Bain, cited by Campbell, 1960, p. 385].

Involvement with tasks for intrinsic rather than extrinsic reasons could foster creative productivity for two reasons. First, as already suggested, it maintains the activity needed to establish the necessary skills or information and to generate the necessary possible solutions. Second, it brings an attitude of mind that allows task requirements to come to the fore. Crutchfield (1962) contrasts this task-involved motivation with extrinsic, ego-involved motivation where the task is not of primary importance, and suggests that creative subjects are resistant to social pressure because of a stronger orientation to task requirements.

A number of studies find eminent creatives characterized by high levels of task involvement. McCurdy (1960) concluded that the childhood pattern of genius involves early finding of pleasure in the world of ideas — a trend encouraged by parents — and separation from or avoidance of peers. He also contended that eminent people are highly independent by virtue of reliance on and commitment to their own ideas. Roe (1952) reported a similar pattern in physical and biological scientists. Social scientists differed, showing early and continuing interest in social relations that became the area of their work. All, however, showed a high level of commitment to their work. MacKinnon's (1964, 1965) creative architects were inclined to strive where independent activity was called for and were guided by self-generated standards of excellence, while less creative architects achieved through conformity to professional standards. This pattern was also found with mathematicians (Helson, 1971; Helson and Crutchfield, 1970b). Taylor and Ellison (1967) and Chambers (1964) found self-initiated, task-oriented striving a distinguishing characteristic of creative scientists; Barron (1963) obtained similar findings for writers. Thus, both theoretical considerations and research evidence suggest that creative individuals are more task oriented or involved in their own ideas or work than are people in general.

Barron (1958) has presented a further formulation concerning motivation supporting creative activity. Creative individuals, he argued, seek complexity, and disorder, from which they can create new simplicities and new orders. The Barron—Welsh Art Scale (revised as the Revised Art Scale, Welsh, 1959), used as a measure of this tendency, has proved effective in discriminating creative from noncreative groups (Golann, 1962; Helson and Crutchfield, 1970a). This concept provides a useful supplement to the concept of task commitment. Task commitment without a preference for situations allowing new conceptualizations may lead to considerable achievements, but they would probably not be creative achievements. In proposing that needs for both quality and novelty are essential for creative production, Maddi (1968) made a similar point.

The list of characteristics presented as typical of high-level creatives is basic and minimum, and it is worth recalling the earlier caveat — that the list cannot do justice to the diversity of creators. Artists, for example, are done less justice than other groups. Current concepts and measures of ability (convergent and divergent) seem less applicable in art than other areas (McNemar, 1964; McWhinnie, 1970). The list could include other dimensions, such as need for novelty, which, though potentially relevant, have not had this relevance clearly established. Others such as introversion (Cattell and Butcher, 1968) and independence of social influence are excluded because of their possibly less central role in creativity, though this is arguable. The latter two characteristics are, however, subsequently considered in relation to divergent thinking in an effort to further examine the convention of calling divergent thinking tests creativity tests.

Dimensions of Creativity in Normal Subjects

With children, there is no consistent convergence between the dimensions typical of eminent creators. Results with college students are more positive. It is concluded that approaches to creativity anchored to products are preferable to the trait-based approach.

If the concept of creativity as a normally distributed trait is to be accepted, measures of divergent thinking, intelligence, task involvement, and preference for complexity must be related positively in unselected samples. It might be argued that discriminant as well as convergent validity should be demonstrated. However, this requirement is difficult to establish for many psychological concepts and may be an unnecessarily stringent one (Jackson, 1969). In any case, convergent validity must be established. Thus, the next step is an examination of relevant research which, as in many areas, is mainly with school children and college students.

It is difficult to find measures of some of the creativity-related dimensions that are completely appropriate for our purpose. Curiosity conveys a sense of intrinsic involvement, but does not fully encompass the concept of task involvement used above. Though curiosity measures seem the most likely measures of task orientation in children, different curiosity measures are not always closely related to each other (Day, 1968; Medinnus and Love, 1965), which makes it unlikely, but not impossible, that they will relate consistently to other relevant creativity dimensions. While the Barron—Welsh Art Scale is used readily enough with children, and Golann (1962) has presented some evidence of its construct validity with boys, it may not be entirely appropriate for young subjects. Also, there could be developmental discontinuities in the psychological significance of preference for complexity, task involvement, and divergent thinking.

Research Evidence

Wallach's (1970) review of the extensive literature on the relation between intelligence and divergent thinking indicates that there is an ideational fluency dimension that is distinguishable from intelligence, though the two dimensions are generally positively related. However, this relationship appears to reflect a method factor: it is not found when divergent thinking is assessed in a context that differs from that in which intelligence is normally assessed (Boersma and O'Bryan, 1968; Nicholls, 1971).

A number of studies found divergent thinking unrelated to the art scale in children (Hetrick, Lilly, and Merrifield, 1968; McWhinnie, 1967, 1969, 1970;

Ward, 1968). Significant positive relations were found with college students (Eisenman, 1969b). Using a polygon measure of preference for complexity with college students, Eisenman and Foxman (1970) and Eisenman and Schussel (1970) found positive relations between divergent thinking and preference for complexity. Eisenman's polygon measure correlated ($r = 0.55$) with the art scale (Eisenman, 1969b), and there is evidence of construct validity (Eisenman and Boss, 1970; Grove and Eisenman, 1970; Taylor and Eisenman, 1964). Thus, though the usefulness of Eisenman's measure in discriminating eminent creatives from uncreatives is not established, there are grounds for considering studies using it.

Relations between curiosity and divergent thinking for children are variable. Day (1968) found two curiosity indexes positively related to divergent thinking. Penny and McCann (1964) found positive relations for sixth but not fourth graders. Maw and Maw (1965) and McReynolds, Acker, and Pietila (1961) obtained nonsignificant results. No studies of curiosity with older subjects were found, but a study by Weissman (1970) is relevant. He found that college students, high on a measure of disposition toward intellectuality, also gained higher scores on one of two divergent thinking tests. However, in a factor analysis neither of the divergent thinking tests loaded on a disposition toward intellectuality factor.

The art scale is not related positively to measures of intelligence (Bieri, Bradburn, and Galinsky, 1958; Harris, 1961; Hetrick, Lilly, and Merrifield, 1968; McWhinnie, 1967, 1969, 1970; Welsh, 1959). (McWhinnie and Bieri *et al.* used Embedded Figures Tests.) Eisenman's polygon measure was also unrelated to intelligence (Eisenman and Robinson, 1967).

Day (1968) found the art scale related to one measure of curiosity but not to another. The art scale loaded on Weissman's (1970) disposition toward intellectuality factor.

Intelligence could be expected to relate to curiosity in children, but Day's (1968) findings are variable, and Maw and Maw found positive relations in one case (1961a) but not in another (1961b). Day and Langevin (1969) found nonsignificant relations for nursing students. This evidence casts some doubt on the relevance of curiosity measures for the present purpose and suggests the need for more adequate measures of intrinsic task commitment.

With two groups of 10-year-olds, the writer examined relations between divergent thinking (measured under both gamelike and testlike conditions), intelligence, the Revised Art Scale, a measure of persistence on an arithmetic puzzle where children were free to stop when they chose, and a rating of involvement in self-initiated intellectual activity in the classroom. The art scale did not relate consistently with any other measure. There was some convergence between intelligence, divergent thinking (testlike assessment), and the two task-orientation indexes. This convergence was largely between measures of performance in the classroom, however, suggesting that a method factor might account for it. If other measures had been taken in a gamelike context, convergence between them and gamelike divergent thinking might have been found. By definition, a trait must show cross-situational generality. Thus, though the study was not comprehensive, it does not support the concept of a trait of creativity, but suggests that a situationally specific dimension of creativity may be found.

As the art scale has proved empirically fruitful with high-level creatives, its failure to relate to the other measures (in this study and those reviewed above) must raise serious doubts about the validity of the concept of a trait of creativity in children. With college students, the evidence is more encouraging. This might reflect a stabilization of the meaning of the dimensions by young adulthood or the restricted range of the college samples. In the latter respect, the studies of college students are similar, and the studies of children dissimilar, to the studies reviewed in the previous section.

Though further and more adequate research might be desirable, the concept of creativity as a normally distributed trait is not well supported by the available evidence. And even if it were better supported, its restricted and variable relevance to creative workers of different types, in different fields, and at different times would have to be acknowledged. As the concept is not necessary for the study of creativity in people in general, approaches anchored to achievement criteria seem preferable. Such approaches can take full account of the differing requirements of performance in different areas and leave open the question of relations between early and late achievement, although there is some evidence that early achievement is predictive of later achievement (Klein and Evans, 1969).

Divergent Thinking as Creative Ability

Further research on divergent thinking confirms that these tests are best not labeled creativity tests. Effects of preconceptions about creativity on divergent thinking research emphasize the need for research unhampered by these preconceptions.

The status of divergent thinking tests as indexes of creativity is not enhanced by the evidence reviewed above. This status can also be questioned because of the absence of positive relations with social independence and introversion. It has been suggested that extraversion is related to divergent thinking, and some findings with divergent thinking tests seem explicable in terms of this (Eysenck, 1967). Three studies found nonsignificant relations between these dimensions (Hudson, 1968; Iwata, 1968; Souief and El-Sayed, 1970), while one found extraversion and divergent thinking positively related (Kobayashi, 1970).

McHenry and Shouksmith (1970) found that children's acceptance of supposed group norms (for names of inkblots) was related positively to divergent thinking. Dacey and Ripple (1969) found that divergent thinking was unrelated to independence of other's opinions. Weisberg and Springer (1961) found that high divergent thinking scorers were no different from low scorers in striving for independence. Long, Henderson, and Ziller (1967) found that children with high originality scores were socially dependent (but there were indications of alienation from salient adults, a trend also observed by Weisberg and Springer, 1961). Wallach and Kogan's data (Cronbach, 1968) also show that social dependency and divergent thinking are related positively.

Thus, the evidence suggests that divergent thinking tests do not provide a meaningful index of creativity. We have not been concerned with the effectiveness of these tests in the prediction of creative achievement, except with high-level or eminent persons. The research on criterion validity of divergent thinking creativity tests in average samples cannot be reviewed here, but validations are not abundant (Vernon, 1967; Wallach, 1970), and negative findings have been reported (Harvey, Hoffmeister, Coates, and White, 1970; Moss and Duenk, 1967). If authors are less likely to submit and editors less likely to accept nil results (Bakan, 1966), the reality may be worse than the appearance. If, as Torrance (1969) found, divergent thinking tests are of value in predicting criteria of creativity in the high intelligence range, this certainly suggests the usefulness of the tests. However, it is fairly safe to predict that intelligence tests will be similarly useful with groups high in divergent thinking. In fact, despite a restricted intelligence range in his sample, Torrance (1969) did find intelligence significantly related to his criteria. Klein and Evans (1969) also found intelligence predictive of creative achievement in adolescents. If both types of tests prove effective in predicting creative achievement, there should be good reasons for calling one, but not the other, a measure of creative ability. Such reasons may exist, but they seem largely of the face validity type (Wallach, 1970), and this form of validity is heavily dependent on the eye of the beholder.

If research evidence on eminent creators is taken as a guide, there is more justification for calling the tendency to become intrinsically involved in tasks creativity than there is for labeling divergent thinking as creativity. Perhaps the identification of divergent thinking rather than task commitment with creativity reflects the popular view of creativity that emphasizes freedom of impulse and absence of constraints (Maddi, 1965; Wyschogrod, 1966). Moderate correlations between teachers' ratings of creativity and creative ability tests (Haddon and Lytton, 1971; Torrance, 1967) could support the claims that divergent thinking ability is creative ability or that the tests have been accepted as creativity tests because they accord with the popular concept of creativity. Popular belief on the nature of creativity might be of interest to psychologists, but it hardly provides a satisfactory basis for naming psychological dimensions.

In view of the importance attached to creativity in society at large, some reflections in psychological thought are not surprising. A number of writers have observed that modern man seeks to achieve meaning for meaningless existence through creativity (Bruner, 1962; Kallen, 1970; Morreale, 1969; Wyschogrod, 1966). When creativity is "deified" (Wyschogrod, 1966) or "designates superior spiritual status" (Kallen, 1970), everybody including the unintelligent must have access to creativity. If not a uniformly, at least a normally distributed trait of creativity is necessary if all are to be saved. It must be possible for psychologists to acknowledge the dignity and value of every person without attempting to bless them with the qualities of eminent creators. . . .

In view of the dubious status of divergent thinking measures as creativity tests, the practice of establishing criterion groups of creatives on the basis of joint status on divergent thinking tests and creativity ratings is questionable, even if ratings are given the greater weighting (Anastasi and Schaefer, 1969; Schaefer, 1969a, 1969b). Further, this practice means that potentially valuable information remains inaccessible to anyone wishing to examine the meaning of divergent thinking behavior. If the correlates of the two indexes used to establish criterion groups were presented separately, clarification of their significance might be achieved. In the same fashion, studies attempting to validate creative ability tests against composite indexes formed from a number of creativity criterion scores do not increase our understanding of divergent thinking as much as they might easily do (Dewing, 1970).

There is a clear need for research on divergent thinking that is not constrained by preconceptions about creativity. Hudson (1966, 1968) suggested that divergent thinking ability relates to personality functioning in a way that is not integrally related to creativity but that is related to arts versus science bias. His work has methodological problems (Kinsbourne, 1968), but other studies more often find students of the arts scoring higher (Cropley and Field, 1968; Pont, 1970; Rump, 1969; Rump and Dunn, 1971) than the same as science students (Haddon and Lytton, 1971). If divergent thinking tests are considered creativity tests, it follows that students of the arts are more creative than those in science. This is analogous to asserting that runners are better athletes than rowers. While the suggestion that majors in the arts are more creative than those in business (Eisenman, 1969a) may have more intuitive appeal, this conclusion tends to imply unnecessary, perhaps questionable, value judgments and, by providing an interpretation of group differences in divergent thinking that is both vague and somehow closes the issue, obscures rather than encourages clarification of the nature of differences between these groups. As has been suggested, Hudson's approach is of some value in interpreting Shapiro's research. The finding that divergent thinking scores relate to quality of imaginative writing (Wodtke, 1964) might also reflect the tendency for arts-biased students to perform better on such tasks than science-biased students. Hudson's approach is one that might be pursued more vigorously if divergent thinking were not identified with creativity.

While it would be hasty to conclude that divergent thinking is not implicated in at least some forms of creativity, there are good reasons for using neutral labels when referring to this aspect of thinking. The continuing use of "creativity tests" is not justified on the grounds "that a test of creativity is not 'creativity' just as a test of intelligence is not 'intelligence' [Dellas and Gaier, 1970, p. 59]." Intelligence tests do not exhaust the meaning of intelligence, but they are valuabFe predictors of many aspects of intelligent behavior. A parallel claim cannot be made for divergent thinking creativity tests.

Yamamoto (1965) accounted for the confusion in creativity research by likening researchers to blind men and creativity to the proverbial elephant. This simile, however, is too simple. There are, in fact, a variety of genuine elephants, and the blind men have in many cases coped with this pretty well. A major source of confusion, however, is the unacknowledged collection of domestic pets that accompany the blind men into the elephant compound.

Pseudocreativity, where creativity is sought to give meaning to life, can be contrasted with genuine creativity, where the creator is guided primarily by the nature of the materials he is working with (Wyschogrod, 1966). This element of genuine creativity has been absent too often in research on "creative ability." A more consistent use of neutral labels for divergent thinking and related processes might lead to research that is freer of preconceptions and, by reducing the plausibility of ready-made explanations for creative production in less-than-eminent subjects, might foster increased task-oriented enquiry in this area also.

References

ANASTASI, A. and SCHAEFER, C. E. (1969) Biographical correlates of artistic and literary creativity in adolescent girls. *Journal of Applied Psychology*, 53, 267–273.

AUSUBEL, D. P. (1964) Creativity, general creative abilities, and the creative individual. *Psychology in the Schools*, 1, 344–347.

BAKAN, D. (1966) The test of significance in psychological research. *Psychological Bulletin*, 66, 423–437.

BARRON, F. (1958) The needs for order and disorder as motives in creative activity. In C. Taylor (Ed.), *The 1957 University of Utah research conference on the identification of creative scientific talent*. Salt Lake City: University of Utah Press.

BARRON, F. (1963) *Creativity and psychological health*. Princeton: Van Nostrand.

BARRON, F. (1969) *Creative person and creative process*. New York: Holt, Rinehart & Winston.

BIERI, J., BRADBURN, W. H. and GALINSKY, M. D. (1958) Sex differences in perceptual behaviour. *Journal of Personality*, 26, 1–12.

BOERSMA, F. J. and O'BRYAN, K. (1968) An investigation of the relationship between creativity and intelligence under two conditions of testing. *Journal of Personality*, 36, 341–348.

BRUNER, J. S. (1962) The conditions of creativity. In H. E. Gruber, G. Terell and M. Wertheimer (Eds), *Contemporary approaches to creative thinking*. New York: Prentice-Hall.

CAMPBELL, D. T. (1960) Blind variation and selective retention in creative thought as in other knowledge processes. *Psychological Review*, 67, 380–400.

CATTELL, R. B. and BUTCHER, H. J. *The prediction of achievement and creativity*. New York: Bobbs-Merrill.

CHAMBERS, J. A. (1964) Relating personality and biographical factors to scientific creativity. *Psychological Monographs*, 78 (7, Whole No. 584).

COVINGTON, M. V. (1967) New directions in the appraisal of creative potential. Unpublished manuscript, University of California, Berkeley.

CRONBACH, L. J. (1968) Intelligence? Creativity? A parsimonious reinterpretation of the Wallach-Kogan data. *American Educational Research Journal*, 5, 491–511.

CROPLEY, A. J. and FIELD, T. W. (1968) Intellectual style and high school science. *Nature*, 218, 1211–1212.

CRUTCHFIELD, R. S. (1962) Conformity and creative thinking. In H. E. Gruber, G. Terrell and M. Wertheimer (Eds), *Contemporary approaches to creative thinking.* New York: Prentice-Hall.

CSIKSZENTMIHALYI, M. and GETZELS, J. W. (1970) Concern for discovery: An attitudinal component of creative production. *Journal of Personality,* 38, 91–105.

DACEY, J. and RIPPLE, R. (1969) Relationships of some adolescent characteristics and verbal creativity. *Psychology in the Schools,* 6, 321–324.

DAY, H. I. (1968) A curious approach to creativity. *Canadian Psychologist,* 9, 485–497.

DAY, H. I. and LANGEVIN, R. (1969) Curiosity and intelligence: Two necessary conditions for a high level of creativity. *Journal of Special Education,* 3, 263–268.

DELLAS, M. and GAIER, E. L. (1970) Identification of creativity: The individual. *Psychological Bulletin,* 73, 55–73.

DEWING, K. (1970) The reliability and validity of selected tests of creative thinking in a sample of seventh-grade West-Australian children. *British Journal of Educational Psychology,* 40, 35–42.

EISENMAN, R. (1969a) Creativity and academic major: Business versus English majors. *Journal of Applied Psychology,* 53, 392–395.

EISENMAN, R. (1969b) Creativity, awareness, and liking. *Journal of Consulting and Clinical Psychology,* 33, 157–160.

EISENMAN, R. and BOSS, E. (1970) Complexity-simplicity and persuasibility. *Perceptual and Motor Skills,* 31, 651–656.

EISENMAN, R. and FOXMAN, D. J. (1970) Creativity: Reported family patterns and scoring methodology. *Psychological Reports,* 26, 615–621.

EISENMAN, R. and ROBINSON, N. (1967) Complexity-simplicity, creativity, intelligence, and other correlates. *Journal of Psychology,* 67, 331–334.

EISENMAN, R. and SCHUSSEL, N. R. (1970) Creativity, birth order, and preference for symmetry. *Journal of Consulting and Clinical Psychology,* 34, 275–280.

EYSENCK, H. J. (1967) Intelligence assessment: A theoretical and experimental approach. *British Journal of Educational Psychology,* 37, 81–98.

FOX, H. H. (1963) A critique on creativity in science. In M. A. Coler and P. A. McGhee (Eds), *Essays on creativity in the sciences.* New York: New York University Press.

GHISELIN, B. (Ed.) (1955) *The creative process.* New York: Mentor.

GOLANN, S. E. (1962) The creativity motive. *Journal of Personality,* 30, 588–600.

GOLANN, S. E. (1963) The psychological study of creativity. *Psychological Bulletin,* 60, 548–565.

GROVE, M. S. and EISENMAN, R. (1970) Personality correlates of complexity-simplicity. *Perceptual and Motor Skills,* 31, 387–391.

GUILFORD, J. P. (1964) Some new looks at the nature of creative processes. In N. Frederiksen and H. Gilliksen (Eds), *Contributions to mathematical psychology.* New York: Holt, Rinehart & Winston.

GUILFORD, J. P. (1967) *The nature of human intelligence.* New York: McGraw-Hill.

HADDON, F. A. and LYTTON, H. (1971) Primary education and divergent thinking abilities— four years on. *British Journal of Educational Psychology,* 41, 136–147.

HARMON, L. R. (1958) The development of a criterion of scientific competence. In C. Taylor (Ed.), *The 1957 University of Utah research conference on the identification of creative scientific talent.* Salt Lake City: University of Utah Press.

HARRIS, T. L. (1961) An analysis of the responses made by adolescents to Welsh Figure Preference Test and its implications for guidance purposes. Unpublished doctoral dissertation, University of North Carolina.

HARVEY, O. J., HOFFMEISTER, J. K., COATES, C. and WHITE, B. J. (1970) A partial evaluation of Torrance's test of creativity. *American Educational Research Journal,* 7, 359–372.

HELSON, R. (1971) Women mathematicians and the creative personality. *Journal of Consulting and Clinical Psychology,* 36, 210–220.

HELSON, R. and CRUTCHFIELD, R. S. (1970a) Creative types in mathematics. *Journal of Personality,* 38, 177–197.

HELSON, R. and CRUTCHFIELD, R. S. (1970b) Mathematicians: The creative researcher and the average PhD. *Journal of Consulting and Clinical Psychology*, 34, 250–257.

HETRICK, S. H., LILLY, R. S. and MERRIFIELD, P. R. (1968) Figural creativity, intelligence and personality in children. *Multivariate Behavioral Research*, 3, 173–187.

HOLLAND, J. L. (1961) Creative and academic performance among talented adolescents. *Journal of Educational Psychology*, 52, 136–147.

HUDSON, L. (1966) *Contrary imaginations*. London: Methuen.

HUDSON, L. (1968) *Frames of mind*. London: Methuen.

IWATA, O. (1968) Some relationships of creativity with intelligence and personality variables. *Psychologica*, 11, 211–220.

JACKSON, D. N. (1969) Multimethod factor analysis in the evaluation of convergent and discriminant validity. *Psychological Bulletin*, 72, 30–49.

JACKSON, P. W. and MESSICK, S. (1965) The person, the product, and the response: Conceptual problems in the assessment of creativity. *Journal of Personality*, 33, 309–329.

KALLEN, H. M. (1970) "Creativity" today. *Philosophy and Phenomenological Research*, 30, 428–435.

KINSBOURNE, M. (1968) The contrary imaginations of arts and science students: A critical discussion. *Developmental Medicine and Child Neurology*, 10, 461–464.

KLEIN, S. P. and EVANS, F. R. (1969) Early predictors of later creative achievements. *Proceedings of the 77th Annual Convention of the American Psychological Association*, 4, 153–154.

KOBAYASHI, M. J. (1970) Relationships of intelligence and creativity to anxiety and extraversion-introversion in ninth-grade Japanese children. *Dissertation Abstracts*, 30 (9–A), 3730.

KRIS, E. (1952) *Psychoanalytic explorations in art*. New York: International Universities Press.

LONG, B. N., HENDERSON, E. H. and ZILLER, R. C. (1967) Self-social correlates or originality in children. *Journal of Genetic Psychology*, 111, 47–57.

MacKINNON, D. W. (1964) The creativity of architects. In C. W. Taylor (Ed.), *Widening horizons in creativity*. New York: Wiley.

MacKINNON, D. W. (1965) Personality and the realization of creative potential. *American Psychologist*, 20, 273–281.

MADDI, S. R. (1965) Motivational aspects of creativity. *Journal of Personality*, 33, 330–347.

MAW, W. and MAW, E. W. (1961a) Establishing criterion groups for evaluating a measure of curiosity. *Journal of Experimental Education*, 12, 57–61.

MAW, W. and MAW, E. W. (1961b) Nonhomeostatic experiences as stimuli of children with high curiosity. *California Journal of Educational Research*, 7, 57–63.

MAW, W. and MAW, E. W. (1965) Personal and social variables differentiating children with high and low curiosity. (Cooperative Res. Proj., No. 1911) University of Delaware.

McCURDY, H. G. (1960) The childhood pattern of genius. *Horizon*, 2, 33–38.

McHENRY, R. E. and SHOUKSMITH, G. A. (1970) Creativity, visual imagination and suggestibility: Their relationship in a group of 10-year-old children. *British Journal of Educational Psychology*, 40, 154–160.

McNEMAR, Q. (1964) Lost: Our intelligence? Why? *American Psychologist*, 19, 871–882.

McREYNOLDS, P. W., ACKER, M. and PIETILA, M. (1961) The relation of object curiosity to psychological adjustment in children. *Child Development*, 32, 366–374.

McWHINNIE, H. J. (1967) Some relationships between creativity and perception in sixth-grade children. *Perceptual and Motor Skills*, 25, 979–980.

McWHINNIE, H. J. (1969) Some relationships between creativity and perception in fourth-grade children. *Acta Psychologica*, 31, 169–175.

McWHINNIE, H. J. (1970) A factor analytic study of perceptual behaviour in 4th and 5th grade children. *Acta Psychologica*, 34, 89–97.

MEDINNUS, G. and LOVE, J. M. (1965) The relation between curiosity and security in preschool children. *Journal of Genetic Psychology*, 107, 91–98.

MEDNICK, S. A. (1962) The associative basis of the creative process. *Psychological Review*, 69, 220–232.

MORREALE, B. (1969) Tales of academe. *Encounter*, 33, 25–32.

MOSS, J., Jr. and DUENK, L. G. (1967) Estimating the concurrent validity of the Minnesota Tests of Creative Thinking. *American Educational Research Journal*, 4, 386–396.

NICHOLLS, J. G. (1971) Some effects of test procedure on divergent thinking. *Child Development*, 42, 1647–1651.

PENNY, R. K. and McCANN, B. (1964) The children's reactive curiosity scale. *Psychological Reports*, 15, 323–324.

PONT, H. B. (1970) The arts-science dichotomy. In H. J. Butcher and H. B. Pont (Eds), *Educational research in Britain 2.* London: University of London Press.

ROE, A. (1952) *The making of a scientist.* New York: Dodd, Mead.

RUMP, E. E. (1969) Comparisons between arts and science students on measures related to divergent thinking ability. Paper presented at 41st Congress of the Australian and New Zealand Association for the Advancement of Science, Adelaide.

RUMP, E. E. and DUNN, M. (1971) Extensions to the study of science students' divergent thinking ability. *Nature*, 229, 349–350.

SCHAEFER, C. E. (1969a) Imaginary companions and creative adolescents. *Developmental Psychology*, 1, 747–749.

SCHAEFER, C. E. (1969b) The self-concept of creative adolescents. *Journal of Psychology*, 72, 233–242.

SHAPIRO, R. J. (1968) Creative research scientists. *Psychological Africana*, Supplement No. 4.

SNOW, C. P. (1966) *Variety of men.* New York: Scribners.

SOUEIF, M. I. and EL-SAYED, A. M. (1970) Curvilinear relationships between creative thinking abilities and personality traits. *Acta Psychologica*, 34, 1–21.

TAYLOR, C. W. and ELLISON, R. L. (1967) Biographical predictors of scientific performance. *Science*, 155, 1075–1080.

TAYLOR, D. W. (1958) Variables related to creativity and productivity among men in two research laboratories. In C. Taylor (Ed.), *The 1957 University of Utah research conference on the identification of creative scientific talent.* Salt Lake City: University of Utah Press.

TAYLOR, R. E. and EISENMAN, R. (1964) Perception and production of complexity by creative art students. *Journal of Psychology*, 57, 239–242.

TORRANCE, E. P. (1967) The Minnesota studies of creative behavior: National and international extensions. *Journal of Creative Behavior*, 1, 137–154.

TORRANCE, E. P. (1969) Prediction of adult creative achievement among high school seniors. *Gifted Child Quarterly*, 13, 223–229.

VERNON, P. E. (1967) Psychological studies of creativity. *Journal of Child Psychology and Psychiatry*, 8, 153–164.

WALLACH, M. A. (1970) Creativity. In P. H. Mussen (Ed.), *Carmichael's manual of child psychology.* (3rd ed.) New York: Wiley.

WALLACH, M. A. and KOGAN, N. (1965) *Modes of thinking in young children.* New York: Holt, Rinehart & Winston.

WARD, W. C. (1968) Creativity in young children. *Child Development*, 39, 737–754.

WEISBERG, P. S. and SPRINGER, K. J. (1961) Environmental factors in creative function. *Archives of General Psychiatry*, 5, 554–564.

WEISSMAN, H. N. (1970) Disposition toward intellectuality: Its composition and its assessment. *Journal of General Psychology*, 82, 99–107.

WELSH, G. G. (1959) *Welsh Figure Preference Test: Preliminary manual.* Palo Alto: Consulting Psychologists Press.

WODTKE, K. H. (1964) Some data on the reliability and validity of creativity tests at the elementary school level. *Educational and Psychological Measurement*, 24, 399–408.

WYSCHOGROD, M. (1966) The cult of creativity. *Teachers College Record*, 67, 618–622.

YAMAMOTO, K. (1965) Creativity: A blind man's report on the elephant. *Journal of Counseling Psychology*, 12, 428–434.

ZIMMERMAN, W. S. (1964) Statistical problems and some related issues in the selection of items for tests of creativity. *Journal of Educational Measurement*, 1, 93–96.

2

The Processes of Creative Thought *

R. B. CATTELL

THE VARIETY of ideas about the causes of creativity in genius are endless, ranging from Moorman's (1940) theory of germ stimulation by tuberculosis (Voltaire, R. L. Stevenson, Bashkirtseff, Keats, Shelley, Sidney Lanier, Hood, Bessemer, Schiller, and others), to Lombroso's "equivalent to crime," to Kretschmer's "warring heredities," to Adler's overcompensation for inferiority, and even to Freud's "evasion of reality."

The modern and quantitative study of genius can be said to begin with Galton (1870), who stressed the centrality of sheer "g," and demonstrated the substantial hereditary connections of that "g". Havelock Ellis may be said to have added the importance of temperament, in his finding from statistical analyses in the National Portrait Gallery (unfortunately not since followed up) that in Britain the Nordic strain (Newton, Kelvin, Edison, Rutherford) expressed itself in mathematics and science, and the Celtic strain (dark-eyed and haired) in religion, history, and verbal-social skills. Kretschmer (1931) followed Nietzsche ("Where is the madness with which you should be inoculated?") and the Greeks in believing that there must be some element of the fanatic in genius. He stressed hybridization of talented races, and, (as followed up later by Sheldon) the importance of temperament, rooted in body build, in deciding the direction of expression, here reaching views essentially consistent with those of Havelock Ellis.

More careful documentation followed, in this tradition, in the work of Cox and Terman (1926), who studied 301 men of genius from the past, and then in Terman (1925) who began that monumental follow-up of children actually selected by intelligence tests to lie within the top 1% of the ability range. The former study fully confirmed the general emphasis by Galton on high absolute magnitude of general intelligence in geniuses. When rated by independent judges operating on childhood biographical data, 84% of the 301 geniuses received, by modern IQ standards (sigma = 15–16), IQs of 120 or more, and 21% of 150 or more. Additionally, Catherine Cox (1926, Vol. 2, p. 218) called attention to the pervasive frequency of "persistence of motive and effort, confidence in their abilities and great strength or force of character," which Galton has also commented on as "great energy and zeal."

---

*Chapter 13 in *Abilities: Their Structure, Growth, and Action*. Boston: Houghton Mifflin (1971), pp. 407–417. Reprinted by permission of the author.

From there, the chief developments have been studies on living subjects: (a) of abilities *other* than general intelligence, by Guilford, Merrifield, and a group of able associates (1961); (b) of the criterion of creative performance in life, by Calvin Taylor and his associates (1963), Barron (1963) and others; and (c) of personality and motivation, in terms of modern, measurable dimensions by Cattell and Drevdahl (1955), Cox (1926), Drevdahl and Cattell (1958), Jones (1959), Sprecher (1959) and others. The second of these lines of research is vitally necessary, for until we know how the actual criteria correlate we do not know whether we are trying to predict one thing or several. Taylor's work shows definitely that among scientists in industry the publication of research articles, the number of patents obtained, etc., are different from and little correlated with the evaluation by peers and supervisors. The personality analyses (in this field and by Lowell Kelly in medical research) give a clue to this discrepancy between criteria, because they show that creative persons are apt to be unpopular. Incidentally, finding firm criteria is the toughest part of this area of research. It is not an intellectually defensible escape from this problem of an objective criterion of creativity to say it cannot be documented and *must* rest on ratings. For "ratings" are merely personal opinions, changing with the cultural affiliations, intelligence, etc., of the rater.

This issue also affects the approach to creativity by measures other than intelligence. Guilford and his co-workers who have gone to abilities beyond intelligence, nevertheless have defined creativity in *the test performance itself*, instead of by some life criterion through which the designation of a test as a "creativity" measure could be validated. The result is that the verdict that a test measures creativity is only a projection of the test constructor's personal view about what creativity is. Thus in the intellectual tests designed by Guilford's students, and many others who have worked on creativity in this decade, creativity has finished up by being evaluated simply as oddity or bizarreness of response relative to the population mean or as output of words per minute, etc. This indeed comes close to mistaking the shadow for the substance. Mere unusualness, without adaptive values, is, as Eysenck shows (1957) actually a good measure of psychopathy or neuroticism, not creativity. Again one must repeat that many creative products are odd; but oddity is not creativity. For some, additional, vital condition must be met by the latter.

Of course, in the last resort, a similar charge of circularity could be brought also with regard to intelligence, if Galton, Terman, and others had not located their geniuses first and *afterward* evaluated their intelligence. Terman found, as we have seen, that geniuses of the past, vindicated by history, were generally of exceptionally high intelligence. But this makes intelligence only a necessary, not a sufficient condition. It was only when Terman came to his study of *living* children of high intelligence and allowed it to be called a study of genius that a doubtful logical assumption crept in. A writer can be the victim of his readers, and in this case perhaps the mistake is in assuming that Terman intended that the label "genius" apply to these bright individuals before later life performances had confirmed their status. Another instance of this dictatorship of the follower may have occurred in the followers of Guilford, whose emphasis on abilities other than intelligence has become for the moment the popular view that intelligence is unnecessary! It remains true, as Burt (1967), Butcher (1969), Thorndike (1943), and Vernon (1960) have reminded neophytes in the field, that general intelligence is *still* the main essential *ability* (apart from personality traits) and that the one, sure, common feature of many and varied tests of creativity is their high "g" saturation. As Burt has pointed out: "the new tests for creativity would form very satisfactory additions to any ordinary battery for testing the general factor of intelligence."

Some Ability and Personality Associates of High Creativity

If, as suggested above, we stand by *actual life performance* (rather than performance in a two-hour test of artificial "creativity measures") as the necessary criterion, then – after intelligence – the most important determiners are unquestionably personality factors. Biographical studies by Roe (1953), Barron (1963), the present writer (1963b) and especially Drevdahl and Cattell (1958) agree with the view inherent in Havelock Ellis, Kretchmer, Terman, Galton, and other shrewd observers that the creative person does possess, over and above intelligence, some very characteristic personality qualities. These may or may not be considered healthy normal qualities – this is often a matter of values – but the psychologist today can at least analyze them as meaningful source traits which point to clear theories of causal action.

Without space to present separately the profiles from the various personality factor surveys of highly creative people in physical science, biology, psychology, art, and literature (see Cattell and Drevdahl, 1955; Drevdahl and Cattell, 1958) – which, incidentally, agree amazingly well, considering the diversity of interest of the groups – we present in Figure VI.1 the composite, central profile found. Its greatest deviations from the average are (apart from intelligence) on high self-sufficiency, introversion, dominance, and desurgency.

The selection of outstandingly creative individuals was made in these cases by committees of peers, and is thus, in essence, the same as, say, a Nobel prize selection procedure. It differs from direct personality rating in that it is made with documents and productions. In the case of the common (three area) scientist's profile the raters also were asked to contrast their choices with choices of equally academically distinguished men (administrators and teachers) *not* creatively gifted. Since abbreviated discussion most easily proceeds with the broader second-stratum level of personality factors (though the more accurate prediction and understanding rest on the primaries), we may point out that at a rough glance these people would be described as introverts (second-order Factor I). They also show high self-sufficiency and dominance in the primaries. Both

Source Trait	Direction		Scientists	Artists	Literary	Artistic and Literary Creators Same or Different from Scientists
			(114)	(64)	(89)	
A	(–)	Sizothyme	3.4*	3.0*	3.9*	S
B	(+)	Intelligent	9.1*	8.3*	8.8*	S
†C	(+, –)	Ego strong and Ego weak	6.9*	5.1*	4.2*	D
E	(+)	Dominant	7.2*	5.6*	6.0*	S
F	(–)	Desurgent	3.5*	3.3*	4.0*	S
G	(–)	Casual	3.4*	5.1*	4.7*	S
†H	(+, –)	Parmic and Threctic	6.5*	5.2*	4.9*	D
I	(+)	Premsic	7.1*	8.9*	7.8*	S
L	(–)	Alaxic	4.1*	5.2	5.4	S
M	(+)	Autious	5.5	8.8*	6.8*	
N	(+)	Unaffected	5.5	4.7*	5.2	
O	(+, –)	Poised and Guilt Prone	3.8*	6.1	6.1	D
Q_1	(+)	Radical	6.2*	6.9*	7.3*	S
Q_2	(+)	Self-Sufficient	6.5*	8.9*	9.2*	S
Q_3	(+)	Strong in Self-Sentiment	6.8*	6.0*	5.9*	S
Q_4	(–)	Low in Ergic tension	5.1*	5.2*	5.3	S

FIG. VI.1 Personality Profile Common to Those Creative in
Science, Art, and Literature (see Appendix VI.1)

*Significantly different from general population at $P < 0.05$ or beyond.
†A plus *and* a minus means above average in one area of creativity and below in another.

The data are from Cattell and Drevdahl, 1955, and Drevdahl and Cattell, 1958, in
nationally eminent U.S. figures.

the intensive *biographical* researches of Anne Roe (1953) and the more discursive
biographical survey by the present writer (1963b) strongly support the main
conclusions of these systematic *test* results. Cavendish hiding from society in a
remote wing of his mansion, Newton forever wandering on "strange seas of
thought, alone," Einstein remote in the patent office library, Darwin taking his
solitary walks in the woods at Down — these are the epitome of the way of life
of the creative person. If this introversion and intensity is the essence, it is easy
to see why a committedly extravert, impulsive and casual society has had to begin
frantically chasing — and vulgarizing — creativity over the last decade.

In this latter connection let us note that acceptance of the idea that measures
of fluency are measures of a creative ability has led to generalizations to the effect
that the temperamental and personality associations of fluency are conditions
of creativity. Thus, inferences drawn from the empirical research of Getzels and
Jackson (1962), for example, (who used certain tests from the Objective–Analytic
Personality Factor Battery, but not enough to measure any one factor) and the
theorizing of Maslow (1954), have led to the picture of the creative person

as an incontinent, unrestrained, over-self-expressive individual. In the latter's descriptions of the self-actualizing personality, one scarcely can escape the impression that, without some daily assault upon convention, such a personality feels futile. That some kind of true *flexibility* of temperament and thinking habits are necessary to genius no one can doubt. But according to personality research, this is a very different trait from the uninhibited (U.I. 17) dimension or the "exuberance" or U.I. 21 dimension. In 1948 Tiner and the present writer (Cattell and Tiner, 1949) completing a decade of study of rigidity (Cattell, 1933a) — defined as a motor-perceptual personality trait — by exploring its intellectual expressions, found that after putting aside the *classical* motor-perceptual rigidity factor (see Luchins and Luchins, 1959), and the general fluency factor (U.I. 21 or g_r), a new behavioral factor remained. This had the pattern reproduced in Table VI.1, and was called Ideational Flexibility-vs-Ideational Inertia or Rigidity, g_x. It suggests some kind of energy, and the question immediately arises whether we are unearthing a new kind of general ability capacity — a "g" — or whether this is some temperamental tendency which expresses itself partly in the cognitive domain. Against the former view is the fact that it has not appeared clearly as a second or third-stratum general power in cognitive measures only. Against the latter is the fact that Table VI.1 shows only one variable that could be definitely temperamental (flicker fusion) and that Guilford and his associates picked up this pattern later in pure ability traits. (It appeared, however, in their data, with that lopping off of part of the pattern which is due to the restriction of their researches to orthogonal rotations, thus making final interpretation somewhat difficult.) . . .

Until factorial searches are made over a wider spectrum of variables, such dilemmas as to ability or temperamental origin will remain. Indeed, we need constantly to be reminded that when tentatively we conceptualize the behavior of rigidity, fluency, and flexibility as expressions of cognitive performances, we are actually in a complex and insufficiently analyzed field in which much of the variance probably will turn out to be due to personality and temperament factors, notably those now indexed as U.I. 16 through U.I. 33. Thus the relation of Guilford's assumed ability factors,such as the above flexibility factor, to temperament, in any adequate sense still has to be investigated. Certainly much of the

TABLE VI. 1 *Behavior in the Dimension of Ideational Flexibility versus Firmness*

Performance and Direction of Measurement	Loading in the Factor
High ability to reconstruct hidden words	0.51
High success in finding solutions to riddles	0.41
Rapid speed of flicker fusion	0.41
Plasticity (changes in exactitudes of repetition of Werner tone rhythm test)	0.34
Good ability to restructure habitual visual perception	0.29

variance in classical motor-perceptual rigidity is due specifically to personality factors U.I. 21, 23, 26, etc., which could readily account for 90% of its variance.

Elsewhere in this volume we have made a more detailed analysis of the concept of flexibility-vs-rigidity. Rigidity is the most overused and under-analyzed term in the whole of personality psychology. . . .

The scientific way out from this mesmerized preoccupation with a word is to take the actual operations by which the various writers would consent to their subjective visions being represented by behavior, and to do an extensive factor analysis covering all manifestations. This has been accomplished up to a point by the work of Coan, the present writer (1933a and b, 1935a and b, 1943, 1946a and b, 1949, 1955a and b, 1965a and c, and 1967a), Damarin, Eysenck, Howarth, Hundleby, Knapp, Pawlik, Peterson, Rethlingshafer, Ryans, Saunders, Scheier and many others with less systematic attacks. The performances have ranged from perceptual (seeing new shapes or objects embedded in old objects) to motor (writing familiar letters in unusual combinations, calling the names of a string of colors by prescribed wrong names), and from physiological (hangover of a visual contrast effect, pulse rate persistence) to social and characterological (instability of attitudes, change of opinion under fact and authority). The verdict is perfectly clear that there is no such factor as general rigidity.

The view which emerges is that the concept has been under-analyzed, both experimentally and in conceptual definition. For example, an appreciable fraction of what the casual psychologist calls rigidity is due in the final place to low g_f, either innate or through brain injury. The mental defective goes on doing the same thing inappropriately because he does not have the relation-perceiving capacity to see that a more effective alternative presents itself. Secondly, the widespread derogation of ridigity (notably by psychiatrists and alleged progressive social issues psychologists) overlooks the fact that much "rigidity" is operationally simple character stability, C factor (such as is notoriously absent in neurotics) in the face of persuasion ("obstinacy" to the tempter). Human learning is based on a certain probability of constancy in the external world. The internal stability of a habit should match the external stability of the world, as Humphreys (1962) and others have shown in more technical detail experimentally. There is an optimum "plasticity" of habits. Probably our habits, if anything, err on the side of being insufficiently rigid, for memory is fallible, and the cue from the fact that would be correct (assuming some constancy in the external world) is lost. Low rigidity is here poor memory.

Strictly in the domain of cognitive process it is questionable whether flexibility-rigidity, in its myriad manifestations, is affected by more than g_f, g_r, and g_m — intelligence, fluency, and memory trace persistence. What emerges very clearly from the broader analyses is that, on the other hand, several distinct personality—temperament factors are involved, and that they determine more of the variance on flexibility—rigidity than do any cognitive factors. For example, the variance on the most widely used perceptual-motor rigidity battery (that investigated by

Pinard, Spearman, Stephenson, Eysenck, and the present writer, and consisting of performing old motor-perceptual tasks in new "interfering" ways) is significantly contributed to by no fewer than five personality factors: U.I. 23, Mobilization-vs-Regression; U.I. 24, Anxiety; U.I. 26, Narcissistic Self-Determination; U.I. 29, Superego; and U.I. 33, Depressive Tendency. These act to determine the total rigidity on this common measure in psychologically understandable ways. For example, the self-exactingness in superego strength, self-determination and depressive guilt work to overcome the tendency of the organism to accept the rigidity of its own natural process ("laziness," pleasure principle). In the case of the large effect of regression (U.I. 23) – and probably the small effect of anxiety (U.I. 24) – however, we see an effect on the very energy resources themselves needed to combat rigidity.

The role of these same personality factors in creativity in the broader sense (as distinct from this operational flexibility–rigidity) remains to be investigated. But if the questionnaire measurement of personality may be temporarily accepted as a guide, we should expect superego (U.I. 29), and what is virtually the self-sentiment (U.I. 26) to act as they do here, contributing to flexibility. In the questionnaire domain, it must not be overlooked that there is also a powerful contribution to creativity . . . from the dimension of radicalism–conservatism first demonstrated by Thurstone and, as Q_1, in the 16 PF, since shown to be broader than the religio–political items in his analysis. It seems to be some kind of temperamental tendency to restless critical adoption of the new, as opposed to a phlegmatic, tolerant conservatism.

The personality factors – other than intelligence – which favor creativity are not, by any means, highly advantageous or even adaptive in other realms of behavior. For example, higher rated mental hospital attendants (psychiatric technicians, see Shotwell, Hurley, and Cattell, 1961) are lower on Q_1, the more radical being presumably unable to tolerate the unreason of lunatics. The higher superego and self-sentiment, on the other hand, would be helpful in most situations. The plasticity contribution which comes from poor memory and high inherent lability, as in the dreamer who forgets his own telephone number, puts on socks of two different colors, and goes tortuously back to basic principles on the simplest decisions, operates in most situations undoubtedly as a defect rather than as a virtue of "flexibility." (Note, for example, in Table VI.1, the failure of the highly flexible to reproduce familiar sounds accurately.) This matter of fields of effectiveness is scrutinized more closely in the next section.

Flexibility is thus of considerable importance, but it is a complex entity traceable to several distinct events. Fluency, on the other hand, seems to be largely a general cognitive trait of ease of retrieval (plus local storage levels, . . . together with whatever impulsiveness or energy is ascribed to the highly inherited temperament trait of exuberance (U.I. 21). These are certainly important in determining the productivity or "divergence of thinking" in a test situation in a fixed short interval of time, as the work of Guilford and his collaborators abundantly proves; but it is still an open question whether g_r and U.I. 21 correlate positively, negatively, or insignificantly with *creativity in life*, over long periods, such as we examined in our leading physicists, biologists, artists, and writers. One suspects the correlation would be positive, but not as high as for the personality traits in Figure VI.1. In real performance, it was doubtless important that Kekulé had the flexibility of thought and the retrieval capacity to conjure up many images from which he culled at last the benzine ring structure, that Newton hearing the apple fall had the notion of universal gravitation, and that Archimedes' principle finally occurred to him daydreaming in his comfortable bath. But in what fraction of a second, after the thud of the falling apple in the still autumn evening, the idea came to Newton, or at what stage of the bath it came to Archimedes matters little. Output per minute is unimportant, compared to quality and aptness. The speed and productivity measures taken on artificial test situations are on a very different and possibly irrelevant level in relation to the productivity we encounter in real life originality.

Evidence on high creativity in life careers points to the necessity first of high intelligence, and second of a very characteristic, "concentrating," personality profile. In respect to life-long and fundamental originality, as shown in problem-solving and cultural contribution, these together are more important than any restricted special abilities or fluencies, and when we look at the personality associations more closely, the psychologist will recognize that our rough intro-ductory interpretation of the creative personality as "introverted" stops far short of all the information contained in the profile of primary personality factors in Figure VI.1. Indeed, first he will notice that there is a curious paradox within the second-stratum introversion pattern itself. For among these researchers, sizothymia (A −), desurgency (F −), and self-sufficiency (Q_2 +) appear strongly in what is normally the right direction for the second-stratum introversion factor, whereas threctia (H −) is in the wrong direction, i.e., creative researchers are parmic (H +). Another, and at present admittedly more speculative, way of saying this is that creative people are those who would constitutionally be extraverts (H +) but who have somehow been made introvert (A −, F −, Q_2 +) by heavy cultural pressures, and an environmental training in the depth-increasing value of inhibition. It is of much psychological interest to ask how − granted their association − the introvert qualities of A −, F −, and Q_2 operate to augment the creativity of the individual.

Let us look at personality dimension A − affectothymia-vs-sizothymia. Compared to the emotionally expressive and responsive affectothyme, the sizothyme according to ratings and questionnaire items, is dry, realistic, sceptical, and even "cranky." He does not see life in terms of easily given promises and of widely humanly acceptable, casual compromises with reality. Occupational data shows that A − makes a person a poor teacher of young children and a hopeless salesman (both high on A +), but a more effective house electrician or physicist (both A −). Considering next the F factor, we encounter, at the F −, desurgent end, the general inhibition component in introversion. Unlike the surgent wit — the happy-go-lucky "life and soul of the party" — the desurgent individual is cautious in statement, aware of many possibilities of failure and possessed of a deep feeling for responsibility. It is the inhibition we call desurgency (F –) that is responsible for his having second, third, and fourth thoughts where the surgent person expresses a superficial originality in the first. The self-sufficiency of the next factor, Q_2, is a very pervasive influence in the creative personality. Here we see the vital set of values necessary for living the kind of life which receives little social reinforcement and requires dogged pursuit of lonely trails. (The "lonely seas of thought" in which Newton confessed he had desired some company.)

To distinguish the precise and measurable pattern of the second-stratum (A, F, H, Q_2–) pattern from the battered popular expression extraversion–introversion, it has been called in personality theory *exvia-vs-invia*. This dimension of exvia-invia has been checked as a second-stratum factor at all post-infancy age levels, and, as the work of Eysenck and the present writer shows, it is very stable in form and characteristically measurable. One can readily see in psychological terms how the inviant adjustment favors intensive concentration on original production. It is interesting also, however, to consider the exvia-invia balance in energy-economic terms by the computer model considered a couple of chapters back. The computer model of abilities has elements of input, storage, processing, and output. If one needs much internal working over a material, the fewer working elements given over to input and output transactions, the better. The individual who is constantly immersed in "journalism" (derived from the French for "the day"), in current fashions in clothes, art, and what else, and in living the lives of all around him (as the A +, F +, H +, and Q_2– individual is) cannot obtain either the quiet or the sustained reserve of "working elements" for the actual processing. As the title of Balchin's novel of the life of scientists characterizes the situation, there is a necessity for living in *The Small Back Room*.

Other personality characteristics which differentiate the creative researcher, writer, and artist from the equally intelligent teacher, administrator, or journalistic writer are higher E (dominance), higher L (protension), and higher M (autia). The higher L — with its egotism and paranoidlike features — is responsible for some of those unpopular features of the scientist which a penetrating and realistic observer like Roe has not hesitated to draw for us (1953), and which incidentally, account for some of the asperity of scientific debates. Rightly or wrongly, most scientists are predisposed to the conviction that theirs is *the* conception needed, and high L helps them to exhaust its possibilities. The higher M, or autia factor, bespeaks a greater intensity and spontaneity of inner mental life (the relation of such inner imaginal activity is obvious). The higher dominance (E factor; see Figure VI.1) combined also with some tendency to higher radicalism, permits the scientist to sustain more comfortably the socially egregious positions into which his original thoughts get him. (Newton perhaps had insufficient of this, for he nearly gave up publishing after all the unpleasant disputes with Linus and Pardies into which his treatise on "Opticks" pitchforked him.)

Obviously the personality qualities that are most functional in enabling high intelligence to produce new ideas and father them to ultimate survival will vary with the social setting of the occupation of the scientist, the writer, and the artist. The setting and incentive system have changed in the last generation appreciably for the scientist; but the required core of personality qualities discussed above seems to remain the same. Without them high ability is only high ability.

Appendix VI.1

The reader may find helpful the following descriptions of Cattell's basic bipolar personality factors (PF). These are used in the 16 PF Questionnaire. The descriptions, culled from several sources, are as follows:

Factor	High Pole (+)		Low Pole (–)
A	Cyclothymia (outgoing, sociable)	vs.	Schizothymia (reserved, aloof)
B	Intelligence (bright)	vs.	Mental defect (dull)
C	Ego strength (stable, mature)	vs.	Dissatisfied emotionality (emotional, immature)
E	Dominance (assertive, aggressive)	vs.	Submission (humble, mild)
F	Surgency (happy-go-lucky, enthusiastic)	vs.	Desurgency (sober, serious)
G	Superego strength (conscientious)	vs.	Lack of rigid internal standards (expedient, casual)
H	Parmia (adventurous)	vs.	Threctia (shy)
I	Premsia (tender-minded)	vs.	Harria (tough-minded)
L	Protension (suspecting)	vs.	Alaxia (trusting)
M	Autia (imaginative, bohemian)	vs.	Praxernia (practical)
N	Shrewdness (sophisticated)	vs.	Naivete (unpretentious)
O	Guilt proneness (insecure, apprehensive)	vs.	Confident adequacy (self-secure, assured)
Q_1	Radicalism (experimenting)	vs.	Conservatism (conservative)
Q_2	Self-sufficiency (resourceful)	vs.	Group dependency (socially dependent)
Q_3	High self-sentiment (controlled)	vs.	Poor self-sentiment (uncontrolled)
Q_4	High ergic tension (tense, excitable)	vs.	Low ergic tension (composed, relaxed)

References

BARRON, F. (1963) *Creativity and Psychological Health*. Princeton: Van Nostrand.

BURT, C. (1967) Intelligence and achievement, *Mensa*, December, 1–20.

BUTCHER, J. (1968) *Human Intelligence: Its Nature and Assessment*. London: Methuen.

CATTELL, R. B. (1933a) Temperament tests: I temperament. *Br. J. Psychology*, 23, 308–329.

CATTELL, R. B. (1933b) Temperament tests: II tests. *Br. J. Psychology*, 24, 20–49.

CATTELL, R. B. (1935a) On the measurement of "perseveration". *Br. J. Educational Psychology*, 5, 76–92.

CATTELL, R. B. (1935b) Perseveration and personality: some experiments and a hypothesis. *J. Mental Science*, 61, 151–167.

CATTELL, R. B. (1943) The measurement of adult intelligence. *Psychological Bulletin*, 40, 153–193.

CATTELL, R. B. (1946a) *The Description and Measurement of Personality*. New York: World Books.

CATTELL, R. B. (1946b) The riddle of perseveration: I. "Creative effort" and disposition rigidity. *J. Personality*, 14, 229–238.

CATTELL, R. B. (1949) The dimensions of culture patterns by factorization of national characters. *J. Abnormal and Social Psychology*, 44, 443–469.

CATTELL, R. B. (1955a) Psychiatric screening of flying personnel. Personality structure in objective tests. USAF School of Aviation Medicine (Project No. 21-0202-0007), Report No. 9, 1–50.

CATTELL, R. B. (1955b) *The Objective-Analytic (O-A) Personality Test*, Champaign: Institute for Personality and Ability Testing.

CATTELL, R. B. (1963a) Theory of fluid and crystallized intelligence: a critical experiment. *J. Educational Psychology*, 54, 1–22.

CATTELL, R. B. (1963b) The personality and motivation of the researcher from measurements of contemporaries and from biography. In C. W. Taylor and F. Barron (Eds), *Scientific Creativity: Its Recognition and Development*. New York: Wiley, Chapter 9.

CATTELL, R. B. (1965a) *The Scientific Analysis of Personality*. London: Penguin Books.

CATTELL, R. B. (1965c) Higher order factor structures and reticular-vs.-hierarchical formulae for their interpretation. In C. Banks and P. L. Broadhurst (Eds), *Studies in Psychology*. London: University of London Press.

CATTELL, R. B. (1967a) The theory of fluid and crystallized general intelligence checked at the 5–6-year-old level. *Br. J. Educational Psychology*, 37 (2), 209–224.

CATTELL, R. B. and DREVDAHL, J. E. (1955) A comparison of the personality profile of eminent researchers with that of eminent teachers and administrators. *Br. J. Psychology*, 44, 248–261.

CATTELL, R. B. and TINER, L. G. (1949) The varieties of structural rigidity. *J. Personality*, 17, 321–341.

COX, C. and TERMAN, L. M. (1926) The early mental traits of 300 geniuses. *Genetic Studies of Genius*, Vol II. Stanford: University Press.

EYSENCK, H. J. (1957) *The Dynamics of Anxiety and Hysteria*. London: Kegan Paul.

GALTON, F. (1870) *Hereditary Genius*. New York: Appleton.

GETZELS, J. W. and JACKSON, P. W. (1962) *Creativity and Intelligence: Explorations with Gifted Students*. New York: Wiley.

GUILFORD, J. P., MERRIFIELD, P. R., CHRISTENSON, P. F. and FRICK, J. W. (1961) Some new symbolic factors of cognition and convergent production. *Educational and Psychological Measurement*, 21, 515–541.

HUMPHREYS, L. G. (1962) The organization of human abilities. *American Psychologist*, 17, 475–483.

JONES, H. E. (1959) Intelligence and problem solving. In J. E. Birren (Ed.), *Handbook of Aging and the Individual*. Chicago: University of Chicago Press.

LUCHINS, A. S. and LUCHINS, E. H. (1959) *Rigidity of Behavior*. Eugene: University of Oregon Books.

MASLOW, A. H. (1954) *Motivation and Personality*. New York: Harper.

MOORMAN, L. J. (1940) *Tuberculosis and Genius*. Chicago: University of Chicago Press.

ROE, A. (1953) *The Making of a Scientist*. New York: Dodd.

SHOTWELL, A. M. HURLEY, J. R. and CATTELL, R. B. (1961) Motivational structure of an hospitalized mental defective. *J. Abnormal and Social Psychology*, 62, 422–426.

SPRECHER, T. B. (1959) A study of engineers' criteria for creativity. *J. Applied Psychology*, 43, 141–148.

TAYLOR, C. W. and BARRON, F. (1963) *Scientific Creativity: Its Recognition and Development*. New York: Wiley.

TERMAN, L. M. (1925) *Mental and Physical Traits of a Thousand Gifted Children*. London: Harrap and Co.

THORNDIKE, R. L. (1943) The origin of superior men. *Scientific Monographs*, 56, 424–433.

VERNON, P. E. (1960) *Intelligence and Attainment Tests*. London: University of London Press.

3

Creative Architects*

D. W. MacKINNON

Ego and Self in Creative Process

THE history of the concepts of ego and self has been a long and confused one, but there is today rather general agreement upon the sense in which each is to be used in psychological theory. In a functionalist psychology of personality the ego is conceived to be a system of regulating functions – inhibition, reality testing, decision-making, scheduling, etc. – which serve to integrate the subsystems of personality. On the other hand, it effects adjustment of the individual to the situation in which he finds himself and, on the other hand, it permits the individual to express himself in creative actions which change the environment and contribute to the actualization of himself through the development and expression of his potentialities. In contrast to the ego, the self is conceived of as an individual's system of perceptions, conceptions, and images of himself as a person. The two systems are intimately related; the regulating functions of the ego are obviously influenced by the complex of percepts, concepts, and images which constitute the self, while the content of awareness that the perceiving individual thinks of as his self is clearly influenced by the quality and quantity of the functioning of his ego.

This is the rationale that led us in our study of creative persons and the creative process to hypothesize that the creativeness with which persons perform in their professional roles is a function of their images of themselves as individuals and as professional practitioners.

The Subjects

The subjects whose creativity and images of the self are here reported are 124 American architects. Forty of them, constituting a nationwide sample and here designated as Architects I, were selected by a panel of five professors of architecture at the University of California, Berkeley, for the unusual creativeness they had shown in the practice of their profession.

The second group, Architects II, consists of forty-three architects so chosen as to match Architects I with respect to age and the geographic location of their

*The Study of Lives. New York: Atherton Press (1964).

practice. Each of them met the additional requirement that he had had at least two years of work experience and association with one of the originally selected creative architects.

The third sample, Architects III, was also chosen to match Architects I with respect to age and geographic location of practice, but, unlike Architects II, the forty-one men in this group had never worked with any of the Architects I.

Architects I, II, and III were selected in this manner in hopes of tapping a range of creative talent sufficiently wide to be fairly representative of the profession as a whole. To determine whether or not we had succeeded, ratings on a seven-point scale of the creativity of all 124 architects were obtained from six groups of architects and architectural experts. . . . The differences are in the expected direction and are statistically highly significant.

. . . The three samples show an overlap in their judged creativity; they are not discontinuous groups, but, combined, approximate a normal distribution of judged creativeness ranging from a low of 1.9 to a high of 6.5 on a seven-point rating scale. . . .

Image of the Self as Person

A major technique employed for the recording of the architects' images of themselves was the Gough Adjective Check List (ACL) (1). Upon its first administration each architect was asked to check on this list of three hundred adjectives those which he judged to be most descriptive of himself, and upon its second presentation to check those which would describe him if he were the person he would like to be. The two images thus obtained were, first, the images of the *real self* and, second, the image of the *ideal self* or *ego ideal*.

Adjective Descriptions of the Real Self

. . . Architects I, more often than either Architects II or III, see themselves as inventive, determined, independent, individualistic, enthusiastic, and industrious; more often than Architects II they say they are adaptable, and have wide interests; and more often than Architects III they describe themselves as artistic, progressive, and appreciative. A strikingly different image of the self is held by both Architects II and III, who more often check as self-descriptive the adjectives responsible, sincere, reliable, dependable, clear-thinking, tolerant, and understanding. More often than Architects I, Architects II say they are forgiving, kind, sensitive, rational and alert; and Architects III, more often than Architects I, say they are peaceable, good-natured, moderate, steady, practical, and logical.

In summary, architects, regardless of the level of their creativeness, tend to think well of themselves, but the quality of the self-image of highly creative architects differs from that of their less creative colleagues. Where the former more often stress their inventiveness, independence, and individuality, and their enthusiasm, determination, and industry, their less creative colleagues are impressed by their own virtue and good character and by their rationality and sympathetic concern for others. . . .

The first variable on the profile sheet is total number of adjectives checked (No Ckd). Though Architects I and II both score higher (53) on this dimension than Architects III (50), the differences are not significant. And in the total sample creativity is not significantly related to the number of adjectives which architects check to describe themselves.

The second variable of the ACL, defense (Df), provides a measure of the defensiveness or guardedness with which one fills out the check list. There is a tendency for the less creative architects to be more defensive in describing themselves; Df correlates -0.21 with rated creativity in the total sample. This greater defensiveness of the less creative architects is not surprising in view of their more frequent attribution to themselves of virtue and good character (see Table VI.2).

The scores on the next two variables of the ACL, the number of favorable adjectives checked (Fav) and the number of unfavorable adjectives checked (Un-Fav), also reveal a more defensive attitude on the part of the less creative architects. Though the mean score on favorable adjectives checked progresses from Architects I (48) to Architects II (51) to Architects III (52), these differences are not significant, nor in the total sample does rated creativity correlate significantly with the number of favorable adjectives checked.

On the other hand, the number of unfavorable adjectives checked correlates $+0.28$ with rated creativity for the total sample, and the mean score on unfavorable adjectives checked for Architects I is significantly different ($\leqslant 0.01$ level) from the mean score for Architects III (46). It is not that highly creative architects are more self-critical than people in general (their standard score is 50), but that

TABLE VI.2 *Adjectives Checked as Self-Descriptive by 80% or More of One Sample but by Less Than 80% of Another*

Checked by $\geqslant$ 80% of I, but < 80% of III	Checked by $\geqslant$ 80% of I, but < 80% of II	Checked by $\geqslant$ 80% of II, but < 80% of I	Checked by $\geqslant$ 80% of III, but < 80% of I
*inventive	*inventive	†responsible	†responsible
*determined	*determined	†sincere	†sincere
*independent	*independent	†reliable	†reliable
*individualistic	*individualistic	†dependable	†dependable
*enthusiastic	*enthusiastic	†clear-thinking	†clear-thinking
*industrious	*industrious	†tolerant	†tolerant
artistic	adaptable	†understanding	†understanding
progressive	interests wide	forgiving	peaceable
appreciative		kind	good-natured
		sensitive	moderate
		rational	steady
		alert	practical
			logical

*Checked by $\geqslant$ 80% of I, but < 80% of II and III
†Checked by $\geqslant$ 80% of II and III, but < 80% of I

the less creative architects are less inclined than their more gifted peers to admit flaws in their character armor.

With respect to self-confidence (S-Cfd) the three groups of architects do not differ significantly one from another, nor in the total sample is self-confidence as measured by the ACL scale significantly correlated with rated creativity; but in self-control (S-Co) the groups do differ, with Architects I scoring below the profile mean (46) and Architects II (54) and Architects III (58) scoring above the mean.

This is congruent with the findings reported above, since high scorers on the self-control scale, according to Gough, "tend to be serious, sober individuals, interested in and responsive to their obligations. They are seen as diligent, practical, and loyal workers. At the same time there may be an element of too much control, too much emphasis on the proper means for attaining the ends of social living. Thus the highest level of ego integration which involves recognition and sublimation of chaotic and destructive impulses, along with the allosocial and life-giving dispositions, may be denied to these individuals." In light of this description it is interesting to note that in the total sample of architects self-control correlated -0.40 with rated creativity.

It is the other way around with lability (Lab) as measured by the ACL, Architects III scoring below the standard score mean at 47, Architects II just slightly above the mean at 52, and Architects I well above the mean at 57, the differences being significant ($\leqslant 0.01$ for I vs. III $\leqslant 0.05$ for I vs. II and II vs. III). . . .

On the personal adjustment scale (Per Adj) Architects I score below the profile mean (46), Architects II at the mean (50), and Architects III above it (52). The differences are significant ($\leqslant 0.01$ level) between groups I and III and between groups I and II ($\leqslant 0.05$ level), but not between groups II and III. The scale . . . measures an attitudinal set of optimism, cheerfulness, an interest in others, and a readiness to adapt to the social situation. . . .

It is interesting to note, then, that personal adjustment as measured by the ACL scale correlates -0.33 with rated creativity in the total sample of architects.

The next fifteen dimensions on the ACL are the need scales developed by Heilbrun to measure variables first conceptualized by Murray. Heilbrun, following Edwards in his development of the Personal Preference Schedule, refers to the conceptualized dimensions as manifest needs within Murray's need-trait system. To be sure, eleven of the fifteen variables — abasement, achievement, affiliation, aggression, autonomy, deference, dominance, exhibition, nurturance, order, and succorance — were listed by Murray as manifest needs. . . .

It is of interest to note first those variables on which architects of different levels of creativeness do not differ. All three groups are above the standard score mean on achievement (Ach) and dominance (Dom) and below the mean on succorance (Suc). Their mean scores on these dimensions are not significantly different one from another. Considering the nature of their profession, the success with which they practice it, the demands it makes upon them, and the kinds of relationships they must establish with clients and builders, this is as one would expect.

Of the remaining scales there are five on which Architects I score higher than Architects II, and Architects II higher than Architects III – namely, heterosexuality (Het), exhibition (Exh), autonomy (Aut), aggression (Agg), and change (Cha). On all but the first of these dimensions Architects I score above the profile mean, while Architects II and III have mean scores below it; and on each of the dimensions the difference in the mean score between Architects I and Architects III is significant at the ≤ 0.01 level, with the exception of heterosexuality, where the difference is significant at or beyond the 0.05 level. In addition, each of the scales, except for heterosexuality, correlates (≤ 0.01 level of significance) with rated creativity in the total sample of 124 architects: exhibition, +0.38; autonomy, +0.37; aggression, +0.36; and change, +0.46.

All three groups have mean scores below 50 on heterosexuality (I, 49; II, 46; III, 44), and in the total sample, heterosexuality is not significantly correlated with the criterion. . . .

Where exhibition, autonomy, aggression, and change are positively correlated with rated creativity in the total sample of 124 architects, these variables are negatively correlated with creativity: endurance, –0.25; order, –0.33; intraception, –0.40; nurturance, –0.31; affiliation, –0.25; abasement, –0.21; and deference, –0.36.

The negative correlations of abasement, affiliation, deference, and nurturance with creativity are as one would predict. Some question might, however, be raised about the inverse relationship of endurance, order, and intraception with creativity.

It would appear that the type of endurance tapped by the Heilbrun scale involves working uninterruptedly at a task until it is finished, sticking to a problem even though one is not making progress, and working steadily at a single job before undertaking others. Endurance of this short-range type is not so characteristic of the highly creative person as is endurance over long periods of time even a lifetime, with much more flexibility in behavior and variation in specific means and goals. In the life-history interview, for example, the more creative architects, more often than those less creative, report turning to another activity when seriously blocked in a task and returning later to it when refreshed, whereas less creative architects more often report working stubbornly at a problem when blocked in their attempts at solution. . . .

As for the negative correlation of order with creativity, this is highly congruent with a large body of data obtained in our own studies as well as in those of others at the Institute of Personality Assessment and Research (2). These data indicate a strong preference on the part of highly creative persons for richness and complexity of stimulation; they prefer the challenge of disorder to the barrenness of simplicity.

We do well to remind ourselves that the variables of personality measured by the Heilbrun scales of the ACL, which so effectively predict creativity, are based upon images of the self which subjects reveal to us through the checking of those adjectives which they consider most descriptive of themselves. It is remarkable that so simple a device as a list of three hundred adjectives can reveal so much about a person. That it can do so is due in large part to the fact that a person's self-image is not a static concept but the focus of a constellation of dispositional trends — needs and their associated affects — in the person. . . .

Adjective Descriptions of the Ideal Self

. . . Table VI.3 lists those adjectives checked by 80% or more of Architects I when describing the ideal self and checked at least twenty percentage points less often when describing the real self. The percentages of subjects checking each adjective when describing his real self and his ideal self, and the discrepancy between the two percentages are shown both for single adjectives and for groups of adjectives.

These adjectives fall into certain natural groupings, which reveal areas of personal functioning in which creative architects feel least satisfied with them-

TABLE VI.3 *Adjectives Checked by 80% or More of Architects I, when describing Ideal Self, which had been Checked at least Twenty Percentage Points Lower when describing the Real Self*

Adjective	Percentage ideal	Percentage real	Percentage discrepancy
Personal attractiveness			
attractive	90	30	60
charming	90	30	60
good-looking	82	25	57
Average	87	28	59
Self-confidence			
adventurous	100	78	22
confident	98	62	36
courageous	98	58	40
masculine	90	70	20
optimistic	88	68	20
self-confident	88	68	20
strong	82	35	47
daring	80	32	48
Average	91	59	32
Maturity			
natural	92	68	24
humorous	88	62	26
mature	85	50	35
Average	88	60	28

Adjective	Percentage ideal	Percentage real	Percentage discrepancy
Intellectual competence			
alert	100	78	22
clear-thinking	98	68	30
thoughtful	95	72	23
resourceful	92	68	24
logical	88	65	23
thorough	85	50	35
versatile	82	62	20
witty	80	42	38
Average	90	63	27
Good social relations			
generous	92	72	20
kind	92	70	22
considerate	88	68	20
forgiving	88	68	20
sociable	88	65	23
sympathetic	88	68	20
affectionate	85	65	20
patient	85	55	30
tactful	85	65	20
warm	82	62	20
Average	86	64	22
High level of energy			
enterprising	92	70	22
energetic	90	70	20
Average	91	70	21
Sensitiveness			
sensitive	95	75	20

selves and most desirous of change. Above all they wish for greater personal attractiveness, checking markedly more often for the ideal than the real self the adjectives attractive, charming, and good-looking.

The average discrepancy scores for these adjectives between the real and the ideal is fifty-nine percentage points. Secondly, they desire greater self-confidence, checking with a mean discrepancy score of 32 the adjectives adventurous, confident, courageous, masculine, optimistic, self-confident, strong, and daring. The cluster with the next largest average discrepancy score (28) — natural, humorous, and mature — suggests a desire for greater maturity of mind and spirit. The creative architect would also ideally have greater intellectual competence — would like to be more alert, clear-thinking, thoughtful, resourceful, logical, thorough, versatile, and witty than he sees himself as being.

It is in the realm of his social relations and interpersonal reactions, however, that the creative architect finds the largest number of favorable adjectives that he wishes were descriptive of him. Ideally he would be more generous, kind, considerate, forgiving, sociable, sympathetic, affectionate, patient, tactful, and warm. Ideally, too, he would have a higher level of energy (energetic, enterprising) and he would also be more sensitive.

Since the intelligence of Architects I as measured by the Terman Concept Mastery Test correlates − 0.08 with their rated creativity, it is questionable whether Architects I would be more creative if their intelligence could somehow be increased, and it is paradoxical that they wish for themselves so many of those mild and gentle traits of social and interpersonal behavior which their less creative colleagues see as so characteristic of themselves.

Actually, discrepancies between adjectives checked to describe the real self and those checked to describe the ideal self reveal all three groups as desiring more personal attractiveness, self-confidence, maturity, and intellectual competence; a higher level of energy; and better social relations. As for differences between the groups, however, Architects I would ideally be more sensitive; and Architects II and III both wish for opposites if not incompatibles − they would ideally be more original but at the same time more self-controlled and disciplined. . . .

The mean correlation of adjectives checked to describe the real self with adjectives checked to describe the ideal self is for Architects I +0.44, for Architects II +0.48, and for Architects III +0.53. . . .

Here again is evidence of a greater defensiveness on the part of the less creative architects and a willingness on the part of their more creative colleagues to recognize and to admit a greater discrepancy between themselves as they are and as they would ideally be.

Image of the Self as Architect

Having seen how creative architects and their less creative colleagues perceive themselves as persons and having seen, too, what additional virtues they would wish to possess, we may now inquire as to how they see themselves in their professional role of architect and how closely they perceive themselves as approximating their ideal for the profession. . . .

A first impression of differences in the architects' professional self-images may be gained by noting the item which each group sorts as most saliently descriptive. For Architects I it is their aesthetic sensitivity and respect for artistic standards. For Architects II it is the holding of exceptionally high standards of professional performance for oneself as well as for others and a superior ability in evaluating and judging architectural plans. For Architects III it is their sense of responsibility and, like Architects II, their superior ability in evaluating and judging architectural plans. Items ranked first by one group are not given markedly discrepant placement by the others − there is fairly good agreement among all three groups as to what most characterizes them as architects − but what *is* revealed by the first-placed items is so congruent with other facets of their self-images as to deserve special notice. . . .

At the other end of the distributions, namely, the five items sorted as least characteristic, there is even better agreement among the three groups of architects. The only difference to be noted is a rather pronounced tendency for Architects I to disclaim any "special talent for solving organizational problems" (rank of 46), whereas Architects II and III less often deny organizational skills (ranks of 39.5 and 33). . . .

It is clear that Architects III take their responsibilities seriously, first to the client (rank of 8.5), then to the profession (18), and lastly to society (34.5). The more concrete and immediately present the individual or the group, the greater the sense of responsibility which Architects III feel toward them. . . .

In contrast, the more creative Architects I see a sense of responsibility to others as much less emphasized in their character. Of the three responsibilities, that to the client comes first (34), then responsibility to society (39.5), and in last place responsibility to the profession (44.5). In his picture of the ideal architect, the creative architect sees each of these responsibilities as more important. It is interesting to note, though, that strongest would be the responsibility to society (21), then responsibility to the client (30.5), and finally responsibility to the profession (33).

In general, and as one would expect, Architects II, in their attitudes toward these responsibilities in themselves and in the ideal architect, are intermediate between Architects I and III. . . .

It is at once apparent that creative architects feel their primary responsibility is to their own high standards of what is right and proper in architectural design. About these standards and their ability to meet them they have no serious doubts. They see themselves as perfectionists devoting endless attention to matters of design, planning, detailing, individualization, industrialization, technology, etc. (14, 33, 26). Not only do they see themselves as perfectionists, but they also recognize that they are hyper-critical of the work of others (34, 45, 47). They are convinced of the worth and validity of their own efforts; indeed they report a "sense of destiny" with respect to their career in architecture (12, 28.5, 26). Convinced that they can accomplish anything they set out to do, they tend less often than their colleagues not to recognize their own professional limitations and consequently may attempt the impossible (31.5, 15.5, 21). In contrast to their colleagues, they more often report putting architectural values above all others, subordinating everything to their architectural goals (31.5, 47, 41.5). They also more often see themselves primarily as idea men content to leave the systematic working out of details to others (26, 36, 44), and they much more often claim to be satisfied only with those ideas which are new and original solutions to design problems (19, 35, 38.5).

Although they believe they influence and help colleagues to be more creative in their endeavors (11, 26.5, 36.5), creative architects do not easily, willingly, or often find that they can accept ideas and help from others in working out their own architectural solutions. In contrast to them, their less creative colleagues report more often being able to take other people's ideas and concepts and fashion them into practical architectural designs and programs (28, 8, 3.5); and when blocked in their work less creative architects more frequently seek the help and advice of others (27, 9, 12.5).

The independence with which creative architects work is revealed in their expressed dislike and avoidance of administrative work (23, 37, 36.5) and in the frequency with which they assert that they are not team men but prefer to work alone (29, 41, 40). Indeed, they see themselves as much less interested than their colleagues in making a serious effort to keep up with current publications and the literature in architecture (39.5, 22.5, 24). . . .

Having examined the images which architects of different levels of creativeness have of themselves in their professional role, we may now ask what, if any, is the relation between satisfaction with one's own professional image and one's creativity.

To begin, we may note that, of the three groups, only Architects I place in first rank in describing the self the same item which they rank first in describing the ideal, namely, "Takes an aesthetic view; is especially sensitive to matters of form and coherence in architectural problems." Creative architects are agreed that the most salient trait of the ideal architect is an aesthetic view and sensitivity to matters of form and coherence. This is the trait which they also see as most characteristic of themselves.

Architects II see themselves as most characterized by high standards of professional performance and superior ability in judging and evaluating architectural plans, but in describing the ideal they give first rank to the item "Has strong powers of spatial visualization." For them the most valued trait of the ideal architect is an intellectual skill rather than an aesthetic sensitivity.

Architects III see their most characteristic traits to be a broadly based, responsible, and comprehensive approach to architectural problems and a superior ability to judge and to evaluate architectural plans; they place in first rank as most characteristic of the ideal architect one of the items which was tied for first place in the self-description of Architects II: "Has exceptionally high standards of professional performance for himself as well as others."

Here again we see difference among the three groups of architects which are highly congruent with the differences revealed in other analyses. . . .

The tendency of creative architects to think especially well of themselves as architects is, however, perhaps most vividly illustrated by the extremely large number of them who, in rating their own creativity and the creativity of the other architects in the total sample, give themselves the highest rating of 7 : 43% of Architects I in contrast to 6% of Architects II and 9% of Architects III.

Ego Functioning, Self-imagery, and Creativity

One is struck by the accuracy of self-perception, by the degree to which architects see themselves as they really are, and by the remarkable consistency with which they conform in their thought and in their behavior to the type of person they see themselves as being.

What is most impressive about Architects I is the degree to which they have actualized their potentialities. They have become in large measure the persons they were capable of becoming. Since they are not preoccupied with the impression they make on others or the demands that others make on them they are freer than the other two groups to set their own standards and to achieve them in their own fashion. It is not that they are socially irresponsible but that their behavior is guided by aesthetic values and ethical standards which they have set for themselves and which have been effectively integrated into their images of themselves and of their ideals. They are perhaps the prototype of the person of strong ego. Confident of themselves and basically self-accepting, they are to an unusual degree able to recognize and give expression to most aspects of inner experience and character and thus are able more fully to be themselves and to realize their ideal.

Architects III, on the other hand, appear to have incorporated into their egos and into their images both of the person they are and the person they would like to be, the more conventional standards of society and of their profession. More dependent upon the good opinion of others for their own good opinion of themselves, their goals and ideals are to an important degree those of the group rather than uniquely their own. Whereas the egos of Architects I are on more intimate terms with the id, the egos of Architects III are more at home with their superegos. It is not that Architects III experience more conflict than Architects I, but that, whereas Architects I have decided that where id was ego shall be, Architects III have determined that superego shall be where ego might have been. . . .

Notes

1. GOUGH, H. G. (1961) *The Adjective Check List.* Palo Alto: Consulting Psychologists Press.
2. MacKINNON, D. W. (1962) The personality correlates of creativity: a study of American architects. *Proceedings of the XIV International Congress of Applied Psychology, Copenhagen, 1961,* II; 11–39. Copenhagen: Munksgaard. Also see F. Barron (1958) The needs for order and disorder as motives in creative activity. In C. W. Taylor (Principal Investigator) *The Second Research Conference on the Identification of Creative Scientific Talent,* pp. 119–128. Salt Lake City: University of Utah Press.

4

Creative Writers *

F. BARRON

THE MAIN body of findings that I shall discuss has emerged from work with a group of 56 professional writers and 10 student writers, and the method of work germane to this comparison has been characterized chiefly by reliance upon our usual psychological tests, interviews, and experiments. Although all these writers were actively engaged in creative work, they did differ widely among themselves in the goals of their work and in the audiences they reached. Thirty of them were writers of wide renown who are generally considered important artists in the field of writing; their names were obtained by asking three faculty members in the English Department and one in the Drama Department at the University of California to nominate writers of a conspicuously high degree of originality and creativeness. Twenty-six others are successful and productive writers who were not nominated as outstandingly creative, but who have clearly made their mark in the field of writing. While I intend to present some comparisons between these two groups, I wish to make it quite clear that I am not suggesting that one group is creative and the other is not. Apart from the fact that my life would be in danger if I were to do so, I must say quite honestly that some of the writers nominated as outstandingly creative appeared to me to be less creative than many of those who were not so nominated, and among the writers who were not mentioned by the nominators (and hence by this exclusion defined simply as representative of their craft) were persons of a high order of creative ability. In brief, the central body of data from which we have drawn generalizations in this particular study comes from the testing and interviewing of 66 persons whose main aim in life was to create meaningful patterns with words.

Writers were chosen for study for several reasons. First of all, writing is probably the most prevalent and most widely understood form of communication of creative interpretations of experience. Then too, the social impact of writers in disseminating information, influencing public opinion, forming public taste, and advancing culture, is very great. Finally, language itself is so much an expression of culture that a study of its use in any particular society provides a unique field for observation of creative forces in the culture itself.

Creative writing was defined for the purpose of the study as the composition of phrases, essays, stories, poems, and plays which communicate a single individual's interpretation of experience in an original manner. The primary aim of the study was to characterize creative writers in terms of abilities and personality, in order to compare them with various other groups of creative individuals as well as with less creative writers and with people in general. A secondary aim was to investigate the process of creation in writing, through careful study of an author's work, through intensive interviews with him about his work, and through tests calling for composition, or providing an opportunity for creative perception and expression. Process was taken to include these aspects of the act most prominently: the conscious intention of the writer; preconscious or unconscious intentions, and determinants of the conscious intention (such as the psychic needs being served, the origins of fantasy, the meaning of the work in relation to the total life cycle of the writer); the choice of form; significant revisions, discarded beginnings, final self-criticism; unexpected or unplanned changes in intention or form, sudden inspiration; temporal and emotional phases in the process (intensity of work and feeling, blocks, distribution of attention, periods of easy flow, alternation of convergent and divergent phases); feeling of completion or incompletion; attitude towards the work when it is finished.

As you might imagine, trying to do justice to these aims proved a large order. Trying to express the conclusions in appropriate detail has proved also to be a difficult task. In what follows, I shall have to depend on summary statement a great deal, with just a few examples. Material from the projective techniques, the interviews, and uncodified observations in the assessment setting itself cannot easily be marshalled in the form of evidence that can be checked in other studies, but I shall nonetheless venture a few generalizations from those sources.

Let me begin by presenting a composite Q-sort description of the writers who were assessed. This composite was arrived at in the following fashion: each member of the assessment staff, without discussing the person with one another, employed the usual 100-item set of sentences to describe each subject at the end of the three days of assessment. The Q-sort deck was constructed especially to allow the expression of clinical inference. Sorting was on a 9-point scale with forced-normal distribution. Item placements were then averaged for the staff as a whole to arrive at a composite description of each subject, and these item placements were in turn averaged to arrive at a composite description of the group.

When this was done, the five items most characteristic of the group of creative writers were these:

> Appears to have a high degree of intellectual capacity.
> Genuinely values intellectual and cognitive matters.
> Values own independence and autonomy.
> Is verbally fluent; can express ideas well.
> Enjoys esthetic impressions; is esthetically reactive.

GE – K

The next eight more characteristic items were:

Is productive; gets things done.
Is concerned with philosophical problems; e.g., religion, values, the meaning of life, etc.
Has high aspiration level for self.
Has a wide range of interests.
Thinks and associates to ideas in unusual ways; has unconventional thought processes.
Is an interesting, arresting person.
Appears straightforward, forthright, candid in dealings with others.
Behaves in an ethically consistent manner; is consistent with own personal standards.

The student writers, as perceived by the assessment staff, differed from these mature creative writers in several important respects. For them, the second most characteristic item was: "Concerned with own adequacy as a person, either at conscious or unconscious levels." Also highly characteristic were these items: "Is basically anxious"; "has fluctuating moods"; "engages in personal fantasy and daydreams, fictional speculations." One might put this down simply to their youth and the problems of ego-identity with which they were grappling, but I am inclined to think that something more was involved. From subsequent observation of these student writers I believe that for them writing was much more a form of self-therapy, or at least an attempt at working out their problems through displacement and substitution in a socially acceptable form of fantasy. They fit closely to the sort of picture Freud gives of the poet in his essay, "The Poet and Daydreaming"; the true artist, however, is of another breed, whatever troubles he may have. Of this I shall try to say more later.

Turning now to the psychometric data from the study of the mature creative writers, we find independent confirmation of several of the staff Q-sort descriptions, which had of course been given before the tests were scored. The creative writers earned an average score of 156 on the Terman Concept Mastery Test; the mean score of the Stanford Gifted group in adulthood is 137, and the mean score of 343 captains in the United States Air Force is 60, where the standard deviation for the general population is about 30. These values cannot be translated precisely into IQ terms, but I think we can say with assurance that distinguished writers possess quite superior verbal intelligence. This perhaps deserves emphasis, for there has been some tendency to misinterpret one of the findings of several studies by the staff of the Institute of Personality Assessment and Research. The finding is that when ratings of the creativity of individuals relative to one another are obtained for all members of a very highly selected and distinguished group of creators, the correlation with measured verbal intelligence is zero, as was true in our study of creative architects. It should not be forgotten that the mean score for the group as a whole is quite high, however. And, of course, because of the extreme restriction of range on the creativity variable one must expect considerable attenuation in the correlation coefficient. Probably a more accurate estimate of the true degree of relationship between creativity and verbal intelligence was given in the military officer sample itself, where scores on a set of creativity measures correlated 0.35 with scores on the Concept Mastery Test. . . .

Where the subject-matter itself requires high intelligence for the mastery of its fundamentals, as in mathematics or physics, the correlation of measured intelligence with originality in problem-solving within the discipline tends to be positive but quite low. Among artists such as painters, sculptors, and designers, the correlation between rated quality of work and measured intelligence is zero or slightly negative. Again, however, it must be remembered that commitment to such endeavors is already selective for intelligence, so that the average IQ is already a superior one. I would suggest a generalization based not only on my own studies and those of my colleagues at the Institute, but upon a number of other researches during the past three years at the University of Minnesota, the University of Chicago, and the National Merit Scholarship Corporation: Over the total range of intelligence and creativity a low positive correlation, probably in the neighborhood of 0.40, obtains; beyond an IQ of about 120, however, measured intelligence is a negligible factor in creativity, and the motivational and stylistic variables upon which our own research has laid such stress are the major determiners of creativity. One of the important stylistic variables is preference for complexity, asymmetry, and the challenge of disorder.

Creative writers obtain very high scores on the Barron–Welsh Art Scale, their average scores being two standard deviations higher than the population average, though nearly a sigma lower than that of successful painters, and lower also than creative architects. Like artists, creative writers prefer figures that are free-flowing, asymmetrical (or at least not boringly balanced), and visually arresting.

One of the tests constructed especially for this study is the Symbol Equivalence Test, in which the subject is given a stimulus image (verbally) and asked to think up a symbolically equivalent image. "Leaves being blown in the wind," e.g., might suggest "a civilian population fleeing chaotically before armed aggression" (i.e., powerless particles blown by the winds of war). Ten test images were presented, and three responses sought to each. The test was scored by typing each response on a separate card for each of the several hundred subjects who took part in the creativity studies, with the name of the respondent removed, and then having three raters independently rate all responses to a given item relative to one another on a 9-point scale on the variable "originality." This was an onerous procedure, requiring more than ten thousand judgments from each rater, but it served to ensure that the results would be free of bias, since neither the identity of the subject nor the sample of which he was a member would be known to the rater. In this test, creative writers proved significantly more original than any other group of creative individuals we studied.

The True–False verbal scale developed from responses of subjects in the Asch study . . . proved quite valuable as a predictor of creativity. The average score of the general population on the Independence of Judgment Scale is 8.12; the group of representative successful writers scored 11.69, the student writers scored 15.2, and the distinguished creative writers scored 15.69. While the distinguished creative writers and the student writers were not significantly different from one another, both differed significantly from representative successful writers at the one per cent confidence level, and they in turn obtained significantly higher scores for independence of judgment than do people in general.

This sort of general trend obtains for a number of other measures as well. Representative writers tend to fall about midway between the general population and distinguished writers, with student writers being much more like the latter that like the former, probably reflecting patterns of identification and of life style as much as of ability proper. This was true for instance, of the Originality scale: distinguished writers scored 67.3 and representative writers scored 61.58, where the mean of the general population is set at 50, and the standard deviation at 10. Another scale that showed this pattern was Flexibility, distinguished writers scoring 60.5; representative writers, 55.65. In this case, student writers were markedly higher than either of the other groups, averaging 72.8. Using this sort of convention or so-called standard score format with the average at 50, scores of 70 or more are higher than those of about 98% of the general population, while a score of 60 places the individual higher than about 84% of the generality. So another way of putting this, which perhaps expresses the pattern better, is to say that the *average* student writer is more flexible than 98% of the general population, while his elders in the field of creative writing are more flexible than about 84% of the general population. However one puts it, the finding is clear: writers as a class are significantly more independent, flexible, and original than most people, and the creative writers who have achieved renown do very well for their years by being almost as flexible as their student counterparts, and a bit more independent.

When one turns to the question of psychological health in relation to creativity the picture is, as our discussion of ego-strength and the unconscious might have led us to expect, by no means a simple one. All three groups of writers earn markedly deviant scores on the scales of the Minnesota Multiphasic Personality Inventory. Since the MMPI was designed to measure the resemblance of those who take the test to certain diagnostic groups in the mental hospital setting, this finding on the face of it suggests that writers and psychiatric patients are indeed like one another in at least some respects. Again, both distinguished writers and student writers are most deviant, with representative writers falling in between them and the general population. . . .

Distinguished writers score particularly high on scales measuring schizoid, depressive, hysterical, and psychopathic tendencies on the MMPI. They are also well above the general population norms in terms of femininity of interest pattern on the CPI (the few female subjects were omitted from the latter calculation).

As I say, however, the picture is not simple, even in unthinking psychometric terms. In spite of obtaining such high scores on measures of pathology, all three groups of writers also obtain distinctly superior scores on the MMPI scale which we developed first of all for prediction of recovery from neurosis, and which other evidence indicates is a good measure of strength of the ego. And that very scale (*Es*), it will be remembered, bears a high negative relationship to the MMPI measures of pathology when general population norms are considered. In brief, if one is to take these test results seriously, the writers appear to be both sicker and healthier psychologically than people in general. Or, to put it in another way, they are much more troubled psychologically, but they also have far greater resources with which to deal with their troubles. This jibes rather well with their social behavior, as a matter of fact. They are clearly effective people who handle themselves with pride and distinctiveness, but the face they turn to the world is sometimes one of pain, often of protest, sometimes of distance and withdrawal; and certainly they are emotional. All of these are, of course, the intensely normal traits indicated by the peaks on their profile of diagnostic scores.

The California Psychological Inventory (which is similar in format to the Minnesota Multiphasic Personality Inventory and built in part from the True–False items of the Minnesota test, but which differs from it in that its purpose is to measure traits related to personal effectiveness rather than psychopathology) bears out the finding regarding greater ego-strength in these creative individuals.

. . . Both these groups of writers are significantly superior to the general population in Social Presence, Self-acceptance, Capacity for Social Status, Psychological-mindedness, and Achievement through Independence. They achieve markedly lower scores in Achievement via Conformance. The highly creative group differs especially from the general population in making rather low scores on Socialization, a performance which in this context I think, is correctly interpreted as resistance to acculturation, for the so-called socialization process is often seen by the creative individual as a demand for the sacrifice of his individuality, which indeed it often is. They score low also on Sense of Well-being, Self-control, and Desire to Make a Good Impression.

One other set of findings, which I shall mention only briefly, concerns the relationship of creative writing ability to such Jungian concepts as extraversion–introversion, feeling–thinking, judging–perceiving, and intuiting–sensing, functions which are seen in Jung's theories as polar opposites. A measure of each of these factors, the Myers–Briggs Jungian Type Indicator, was used in our studies. Both groups, distinguished writers and representative writers, show much the same pattern; they are distinctly more *introverted* than *extraverted*, more *feeling* than *thinking*, and more *intuitive* than oriented to *sense experience*. The latter finding is particularly marked. Only two distinguished writers, and only four representative writers, were not classified by the test as intuitive; overall, 89% of the writers studied were intuitive, as compared with about 25% of the general population.

The really striking differences between writers and other groups, however, lies in the general area of fantasy and originality of perception. One of our interviews was devoted especially to the fantasy life, from day dreams and night dreams and hypnagogic experiences to transcendental experiences in full and acute consciousness. An unusually high percentage (40%, in fact) of creative writers claimed to have had experiences either of mystic communion with the universe or of feelings of utter desolation and horror. The prologues to these experiences were frequently described with considerable vividness in the interview, and this statistic does not represent a checking of "Yes" or "No" to a question such as "Have you ever had a mystical experience?" Other experiences of an unusual sort were also described, such as being barraged by disconnected words as though one were caught in a hailstorm, with accompanying acute discomfort, or seeing the world suddenly take on a new brightness while sun or moon remained the same. A high frequency of dreaming was also reported, as well as a high frequency of dreaming in color, as compared with student groups we have studied.

Most impressive of all, however, was the extent to which motivation played a role, both in the writer's becoming a writer and in the way in which creative writing served a more general philosophic purpose. Almost without exception the successful creative writer had had to suffer considerable hardship in holding to his calling. The hardships included criticism from family and friends, periods of intense self-doubt, financial adversity, sacrifice sometimes of important personal relationships, and even public censure or ridicule. By the time the writer got to us he was past many of these adversities, although poets (even internationally famous ones) were generally living in very modest circumstances, and there were some surprising (to us) instances of distinguished writers of fiction who still had to take other jobs occasionally to stay afloat. One of the poets in our sample, whose work was reviewed recently in *The London Times Literary Supplement* and was hailed as "the most remarkable body of poetry to come from America in the past decade," was earning his living working in a gymnasium and occasionally as dock worker, while still another was typing term papers for undergraduates. At the other extreme there were several novelists whose earnings were in the millions of dollars. Yet to all of them the economic question was of secondary importance; this is true of all of our groups of creative individuals. On the Economic values scale of the Allport–Vernon–Lindzey Scale of Values, creative individuals consistently earn their very lowest score. It is quite apparent that they are playing for other stakes. What then are the stakes, and if there are stakes, just what is the game?

The game, I believe, centers upon the nature of intellect itself and upon the meaning of human life. In reviewing the performance of creative writers on the Symbol Equivalence test I was struck by the rapidity with which they moved from the commonplace stimulus image to the cosmic metaphor. Their concerns, as shown in projective tests like the Thematic Apperception Test and the Rorschach, are with mythical themes — with death, with great inanimate forces, with the symbolic rather than the literal meaning of shapes and colors. The freedom–determinism question arises again and again both in their work and in their fantasies. The nature of man in relation to the cosmos is the engaging problem.

The commitment, in brief, is to larger meanings of an esthetic and philosophical sort which can find expression in the life work that the individual has chosen for himself (or, as some have put it, in the life work that has chosen him). As an aside, one may recall here Goethe's statement: "I did not make my songs, my songs made me." In brief, such individuals are involved constantly in the creation of their private universes of meaning; they are cosmologists all. I am convinced that without this intense cosmological commitment no amount of mental ability of the sort measured by IQ tests will suffice to produce a genuinely creative act. Without wishing to be overly dramatic in this matter, I believe it is literally true that the creative individual is willing to stake his life on the meaning of his work. We think we have observed this in the personal accounts given in intensive interviews with subjects in our own studies, and certainly the many biographies and autobiographical writings of the great artists and scientists bear the conclusion out. Indeed, as Crombie concluded from his survey of the scientific revolution, regulative beliefs of an almost metaphysical sort lie behind the most dedicated quests for new theoretical formulations.

Creative vision, whether in art or in science, has always involved an act of rejection preceding the act of construction; the structure of the world as most people see it must be broken or transcended. William Blake, a great artist both in writing and in painting, has spoken of "four-fold vision." For him, single vision is simply what ordinary physical eyesight enables us to see: the world that the consensus of opinion based on a limited use of senses would affirm as real. A tree is a tree, an inkblot is an inkblot, the sky is blue, and so on. Two-fold vision is the still-limited act of imagination; a cloud formation looks like two lions fighting, or an elephant pushing a Mack truck; the inkblot "might be" two dancers, or a bird in flight, or a monk kneeling in prayer. In three-fold vision, we do not see the mean thing-in-itself as in single vision, nor the thing as it might be if it were a little or even a lot different, as in two-fold vision, but we see the thing as symbol. Recall again the heavenly chorus at the conclusion of *Faust*:

> All things transitory
> but as symbols are sent;
> Earth's insufficiency
> *Here* grows to event.

The symbol presents a reality transcended. It is the medium through which a superior vision of reality is sought; it amplifies the poor real world by an act of imagination. The symbol, the play, the dream: these are the manifestations of three-fold vision.

Four-fold vision is still a step beyond. It is the vision of the mystic, the seer, the prophet; it is vision suffused with the most intense feeling: horror, awe, ecstasy, desolation. A passage from Blake himself illustrates it well:

> I assert for myself that I do not behold the outward creation, and that to me it is hindrance and not Action ... "What," it will be Questioned, "When the Sun rises, do you not see a round disk of fire somewhat like a Guinea?" Oh, no, no, I see an

Innumerable Company of the Heavenly host crying, "Holy, holy, holy is the Lord God Almighty." I question not my corporeal or Vegetarian Eye any more than I would Question a Window concerning a Sight. I look through it and not with it.

In this research we have attempted through a variety of techniques to understand the vision of the world that these our subjects had. Their work itself, of course, is their primary testament, and moral vision is what it communicates above all. . . .

My own conclusion, then, is that creative writers are persons whose dedication is to nothing less·than a quest for ultimate meanings. Or perhaps it is not so much that they are dedicated as that they understand themselves to have been elected and have accepted the office. What is enjoined upon them then is to listen to the voice within and to speak out. What they speak is to be the truth, but it need not be everyone's truth, or even anyone else's. In these essentials, omitting writing as the specific form, I believe creative writers are no different from creative individuals in all walks of life, including those whose business it is to be silent.

5

Creative Mathematicians*

R. HELSON

THERE were several reasons for choosing mathematics as an area in which to study creativity in women. The very fact that there were only a few creative women mathematicians seemed advantageous. It might be possible to study not just a sample but virtually all of them. Perhaps these women would show particularly clearly the essential traits of the creative person, of either sex, and surely such an investigation would contribute to the appraisal of creativity in women and of women's potential for scientific accomplishment. A felicitous development was that Richard Crutchfield, who was also at IPAR, undertook a study of male mathematicians, so comparisons of men and women became possible. . . .

Design of The Study of Women Mathematicians

Sample and Criterion of Creativity

In the period of planning the study it soon became evident that creative women mathematicians did not always have a regular position at a university and that it would not be possible to constitute an adequate sample by simply drawing up a list of women from the directories of institutions of higher education. Instead, names of women who had attended graduate school and obtained the Ph.D. degree in mathematics between 1950 and 1960 were requested from a sample of institutions (Helson, 1971). Mathematicians at these and other universities provided additional names, particularly of women they considered creative.

Of fifty-three invitations extended, forty-four (83%) were accepted. Three women were tested later than the others and are not included in all analyses. Three wives of faculty members at the University of California at Berkeley were asked to provide data only about their research style. The number of subjects thus varies between forty-one and forty-seven.

The appropriate criterion of creativity for these women seemed to be the *quality* of the individual's research. Number of publications or general reputation

---

Women and the Mathematical Mystique. Baltimore: The Johns Hopkins Press (1980).

and influence, though easier to measure, would be less suitable as a criterion for a group so marginal in the profession. Therefore, ratings for each mathematician were obtained from a group of specialists in her own area of mathematics. A seven-point scale was used, a rating of 4.0 signifying that the subject was about as creative as the author of an average research paper in a mathematical journal. The ratings were highly reliable. Subjects rated above 5.0 were classified as "creative."

The subjects ranged in age from twenty-four to sixty-four, the average age being forty-one. Two thirds were married. One third had Jewish parents, and most of the rest were from a Protestant background. Creative and comparison women did not differ in these respects, nor in the quality of their graduate school. As in the sample of male mathematicians, foreign cultural influence was strong. Half of the creative women were born in Europe or Canada, and almost half of the native-born subjects had at least one parent born in Europe. The difference in the number of foreign births in the creative and comparison groups is significant at the 10% level. However, foreign-born and native-born creative women do not differ in the characteristics that will be reported as significantly differentiating creative from comparison subjects.

Measures

A great many tests and measures were obtained during the assessment weekend. The following discussion will emphasize several measures of personality and one measure of self-reported mathematical style.

One category of measures for assessing personality consists of two paper-and-pencil inventories, the California Psychological Inventory (Gough, 1957) and the Adjective Check List (Gough and Heilbrun, 1980). A second category of measures is observations of the assessment staff, recorded in various ways. For example, the hundred-item Clinical Q-sort (Block, 1961) comprises statements about personality that are sorted in a prescribed normal distribution according to how characteristic or uncharacteristic of the person being described each item is. A third source of information about personality is the personal-history questionnaire . and interview. The questionnaire was answered by the subject. The interview was unstructured, but afterwards the interviewer made ratings, commented on various questions, and wrote a personality sketch.

Mathematical style was assessed by the Mathematicians Q-sort, consisting of fifty-six items about work attitudes and research habits that the mathematicians sorted to describe themselves (Helson, 1967). . . .

These measures of personality and mathematical style will be utilized repeatedly in this paper. Measures of intelligence, interests, esthetic ability, and other aspects of personality or life history that receive mention are described more fully elsewhere (Helson, 1971).

Women Mathematicians and the Creative Personality

Introductory Overview of the Sample

The California Psychological Inventory (CPI) yields scores on eighteen scales, which are intended to give a comprehensive picture of the interpersonal and intellectual characteristics of the individual. The scores for an individual or group may be plotted as a personality profile. . . . Harrison Gough, the author of the CPI, has provided this interpretation of the group profile of the women mathematicians: "Two implications stand out at once. The first has to do with superior intellectual functioning, an unusual combination of perseverance, adaptiveness, and sensitivity to the new and unforeseen. The second has to do with temperament, which in this case appears to be moderate and even subdued, and yet without loss of individuality or spark. The basic portrait is of a perceptive, cognitively open, highly intelligent individual, reflective and reserved, yet capable of responding creatively to her personal world."

Another group portrait of the women mathematicians comes from the items from the Clinical Q-sort that the assessment staff placed as most salient in their personalities: "Genuinely values intellectual and cognitive matters"; "appears to have a high degree of intellectual capacity"; "values own independence and autonomy"; "is a genuinely dependable and responsible person"; "prides self on being objective and rational."

Differences between Creative and Comparison Women

The subjects whose work was rated above average in creativity were compared with other women mathematicians. The findings reported are significant beyond the 0.05 level of confidence.

Validation of the criterion ratings

Findings from the professional-history data bank supported the validity of the criterion ratings in showing that the women classified as creative had been performing at a level superior to that of the comparison women. They received the Ph.D. at an earlier age, submitted their first paper for publication before the Ph.D. rather than after, published more papers, and received more grants and fellowships after graduate school (Helson, 1971).

Personality characteristics

On the CPI, the creative subjects scored higher than the comparison subjects on the flexibility scale and lower on the communality and the achievement-via-conformance scales. In combination with other features of their profiles, these findings indicate that the creative subjects were strongly motivated to create their own forms and to express and validate their own ideas but did not enjoy routine duties or working within a highly structured framework.

Welsh (1975) has developed measures of two personality traits, labeled "origence" and "intellectence," that he postulates to be fundamental in creative personality. . . . Standard scores for the two groups differ significantly on these two scales, indicating that the comparison women describe themselves as rational, astute, and self-disciplined, whereas the creative women perceived themselves as more self-preoccupied, autonomous, unorthodox, and temperamental.

The findings based on the subjects' self-descriptions on personality inventories are supported by the IPAR staff observations. The staff observers did not know the women's creativity ratings, but analyses show that they judged the following Clinical Q-sort items to be more descriptive of the creative subjects than of the comparison subjects: "Thinks and associates to ideas in unusual ways"; "has unconventional thought processes"; "is an interesting, arresting person"; "tends to be rebellious and nonconforming"; "genuinely values intellectual and cognitive matters"; "appears to have a high degree of intellectual ability"; "is self-dramatizing, histrionic"; "has fluctuating moods." The statements judged to be more descriptive of the comparison women were: "Judges self and others in conventional terms like 'popularity,' 'the correct thing to do,' social pressures, etc."; "is a genuinely dependable and responsible person"; "behaves in a sympathetic or considerate manner"; "favors conservative values in a variety of areas"; "is moralistic."

Mathematical style

The creative subjects described themselves as more involved in research than the comparison women did, and they seemed to employ less fully conscious cognitive processes ("must exert effort to express a mathematical train of thoughts in words"; "solution to a problem often comes from an unexpected direction"). They also describe themselves, however, as inventive and ingenious. Comparison women were more interested in teaching, salary, and understanding the ideas of others; and they described themselves as more organized and efficient in their work style (Helson, 1971).

Interests

The creative women expressed strong interest in leisure activities that were primarily intellectual in nature: attending concerts, listening to classical records, going to plays, reading classics, and hiking. The comparison subjects were more heterogeneous in their strong interests and had a larger number of moderate interests than the creative subjects. The creative women seem to have simplified their lives to a few things about which they cared very much. They spent most of their time in research and homemaking; they spent less time than the comparison subjects in teaching, administration, community activities, and politics.

Esthetic sensitivity

The creative and the comparison women were asked to make mosaic designs. The designs made by the creative subjects were judged by a panel of experts as having more artistic merit and as more pleasing than those of the comparison subjects.

Intelligence and cognitive abilities

The creative and the comparison women appear not to have differed on the Wechsler Intelligence Scale, though only part of the sample was tested (MacKinnon and Hall, 1973). On the Concept Mastery Test, developed by Terman to assess high intelligence as it has been utilized and enriched in adult cultural experience, the creative subjects did somewhat better than the comparison subjects ($p < 0.10$). Their average score of 144 is higher than that of the Stanford Gifted subjects (137), industrial research scientists (118), and military officers (60) and essentially the same as that of the creative male mathematicians (148). It has been suggested that sex differences in the understanding of physical and mechanical relationships contribute to the disinclination of women for mathematics and the sciences. Thus, creative women might show an unusual facility in this area. Creative and comparison subjects, however, did not differ on the Bennett Mechanical Comprehension Test. Both groups did well in comparison with most women but less well than men (Helson, 1971).

Childhood background

More creative women had fathers who were professional men, and in the opinion of the personal-history interviewers, they were more identified with their fathers than the comparison women. Although the women mathematicians as a whole came disproportionately from families of girls, the creatives, unless they came from very large families, were particularly likely not to have brothers. A number of the women mathematicians seem to have been adopted as the "son" of an intellectual father.

Summary

The outstanding finding of this study is the striking difference in personality between the creative and comparison women. The creatives differ from the comparison women in a strong intellectual orientation more than in "raw intelligence." On a variety of measures and in a variety of areas, they show strong symbolic interests, introversion, independence, and lack of constriction. These characteristics have all been attributed to the "creative personality," and the creative women mathematicians actually demonstrate them more clearly than the men (Helson and Crutchfield, 1970). Perhaps social pressures make it so difficult for a woman to be a creative mathematician that only those who persist are introverted individualists with a deep inner motivation.

Differences between Men and Women Mathematicians

Although the creative women clearly have more of a "creative personality" than less creative women, the important comparison in real life is usually with creative men. The male mathematicians did not participate in the assessments, but their scores on measures such as the CPI and the Mathematicians Q-sort can be compared with those of the women.

On the CPI, the comparison men and women are quite similar in personality . . . but the creative men score significantly higher than the creative women on several measures of social ascendancy and on intellectual efficiency (see Figure VI.2).

On the Mathematicians Q-sort both the creative men and the creative women had a pattern of characteristics that differentiates them from all other mathematicians. The creative men described themselves as having confidence, initiative, ambition, impact on the environment, and intellectual balance and soundness.

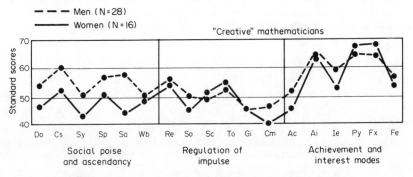

FIG. VI.2 Profiles of men and women mathematicians on the
CPI: creative subjects

KEY: Do (dominance); Cs (capacity stat.); Sy (sociability); Sp (social pres.); Sa (self-accept.); Wb (well-being); Re (responsibility); So (socialization); Sc (self-control); To (tolerance); Gi (good impress.); Cm (communality); Ac (achiev. via conformance); Ai (achiev. via independence); Ie (intellectual efficiency). Py (psychological-mindedness); Fx (flexibility); Fe (femininity)

In contrast, the creative women described themselves as nonadventurous and inner-focused. In the work style of the creative women the self is totally committed, unconscious as well as conscious processes are involved in the creative effort, and emphasis is directed toward developing what is within rather than toward exploring or mastering the environment (Helson, 1967). Comparison men and women differed very little in the way they described their work style.

What are we to make of the fact that the creative men and women differ from each other more than the comparison men and women do and how are we to understand their distinctive styles, particularly that of the women? It is surely relevant that although the creative men and women had careers that were quite similar through graduate school, their lives at the time of testing were very different. The men had published more papers and held important positions at prestigious places. Only two or three of the women taught graduate students, and one third, including some of the most highly rated, had no regular position at all. Most of the married women were married to mathematicians, and nepotism was a frequent problem. Also, half of the creative women had young children.

One could argue that the inner-focused, emotional, low assertive style of the creative women was a strategic adaptation to a life situation in which they worked in relative isolation, often distracted by their responsibilities as home-makers and mothers (Helson, 1975). If so, one might see the style of the creative men as also a strategic adaptation to their life situation, in which they occupied positions that rewarded them and put heavy demands on them for competitive exertion and intellectual leadership. The men and women comparison subjects could be seen as adopting strategies that sacrificed creativity for the more tangible, immediate, or congenial necessities of teaching and earning a living.

There are, however, other factors to consider. As suggested earlier, creative women who persevere in mathematics may be more introverted, unconventional, and less adaptable than the creative men, or there may be sex differences in the creative personality not confined to mathematics that are not attributable to one's job situation. In order to weigh these various factors, it would be helpful to know something about sex differences in a field that imposes less divergent conditions of life on its creative men and women than mathematics does.

Sex Differences among Mathematicians and Writers

Unlike mathematics, literary fantasy for children is a field to which men and women have contributed in about equal numbers. Also, institutional organization is minimal. Writers usually work at home. Like mathematics, however, writing attracts highly creative individuals.

Criterion ratings of creativity, the CPI, and a Writers Q-sort were available for fifty-seven authors of literary fantasy for children (Helson, 1977). These men and women were compared with the men and women mathematicians.

Personality Characteristics and Work Style

An analysis of variance on CPI scales was conducted to find out whether the two groups of creative women and the two groups of creative men differed in similar ways from their respective comparison groups. Other analyses investigated the similarity between the creative men and women writers and between the creative men and women mathematicians (Helson, 1978).

The results are clear. The two groups of creative women have the most in common. Both appear to be somewhat stubbornly unconventional and individualistic and tend not to be social leaders but to have an original and engrossing inner life.

The two groups of creative men scored similarly on only one scale (self-control). Both groups scored low and thus appear to have more access to anger and negative emotion than comparison men.

The two groups of creative writers, men and women, have much in common, including the same core of traits that characterized the creative women. On the other hand, the two groups of creative mathematicians, men and women, scored similarly on only one scale (flexibility). On three scales (sociability, self-acceptance, and achievement via conformance) the creative men and women mathematicians scored significantly *differently* in relation to their comparison groups.

The set of findings, then, informs us that the creative male mathematicians are different from the other groups. They have a personality in which there is relatively more social assurance and assertiveness and less conflict with conventional channels of expression and achievement.

By examining comparable items from the Mathematicians *Q*-sort and the Writers *Q*-sort, it can be shown that the creative writers of both sexes describe their work style in a way that resembles that of the creative women mathematicians more than it does that of the creative men mathematicians (Helson, 1978). That is, there is more emphasis on emotional involvement and participation of the unconscious than on initiative and mastery.

There is, however, one area in which the two samples of creative men differ from other subjects in one way, while the creative women differ in another way. Creative men emphasize their ambition to do great things, whereas creative women convey the strength of their motivation by their willingness to set aside other things for their work (see Table VI.4).

Summary

These comparisons of writers and mathematicians show us that the creative style of the women mathematicians is not peculiar to them; they share it with creative writers. And yet, is it an appropriate style for mathematics? Why are the creative women in mathematics different from the creative men? We still do

TABLE VI.4 *Placement of Q-sort items about ambition and commitment by men and women mathematicians and writers*

	Mathematicians ($N = 111$)			Writers ($N = 54$)		
	Creative Mean	Comparison Mean	t	Creative Mean	Comparison Mean	t
	"Has an earnest desire to make a mark in mathematics" ("has a keen desire for fame and immortality in literature").					
Women	2.83	3.00	−0.56	3.00	2.73	0.58
Men	3.94	3.03	4.25***	3.75	2.73	2.43*
t	−4.58***	−		−1.93	−	
	"Subordinates other things to research (literary) goals; puts these values before others."					
Women	3.44	2.43	3.24**	3.67	2.27	3.89***
Men	3.03	2.65	1.28	2.92	2.67	0.54
t	1.24	−		1.60	−	

*$P < 0.05$.
**$P < 0.01$.
***$P < 0.001$.

not know to what extent the inner-focused, low assertive style is a function of life situation and to what extent it is rooted in basic personality characteristics. A useful approach at this juncture would seem to be to study individual differences among the mathematicians and factors associated with differences among subgroups.

Subgroups of Women Mathematicians

Designation of Subgroups

There are many ways of differentiating among people. . . . The Mathematicians Q-sort was chosen to provide a basis for the identification of subgroups.

A cluster analysis (Tryon and Bailey, 1970) of the data from the entire sample of 109 men and women produced four clusters (Helson, 1967). The first two clusters – which were all that were readily manageable – are shown in Table VI.5. The first cluster contrasts orderliness with a free, messy, and emotional attitude toward mathematics. The second cluster contrasts an inventive, confident, ambitious, and intellectually flexible attitude with its opposite – cautious, inner-oriented, shy, and settled.

These cluster dimensions would seem to represent two antitheses that are of general importance for creativity in mathematics, and probably in science generally. There is an "essential tension" (Kuhn, 1963) between the scientist's need to respect the order of the past, to uphold it and build upon it, and the need to destroy this order or to live in chaos until a new synthesis is created.

TABLE VI.5 *Clusters of the mathematicians Q-sort for men and women mathematicians (N = 109)*

Characteristics	Oblique factor coefficient
Cluster 1	
Is neat and orderly in his habits and manner of work.	0.85
Enjoys the freedom of working in a messy terrain.	−0.49
Has an active, efficient, well-organized mind.	0.48
Prefers to get miscellaneous chores out of the way before settling down to research.	0.47
Feels emotionally tense when a result becomes imminent.	−0.38
Cluster 2	
Work is characterized by inventiveness and ingenuity.	0.75
Lacks confidence; is afraid to strike out in new directions.	−0.71
Is flexible and adaptable in his thinking, able to shift and re-structure easily.	0.49
Does not work on problems known to be very difficult.	−0.48
Reacts quickly to research problems; immediately generates a great number of ideas.	0.42
Research interests lie within a rather narrow range.	−0.40
Research problem is likely to originate in attempt to extend known proofs or results rather than in attempt to clarify a nebulous area.	−0.39
Work is characterized by intuitive power.	0.37
Easily distracted; tries to secure optimum conditions for concentration.	−0.35

There is a second antithesis between inner contemplation and outer mastery. Mathematicians are known to be introverted (Campbell, 1974; Helson and Crutchfield, 1970), and there is a general negative relationship between interest in science and leadership (Holland, 1973). And yet, original contributions usually require an element of risk-taking and initiative in the outer world.

In the present sample of men and women mathematicians, creative subjects score lower than comparison subjects on cluster 1, and men, especially creative men, score higher than women on cluster 2. In fact, the emergence of these two clusters in the cluster analysis is probably attributable to the fact that creativity and sex were major variables in the sample. But of course they are very important variables. All in all, it seems worthwhile to explore the possibility that different patterns of scores on these two cluster dimensions will identify an important and revealing set of subgroups of mathematicians. . . . These groups will be designated Group I, Group II, Group III and Group C (or core comparison group) respectively. . . .

Work Styles

As one might anticipate, the several groups emphasized different items from the Mathematicians *Q*-sort in describing their work styles (see Table VI.6). Group I emphasized excitement, curiosity, and pleasure in working in a "messy

TABLE VI.6 *Characteristic features of work style for subgroups of women*

Characteristics rated highest	Mean placement (5-point scale)
By group I	
Feels emotionally tense when a result seems imminent.	4.2
Enjoys the freedom of working in a messy terrain.	3.9**
Has a lively sense of mathematical curiosity and inquiringness; a desire to know and understand.	3.8
By group II	
Research interests lie within a rather narrow range.	4.7**
Finds it difficult to read the works of others and prefers to spend her energies on own work.	4.4**
Feels emotionally tense when a result seems imminent.	4.0
Is somewhat deficient in command of basic sources and technical literature in the field.	4.0
Takes an esthetic view; is sensitive to matters of form and elegance in research problems.	3.9
Lacks confidence; is reluctant to strike out in new directions.	3.8
By group III	
Prefers to work on problems that lend themselves to elegant and exact solutions.	4.2
Research interests lie within a rather narrow range.	4.1
Has a lively sense of mathematical curiosity and inquiringness; a desire to know and understand.	4.0
By group C	
Has a need to teach; enjoys instructing and working with students.	4.4
Takes an esthetic view; is sensitive to matters of form and elegance in research problems.	3.8
Research problem is likely to originate in an attempt to extend known proof or results rather than in an attempt to clarify a nebulous area.	3.8
Prefers to get miscellaneous chores out of the way before settling down to research.	3.8
Can imagine enjoying work other than mathematics.	3.8

**P < 0.01 (*t* test for difference between group indicated and Group C).

terrain." Members of Group II described themselves as emotionally involved with their own work and uncomfortable or inadequate in relation to the outside world. Group III expressed a preference for elegant and exact solutions. They had narrow research interests but a lively mathematical curiosity. The core comparison group had less interest in research than the other groups.

Personality Characteristics

The personality characteristics of the groups are consistent with their mathematical styles. Figure VI.3 shows the distinctive profiles of the three creative groups on the Gough–Heilbrun "need" scales of the Adjective Check List. The peak score for Group I is on the autonomy scale; for Group II it is on the abasement scale; and for Group III, on the order scale. The profile of Group C is

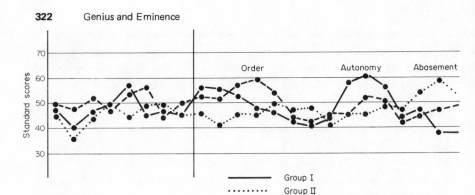

FIG. VI.3 Profiles of three subgroups of women mathematicians on the Adjective Check List

not shown, but it is very similar to Group III's, except exaggerated — the peak
on order is much higher, and scores for heterosexuality, affiliation, and change
are much lower.

The ACL manual says that those who score high on autonomy are independent,
assertive, and self-willed, heedless of the preferences of others when they themselves wish to act. In contrast, those with high scores on abasement are self-
effacing and may have problems with self-acceptance. They face the world with
anxiety and foreboding, and their behavior is often self-punishing, perhaps in the
hope of forestalling criticism and rejection from without. Those who score high
on order seek objectivity and rationality and are firm in controlling impulse.
These remarks are not offered as descriptions of the subgroups of women
mathematicians (because their peak score on the ACL is not all there is to know
about them) but as a designation of some important dimensions of difference in
their personalities.

Differences in the way the groups describe themselves were borne out and
elaborated by differences in the way the IPAR staff saw them. For example,
results from the Clinical Q-sort showed that the IPAR staff described members
of Group I — more than the other women — as having a clear-cut and internally
consistent personality, being relatively free of self-concern, initiating and responding to humor, being productive, having insight into their own motives, expressing
hostility directly, and characteristically pushing and trying to stretch limits.
They behaved in a less feminine manner.

Characteristics seen as more salient in Group II than in other women included
a propensity to fantasy and daydreams, unpredictability and fluctuating moods,
a brittle ego-defense system, and an interesting, arresting personality. They were
seen as less cheerful than the other women.

Group III was seen as genuinely valuing intellectual and cognitive matters and
as enjoying sensuous experiences (including touch, taste, and smell).

Group C was described as uncomfortable with uncertainty; judging self and others in conventional terms; favoring conservative values; alert to differences between self and others; genuinely dependable and responsible; priding self on objectivity and rationality; moralistic; fastidious; and over-controlled. They were seen as less intellectual and as having less intellectual capacity.

The subgroups also differed significantly on cognitive tasks. Group I scored highest on the Unusual Uses test of originality; Group II scored highest on the Terman Concept Mastery and the Gottschaldt Figures, a measure of ability to break configural set; Group III scored lowest on Unusual Uses and the Gottschaldt Figures; and Group C scored lowest on the Terman Concept Mastery and on a perceptual-cognitive test designed to measure ability to change figure-ground relationships. These results showed that the groups who described themselves as low in orderliness tended to score higher on measures of originality and cognitive flexibility than groups who described themselves as high in orderliness.

It would be very interesting to be able to show that the subgroups differed in mathematical speciality. The only difference that has been established is that Groups I and II were less often specialists in algebra or analysis than Groups III and C. Group I led in applied interest, and Group II led in logic, but these differences did not reach significance.

Some Background Findings

The work of Datta (1973), Lesser (1976), Rosenberg (1965), Sarason (1973), and others suggests the importance of ethnic background for the development of cognitive styles and self-esteem. In this study, religious background of parents is one of several demographic variables that distinguish among the subgroups of women mathematicians. Groups I . . . and C were predominantly Protestant, and Groups II and III were predominantly non-Protestant (see Table VI.7). Thus, Protestants who were rated at least average in creativity were generally high in confidence and inventiveness, while non-Protestants with comparable ratings on creativity were generally more cautious and inner-oriented. Also, most subjects low in creativity were Protestants.

TABLE VI.7 *Some background characteristics distinguishing Groups I . . . and C from Groups II and III*

| Groups | Religious background[a] | | Father's education[b] | | Difference in parents' education[c] | |
	Protestant	Non-Protestant	College	Non-college	Father more educated	Father not more educated
I . . . and C	19	6	8	16	4	20
II and III	7	13	15	4	15	3

[a] $\chi^2 = 7.81, P < 0.01$.
[b] $\chi^2 = 8.87, P < 0.005$.
[c] $\chi^2 = 16.68, P < 0.001$.

Another characteristic that co-varied with religious background in this sample of mathematicians was education of father. Fathers of Groups II and III, the non-Protestant groups, were the most highly educated. Group I fathers were intermediate, and Group . . . C had fathers with the least education (see Table VI.7). As one might expect, the highly educated fathers were professional men, so that Groups II and III abounded in women whose fathers were professors, engineers, or physicians. Fathers of members of the other groups were usually in business, large or small, the lesser professions, or perhaps skilled trades or farming. Another variable related to education of the father was the difference in education between father and mother. Groups II and III came from homes in which the father was almost always better educated than the mother; the other groups came from homes in which the parents usually had the same education.

Finally, there is some evidence that more families of Groups II and III were "incomplete" or considered "foreign" in their communities. Four of five women in whose homes there was death or divorce in the subject's childhood were from Groups II and III. Although Groups I, II, and III do not differ in the number of foreign-born, more members of groups II and III moved with their families from their native country when they were children or adolescents.

Some Hypotheses

It seemed puzzling that there should be striking demographic differences among the subgroups. Three hypotheses will be advanced to explain the relationships. . . .

The first hypothesis is that clusters 1 and 2 reflect dispositions acquired in early stages of development. Cluster 1 assesses alternative attitudes toward authority and toward feelings of shame and self-doubt (Erikson, 1963) that are associated with the parents' attempt to control the young child's bowels, bodily exploration, and locomotor activity. Cluster 2 taps introversion versus extraversion and masculinity versus femininity, but along with these it assesses a confidence and initiative in dealing with the outside world that may be interpreted in a developmental context. In Erikson's version of psychoanalytic theory, to gain this initiative the child must surmount "Oedipal" conflicts. His or her success in doing so depends in part on the severity of conflictful and guilty feelings toward parents but also on the degree to which these conflicts can be transferred, transformed, and worked out in school and in other areas of the world outside the family.

A second hypothesis is that the predominantly Protestant groups developed vulnerabilities in the course of their socialization that were different from those developed by Groups II and III and that important factors in the socialization experience were (1) Protestant or non-Protestant values and (2) the degree of integration of the family into the wider society. Briefly, it is hypothesized that Groups I and C experienced more vulnerability in the area of order versus disorder, because of Protestant emphases on cleanliness, independence, and emotional control, and that Groups II and III experienced more vulnerability in the area of initiative and confidence, because the barrier between the family and the outer world reduced opportunities for working out attitudes toward parents and siblings by means of identifications and interests outside the family. Especially for bright and introverted little girls, the combination of the barrier between family and outer world and the superior education and status of the father would have intensified Oedipal conflicts.

It would be a mistake to construe the main variables too narrowly in terms of religious background. Some of the women who are atypical of their quadrant in ethnicity seem to have had psychological experiences similar to those of their fellows. For example, one of the Protestants in Group II grew up in an enclave within a Catholic culture. Another Protestant in Group II had no father in the home to help her separate from her loving but moody mother, a factor likely to create difficulties in the development of initiative and management of guilt.

The third hypothesis is that differences between groups with similar socialization pressures may be understood in terms of their having reacted to these pressures in different ways. Members of Group I rebelled against adult control, at least inwardly, and reacted counteractively to shame and self-doubt; they emphasized their autonomy and the value of their own productions. Group C internalized parental dictates and tried to obtain approval by strict control and good behavior. Because of the Protestant emphasis on independent achievement and the social integration of their families in the community, members of Group I were likely to show initiative and confidence in competition at school. On the other hand, Group C found their initiative restricted by dutifulness, self-doubt, and ambivalence toward parental figures.

It has been hypothesized that both Groups II and III were handicapped in the development of initiative by guilt feelings toward parents. As Group II tends to undercontrol and Group III to overcontrol (low vs. high scores on cluster 2), perhaps the difference was that members of Group II remained outwardly dependent in many ways but sought to work out their dilemmas by developing the fantasy and imagination that is characteristic of the period of initiative vs. guilt (Erikson, 1963). Group III became at least superficially self-sufficient by suppressing personal feelings or subjecting them to strict control.

Parents and Early Development

Several kinds of information were analyzed to discover their consistency with the above hypotheses. One of these was the subjects' descriptions of their parents on dimensions of a semantic differential (Osgood, Suci and Tannenbaum, 1957). Three dimensions each were chosen to assess (1) Protestant values and/or social integration (strong–weak, stable–unstable, clean–unclean) and (2) personal qualities not closely related to Protestant values and social integration (deep–

shallow, pleasant—unpleasant, warm—cold). One dimension (safe—dangerous) was chosen on the grounds that it might relate to Oedipal problems common to the period of initiative versus guilt. Hypotheses were that parents of Groups I and C would have modeled the first set of values more strongly than parents of Groups II and III, that there would be no difference or less difference on the second set, and that Groups II and III would perceive their parents as having been less "safe."

. . . Groups I and C described their parents as stronger, safer, and somewhat more stable than did Groups II and III. Differences on the other dimensions were not significant. The only contradiction to the hypotheses occurred on the clean—unclean dimension. Although Group II differed significantly from the other groups, describing their parents as somewhat less than perfectly clean, Group III described theirs as the cleanest of all.

Another source of information relevant to the hypotheses was the personal-history interviewers' ratings of the most likely childhood precursors of interest in mathematics. The items rated were a set of defense mechanisms from the psychoanalytic repertoire. "Reaction-formation to primitive body expressiveness" and "need for autonomy in fantasy" were items that seemed to represent (alternative) methods of coping with the problem of autonomy versus shame and self-doubt. The predominantly Protestant groups (I and C) would be expected to receive significantly more high ratings on this pair of items. "Sublimation of sexual curiosity or curiosity about the body and its functioning," "sublimation of hostility," and "redoing" seemed more appropriate for problems of initiative versus guilt. The predominately non-Protestant groups (II and III) would be expected to receive high ratings on these. No prediction was made about a sixth item, "withdrawal."

Results showed that Groups I and C did have more high ratings on the predicted items, and Groups II and III received more high ratings than Groups I and C on "sublimation of hostility" and "redoing." The addition of "sublimation of sexual curiosity," however, reduced the discrimination.

The third hypothesis asserts that Group I differed from Group C, and Group II from Group III, in their ways of dealing with similar problems (shame and self-doubt in the first case, guilt and dependence in the second). Because of the small size of the sample, to test this hypothesis, each group was compared with all other subjects, and the best pair of differentiating items was determined. For Group I this pair was "need for autonomy" and "sublimation of sexual curiosity." For Group C, it was "reaction-formation to primitive expressiveness" and "withdrawal." For Group III, the best pair of items was "sublimation of hostility" and "redoing." Group II could not be differentiated from the other women at the 5% level of significance. However, when Group II was combined with Group I, the two groups together received more high ratings on "sublimation of sexual curiosity."

Finally, the groups were compared on two Transactional Analysis scales

(Williams and Williams, 1980) that can now be scored on the ACL. The free-child and the adapted-child scales are considered to assess ego states carried over from childhood. Persons in the ego state of the "free child" are ebullient and not inclined to hold themselves in check or postpone gratification. Low scorers on the free-child scale are conservative, self-denying, and lacking in zest. A person in the state of the adapted-child has difficulty in overcoming dependent role behaviors, dislikes confronting contemporary reality, and seeks satisfaction in dreams and fantasy. Low scorers on the adapted-child scale have achieved more independence, apparently by suppressing their feelings or developing an insensitivity to those of others (Gough and Heilbrun, 1980).

It was hypothesized that Group I would score higher than Group C on the free-child scale and that Group II would score higher than Group III on the adapted-child scale. Table VI.8 shows that these hypotheses were confirmed and that the designated groups have the extreme scores on each scale.

TABLE VI.8 *Comparisons of subgroups on free-child and adapted-child ego state (ACL)*

Scale	Group I	Group II	Group III	Group C	t
Free-child	54.1	44.8	46.0	38.2	3.12[a]
Adapted-child	51.0	60.3	46.7	50.7	3.09[b]

[a] $P < 0.01$, Group I versus Group C.
[b] $P < 0.01$, Group II versus Group III.

Summary

These findings from three different sources — the subjects' descriptions of parents, the life-history interviewers' inferences about developmental patterns, and scales developed to assess ego-states carried over from childhood — tend to support the hypotheses. . . .

Current Conditions of Life

The preceding material pertains to the hypothesis that patterns of mathematical style reflect influences from the past. To what extent may factors of the present be influencing research style?

Two important ways in which the groups differed were with respect to age and responsibility for child-rearing. The extremes are represented by Group C, whose mean age was 44 and of whom 75% were childless, and Group II, whose mean age was 34 and of whom 70% had children. Though 60% of Groups I and III had children, Group II had *more* children, *younger* children, and included more single young women that the rest of the sample. It is evident that these facts of life situations must have contributed to the lack of confidence and initiative in Group II (even though the personality characteristics of Group II may also have made them vulnerable to role conflicts). . . .

Summary and Discussion

The outstanding finding of the first study was the striking difference in personality between women mathematicians rated high in creativity and other women mathematicians. The creative women had strong symbolic interests and were introverted, original, and independent. The comparison subjects were much more orderly and conventional. Differences in intelligence and specific cognitive abilities were less evident than the differences in personality.

Comparisons of men and women mathematicians showed that the less creative men and women were more similar in personality than the creative men and women. Whereas the creative men had more initiative and assertiveness in their research style than other subjects did, the creative women were inner-oriented and low in assertiveness. Comparisons of creative mathematicians and writers, relative to comparison groups, showed that the personality and style of the creative women mathematicians resembled that of creative writers of both sexes. The creative women mathematicians were not complete mavericks, then. But why were the sex differences in creative style greater among mathematicians than among writers? The creative male mathematicians had responsible, prestigious positions at high-pressure institutions, while few of the creative women had contact with graduate students, one third had no regular job, and half had young children to take care of. Many of the men and women writers worked at home, so their life styles tended to be less dissimilar than those of men and women mathematicians.

On the other hand, such facts did not refute the hypothesis that there are two primary creative styles, one high in ego-assertiveness and the other low, and that although some men incline to the first and others to the second, most women show the low-assertive style (Helson, 1967, 1968, 1978). If the low-assertive style is not appropriate for mathematics, then as long as such sex differences exist, are creative women doomed to a low level of accomplishment in this field?

A next step in the exploration of this issue was to study factors associated with the adoption of different research styles within each sex. Two main dimensions of variation in research style were (1) orderliness versus an emotional, disorderly attitude and (2) confident inventiveness versus constriction and inner focus. Creative mathematicians of both sexes scored lower on the first dimension, and men, especially creative men, scored higher on the second. . . . Few women scored high on both dimensions, and few men scored low on both. . . .

Among women, confident inventiveness seems to have been encouraged by family values and by social support in achieving independence from ties to parents. This fact is important because it suggests that the sex difference in confident inventiveness may also have a significant social component (Block, 1973; Mitchell, 1974).

Each of the three creative subgroups of women had its strengths and its weaknesses; each met with discrimination or handicap because of sex. The fact that there were three creative subgroups shows that women with a variety of personality syndromes can do creative work in mathematics. Reducing the rigidity of sex roles should be helpful for all of them.

Nevertheless, Group I, the women high in confident inventiveness, has been the most productive. A style low in ego-assertiveness may be very creative, and it may be the only one available to individuals who, for one reason or another, are excluded from full participation in their society. Women as a group have been in this position. The low-assertive style needs protection and respect; with it individuals may reach insights that others would not. However, it does not fit well into the high-pressure academic setting. Many of the creative women mathematicians would have been more productive if their personal motivations had been supported by institutional nutriment; and they could have obtained this support more readily if they had been less ambivalent or less aloof. Understanding and experiment are needed on both the institutional side and the individual side.

The women of Group II, low on both order and confident inventiveness, are of special interest, not only because their research style is the least common among male mathematicians but also because they were found to be younger and to have had more responsibility for young children than the other women in the sample. Most members of Group II finished graduate school during the 1950s, so they present an interesting case of the interaction between a personality syndrome and a social context at a particular stage in the life cycle. The Group II women vary considerably in the degree to which they have become assimilated into academic life. Unfortunately, the present study does not help us to understand individual differences within subgroups.

Members of Group C, the core comparison group, were older on the average than other subjects and were the most likely to be childless. These demographic characteristics point to another distinctive cohort of women. One may imagine a succession of cohorts, each coming into mathematics with motivations that articulate with the subject-matter, conditions of employment, and social climate at a given time. Mathematics may have a "demand character" such that the personality types attracted to it are limited. If so, one would expect to find over time a varying distribution across a few personality syndromes rather than a succession of new syndromes. Today there is a generation of young women mathematicians with new options, new pressures, perhaps a new ethnic composition. How different it is in personality and research style is an interesting question.

References

BARRON, F. X. (1960) *Creative person and creative process.* New York: Holt, Rinehart & Winston.

BLOCK, J. (1961) *The Q-sort method in personality assessment and psychiatric research.* Springfield: Charles C. Thomas.

BLOCK, J. (1973) Conceptions of sex role: some cross-cultural and lingitudinal perspectives. *American Psychologist,* 28, 512–526.

CAMPBELL, D. P. (1974) *Manual for the Strong-Campbell interest inventory: T325 (merged form).* Stanford: Stanford University Press.

DATTA, L. (1973) Family religious background and early scientific creativity. In *Science as a career choice: Theoretical and empirical studies,* ed. B. T. Eiduson and L. Beckman, pp. 94–102. New York: Russell Sage Foundation.

ERIKSON, E. (1963) *Childhood and society.* New York: Norton.

GOUGH, H. G. (1957) *Manual for the California Psychological Inventory.* Palo Alto: Consulting Psychologists Press.

GOUGH, H. G. and HEILBRUN, A. B., Jr. (1980) *The Adjective Check List manual.* Rev. ed. Palo Alto: Consulting Psychologists Press.

HELSON, R. (1967) Sex differences in creative style. *Journal of Personality,* 35, 214–233.

HELSON, R. (1968) Generality of sex differences in creative style. *Journal of Personality,* 36, 33–48.

HELSON, R. (1971) Women mathematicians and the creative personality. *Journal of Consulting and Clinical Psychology,* 36, 210–220.

HELSON, R. (1975) Personality characteristics and sex, in science. In *Research issues in the employment of women: Proceedings of a workshop,* pp. 61–82. Washington, DC: National Research Council.

HELSON, R. (1977) The creative spectrum of authors of fantasy. *Journal of Personality,* 45, 310–326.

HELSON, R. (1978) Creativity in women. In *The psychology of women: Future directions of research,* ed. J. Sherman and F. Denmark, pp. 553–604. New York: Psychological Dimensions.

HELSON, R. and CRUTCHFIELD, R. S. (1970) Mathematicians: The creative researcher and the average Ph.D. *Journal of Consulting and Clinical Psychology,* 24, 250–257.

HOLLAND, J. L. (1973) *Making vocational choices: a theory of careers.* Englewood Cliffs: Prentice-Hall.

KUHN, T. S. (1963) The essential tension: Tradition and innovation in scientific research. In *Scientific creativity: Its recognition and development,* ed. C. W. Taylor and F. X. Barron, pp. 341–354. New York: Wiley.

LESSER, G. S. (1976) Cultural differences in learning and thinking styles. In *Cognitive styles and creativity in higher education,* ea. S. Messick, pp. 137–160. San Francisco: Jossey-Bass.

MacKINNON, D. W. (1962) The nature and nurture of creative talent. *American Psychologist,* 17 (7), 484–495.

MacKINNON, D. W. and HALL, W. B. (1973) Intelligence and creativity. In *Science as a career choice: Theoretical and empirical studies,* ed. B. T. Eiduson and L. Beckman, pp. 148–152. New York: Russell Sage Foundation.

MITCHELL, J. (1974) *Psychoanalysis and feminism: Freud, Reich, Laing, and women.* New York: Pantheon.

OSGOOD, C. E., SUCI, G. S. and TANNENBAUM, P. (1957) *The measurement of meaning.* Urbana: University of Illinois Press.

ROSENBERG, M. (1965) *Society and the adolescent self-image.* Princeton: Princeton University Press.

SARASON, S. B. (1973) Jewishness, Blackishness, and the nature-nurture controversy. *American Psychologist,* 28, 962–972.

TRYON, R. C. and BAILEY, D. E. (1970) *Cluster analysis.* New York: McGraw-Hill.

WELSH, G. S. (1975) *Creativity and intelligence: A personality approach.* Chapel Hill: Institute for Research in Social Science, University of North Carolina.

WILLIAMS, K. B. and WILLIAMS, J. E. (1980) The assessment of transactional analysis ego stages via the Adjective Check List. *J. Personality Assessment,* in press.

6

Creative Psychologists: Gifted Women*

L. M. BACHTOLD and E. E. WERNER

IN TWO recent studies of personality factors of talented boys and girls in middle childhood and adolescence by the authors (Werner, 1966; Werner and Bachtold, 1969), the personality profile of the gifted boys showed a striking resemblance to that of recognized creative persons (artists, writers, and scientists) in the adult population (Cattell and Drevdahl, 1955; Drevdahl and Cattell, 1958) and of college students nominated for creative potential (Drevdahl, 1956). The findings, for the gifted boys, were generally applicable, regardless of age group, method of selection, type of educational program, and special area of interest.

This trend did not hold for the gifted girls. Their personality profiles, both in middle childhood and adolescence, were less characteristic of the distinguishing traits found for creative adults, and fewer personality factors differentiated the gifted girls from the norm group of their age and sex. The question arose whether these findings reflected the special selection procedure used for the education of gifted students, or whether there were consistent sex differences in personality factors among the gifted in childhood, college, and adulthood.

The reference groups for Cattell and Drevdahl's studies of creative artists and writers and eminent researchers, teachers, and administrators in physics, biology, and psychology, and the other major studies of distinguished scientists (reviewed by Taylor and Barron, 1963) did not differentiate between men and women.

A search of the literature revealed that studies of the personality characteristics of creative women have been exceedingly rare. The exception is a series of reports by Helson (1961, 1966, 1967a, 1967b), who studied the personality traits, cognitive style, and developmental history of college women nominated as high in creative potential in the arts, sciences, and humanities in their senior year and five years after graduation, and who compared women mathematicians considered creative by their peers with less creative women mathematicians and creative men. Personality characteristics in these studies were assessed with the California Personality Inventory (CPI), the MMPI, and by Q-sort and staff ratings. Senior women with creative potential scored significantly higher than their classmates of similar scholastic aptitude in complexity of outlook, flexibility, originality, independence of judgment, psychological-mindedness, and level of noncon-

*American Psychologist, (1970), 25, 234–243. Copyright 1970 by the American Psychological Association. Reprinted by permission of the publisher and author.

formity. Five years later the creatives showed more increase in these characteristics than the noncreatives, with the "active" creatives, both married and single, registering the greatest growth. Creative women mathematicians had higher scores than comparison women on flexibility and lower scores on commonality and achievement by conformity. In contrast to the creative men, however, creative women mathematicians were less self-confident and less sociable, and had a narrower range of interest. A similar finding has been reported by Kurtzman (1967) in a study of creative ninth-grade boys and girls.

There are, as yet, no published studies of the personality characteristics of successful academic women in the fields first explored with men via projective tests by Roe (1953) and with the Sixteen Personality Factor (16 PF) Questionnaire by Cattell and Drevdahl (1955; Drevdahl and Cattell, 1958): scientists in psychology, physics, and biology, and artists and writers.

One study of the vocational interests of women psychologists (Campbell and Soliman, 1968) suggested that psychology as a career, now as a generation ago, attracts women who have more intellectual, scientific, and verbal linguistic interests than the average women, and fewer interests in the traditional feminine role. A study of femininity and creativity among high school students in physics (Walberg, 1969) raised the question whether the very factors that correspond to the successful feminine and student role may penalize the girl's chances for later eminence in science.

The present study is the first in a series conducted with the 16 PF Questionnaire to fill the gap in our knowledge about the personality characteristics of successful and productive adult women in the social and natural sciences, arts, and humanities.

It was undertaken with the hope that the identification of personality factors that enable women to succeed in the sciences and in academia, in spite of powerful sex-role expectations to the contrary, will contribute to the recognition and development of potential creativity among gifted girls.

A need for further knowledge in this area is indicated as we witness the steady decline of the proportion of women awarded higher degrees, in the sciences (Rossi, 1965b) and in academic positions (Barnard, 1964) in the very decade that has seen such a surge in research on cognitive functions, creativity, and sex-role expectations.

Procedure

It was the purpose of this study to obtain a personality profile of academic women in psychology in order to compare them (*a*) with the general female population, (*b*) with college women, (*c*) with the "successful academic men" described by Cattell and Drevdahl (1955), (*d*) with the psychologists among the academic men, and (*e*) to determine differences in women's profiles in relation to their area of vocational interest, productivity, and major activity.

The directory of the American Psychological Association provided a selected group of professional women who could be compared with the "successful academic men." Criteria of success were attainment of a doctoral degree and affiliation with a college or university. Choice of age levels was influenced by Barnard's (1964) report on academic women, wherein she noted that trends in the proportion of academic personnel who are women appeared closely related to trends in the proportion of higher degree winners who are women. She found these trends to be up from 1910 to about 1930, and down thereafter. By setting the latest year of birth at 1910, it was anticipated that the group of women in this study would represent a generation that (*a*) had sufficient vocational maturity to demonstrate maximum attainment and (*b*) were minimally affected by social factors related to the drop in proportion of academic personnel who are women.

In order to allow for direct comparison with the personality profile of the male group, personality characteristics were measured by the test used by Cattell and Drevdahl, the 16 PF Questionnaire. The handbook for the 16 PF Questionnaire (Cattell and Eber, 1957) provides descriptive information on each factor, which is presented as a bipolar measure, and is summarized with a high score corresponding to the description on the left, and a low score to the behavior on the right, as follows:

A	cyclothymia; sociable	vs. schizothymia; aloof
B	intelligence; bright	vs. mental defect; dull
C	ego strength; mature	vs. dissatisfied emotionality; immature
E	dominance; aggressive	vs. submission; mild
F	surgency; enthusiastic	vs. desurgency; serious
G	superego strength; conscientious	vs. lack of rigid internal standards; casual
H	parmia; adventurous	vs. threctia; shy
I	premsia; sensitive	vs. harria; tough
L	protension; suspecting	vs. relaxed security; accepting
M	autia; bohemian introverted	vs. praxernia; practical
N	shrewdness; sophisticated	vs. naiveté; unpretentious
O	guilt proneness; insecure	vs. confident adequacy: self-secure
Q_1	radicalism	vs. conservatism of temperament
Q_2	self-sufficiency; resourceful	vs. group dependency; sociably group dependent
Q_3	high self-sentiment formation; controlled	vs. poor self-sentiment formation; uncontrolled
Q_4	high ergic tension; excitable	vs. low ergic tension; composed

To provide bases for comparisons among the female group, information was requested on areas of vocational interest, major activities in the field of interest, and number of publications in professional journals. Areas presented were counseling and guidance, clinical, developmental, educational, experimental, industrial, learning, statistics, social, and school psychology to be ranked by number if there were more than one. Activities to be checked according to percentage of time spent were teaching, research, clinical and consulting, and administration. Respondents were also asked to indicate the number of publications for which they were senior author or coauthor. It was suggested that all material be submitted anonymously.

The survey materials were mailed to all women members of the APA in 1965 whose biographical information met criteria, that is, the doctoral degree, affiliation with a college or university, and birth in 1910 or earlier. Names of 296 women were thereby obtained. Even though addresses were checked in the 1967 APA directory supplement, 63 surveys were returned because of unknown address. An additional 6 were returned because of death or disability. Data were supplied by 124 respondents.

Results were analyzed by a computer program that provided means and standard deviations of raw scores for the total group and for subgroups; since no directionality of differences was hypothesized, all t tests were two-tailed tests. Within-group differences of the women were reported in terms of significant differences between raw score means. Because a revised form of the 16 PF Questionnaire (Cattell and Eber, 1962; Form A) was used, comparisons between male and female groups were based on standard scores. Standard scores are expressed in stens (Cattell and Eber, 1957). Sten scores range from 1 to 10, with a mean of 5.5 and a standard deviation of 1. To compare the similarity of sten profiles between men and women, a pattern similarity coefficient (r_p) was obtained.

Results and Discussion

The psychologists who provided the personality profile of the "successful academic women" represent a generation with an increasing proportion of women winning doctorates and entering the academic field. Despite their increasing numbers, access to areas considered the province of men was not generally approved nor readily gained. It would therefore be anticipated that these women would differ from women in general in a number of personality characteristics.

Since the youngest was 58 at the time of the study, and 65.7 was the mean age for the group, it must be also assumed that for most their peak in professional attainment and productivity had been achieved. Responses on the distribution of time spent in activities revealed that for 49% the major portion of their time involved teaching; for 34%, counseling and consulting; for 14%, administration; and for 8%, research. The rank order of activities compares closely with the "main phases of work" reported by 129 women psychologists in colleges and universities two decades ago (Fjeld and Ames, 1950). Teaching was given considerably greater emphasis than guidance-related work such as counseling and testing, while considerably less emphasis was noted for research and administration. In 1950, 24% reported research as a major emphasis of work, while in the present study the proportion of women in research was considerably smaller. The apparent drop in research activity over a 20-year period for this age-selected group raises a question of whether research tends to be a function assigned to women early in their career, or whether this activity has become increasingly the domain of men.

Major interests were distributed as follows: 24%, clinical; 20%, counseling and guidance; 22%, developmental; 10%, educational; 2%, experimental; 1%, industrial; 3%, learning; 1%, statistics; 3%, social; 5%, school psychology; and 9% in diverse areas of specialization, such as exceptional children.

A wide range in number of publications was reported. It is understandable that full-time teaching, counseling, or administration, or combinations thereof would limit if not preclude opportunities for writing. Thus, productivity in terms of senior authorship was zero for 22 respondents, yet soared to a prodigious 275 for one psychologist.

Comparisons with the General Female Population

Contrasted with the norm group of women (Cattell and Eber, 1962), the psychologists differed significantly on 14 of the 16 personality factors. Means and standard deviations are shown in Table VI.9 for the psychologists, with significance of differences between psychologists and (a) women in general and (b) college women.

Because age trends in relation to the personality factors have not been demonstrated, no age corrections on scores were made. However, an assumption of

TABLE VI.9 *Means and Standard Deviations for Women Psychologists and Significance of Differences between the Psychologists and Average Women, and College Women*

Factor	M	SD	Differences from average women	t	Differences from college women	t
A	9.37	3.57	−2.51	8.20*	−2.39	7.05*
B	9.85	1.56	+3.93	20.79*	+2.13	12.59*
C	15.91	4.11	−0.12	0.31	+1.14	3.03*
E	12.49	3.93	+2.95	6.77*	+1.80	4.85*
F	11.45	3.77	−1.90	4.75*	−3.91	9.41*
G	12.48	3.29	−1.16	3.83*	−0.40	1.24
H	14.22	4.84	+1.91	4.09*	+1.91	3.94*
I	13.23	2.90	+1.39	5.15*	+1.47	5.17*
L	6.67	2.51	−1.74	6.17*	−1.92	6.70*
M	13.71	2.99	+0.97	3.19*	+1.25	3.85*
N	11.34	2.66	+0.70	2.94*	+0.89	3.47*
O	7.67	3.28	−3.03	8.56*	−2.94	8.31*
Q_1	12.12	2.47	+3.35	13.14*	+3.48	12.97*
Q_2	12.54	3.31	+2.52	7.94*	+2.85	8.65*
Q_3	11.72	2.80	+0.20	0.72	+1.09	3.90*
Q_4	10.05	4.47	−2.87	6.26*	−2.75	5.95*

*$p < 0.01$.

stability in personality characteristics after maturity was supported by Roe's (1953, p. 226) study in which she found a "practically negligible" effect of age on the personality of scientists. More recently, Helson (1967a), in her study of creative women, demonstrated that personality patterns become consolidated with maturity.

The following comparisons are expressed in the descriptive terms provided by Cattell and Eber (1957) for persons scoring above or below the norm on each factor. No significant differences appeared on ego strength (C) and self-control (Q_3). In these respects the academic women scored in the normal feminine range of emotional maturity and will power.

It is not surprising to find these college-affiliated women more intelligent (B+), and liking words, working alone, and intellectual companionship (A–). Such characteristics seem essential for the years of concentrated study required in their professional preparation. That they also are more silent and introspective, more serious and concerned (F–) than the average woman is understandable for the same reason. Involved with the manipulation of ideas rather than action-oriented processes, social scientists tend to be more introverted than extraverted, a characteristic that is further described by a high M score. The M+ person is characterized as having intense subjectivity and inner mental life.

These personality characteristics could lead to a premature conclusion that here is a recluse. On the contrary, academic women psychologists as a group are imaginative in inner life and conversation, with a liking for new experience (I+). Accepting and adaptable, open, and ready to take a chance (L–), they are also more inclined to experiment with problem solutions, more radical, and less inclined to moralize (Q_1+). The implied tolerance for ambiguity may explain a G score that is below the mean for the general population. It is probable that a "loosening" of rigid internal standards (G–) is a requisite for a sensitivity to problems and the freedom to experiment with problem solutions.

The "successful academic women" scored high on assertiveness and self-assurance (E+), supporting an inference by Maccoby (1963) that dominance appears to be a prerequisite in analytic thinking.

Independence is indicated by the high Q_2 score, indicating that the women psychologists as a group are self-sufficient, and accustomed to making their own decisions. Decision making is enhanced by having an exact, calculating mind, a flexible view-point, and insight regarding self and others (N+). Dominance and self-sufficiency are qualities that the culture apparently does not seem to foster in the growing female. How, then, did the academic women overcome apparent cultural influences toward dependency?

A partial answer may be given by the high H score; the H+ person is described as adventurous, impulsive, showing little inhibition by environmental threat. Additional strength for resisting environmental pressure is provided by the strong self-confidence (O–) and low anxiety level (Q_4–) of the study group. Of all the factors, it is probable that these three characteristics were most sustaining to these academic women of a generation that took a predominantly negative view of females in higher education.

In summary, the composite profile describes the academic woman psychologist as an introspective person, with an imaginative inner mental life. Although she enjoys working alone and is independent and self-sufficient, she is ready to take a chance and welcomes new experiences. Self-assertive, she is also insightful regarding herself and others, and not inclined to moralize. Without rigidity in standards, she is flexible in viewpoint and adaptable. Emotionally stable and with adequate self-control, she also seems fairly free from general anxiety.

Similarities are observed with earlier studies of young bright adults. Helson (1961) described her group of women mathematicians as serious, introverted, highly intelligent, and independent-minded. In their study of very bright adults, Southern and Plant (1968) found their women, compared to the norm, to be significantly more theoretically, aesthetically, and independently oriented, and also relatively impulsive and uninhibited.

Comparisons with Women College Students

The academic women differed from the college women as they did from the general population norm on all factors, except C, Q_3, and G. Differences were significant for every factor except G, superego strength, as shown in Table VI.9.

Although the academic women did not differ from women in general in ego strength (C) and will power (Q_3), they were significantly more emotionally mature and controlled than the women college students. It seems probable that age difference might account for the greater emotional stability and self-control of the older women. . . .

Comparisons with Successful Academic Men

Cattell and Drevdahl's (1955) groups of leading scientists differed markedly from the norm for the general population. In Figure VI.4 mean sten scores for the "successful academic men" are presented with mean sten scores for the "successful academic women." The profiles are strikingly similar. . . .

Both groups differ from the general population in their aloofness (A-), intelligence (B+), assertiveness (E+), seriousness (F-), lack of rigidity (G-), adventuresomeness (H+), sensitivity (I+), adaptability (L-), self-confidence (O-), radicalness (Q_1+), and self-sufficiency (Q_2+). Computation of the pattern similarity coefficient (Cattell and Eber, 1957) showed an r_p of 0.70, indicating a high correlation of profiles.

However, observation of the somewhat greater distances between the successful academic male and female on stens B, C, F, G, Q_1, and Q_3 suggests possible differences. Relative to intelligence Barnard (1964) observed, "women who receive the doctor's degree are, on the usual types of measure, intellectually

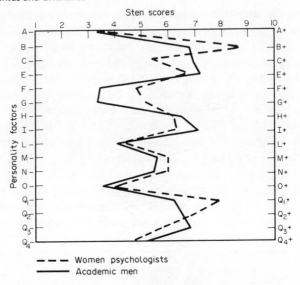

FIG. VI.4 Personality profiles of academic men and women
psychologists.

superior on the average to men who do [p. 78]." Although the profile of eminent
men manifests well above average intelligence (B+), the higher sten for the
academic women suggests that they may need even greater intellectual power
than the men to compete in scientific and academic attainment. On the other
hand, while above average ego strength (C+) and will power (Q₃+) were not
indicated as components in feminine success, the academic men seem to have
particular emotional maturity and stability and more exacting will power.

The academic women show a tendency to be less serious (F) and somewhat
more rigid in internal standards (G). Although the academic men are less conservative (Q₁) than average, the women seem considerably more radical, a
characteristic no doubt essential to their departure from the typical female
image.

Comparisons with Psychologists among the Successful
Academic Men

It is of particular interest to note the profile of the women psychologists as
compared with Cattell and Drevdahl's (1955) group of 107 eminent psychologists
in higher education presented in Figure VI.5.

Although the profiles bear marked resemblance when measured against their
professional colleagues, the women seem more aloof (A), less dominant (E), less
adventurous (H), and more self-sufficient (Q₂). These differences may be related

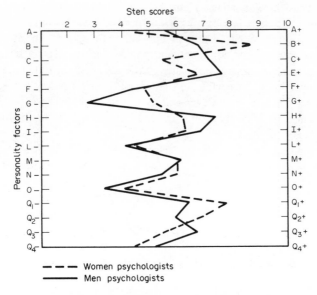

FIG. VI.5 Personality profiles of psychologists — men and
women.

to the composition of male and female groups. Of the men psychologists, 49%
were engaged in research, 26% in administration, and 25% in teaching; whereas
only 8% of the women spent the major portion of their time in research, 14% in
administration, and 49% in teaching. Furthermore, 34% of the women were
involved in clinical and consulting activities that were not represented in the
male group. Personality differences·may, therefore, be more closely related to
variations in vocational activity than to differences between male and female
psychologists in general.

Of perhaps greatest importance is the strong similarity between the men and
women psychologists, indicated by the pattern coefficient of similarity which
was the same as for Figure VI.4, r_p 0.70.

Differences in Personality Factors among Women Psychologists in Different Interest Groups

The analysis of differences in personality factors between interest groups
includes counseling and guidance, clinical, and developmental psychologists.
There were too few in each of the other areas of specialization among the women
of this generation to justify statistical comparisons. There were many more
similarities than differences in personality factors among the women who
specialized either in clinical, counseling, or developmental psychology.

Differences in the greatest number of factors (A, H, O, Q_2, and Q_4) were found between the women who identified themselves as counseling and guidance psychologists and those who considered themselves developmental psychologists. These two groups seem to represent two ends of a continuum ranging from a more adventuresome and confident, warm and sociable, relaxed, but also more group-dependent personality (the counseling psychologists) to the more socially aloof, intellectually independent, tense, and self-sufficient developmental psychologists. There were only two significant differences between the counseling and the clinical psychologists (on Factors H and O), with the counseling psychologists scoring higher on adventuresomeness and self-confidence than the clinical psychologists. In turn, the clinical psychologists differed from the developmental psychologists on only *one* factor: they were, as a group, more sociable than the developmental psychologists. . . .

The differences found in the present study among women psychologists point to a more "action and social relations" oriented personality among the counseling and educational psychologists, a less "secure" personality among the clinical psychologists, and a more "intellectually independent, reflective, and self-sufficient" personality among the developmental psychologists. . . .

Differences in Personality Characteristics between Women Psychologists with Few and Many Scientific Publications

For purposes of comparison we chose 30 women with no publication or only one and compared them with 30 women psychologists with the largest number of publications (26–275) – senior authors only. They represented the bottom and top quartile of the publication distribution among the respondents.

A comparison of the 16 PF Questionnaire profiles of the "high" and "low" publishers among these women psychologists reveals significant differences on only *one* personality factor: A. . . . The more productive women psychologists as a group preferred contemplation over social relationships, liked working alone, intellectual companionship, and rigor of thought. In this they resemble strongly the "significant contributors" to American psychology studies by Clark (1957), 95% of whom were men. As a group the highly productive women psychologists also scored higher on Factor B (intelligence) and lower on Factor Q_4 (less unresolved tension and anxiety), but the differences on these two factors between the high and low publishers did not reach the 0.05 level of confidence.

The largest proportion of women psychologists with many publications (about 40%) came from the area of developmental psychology; the lowest proportion came from the area of clinical and counseling psychology (15% each). . . .

However, only about 20% of the women with a significant number of publications worked full-time in one activity; nearly half of the productive women psychologists spent their time divided between teaching and other activities. In contrast, nearly 90% of the women with no or only one publication during their professional lifetime were full- or at least three-quarters time engaged in the pursuit of one job activity, and found or took little time for writing.

The more varied the activities were that the women psychologists engaged in, the greater the likelihood for their productivity. In this they resembled the significant contributors to psychology among the men (Clark, 1957).

Both Clark's (1957) assessment of American psychologists and Drevdahl's (1964) studies of personality characteristics of productive and nonproductive psychologists raised the question whether the lack of productivity of the practicing clinician (as measured by contributions to the scientific literature) might be due to the kind of person he is, his orientation to life and people, and his preference for social action over contemplation, rather than to any educational experience. Clark (1957) suggested:

> The psychologists who do not achieve eminence have the same sort of motivation for service to society but express this to a much greater extent through face-to-face contact with individuals and helping persons achieve solutions to personal problems. Any great expenditure of time in this kind of enterprise would prevent a person from engaging in activities which would call him to the attention of other psychologists around the country. Thus it very well may be that what we observe are differences in manner of achieving a solution to human problems rather than differences in attitude about the need for such solutions [p. 95].

This difference in orientation is also apparent among the women psychologists who represent different fields of *interest*. The great similarity, however, in the personality profiles of the "high" and "low" publishers among the women psychologists makes one wonder whether opportunities and restrictions of the major fields of *activity* play a greater role in scientific productivity than differences in personality factors among this group of successful academic women. Barnard (1964) concluded that academic position is "inextricably related to productivity [p. 154]." Rossi (1965a) has pointed out that self-selection works much more strongly among women so that at each higher level of education, women probably have a greater potential for significant achievement than men, but greater claims are also made on their "instant availability" in social interaction and service for others. It is a much rarer social phenomenon to find women than to find men with intense channeling of energy in professional work and tolerance of and preference for social isolation.

Differences in Personality Factors among Women Psychologists Engaged in Different Types of Activities

Again, there were many more similarities than differences among the personality profiles of women psychologists who were engaged in different types of professional activities. . . .

With a single exception, there were *no* significant differences among the women psychologists who were predominantly engaged in administrative, consulting, or research work. On one factor, N, the women in administration indicated greater social alertness than those in a consulting or clinical function. Women whose major activity was college teaching, however, differed from the other groups on a number of personality factors. When compared with women psychologists in administration, they appeared less dominant (E), less self-assured (O), and more anxious (Q_4). When compared with women psychologists who were engaged in counseling, they were more serious and exacting (F; Q_3) and less dominant (E). When compared with women psychologists engaged full-time in research, they appeared more controlled and exacting. There was a greater similarity in personality profiles between the women psychologists whose major activity was college teaching and those whose major activity was research than between the college teachers and the other two groups (administration, counseling). A study of college teachers in the sciences (Eckert and Stecklein, 1961) had shown that women teachers seem more psychologically dependent on comfortable relations with other people, both peers and the young. This, together with their decided minority status in the academic field (less than 10% of all academic positions, only 1% of the professorships in the biological and social sciences are held by women; Mattfeld and Van Aken, 1965), may explain why, in spite of greater will power, women psychologists in college teaching may appear less confident and secure than women choosing other activities within the academic setting. The most dominant and self-assured would be most likely, over a professional lifetime, to achieve administrative positions.

Cattell and Drevdahl's (1955) 16 PF Questionnaire study of teachers, administrators, and researchers among men in several scientific fields likewise found no significant differences between teachers and researchers among the academic men in psychology. The differences between teachers and administrators among the men were in the direction of greater adventuresomeness (H), unconventionality (M), will control (Q_3), and anxiety (Q_4). These differences also appear in our comparisons between academic women who were college teachers and those who were administrators.

Conclusions

The women in this study were selected to represent a sample of academic women who had reached their peak attainment in a scientific profession. Generalizations from the findings, therefore, are intended for this particular reference group. Successful academic women in psychology differ from adult women in general and from women college students in many of the same personality characteristics in which they resemble successful academic men. As a group, they tend to be more intelligent, socially aloof, dominant, serious, adventuresome, sensitive, flexible, imaginative, insightful, unconventional, secure, and self-sufficient than adult women in the general population and women in college, and less anxiety prone. They score within the normal adult feminine range in emotional maturity and will power, but appear significantly more emotionally mature and controlled than women college students.

The great number of significant differences between the personality profiles of the college women and the successful academic women and the lack of similarity between the personality profiles of gifted girls in special education programs and recognized creative people, both men and women, seem to indicate that a selection strictly on the basis of intelligence and achievement tests does not lead to the discovery and encouragement of potentially creative girls in special classes from the elementary to the college level.

In spite of a striking similarity between the 16 PF Questionnaire profiles of successful academic men and women and the men psychologists, the women psychologists score, as a group, higher than the successful academic men on intelligence, superego strength, and unconventionality (radicalism), and lower than the academic men on self-sentiment.

Of the three major interest groups represented among the respondents, the developmental psychologists among the women of this generation contained the greatest proportion of significant contributors to the scientific literature. The counseling and guidance psychologists were more "social action and people oriented"; the clinical psychologists had more conflicting and less secure personality profiles. Both groups contributed a much smaller proportion of scientific articles.

Differences between high and low publishers centered on Factor A; the significant contributors among the women psychologists were more socially aloof and exacting. More productive women were college teachers, and more shared their professional time between teaching and other activities. Women in clinical and administrative work contributed relatively fewer publications. Demand made on the women's time or type of assignments appeared more important than differences in personality characteristics among these women whose self-selection would yield a greater percentage with potential for scientific contributions.

References

BARNARD, J. (1964) *Academic women*. New York: World.

CAMPBELL, D. P. and SOLIMAN, A. M. (1968) The vocational interests of women in psychology: 1942–1966. *American Psychologist*, 23, 158–163.

CATTELL, R. B. and DREVDAHL, J. E. (1955) A comparison of the personality profiles of eminent researchers with those of eminent teachers and administrators and the general population. *British Journal of Psychology*, 46, 248–261.

CATTELL, R. B. and EBER, H. W. (1957) *Handbook for the Sixteen Personality Factor Questionnaire*. Champaign, IL: Institute for Personality and Ability Testing.

CATTELL, R. B. and EBER, H. W. (1962) *Supplement of norms*. Champaign: Institute for Personality and Ability Testing.

CLARK, V. E. (1957) *America's psychologists*. Washington, DC: American Psychological Association.

DREVDAHL, J. E. (1956) Factors of importance in creativity. *Journal of Clinical Psychology*, 12. 21–26.

DREVDAHL, J. E. (1964) Some developmental and environmental factors in creativity. In C. W. Taylor (Ed.), *Widening horizons in creativity*. New York: Wiley.

DREVDAHL, J. E. and CATTELL, R. B. (1958) Personality and creativity in artists and writers. *Journal of Clinical Psychology*, 14, 107–111.

ECKERT, R. E. and STECKLEIN, J. E. (1961) Job motivations and satisfactions of college teachers. *Cooperative Research Monographs*, 7. United States Department of Health, Education and Welfare, Office of Education.

FJELD, H. A. and AMES, L. B. (1950) Women psychologists: Their work, training and professional opportunities. *Journal of Social Psychology*, 31, 69–94.

HELSON, R. (1961) Creativity, sex and mathematics. In D. W. MacKinnon (Ed.), *Proceedings of the conference on the creative person*. Berkeley: University of California Extension.

HELSON, R. (1966) Personality of women with imaginative and artistic interests: The role of masculinity, originality and other characteristics in their creativity. *Journal of Personality*, 34, 1–25.

HELSON, R. (1967a) Personality characteristics and developmental history of creative college women. *Genetic Psychology Monographs*, 76, 205–256.

HELSON, R. (1967b) Sex differences in creative style. *Journal of Personality*, 35, 214–233.

KURTZMAN, K. A. (1967) A study of school attitudes, peer acceptance and personality of creative adolescents. *Exceptional Children*, 33, 157–162.

MACCOBY, E. E. (1963) Women's intellects. In S. M. Farber and R. H. L. Wilson (Eds), *The potential of women*. New York: McGraw-Hill.

MATTFELD, J. A. and VAN AKEN, C. G. (Eds) (1965) *Women and the scientific professions*. Cambridge: M.I.T. Press.

MERENDA, P. and CLARK, W. (1963) Comparison of concepts of multiple inferential selves between clinical psychologists and school guidance counselors. *Journal of Clinical Psychology*, 19, 355–359.

ROE, A. (1953) *The making of a scientist*. New York: Dodd, Mead.

ROSSI, A. S. (1965a) Barriers to the career choice of engineering, medicine or science among American women. In J. A. Mattfeld and C. G. Van Aken (Eds), *Women and the scientific professions*. Cambridge: M.I.T. Press.

ROSSI, A. S. (1965b) Women in science: Why so few? *Science*, 148, 1196–1199.

RUBIN, S. (1957) A study of the self-concept and functions within the profession counseling psychology. *Dissertation Abstracts*, 17, 1587.

SOUTHERN, M. L. and PLANT, W. T. (1968) Personality characteristics of very bright adults. *Journal of Social Psychology*, 75, 119–126.

TAYLOR, C. W. and BARRON, F. (1963) A look ahead. In C. W. Taylor and F. Barron (Eds), *Scientific creativity: its recognition and development*. New York: Wiley.

WALBERG, H. J. (1969) Physics, femininity, and creativity. *Developmental Psychology*, 1, 47–54.

WERNER, E. E. (1966) CPQ personality factors of talented and underachieving boys and girls in elementary school. *Journal of Clinical Psychology*, 22, 461–464.

WERNER, E. E. and BACHTOLD, L. M. (1969) Personality factors of gifted boys and girls in middle childhood and adolescence. *Psychology in the School*, 2, 177–182.

VII

Personal Dynamics and Difficulties in Exceptional Achievement

THE QUESTIONS that are most constantly asked regarding exceptional achievement are: How smart must one be? How "lucky" (fated)? Why the infrequent number of eminent women? However, the oldest and most frequent question is how "crazy" or mentally ill are persons who are noted for their exceptional achievements. From its very beginning, genius and exceptional achievement has been dramatic and material for fantasy. Nothing is as dramatic as the gifted youth who unaccountably fails or whose promise is cut short. It excites us as it saddens us. Yet such lives are far more infrequent than promises kept — if too much is not expected or promised. Chapter VII shows us the difficulties, as well as the courage, that talented persons must call upon during their careers. Although several of the papers (VII-1 and VII-2) do suggest that often these lives verge on psychopathology, all point to one conclusion: alongside turmoil and difficulties such lives display remarkable inner resources and great dignity.

Woody and Claridge (VII-1) report a highly significant statistical relationship between 100 university students' scores on a test of psychoticism and their performance on a standard measure of creative potential. The relationship between psychoticism and measures of different types of thinking appears quite specific in this population, being highly positive and significant for divergent thinking but not significantly associated with convergent thinking. If one recalls earlier comments by several authors questioning whether or not divergent thinking is representative of "creativity", one can appreciate the intriguing nature of Woody and Claridge's findings. Clearly, we have a "puzzle" here. By putting together the articles by MacKinnon (III-4), Nicholls (VI-1), and Barron (VI-4), with the present article, one has an example of the complex questions often involved and the difficulty scientists have in sorting out the truth and the error in long-standing myths.

We have already mentioned Berrington's article (VII-2). It is a profound argument for considering eminent persons as *persons* as well as *achievers*. To know them as persons is to fully appreciate them rather than to use them as stereotypes. Berrington tells us the personal "price" paid by a majority of British Prime Ministers; he tells us also about the often harsh origins of ambition. Nowhere are the lifelong, deeply-personal springs of eminence and career choice more dramatically recorded than in the life and career of William James. After reading Strout (VII-3) it should be extremely difficult to minimize the fact that what we become in adulthood, famous or not, is as much a continuous working through of our earlier family experiences and identities as it is the result of early giftedness, education, and social channels. In this article, we come face-to-face with the question of how important are deeply-set personal ideals and perseverance to the attainment of eminence. Apparently they are as critical and demanding as giftedness.

Having spent some effort pointing to the difficulties and risks that the achievement of eminence requires, we believe such pitfalls need to be put in perspective. For this purpose the book closes with Hardy's wise advice (VII-4). It is simply stated with an elegance equal to mathematical precision. I have not come upon a better-stated or more clearly demonstrated prescription for eminence than Hardy's. It reminds us that to try to become eminent is to be socially responsible and personally honorable, and worthy of respect.

1

Psychoticism and Creativity*

E. WOODY and G. CLARIDGE

Abstract

In view of evidence linking psychosis with high creative ability, an attempt was made to evaluate the relationship between abilities and personality traits. Tests of divergent thinking and convergent thinking were administered, along with the Eysenck's Personality Question-naire, to 100 university students. The hypothesis that "psychoticism" is related to divergent thinking was strongly confirmed. The hypothesis that psychoticism would be related inversely to speed in a convergent-thinking task was rejected. No evidence was found for any relation-ship between extraversion–introversion or neuroticism–stability and either thinking style.

RECENT scientific evidence relating psychosis and creativity has tended to sub-stantiate two old lines of speculation: first, that creativity and psychopathology are of similar origin; and, secondly, that psychotics and highly creative normal individuals share certain personality characteristics and thinking styles.

Evidence that creativity and psychosis have similar origins has come from a number of genetic studies. In a study of foster-raised offspring of schizophrenic mothers, Heston (1966) found that although about half showed psychosocial disability the remaining half were notably successful adults, possessing artistic talents and demonstrating imaginative adaptations to life which were uncommon in the control group. Karlsson (1968) examined seven generations of pedigrees for an Icelandic kindred. He found that among relatives of schizophrenics there was a high incidence of individuals of great creative achievement. McNeil (1971) studied the occurrence of mental illness in highly creative adoptees and their biological parents. The mental illness rates in the adoptees and in their biological parents were positively and significantly related to the creativity level of the adoptees. Such findings lend support to speculations by Hammer and Zubin (1968) and by Jarvik and Chadwick (1973) that there is a common genetic basis for great creative potential and psychopathological deviation. Thus the schizo-phrenic genotype may be thought of as a producer of highly unusual behavior which under certain conditions, both in terms of genetic modifiers and suitable cultural settings, may be very advantageous. This view supports the notion of schizophrenia as a genetic morphism (Huxley, Mayr, Hoffer and Osmond, 1964), whose frequency results from a balance between selectively favourable and un-favourable properties.

*British Journal of Social and Clinical Psychology, (1977), 16, 241–248.

Research concerning similarities between psychotics and highly creative normals has tended to develop along two lines: first, that the thought disorder of psychotics is similar to normal creative thinking; and secondly, that highly creative normals have psychotic-like personality traits.

McConaghy and Clancy (1968) demonstrated that the "allusive" thinking characteristic of many schizophrenics on object sorting tests exists widely in a less exaggerated form in the normal population. In addition, they showed similar familial transmission of allusive thinking in schizophrenics and non-schizophrenics, and suggested that such thinking is akin to highly creative thinking. In a recent study, Dykes and McGhie (1976) actually demonstrated that highly creative normals score as highly on the Lovibond object sorting test as do schizophrenics. Low creative normals tended to produce conventional, unoriginal sortings, while the highly creative normals and the schizophrenics tended to give an equal proportion of unusual sortings. The mean scores of the highly creative and schizophrenic groups differed from that of the low creative group at the 0.001 level. Thus there is a strong evidence that a common thinking style may lead to a controlled usefulness in normals and an uncontrollable impairment in schizophrenics.

Some researchers have claimed that there are indications of psychopathology in the personalities of highly creative individuals. MacKinnon (1962) and Barron (1972) found the tendency for individuals rated as highly creative to obtain several psychopathological scores on scales of the MMPI, particularly Pd (psychopathic deviate) and Sc (schizophrenic). Barron suggested that such MMPI scores indicate that creative people can maintain high intellectual functioning along with psychotic-like experiences. He also summarized some apparent similarities between schizophrenics and highly creative normals: both report odd sensory and perceptual experiences, feelings of restlessness and the inclination towards impulsive outbursts, the preference for solitude, rejection of common social values, and highly unusual or "mystical" experiences. Cattell and his co-workers have investigated the personality factors characteristic of highly creative individuals and produced similarly suggestive results. For example, Drevdahl (1956) found differences in schizothymia, self-sufficiency, and radicalism between creative and non-creative students. Drevdahl and Cattell (1958) studied creative artists and writers and found that they demonstrated traits of radicalism, self-sufficiency, bohemianism, and dominance, along with low surgency and low cyclothymia. On the basis of these findings, they claimed that the creative individual was, on the whole, not well adjusted. Generally, then, the creative individual emerges as a solitary person with asocial attitudes and a lack of concern with social norms; and it is suggested that he is dominant and perhaps aggressive as well. The traits are highly congruent with Eysenck's (1972) theoretical formulation of the trait of "psychoticism", a personality factor hypothesized to be indicative of a predisposition to psychotic breakdown. Claridge (1972) has noted that the traits on which the creative thinker deviates from average appear to parallel closely those which may reflect an increased loading on an underlying personality factor associated with schizophrenia.

Finally two recent studies may be cited which support the notion that a personality dimension of "psychoticism" is associated with creativity. Claridge (1973) used a nervous typological assessment of psychoticism based on a principal components analysis of a wide range of psychophysiological parameters which had been found to discriminate psychotics from controls. In normal individuals, psychoticism so defined was significantly related to scores on the Guilford divergent-thinking tests. Similarly, Farmer (1974) was able to demonstrate that the psychoticism score on the Eysenck's Personality Questionnaire was very significantly related to the originality score on Guilford's "consequences" test.

The principal aim of the present study was to produce more conclusive evidence for a relationship between "psychoticism" as a personality trait in normal individuals and creativity. In addition, an attempt was made to assess speed and accuracy on a convergent-thinking task, with the hope of relating these cognitive abilities to psychoticism and creativity. There are two reasons why these intelligence variables are particularly interesting in the present context. First, it has been found (Eysenck, Granger and Brengelmann, 1957) that slower speed scores significantly distinguished psychotics from normals and neurotics, while level tests, measuring general cognitive ability, did not. Hence, it is reasonable to look for speed differences in normal subjects scoring high and low on psychoticism, the implication being that high-P normals may have a psychotic-like slowness. Second, Payne (1961) argued that the overinclusive thinking which schizophrenics show on object sorting tests may partly explain their tendencies towards abnormal numbers of errors and abnormal slowness on cognitive tests. Crowcroft (1967), too, pointed out that such thinking produces a slowing down of effective mental speed. Since highly creative normals tend to show overinclusive or "allusive" thinking as well, it would be interesting to see if there is a similar overall slowing of mental speed in them, too. The basic intentions were to investigate whether the highly creative normal has any schizophrenic-like cognitive disadvantages in conjunction with his widely divergent, allusive thinking ability, and to get a more complete picture of the cognitive abilities possibly associated with psychoticism.

Method

Subjects

The subjects in this study were 100 university students, both undergraduate and graduate, at Oxford. The mean age was 20.5 years (range = 16–26 years, S.D. = 1.99). In view of Hudson's (1966) suggestion that science specialists and arts specialists may differ in thinking abilities, an effort was made to obtain a wide sampling of the various fields of specialization at the university.

While such a sample obviously has its limitations, there are compelling reasons to think that it is an especially suitable sample, at least initially, in which to look for a relationship between psychoticism and creativity. First, in such a group, intelligence may be assumed to be above a high cut-off level. This aspect is most important as a control for any relationship between intelligence and creativity, particularly in view of the widely expressed hypothesis that creativity is significantly related to IQ up to about IQ 120, whereas it become independent of IQ above this level. Canter's (1973) careful analysis of results provides a good example of how relationships with IQ may contaminate studies of the correlates of creativity, producing spurious results and even preventing any results from emerging clearly. Second, in such a group motivation may be assumed to be consistently high. This aspect is of obvious importance for meaningful results on open-ended, untimed tests, in which the subject is asked to respond exhaustively. It is perhaps clearer that such a sample is highly motivated on a test of "psychological ability" than any other sample. Thirdly, the restriction of age range is important for comparing subjects' scores on the PQ, since P shows a very marked regression with age, especially for males (Eysenck and Eysenck, 1975). Fourthly, use of a student sample allows the inclusion of a wide range of different intellectual "talents" while at the same time ensuring a reasonably consistent common background. The former aspect is important to ensure some generality in the results, since, for example, arts and science specialists may tend to think differently. The latter aspect is important in deriving "uniqueness" or originality scores on the creativity tests, since the rarity of an individual's responses is judged by their frequency of occurrence in the sample as a whole. It is not clear that such scores would have much meaning in a very heterogeneous sample.

Tests

The tests used in this study were the Personality Questionnaire by Eysenck and Eysenck, the Wallach–Kogan creativity tests, and the Nufferno speed test.

The Personality Questionnaire is Eysenck and Eysenck's unpublished penultimate attempt to devise a questionnaire incorporating a psychoticism (P) scale as well as the widely used scales for extraversion (E), neuroticism (N), and dissimulation (L). On the version of the PQ given here, the P scale consisted of 29 items, the E scale of 22 items, the N scale of 23 items, and the L scale of 21 items.

Although the general instructions given in the original tests of creativity by Wallach and Kogan (1965) were modified for use with the present sample, the actual items were retained exactly as in the original. Including both verbal and visual stimuli, the tests consist of five different tasks. These are Instances, Pattern Meanings, Uses, Similarities, and Line Meanings. Each task is evaluated in terms of two related variables: the number of unique responses produced by the subject, and the total number of responses produced by the subject. In the present study, the test items were administered individually on index cards, and the subject was required to write down his responses. Previous studies (Cropley, 1968; Cropley and Field, 1969; Dykes and McGhie, 1976) have demonstrated that these tests of creativity retain the properties of internal consistency, independence of IQ, and reasonable validity when used with a university student sample. In the present case, it was clear that the subjects could respond very imaginatively to the test items in spite of the apparent simplicity of the items. For example, to the item "Name all the things you can think of that move on wheels", subjects responded with such things as "ball-point pens", "clay pots being thrown", "can openers", "fortune", "meals", "hamsters", and so on.

The Nufferno tests of inductive reasoning are predicated on the hypothesis that intelligence tests measure the results of at least three reasonably independent determinants: speed, accuracy, and continuance (Furneaux, 1952). The Nufferno speed tests yield separate scores for speed and accuracy as independent aspects of problem-solving ability (Furneaux, 1956). The test problems are of the letter-series type. In the present research, form B(1) was used on Nufferno sheet 2. Test B(1) is composed of problems of a higher level of difficulty than the other speed-test problem sets, and is expressly suitable for use with a university-student sample. The manual gives several ways of administering and timing the test. In this case, the test was administered individually and every problem was timed separately.

Procedure

The tests were administered to each subject individually, every subject completing all the tests at one sitting. The order of administration of the tests was as follows: Instances, Pattern Meanings, Alternate Uses, PQ, Similarities, and the Nufferno speed test.

With regard to the creativity tests, two aspects of the testing procedure deserve mention. Every reasonable effort was made to provide a comfortable and informal setting for the subject, in accordance with the type of atmosphere Wallach and Kogan have hypothesized to be conducive to creative performance. In addition, no time pressure at all was exerted on the subject. In fact, if the subject spent a particularly short period of time on the first item or two, the experimenter made a point of asking, "Are you sure you're writing down *everything* that you can think of?" The time taken by subjects for the five creativity tests ranged from half an hour to 5½ hours, with a mean of about two hours (S.D. = 50 min).

Results

Table VII.1 shows the means and standard deviations for all of the measures over the total sample. Initially, an analysis was carried out to determine whether

TABLE VII. 1 *Means and standard deviations of the test measures*

	Score	Mean	S.D.
(a) *The Personality Questionnaire*			
Scale			
P		6.17	3.04
E		13.29	5.14
N		11.80	5.58
L		4.53	2.92
(b) *The Wallach–Kogan Creativity Tests* (raw scores)			
Task Instances	Number	65.00	43.19
	Uniqueness	9.72	19.22
Pattern Meanings	Number	52.30	32.52
	Uniqueness	17.80	18.81
Uses	Number	55.79	25.35
	Uniqueness	6.50	8.79
Similarities	Number	59.86	24.22
	Uniqueness	4.70	6.85
Line Meanings	Number	53.21	40.77
	Uniqueness	11.85	18.44
(c) *The Nufferno Speed Test* (raw scores)	Accuracy	17.20	1.03
	Speed	110.11	14.98

it was reasonable to pool all subjects into one group to determine the results. It was found that there were no significant differences between the means for males and females on any of the variables, while the only clear difference for arts and science specialists was on the Nufferno speed measure. The latter score for science specialists was 105.59 (S.D. = 36) and for arts specialists 113.25 (S.D. = 14.71). The lower raw speed score for the science specialists indicates that they were significantly faster than the arts specialists (t = 2.56, $P<0.02$). When the relationship of speed to the other variables was considered separately in these two groups, the only correlations which reached significance – at the 5% level – were those between speed and N; the correlations being of opposite sign in the two groups. From this analysis it was concluded that the sample was relatively homogeneous and all 100 subjects were subsequently considered together as a single group.

Correlations Between Experimental Measures

On the Nufferno test the speed and accuracy scores were independent, the correlation being –0.08. Similarly the personality questionnaire scales were relatively independent of one another, the only significant correlations being those involving the L scale. By contrast, the ten indices of creativity (five number and five uniqueness scores) were all highly intercorrelated. (To correct for considerable positive skew in the creativity scores, they were all transformed into log values.) Correlations there ranged from +0.37 to +0.83, all significant beyond the 0.001 level. Thus it appeared that the tests were tapping a unitary factor.

The correlations between psychoticism and the ten indices of creativity are shown in Table VII.2. It can be seen that all of the correlations are positive and highly significant – beyond the 0.001 level. Table VII.3 shows the comparable correlations for the other three PQ scales. Clearly, creativity as measured by the present tests is independent of extraversion. For neuroticism, the only significant correlations were those with the two scores on the Line Meanings test. Considering that this task came as the last of a very lengthy battery, and that there was no discernible relationship between N and the scores on the very similar Pattern Meanings task, it seems most likely that the correlations with N reflect a fatigue or motivation effect, rather than something intrinsic to the creative process.

Finally, some comment is necessary about the correlations between creativity test performance and the lie scale of the PQ. As can be seen from Table VII.3, seven of the ten correlations were significantly negative. It is also of interest that P and L were themselves correlated significantly and negatively ($r = -0.25$, $P<0.01$). Since it is conceivable that low L scores denote a degree of unconventionality, it is possible that part of the relationship between P and creativity was due to a willingness, by some individuals, to be unconventional. However,

TABLE VII. 2 *Pearson correlation coefficients between P and creativity scores*

	Instances	Pattern Meanings	Uses	Similarities	Line Meanings
Number score	0.32	0.37	0.45	0.36	0.38
Uniqueness score	0.61	0.64	0.66	0.68	0.65

For all correlations, $P<0.001$.

TABLE VII.3 *Pearson correlation coefficients of E, N and L with creativity scores*

Task	Score	E	N	L
Instances	Number	−0.05	0.13	−0.08
	Uniqueness	−0.08	0.11	−0.11
Pattern Meanings	Number	0.00	0.08	−0.21*
	Uniqueness	0.00	0.05	−0.23*
Uses	Number	0.03	−0.03	−0.23*
	Uniqueness	−0.05	0.00	−0.21*
Similarities	Number	−0.08	0.07	−0.12
	Uniqueness	−0.08	0.12	−0.20*
Line Meanings	Number	−0.1	0.21*	−0.20*
	Uniqueness	0.03	0.21*	−0.22*

*$P<0.05$.

compared with the correlations with the psychoticism scale, those with L were very weak and seem unlikely to provide a complete explanation of the results.

The speed score of the Nufferno test failed to correlate significantly with any of the creativity and personality variables. Nor did the accuracy score show any clear relationship with the creativity scores or with the three personality variables. However, accuracy was significantly correlated with P ($r = -0.23$, $P = <0.01$), suggesting a very slight tendency for high-P subjects to be poor at error checking.

In order to examine the relationship between psychoticism and divergent thinking in more detail a further extensive analysis of the P scale and creativity data was undertaken. Space does not permit a complete account of that analysis and only the main finding will be mentioned here. A series of multiple linear regressions were calculated in order to determine the optimum combination of creativity scores capable of predicting psychoticism. It was found that an equation using the uniqueness and number of scores of two of the creativity tests was virtually as good as the equation using scores for all five tests. Thus, the following equation accounted for 64% of the variance in P (multiple $r = 0.80$, standard error = 1.87):

$$P = - 3.54S_n + 3.96S_u - 6.58PM_n + 5.08PM_u + 16.22,$$

where S_n = logged number score on similarities,
$\quad S_u$ = logged uniqueness score on similarities,
$\quad PM_n$ = logged number score on pattern meanings, and
$\quad PM_u$ = logged uniqueness score on pattern meanings.

The best equation using all ten creativity indices accounted for 70% of the variance in P (multiple $r = 0.84$, standard error = 1.74). Thus, it would appear that in future studies of the relationship between P and creativity, the Similarities and Pattern Meanings tests may be used in preference to the others, at a very great saving of time and without any real loss of results. It is also noteworthy that the number scores, which showed *negative* weights in the regression analysis, act as suppressor variables in conjunction with the uniqueness scores. This suggests that high-P individuals give relatively few commonplace responses as well as relatively many unusual ones.

Discussion and Conclusions

The results reported here strongly support our prediction that there should be a significant relationship between Eysenck's P scale and measures of creative thinking; though, surprisingly enough, that relationship seems to be quite independent, in this sample at least, of other important factors of personality and intellectual ability. In particular, high-P individuals showed no evidence of schizophrenic-like cognitive slowness; while, confirming Dykes and McGhie's (1976) result, high creativity did not affect speed of convergent thinking.

There are basically two ways in which the present results could be interpreted, though unfortunately to insist on both of them does involve somewhat circular reasoning. On the one hand, the data could be said to provide evidence validating the P scale, whose status in that regard might otherwise be said to be rather weak. The previous studies, reviewed earlier, which led us to carry out the present experiment, certainly suggest that a measure of genetic predisposition to psychosis should have thinking style as a correlate. From that point of view, the present results strengthen the P scale's claim to be such a measure, while adding to it validation data supplementing that derived, for example, from psychophysiological experiments (Claridge and Chappa, 1973) and more recently, from the study of the symptomatic correlates of the Eysenck questionnaire (Reichenstein, 1976).

On the other hand, if it is considered that independent evidence for the validity of the P scale is already strong, then the present results offer substantial support for the hypothesis that creativity is related to pyschosis. Then the findings might be considered particularly convincing since they emerge from an approach to the hypothesis that is very different from those taken previously. Whether the approach is through genetic studies, studies of schizophrenic thought disorder, personality profiles of creative individuals, or by investigations of the dimensional view of psychosis, the conclusion to be reached seems to be the same: that psychotic and normal creative thinking have certain underlying characteristics in common. If this interpretation is accepted then further studies on individual differences in cognitive style – in normal and clinically psychotic subjects – should provide a powerful way of establishing and elaborating a dimensional model of schizophrenia.

Having said this it has to be admitted that a more banal interpretation of the results is possible. Thus it is evident from the nature of open-ended creativity tests and from the item content of the P scale that both may tap a common factor associated with the willingness to be unconventional or engage in mildly antisocial behaviour. The explanation would find some support in the negative correlations of the lie scale with both P and creativity. However, it will be recalled that the latter were very weak compared with the very high correlations between creativity and psychoticism. Further, in a sense an explanation in terms of such a response set begs the question since unconventionality and antisocial behaviour could in themselves be regarded as characteristics of psychoticism.

Clearly, future studies will need to address themselves to this and a number of other questions which we made no attempt to answer here. One of some importance concerns the extent to which the present results would hold up over a wide range of general intelligence. Or, more specifically, given the uncertain relationship between IQ and creativity test performance, how do psychoticism, general intelligence and divergent thinking interact? The answer to this might partly resolve a paradox that is already evident in the theorizing in this field; namely the attempt, at one and the same time, to relate to schizophrenia both the intellectual excellence usually associated with creative thought and the cognitive deficit — including poor intelligence test performance — frequently found in psychotic patients. We have speculated elsewhere (Claridge, 1972) that intelligence might act as a moderator variable influencing the threshold for actual psychotic breakdown, increasing vulnerability in the dull but affording protection to the intellectually gifted whose equally divergent thinking style may be turned to creative ends.

It is felt that the present results provide some encouragement for examining this possibility experimentally, using the twin strategies of clinical and normal individual differences research.

References

BARRON, F. (1972) The creative personality: Akin to madness. *Psychol. Today* 6, 42–44, 84–85.

CANTER, S. (1973) Some aspects of cognitive function in twins. In G. S. Claridge, S. Canter and W. I. Hume (eds), *Personality Differences and Biological Variations: A Study of Twins.* Oxford: Pergamon.

CLARIDGE, G. S. (1972) The schizophrenias as nervous types. *Br. J. Psychiat.* 121, 1–17.

CLARIDGE, G. S. (1973) A nervous typological analysis of personality variation in normal twins. In G. S. Claridge, S. Canter and W. I. Hume (eds), *Personality Differences and Biological Variations: A Study of Twins.* Oxford: Pergamon.

CLARIDGE, G. S. and CHAPPA, H. J. (1973) Psychoticism: A study of its biological basis in normal subjects. *Br. J. soc. clin. Psychol.* 12, 175–187.

CROPLEY, A. J. (1968) A note on the Wallach–Kogan tests of creativity. *Br. J. educ. Psychol.* 38, 197–201.

CROPLEY, A. J. and FIELD, T. W. (1969) Achievement in science and intellectual style. *J. app. Psychol.* 53, 132–135.

CROWCROFT, A. (1967) *The Psychotic – Understanding Madness.* Harmondsworth: Penguin.

DREVDAHL, J. E. (1956) Factors of importance for creativity. *J. clin. Psychol.* 12, 21–26.

DREVDAHL, J. E. and CATTELL, R. B. (1958) Personality and creativity in artists and writers. *J. clin. Psychol.* 14, 107–111.

DYKES, M. and McGHIE, A. (1976) A comparative study of attentional strategies of schizo-phrenic and highly creative normal subjects. *Br. J. Psychiat.* 128, 50–56.

EYSENCK, H. J. (1971) Relation between intelligence and personality. *Percept. mot. Skills* 32, 637–638.

EYSENCK, H. J. (1972) An experimental and genetic model of schizophrenia. In A. K. Kaplan (ed.), *Genetic Factors in Schizophrenia.* Springfield: Thomas.

EYSENCK, H. J. and EYSENCK, S. B. G. (1975). *Manual of the Eysenck Personality Questionnaire.* London: Hodder & Stoughton.

EYSENCK, H. J., GRANGER, G. W. and BRENGELMANN, J. C. (1957) *Perceptual Processes and Mental Illness.* Maudsley Monographs No. 2. London: Institute of Psychiatry.

FARMER, E. W. (1974) Psychoticism and person-orientation as general personality charac-teristics of importance for different aspects of creative thinking. BSc Thesis, University of Glasgow.

FURNEAUX, W. D. (1952) Some speed, error, and difficulty relationships, within a problem solving situation. *Nature, Lond.* 170, 37.

FURNEAUX, W. D. (1956) *Manual of Nufferno Speed Tests.* London: National Foundation for Educational Research.

HAMMER, M. and ZUBIN, J. (1968) Evolution, culture, and psychopathology. *J. gen. Psychol.* 78, 154–175.

HESTON, L. L. (1966) Psychiatric disorders in foster home reared children of schizophrenic mothers. *Br. J. Psychiat.* **112**, 819–825.

HUDSON, L. (1966) *Contrary Imaginations.* London: Methuen.

HUXLEY, J., MAYR, E., HOFFER, H. and OSMOND, A. (1964) Schizophrenia as a genetic morphism. *Nature, Lond.* **204**, 220–221.

JARVIK, L. F. and CHADWICK, S. B. (1973) Schizophrenia and survival. In M. Hammer, K. Salzinger and S. Sutton (eds), *Psychopathology.* New York: Wiley.

KARLSSON, J. L. (1968) Genealogic studies of schizophrenia. In D. Rosenthal and S. S. Kety (eds), *The Transmission of Schizophrenia.* Oxford: Pergamon.

MacKINNON, D. W. (1962) The personality correlates of creativity: A study of American architects. In P. E. Vernon (ed.), *Creativity.* Harmondsworth: Penguin.

McCONAGHY, N. and CLANCY, M. (1968) Familial relationships of allusive thinking in university students and their parents. *Br. J. Psychiat.* **114**, 1079–1087.

McNEIL, T. F. (1971) Prebirth and postbirth influence on the relationship between creative ability and recorded mental illness. *J. Personality* **39**, 391–406.

PAYNE, R. W. (1961) Cognitive abnormalities. In H. J. Eysenck (ed.), *Handbook of Abnormal Psychology.* New York: Basic Books.

REICHENSTEIN, S. (1976) A pilot study into the incidence of schizophrenic symptoms in a normal population. Undergraduate research dissertation, University of Oxford.

WALLACH, M. A. and KOGAN, N. (1965) *Modes of Thinking in Young Children.* New York: Holt, Rinehart & Winston.

2

Prime Ministers and the Search for Love*

H. BERRINGTON

"Life is all opposites, and a child born with a silver spoon may have to swallow many spoonfuls of bitterness." (The childhood nurse of Sir Henry Page Croft MP, quoted in *My Life of Strife* by Sir Henry Page Croft – later Lord Croft.). . .

THE LONG and meandering road that ends at 10 Downing Street begins its course in an unhappy home; that, in short, is the message of Lucille Iremonger's *The Fiery Chariot*.(1) British prime ministers have come not from the ranks of the extrovert, the equable and the easy-going but from the introspective, the moody and the hyper-sensitive. Our most eminent political leaders have been distinguished, to an exceptional degree, by childhood bereavement and personal isolation. "I recall a particularly poignant conversation late one night, 17 years ago, with Aneurin Bevan", wrote Desmond Donnelly, in his own review of Mrs. Iremonger's book. "I was saying that he must make a more charitable judgement of 'X' (later to hold high office in the Wilson administration) because this person was desperately unhappy. Bevan, always a sensitive man himself, replied quietly 'So are most of us in politics'."(2) If Bevan's diagnosis, and Mrs Iremonger's thesis, are accurate, her book is of deep significance for the student of British politics.

In an obvious but profoundly important sense it is clear that Members of Parliament are psychologically untypical of their electors. For the ordinary voter, politics is usually a matter of peripheral concern; for MPs it is their chief, for some their only, interest in life. The MP possesses skills and aptitudes that ordinary voters do not have. His stock of political information is generally much larger, far more diverse and vastly more detailed than that of the average elector. His belief system, however shallow when measured by some ideal standard, is likely to be much more complex than that of the passive citizen. His intellectual processes, his style of political discourse are likely to be remote from, if not alien to, the modes of thought and political expression of most of his fellow-countrymen.

Perhaps, however, politicians are psychologically unusual in a deeper sense of the term. The evidence is contradictory and often impressionistic, but a political career usually demands such an inordinate degree of ambition, lays such burdens on the private lives of those who follow it and can impose such heavy costs, both

British Journal of Political Science, (1974), 4, 345–369 (edited). Cambridge University Press. Reprinted by permission of the author and the publisher.

psychic and material, that it seems plausible to assume that politicians are psychologically unrepresentative of their electorates.

Barber, in his notable book *The Lawmakers,* did infer that politicians were likely to differ psychologically from other citizens, and reached the tentative conclusion that elected public officials "possess either rather high or rather low levels of self-esteem compared with other persons who have the same social characteristics".(3) Men who came into politics were exceptional *either* in their high abilities *or* their strong needs. Barber argued reassuringly that politicians with realistically high self-esteem would become the political leaders – the men who shaped legislative strategy and planned committee programmes. Those with high competence and a realistic appreciation of their capacities would occupy the seats of legislative power and give leadership to less able and less secure colleagues. Mrs. Iremonger's book is far more disquieting in its implications than Barber's study; for whilst Barber located the insecure and the inadequate amongst the second-rank and less active politicians, Mrs. Iremonger finds that it was those who reached the political summit who most clearly displayed signs of emotional vulnerability. . . .

A cynic might aver that the amount of intellectual energy devoted to understanding the behaviour of political participants varies inversely with their importance. In the last twenty-five years, scholars and polling organizations have accumulated a vast amount of information about the motives and opinions of ordinary electors. We know, however, very little of a *systematic* kind about top decision-makers, except that they are drawn disproportionately from the well-educated and the well-to-do. This gap is the more surprising, because the influence of voters on policy is intermittent, remote and usually oblique whilst that of ministers is continuous, immediate and direct. The psychology of political leaders is a proper and indeed a crucial area of interest for the political scientist.

The Phaeton Complex

The Fiery Chariot began, it seems, as a chatty account of the private lives of British prime ministers, designed for popular consumption. But on reading the biographies of prime ministers in preparation for her own book the author was struck by the frequency with which these men had suffered the loss of a parent in childhood; indeed no fewer than 61% had done so. The regularity of this occurrence seemed to preclude chance, and Mrs. Iremonger, while speculating on the reasons for this apparent link between political success and childhood deprivation, was drawn to the work of Maryse Choisy, a French disciple and revisionist of Freud.

The argument of the book, quite simply, is that lack of "normal affection" in childhood stimulates – or is in some sense the cause of – the growth of abnormal ambition. The child who is deprived of love in the family circle quests after power and acclaim in the political arena. The abnormally ambitious constitute the available men from whom prime ministers are drawn: "there is no such thing as becoming a Prime Minister by accident, in the sense that the choice must be made from among a few, and those few are not there by accident" (1, p. 325). To these propositions we may add another, not explicitly made by the author, that such a man, having achieved political pre-eminence, finds it hard to keep his place. The weaknesses of personality, which are the obverse of the strengths he displays on his way to the top, hinder his retention of power.

Freud, in explaining the development of the super-ego or conscience in the male child, had emphasized the Oedipal conflict between the boy and his father, competitors for the affection of the mother. The super-ego developed out of the resolution of this conflict: "here we have" said Freud,

> in this ego ideal or super-ego, the representative of our relation to our parents. When we were little children we knew these higher natures, we admired and feared them; and later we took them into ourselves.
>
> The ego ideal is therefore the heir of the Oedipus complex, and thus it is also the expression of the most powerful impulses and most important libidinal vicissitudes of the id (4).

Choisy asked herself about the condition of the fatherless and, more specifically, of the illegitimate child. Her work showed that bastards, so far from lacking a super-ego, as might have been inferred from Freudian theory, tended to have exceptionally harsh and rigid ones. Narcissistic, omnipotent in fantasy if helpless in reality, dominated by the sense of their own "specialness", bastard children hark back not to the legend of Oedipus but to the myth of Phaeton.

Phaeton was the son of Phoebus, the sun, and Clymene, a sea-nymph — the child, in more recent parlance, of a backstairs liaison. Venus fell in love with Phaeton, and Phaeton "Growing vain and ambitious, . . . brought on himself rebukes for this arrogance, and slighting insinuations about his birth" (1, p. 13). Angry and resentful, he sought out his father in the Palace of the Sun, asking for proofs that Phoebus loved him and was indeed his father. Phoebus swore that he would give his son whatever he asked. Phaeton, to his father's horror, then asked leave to drive his chariot, the sun, across the skies for a day. Phoebus tried to dissuade him from such a foolhardy deed, but Phaeton refused to listen and held his father to his oath. Unable to restrain his son, Phoebus tried to teach him how to guide the chariot but as soon as Phaeton was seated in the chariot box, the horses, realizing the inadequacy of the driver, went out of control, and the chariot "plunged from the track" (1, p. 14). Heaven and earth were threatened with a conflagration when, to avert this disaster, Jupiter struck Phaeton with a thunderbolt. Phaeton fell into the river Po where his charred body was recovered and buried by local nymphs.

The bastard, wrote Choisy, never grows up to be a normal member of society. Emotionally he remains an infant, cherishing the fictitious omnipotence of early childhood, attracted to magic and the supernatural. Like Phaeton, he seeks to compensate for the inferiority of his birth by a dramatic stroke — by an act whose fulfilment is beyond his powers, and which leads him to catastrophe. Slighted and disregarded in childhood, he cannot tolerate this neglect in adult life. He wants, compulsively, to be recognized, or as Canning put it: "To speak honestly, I would rather be abused a little, if I had my choice, than have nothing at all said about me" (1, p. 63). Drawn by this need, he sets himself a task beyond his capacity. Deprived of love in childhood, he is unable to accept it in adult life; he can absorb only its surrogates, the kingdoms of this world and their glory.

Choisy was writing specifically of the psychology of the bastard. In doing this, had she not, asked Mrs. Iremonger, drawn her boundaries too rigidly? There are more ways than one of not having a father; there was only one admitted bastard amongst her prime ministers but many had lost a father, and most of them one or other parent, in childhood. Moreover, there were those, like Churchill, who suffered rejection and neglect without actually being bereaved as children. Deprivation of love in early life from whatever cause — bastardy, bereavement or parental indifference — might be the critical experience which would lead the Phaetons to seek "attention, acclaim and adoration" (1, p. 24), which would explain their isolation, their sensitivity, their commitment to the attainment of power coupled with occasional recklessness.

Childhood Bereavement

Deprivation of love is difficult to measure, whether it be amongst prime ministers or their fellows; childhood bereavement is easier to assess. A *prima facie* case for the thesis must depend on whether the incidence of bereavement amongst prime ministers was greater than amongst the general population or, more appropriately, amongst the strata from which prime ministers normally came.

But to gauge the degree of childhood bereavement amongst similar social groups poses serious problems. In the first place, the prime ministers Mrs. Iremonger studies span a total of 131 years, from Spencer Perceval, who took office in 1809, to Neville Chamberlain, who resigned in 1940. As there were important developments in medicine, and as general standards of health improved sharply between these dates, it would be unsafe to assume that the chances of losing a parent in childhood remained the same throughout the period.

The second problem relates to the social classes from which prime ministers were drawn. Prime ministers have come, for the most part, from the upper and upper-middle strata of society and it would be wrong to compare their rate of bereavement with figures derived from the total population. It would be surprising if the rate of bereavement amongst the well-to-do was not considerably lower than that amongst the working classes. The snag is that we seem to have no figures for the degree of bereavement during the nineteenth century.

We do, however, have some data from the Census of 1921. Statistics of orphanhood were collected in 1921 in order to assess the needs arising from the carnage of the First World War. Mrs. Iremonger cites these figures, early in her study, in support of her argument that the rate of bereavement amongst prime ministers – 61% – was exceptional. . . .

Perhaps a better way of assessing whether the experience of prime ministers was exceptional is to compare them with similar elite groups at different points of time. For this purpose, a 10% sample of peers in 1900 was taken, and a further 10% sample of peers in 1841. Table VII.4 shows the distribution of bereavement in the various categories. The median date of birth of the combined and un-equal samples of peers was 1825 whereas that of the prime ministers was 1801. Nevertheless, these samples provide a good yardstick of the incidence of bereavement amongst the high status groups from which prime ministers usually came.

Both the control samples, and the prime ministers, reveal a higher rate of bereavement of fathers than of mothers. Amongst those peers in the 1841 sample for whom full information is available, five lost their fathers, four their mothers, and two both: of three more known to have lost at least one parent, all lost their fathers, no data for the mothers having been traced. Of the 1900 sample, eight lost their fathers and five their mothers. Amongst the prime ministers, Aberdeen lost both parents in childhood and MacDonald was illegitimate; of the remaining twenty-two, eight lost a father and six a mother.

Childhood bereavement, then, was not uncommon during the late eighteenth and nineteenth centuries; indeed if, as is probable, the rate of bereavement was higher amongst the lower-middle and working classes we must draw the sombre conclusion that for the mass of the population the loss of a parent in childhood was a frequent, perhaps a typical, occurrence. Yet it is also clear that the rate of

TABLE VII.4 *The Incidence of Parental Loss Amongst Peers and Prime Ministers*

	Lost Parent Before Age of 16 (inc. illegitimacy)*		Normal Childhood		Not Known†	
	No.	%	No.	%	No.	Total
Peers, 1841	14	36	25	64	4	43
Peers, 1900	13	26	37	74	3	53
PMs (Perceval to Chamberlain)	16	67	8	33	–	24

*It should be noted that the figures, in order to be comparable with those given by Iremonger, include bereavement up to the age of sixteen, whereas the Census only covers bereavement up to fifteen.

†The "Not Known" figure for the peers of 1900 consists of four in whose cases the mother's date of death has not been traced; the fathers of all four were still living by the son's sixteenth birthday. In three of the four "Not Known", amongst the peers of 1841, data about the mother is lacking and in one case no information about either the father's or mother's date of death has been found. The "Not Knowns" have been excluded when calculating the percentage. Scottish and Irish peers are included, but not Royal Dukes.

bereavement amongst prime ministers was exceptionally high. Two-thirds of the prime ministers from Spencer Perceval to Neville Chamberlain lost a parent in childhood, through death or illegitimacy, compared with 36% of the earlier, and 26% of the later, sample of peers. If Mrs. Iremonger has greatly underestimated the extent of childhood bereavement over this period, she has nevertheless shown that the percentage of the bereaved amongst prime ministers was unusually high. . . .

If the men who reached 10 Downing Street came to a disproportionate extent from the bereaved, the same feature should be found, though perhaps in a less pronounced form, amongst other active politicians. The numbers in any one late-nineteenth-century Cabinet are small, and are reduced for comparative purposes by those for whom full information is not available. Thus the appointment of one bereaved man to Cabinet office can make a difference of between 5 and 8%. What is striking, however, is the *consistency* with which the proportion of the bereaved runs above the percentages in the samples of peers. Thus, for the Gladstone Cabinet of 1868 the figure is 42%; for his second Cabinet in 1880, 50%; for the Unionist Cabinet of 1895, 47%; for that of 1900, 39%. The proportion in Campbell-Bannerman's Cabinet (claiming no benefit from John Burns, whose father deserted him in infancy) falls to 31%, but this figure includes three of its leading ministers: Asquith, Chancellor of the Exchequer, Grey, the Foreign Secretary, and Lloyd George, at the Board of Trade. Salisbury's administrations were dubbed "the Hotel Cecil" because, it was alleged, he appointed so many of his relatives to ministerial office; the Governments of the late nineteenth century might have been dubbed, with more justice, "Hotel Barnardo". Indeed, in 1849 the leaders of all three British (i.e. non-Irish) parties — Rosebery, Salisbury and Devonshire — had been bereaved in childhood, whilst the sole representative of Independent Labour, Keir Hardie, was an admitted bastard.

Anxiety and Neurotic Response

Any hypothesis which attempts to relate deprivation of love in childhood to political eminence must be able to explain why those who suffered in this way should strive to achieve it. Mrs. Iremonger herself seeks to extend Choisy's interpretation of illegitimacy to all who are deprived of love in childhood. Perhaps a more comprehensive theory can be found in the work of Karen Horney (5). For Horney, "the basic evil is invariably a lack of genuine warmth and affection"(6). Such a situation leads to "basic anxiety" — "a feeling of being small, insignificant, helpless, deserted, endangered, in a world that is out to abuse, cheat, attack, humiliate, betray, envy"(7). The anxious person can protect himself in three ways: by affection, by power, or by withdrawal (8). The neurotic can cope with his anxiety by soliciting and obtaining the love of others, but his will be a compulsive demand for unconditional affection. The second, and for our purpose the most relevant, way of obtaining protection is through power. The motto, says Horney, is: "If I have power, no one can hurt me". The third means is that of withdrawal, of achieving independence from others. The tragedy of the neurotic is that he strives for reassurance in several ways which are often incompatible with each other. "The two attempts which most frequently clash are the striving for affection and the striving for power"(9).

The wish to dominate, to win prestige, to acquire wealth is not in itself, says Horney, neurotic. "The feeling of power, for example, may in a normal person be born of the realization of his own superior strength . . . The neurotic striving for power, however, is born out of anxiety, hatred and feelings of inferiority. To put it categorically, the normal striving for power is born of strength, the neurotic of weakness"(10). The quest for power is a protection against both helplessness and insignificance; the quest for prestige is essentially a search for protection against insignificance. "The neurotic that falls into this group develops a stringent need to impress others, to be admired and respected . . . His entire self-esteem rests on being admired, and shrinks to nothing if he does not receive admiration. Because of his excessive sensitivity, and because he is continually sensing humiliations, life is a constant ordeal"(11).

The striving for power and prestige can also serve as a means of releasing hostility. This hostility can take the forms of a tendency to domineer, or to humiliate. The compulsion to domineer means that such a neurotic is unable to have any "give and take" relationships: "He either has to lead or he feels entirely lost, dependent and helpless"(12). In those in whom the craving for prestige is uppermost, hostility will usually take the shape of a desire to humiliate others. "This desire is paramount in those persons whose own self-esteem has been wounded by humiliation and who have thus become vindictive"(13).

The loss of a parent in childhood or the lack of a father because of bastardy are not the only ways of being deprived of affection, as Mrs. Iremonger fully recognizes. The deprivation can often be attributed to cold, indifferent and negligent parents. The Young Churchill's poignant letters from Harrow bear witness to the callous way in which he was treated by his father (whose own career so closely resembled the Phaeton model) and by his pleasure-seeking mother (14). Disraeli's most recent biographer, Robert Blake, says that "something went wrong" in the relationship between the young Disraeli and his mother. "There is no record of his ever talking about her after her death, and no reference to her in the numerous autobiographical fragments which survive among his papers. Indeed, one might almost think that he wished to obliterate her memory." "Disraeli," writes Blake, "with his intense vanity, his supreme egoism, craved from his mother a degree of admiration and adulation which was never forthcoming"(15).

Bereavement, however, has the merit of being a hard, objective fact, whose incidence both amongst prime ministers and the class from which politicians usually come can easily be measured. The opportunities, so tempting in psychodynamic commentary, to interpret every occurrence in a manner favourable to the starting hypothesis, to ignore every vestige of evidence that may point in a contrary way, to conjure away every inconsistency with the verbal wand of "contradiction", are at a minimum. The meaning of parental deprivation is complex, and the consequences are still not completely clear; but there is considerable evidence to support the not unreasonable view that the loss of a parent in childhood can have serious consequences for later emotional stability and behaviour (16). It would be unwise to accept, without further question, that the results of parental bereavement for an upper-class boy in the nineteenth century are necessarily the same as for a working-class or lower-middle-class child today; the "nanny", for instance, might often serve as a substitute mother. That bereavement would have adverse repercussions of some kind is, however, a plausible starting-point.

Bereavement, therefore, is neither a necessary nor the only condition of being deprived of normal love; but it is unlikely that other, less measurable forms of deprivation would have been more highly represented amongst our control samples of peers than amongst the prime ministers. The high incidence of bereavement amongst prime ministers must be regarded as significant.

These figures afford almost the sole hard data we have about the psychological development of British prime ministers. Nevertheless, Mrs. Iremonger, by exploiting the biographies is able to enlarge and illustrate her thesis. Her evidence is remarkable, not only for its general consistency, but because the temperaments of prime ministers, both in boyhood and in adult life, diverge so starkly from the popular image of the successful politician.

Prime Ministers: Expectations and Reality

It is not easy to spell out a comprehensive list of the qualities a prime minister should have. On the face of it, a successful politician ought to be at ease with his fellows. Quite literally, he has to walk with kings and mix with crowds and we would therefore expect him to be "a good mixer". Indeed, Katz and Lazarsfeld (17) indicate that political opinion leaders were more sociable than other citizens, whilst Kavanagh (18) shows that parliamentary candidates appeared to derive considerable enjoyment from election campaigns. He should be extrovert, sociable if not gregarious, realistically self-confident, able to bear the calumnies of political life without pain and its disappointments without rancour. Without being obsequiously pliable, he should be able to adjust his own opinions to those of his colleagues and to work in harmony with them.

A prime minister must, in addition, have certain specific qualities over and above those he presumably shares with other politicians. Political decisions depend, not so much on reality itself, as on the politician's perceptions of reality. The more distorted these perceptions are, the more costly the results. The very notion of reality, of course, poses deep philosophical questions but, without becoming entangled in problems of this kind, we may note that a prime minister ought to be free of those neurotic misconceptions which colour and indeed transform the way a man sees the world.

A robust and phlegmatic temperament, if not essential in a prime minister, might well, then, be regarded as conferring a special qualification for the post. In fact, few realities stand in sharper antithesis to such reasonable expectations. Prime ministers tended to be unhappy in childhood, lonely and sensitive in adult life. Middle-class socialists may, to an exceptional degree, have found life at their public schools solitary, nasty, brutish and unmercifully prolonged, but this experience was not peculiar to them. . . .

Some, amongst the minority of prime ministers who were not bereaved in childhood, enjoyed their schooldays; Gladstone was happy at Eton (19) whilst Melbourne "forty years later . . . could never hear a clock like the Eton clock without a lift of happiness at his heart"(20). Of those who were bereaved, Rosebery was unusual in consistent devotion to his old school, even arranging that he should die to the strains of a gramophone playing "The Eton Boating Song"(21).

Churchill, however, deprived in a less dramatic way, made clear his unhappiness at Harrow in a letter to his mother. "I hope you don't imagine that I am happy here. It's all very well for monitors and Cricket Captains but it's quite a different thing for fourth form boys. Of course what I should like best would be to leave this [hell of a] place but I cannot expect that at present"(22).

Students of British political culture have often emphasized the role, in political socialization, of team games, which, it is said, simultaneously foster the habits of co-operation and of good-humoured competition, and accustom the boy to subordinate his own inclinations for the greater good of his team. Guttsman, discussing the aims and ethos of the Victorian public school, stresses the importance of team games along with other features of school life: "An educational system, which puts such a high value on the exercise of individual superiority — often callous and brutal in its forms — and on the leadership of the daring and imaginative, and which recognizes existing social distinctions, is a good training ground for a political élite in a status society." It is the more surprising, therefore, that Britain's political leaders should have been marked by a strong aversion to, or incompetence at, organized sport; it is perhaps noteworthy that those games they have played and enjoyed have usually been of an individualistic and, relatively speaking, of a physically undemanding character such as golf or tennis. It is difficult to know how much significance should be attached to the dislike of games evinced by some of the earlier prime ministers, because the nature of games at British public schools may have changed during the century; but the distaste for, or lack of proficiency in, school sport is striking . . . and it is rare indeed to find a prime minister who was both good at, and enjoyed, team games. . . .

The sociable child who seeks high political office would appear from the record to have an immediate handicap. Some prime ministers enjoyed their schooldays, a few liked team games, but only exceptions like Palmerston can be described as gregarious. If any one feature of prime ministerial temperament stands out above all others, it is that of solitariness. If it is stretching the evidence too far to say that most prime ministers were neurotic, it seems clear that most of them were lonely. Shyness, reserve and in some cases isolation were prominent features of the childhoods of British prime ministers. Wellington "was solitary, shy and friendless", Peel "reserved and isolated and hypersensitive", Aberdeen "shy, quiet, reserved . . . and always buried in his books", Salisbury a "nervous and peculiar boy, moody, retiring . . . bad-tempered, uncompanionable, isolated", Balfour, initially unhappy at Eton, was a solitary child, Neville Chamberlain was solitary, going his own way at school, "never seeking friends" (1, pp. 87, 99, 120, 133, 163, 294). Rosebery, despite enjoying his years at Eton, was "a quiet and, indeed, a solitary child"(23). Harold Macmillan, later to be admired as "unflappable" could write of his childhood, "Yet I always felt that, on the whole, the world was something alarming, and people of all ages would be more likely to be troublesome than agreeable. Hence I grew up shy and sensitive"(24).

Moreover, the same qualities occur amongst other high-ranking political leaders, who, whilst not attaining the premiership, almost certainly desired it. Devonshire's biographer, Bernard Holland, saw in Devonshire (who was twice offered the premiership and who probably wanted it) "a certain innate tendency towards shyness and silence, and an indisposition for exchange of ideas"(25). The same loneliness appears in Aneurin Bevan's boyhood. . . .

This shyness, sensitivity and in many cases isolation, usually continued into adult life, often co-existing, by a strange dialectic, with an apparent sociability. According to Mrs. Iremonger, Perceval was "a clear example of the conflict found consistently in our Prime Ministers between the necessity to appear genial and sociable and the intense sensitivity, isolation and solitariness of their true natures". Liverpool, "Clearly a solitary . . . wanted, and made few friends at Oxford − or all his life", Goderich was "Appallingly thin-skinned, despite a cultivated bonhomie", Russell was called "aloof, cold, arrogant" all his life, and he often snubbed those who tried to melt his iciness. Salisbury "avoided personal contacts, rebuffed strangers, and could be insufferably rude . . . All his life he would be incapable of believing himself socially welcome". . . .

Macmillan, on his own account, was able to overcome his shyness and sensitivity by "a long self-training": "I have hardly ever had to make an important speech without feeling violently sick most of the day before . . . Perhaps the reason that I was able to conceal if not to overcome this nervousness was because I had learnt from childhood that these anxieties were natural, inevitable, and must somehow be endured"(26).

Of others who aspired to, or still hope for, the premiership, Enoch Powell's reserve has been recorded by Andrew Roth. "Among the secretaries at the

Parliamentary Secretariat . . . he had the name of an unsmiling man who could not bring himself to say 'Good morning' or exchange any of the small talk . . . which is the lubricant of social life in British offices", or again of Powell's campaigning he writes: "the worst ordeal for Powell was the need to knock on door after door 'cold' and make conversation with strangers he was trying to convert into supporters"(27). . . .

We have no means of assessing with any precision either the magnitude or distribution of such qualities as dislike of team games, shyness, sensitivity and loneliness amongst the population at large or, more pertinently, amongst the relevant social classes. Nor can we assign any numerical value to the isolation, moodiness or reserve displayed by politicians most of whom are long since dead. What is extraordinary is that the most eminent politicians should have lacked the qualities which, on the face of it, seem so important to the career they chose and the office they desired. What is convincing about Mrs. Iremonger's thesis is the cumulative portrait she draws of men who, to a remarkable degree, lacked the very attributes which, it might be supposed, the politician needed in abundance. . . .

Mrs. Iremonger emphasizes this strange divergence, with compelling clarity, in the draft advertisement for the office of prime minister, which she compiled, with perhaps some exaggeration, on the basis of the records of former incumbents.

> The successful Candidate will have lost one or more parents in childhood, though he may exceptionally be an admitted or suspected bastard. He will suffer from other crippling handicaps, whether physical (such as a stammer, poor health, or marked unprepossessingness of manner and appearance) . . . He will be of a hypersensitive nature, and will suffer from incapacitating psychosomatic illnesses, often at times of greatest stress. He will remain throughout his life isolated from his fellow men, nauseated by their junketings, and exhausted by their relaxations. He will have been miserably unhappy at his school, and possibly so much so that he will never be able to bring himself to revisit it after leaving it. His antipathy to sport, particularly team games, will be lifelong. His few friends will be orphaned or deprived like himself, and he may well be married to an orphan who will be very like him in nature . . . He will be subject to fits of prostrating depression. He will, if bereaved, be so desolated by grief as to render him totally incapable of maintaining his grip on life for a period, will immediately seek to resign from public life, and will suffer from its after effects for ever. He may be of a marked natural timidity and shyness, for which he will so over-compensate as to present on occasions an excessively aggressive front. He will possibly be peculiarly superstitious and credulous about magic and the supernatural . . . He will be haunted eternally by a compulsive and obsessive need for total love and adoration and support from another, and will continue to seek it until death, disregarding all else, even, on occasions the security of state secrets, in his pursuit of it or its shadow, and probably writing a million words, to wives, mistresses or sisters, in his search. He will manifest a periodic recklessness, whether in love or other affairs, of a suicidal nature. He will be a devotee of Sir Walter Scott (1, pp. 308–9).

Musings and Reservations

We have to ask why it is that the most successful politicians should be those who, at first glance, appear in some ways so unsuited to the demands of political life. Enquiry might show that the highest ranks in any profession have a disproportionate share of the neurotic and the lonely. If Horney's analysis is correct, however, it is easy to see why eminence in politics, rather than in other fields, should be distinctively, perhaps peculiarly, linked with personal maladjustment.

Success in politics offers a peculiar combination of rewards, amongst which both power and acclaim rank high. For Horney, it will be recalled, power offers protection against feelings of helplessness and insignificance: "If I have power no one can hurt me". Prestige affords a reassurance against the sense of insignificance. A man unable to find good cause for "healthy self-esteem" within himself will fall back upon some external source of validation. If people cheer me, so he may argue, I must be important. To an unceasing search for power after power, we must add an unending quest for fame after fame.

Yet, as Horney says, the tragedy of the neurotic is that,though he can choose from three distinct strategies in coping with his anxiety, he will be unlikely to pursue any one of these single-mindedly. Although at a given time one solution may predominate, the neurotic is driven to follow incompatible courses. The quest for affection clashes with the search for power, the wish to submit clashes with the need for prestige, the clamour for attention with the desire to withdraw. It may be objected that a theory like Horney's is only able to appear convincing because, by the device of the term "contradiction", it can account for any cluster of symptoms. To this we can reply only that the careers of so many prime ministers seem founded upon a contradiction between the apparent requirements of the office and the temperament of its holder. Dangerously seductive though the temptations of this kind of analysis may be, some such concept is necessary if we are to explain the extraordinary contrast between the apparent demands of the post and the actual qualities of so many of those who filled it. . . .

Chief amongst the contradictions is the relative success of prime ministers on the public platform and their inability to establish easy relationships at a personal level. As Lasswell (28) has argued, the satisfaction of emotional responses on a mass scale may be a substitute for those arising from face to face relationships. Again, noting the reserve and indeed the loneliness of so many prime ministers, it is hard to resist the kind of explanation offered by Horney — they attempted to cope with their anxieties by following two contradictory courses of action: by withdrawing from close personal relationships, and at the same time by trying to exercise power over, and obtain admiration from, mass audiences through the gifts of rhetoric and argument.

So far we have considered only the psychological rewards obtained from political life by men with certain psychic needs. We have ignored the costs. These costs can be considerable for the most equable; they must be particularly great for the lonely and anxious figures who so often attain high political office. Conspicuous politicians must learn to suffer much: the malice of the press, the cruel gossip of their colleagues, the jeers of the opposition: ". . . even the end of seven years of Premiership" wrote Harold Macmillan, "I had the same painful anticipation about Parliamentary Questions as men feel before a race or a battle. I always made it a rule on Question Days, Tuesdays and Thursdays, to lunch alone"(26). If men seek office so eagerly, and hold on to it so tenaciously despite these costs, it must be because the need for the gratifications politics can offer is so acute. As James Barber has put it, "Our hypothesis must be that they are attracted to politics by forces strong enough to overpower all the objections they are aware of"(29). It is, of course, impossible to rebut the argument that, in our present state of knowledge, such a hypothesis is circular and untestable. We can plead only that such an objection does not prove that the argument is wrong. The kind of psychic gratification afforded by political life, then, is such that politics may be unique in attracting to it men who suffer from special disabilities. . . .

It may be asked whether these considerations are of general validity or are peculiar to British politics. American presidents, to an even greater extent than British prime ministers, combine the dignified and efficient roles of the constitution. What is true of prime ministers should hold good *a fortiori* of presidents. The fates of Lincoln, whose mother died when he was nine, and of Hoover who had lost both parents by the age of eight, spring to mind. Coolidge, too, lost his mother in boyhood whilst Hayes was a posthumous child. But the overall evidence is less clearcut. Some recent presidents, such as Nixon and Woodrow Wilson, fit easily into the "loner" type. Others, like Eisenhower, Kennedy and Franklin Roosevelt, do not. Perhaps the sensitive and lonely men who have so often become prime minister have been able to survive because they have been protected, to some extent by the national ethos of deference, from the need to mix too closely with ordinary people. The American political culture, with its more open and egalitarian style, may discourage the emergence of the shy and the introspective. . . .

There remains, . . . a stubbornly recurring feature which impairs the symmetry of Mrs. Iremonger's argument. Some of her prime ministers were exceptionally happy in their married life and with their own children. Perceval "took a wonderful pleasure and satisfaction" in his own family (1, p. 47). Canning's regard for his children was "selfless" (1, p. 66). Peel and his wife "were devoted to each other; and in love to the end" (1, p. 102). Russell and his first wife were "very happy" and his second marriage "was at least as happy as his first had been" (1, pp. 113–114). Aberdeen's first marriage was "wonderfully happy" (1, p. 123). Salisbury's "moments of greatest happiness were when he sat at the head of the big dining-room table with all his family around him; or looked on at the yearly gathering of children round the Christmas tree" (1, p. 142). This happiness can be explained, as Mrs. Iremonger explains it, as the fulfilment of a "compulsive and obsessive need for total love and adoration and support from another" (1, p. 309); it can equally be interpreted as the domestic contentment of the normal, well-adjusted man.

Moreover, the general evidence is capable of a more sympathetic interpretation. Toynbee in his *Study of History* attributes the rise of civilization to a response to a harsh environmental challenge; in much the same way, the later eminence of the solitary and often unhappy children studied by Mrs. Iremonger could be ascribed to a singular, but in no sense morbid, resolution to overcome early handicaps.

"It is said", wrote Winston Churchill in his *Life of Marlborough,* "that famous men are usually the product of an unhappy childhood. The stern compression of circumstances, the twinges of adversity, the spur of slights and taunts in early years, are needed to evoke that ruthless fixity of purpose and tenacious mother-wit without which great actions are seldom accomplished"(30). Perhaps these men achieved what they did because of their unusual resources rather than their exceptional needs. The character of the prime ministers in later life gives strong credence to the Iremonger thesis; but the choice of interpretation clearly makes a vast difference to whatever implications her study may have for the working of government and it would be rash, at this stage, to exclude the more generous and less disquieting assessment.

One quality on which Mrs. Iremonger lays emphasis is the recklessness supposed to be a special feature of the "Phaeton" complex. In their relations with women, Balfour, Asquith and Lloyd George all behaved with remarkable imprudence, whilst Lloyd George displayed a similar foolhardiness in the Marconi affair. Dilke, often spoken of by his contemporaries as a potential prime minister and bereaved in childhood, ruined his career by his sexual indiscretions. So, too, did the Irish Nationalist leader, Parnell, who lost his father when he was twelve. Politically, Rosebery and Neville Chamberlain displayed in different ways an incautious obstinacy that was to destroy them both. Perhaps the political career which gives the most dramatic evidence of this quality is of one who was not bereaved, Lord Randolph Churchill. . . .

The Implications for British Government

The implications of Mrs. Iremonger's work are far-reaching. Historians, unable to attribute critical decisions and momentous changes to broad social or political trends, have often had to take refuge in "an accident of personality". It has been contended, for example, that it was an "accident of personality" which destroyed the Liberal Party after 1918. But, if Mrs. Iremonger's thesis is correct, such events are not "accidental"; it was not fortuitous that Asquith succeeded Campbell-Bannerman, nor that he should have been brought down by Lloyd George; political leadership attracts to it men with special needs, needs which may threaten the unity of parties and the harmony of Cabinets.

Consider, in this context, the record of the ten prime ministers from the resignation of Gladstone in 1894 to the fall of Neville Chamberlain in 1940. Of these ten, no fewer than seven lost a parent in childhood, and an eighth,

MacDonald, was illegitimate. The remaining two, Campbell-Bannerman and Baldwin, both survived in office until death or voluntary retirement (Campbell-Bannerman dying after only two years in office). . . .

For the political scientist, studies such as *The Fiery Chariot* have two main implications. Such enquiries add an important psychological dimension to studies of political recruitment, and they also suggest important consequences for the workings of British government. At the outset, however, we must recognize that whatever deficiencies of temperament British prime ministers may have had, they have usually been men of outstanding capacity. If their extraordinary ambition was developed in the cold wastelands of parental neglect, few could have satisfied that ambition, held office for so long and achieved what they did, unless they had been men of exceptional talent. . . .

There will be the rare occasion when the very faults of a neurotic or depressive leader may be turned to advantage. Anthony Storr has argued, in a persuasive way, that it was Churchill's defects, as a man, which saved the nation in 1940 (31).

> At one period in his life, he was fortunate. For, in 1940, his inner world of make-believe coincided with the facts of external reality in a way which very rarely happens to any man . . . In that dark time, what England needed was not a shrewd, equable, balanced leader. She needed a prophet, a heroic visionary, a man who could dream dreams of victory when all seemed lost. Winston Churchill was such a man; and his inspirational quality owed its dynamic force to the romantic world of phantasy in which he had his true being.

It is easy to find fault with Mrs. Iremonger's book. Her statistics are marred by error and, like most commentators in this field, she exploits every ambiguous report or equivocal event in a way favourable to her own hypothesis. Yet these shortcomings must be set against her considerable achievement. She has shown for the first time in a systematic way the extraordinary degree to which the highest political office in Britain has, paradoxically, summoned to it men who might by temperament have been deemed to be singularly unfitted to bear some of its burdens and discharge some, at least, of its duties. After her book, we need, tentatively at least, to cast Barber's verdict in a new form: political candidacy at this level draws towards it men who are exceptional both in their high abilities *and* in their strong needs. If it is lonely at the top, it is because it is the lonely who seek to climb there.

Notes

1. IREMONGER, L. (1970) *The Fiery Chariot: A Study of British Prime Ministers and the Search for Love.* London: Secker & Warburg.
2. DONNELLY, D. (1970) *Daily Telegraph,* December 3.
3. BARBER, J. D. (1965) *The Lawmakers: Recruitment and Adaptation to Legislative Life.* p. 225. New Haven and London: Yale University Press.
4. FREUD. S. (1961) *Complete Psychological Works Vol XIX 1923–25: The Ego and the Id and Other Works.* p. 36 (translated by J. Strachey *et al.*) London: Hogarth Press.
5. HORNEY, K. (1937) The Neurotic Personality of Our Time. New York: W. W. Norton.

6. *Ibid.*, p. 80.
7. *Ibid.*, p. 92.
8. *Ibid.*, p. 96.
9. *Ibid.*, p. 101.
10. *Ibid.*, p. 163.
11. *Ibid.*, p. 171–172.
12. *Ibid.*, p. 175.
13. *Ibid.*, p. 178.
14. CHURCHILL, R. S. (1966) *Winston S. Churchill, Vol. 1, Youth 1874–1900.* London: Heinemann.
15. BLAKE, R. (1969) *Disraeli.* pp. 15–17, London: University Paperbacks.
16. BOWLBY, J. (1953) *Child Care and the Growth of Love.* Harmondsworth: Penguin. RUTTER, M. (1973) *Maternal Deprivation Re-Assessed.* Harmondsworth: Penguin.
17. KATZ, E. and LAZERFELD, P. F. (1964) *Personal Influence.* New York: The Free Press.
18. KAVANAGH, D. (1970) *Constituency Electioneering in Britain.* pp. 81–84. London: Longmans.
19. MAGNUS, P. Sir (1963) *Gladstone.* p. 5. London: John Murray.
20. CECIL, D., Lord (1955) *Melbourne.* p. 25. London: The Reprint Society.
21. JAMES, R. R. (1963) *Rosebery.* p. 486. London: Weidenfeld & Nicolson.
22. CHURCHILL, R. S. (1966) *Winston S. Churchill, Vol. 1,* p. 128. London: Heinemann.
23. JAMES, R. R. *op. cit.*, p. 15.
24. MACMILLAN, H. (1966) *Winds of Change 1914–39.* p. 42. London: Macmillan.
25. HOLLAND, B. (1911) *Life of the Duke of Devonshire, Vol. 1* (2nd edn). London: Longmans & Green.
26. MACMILLAN, H. *op. cit.*, p. 41.
27. ROTH, A. (1970) *Enoch Powell: Tory Tribune.* p. 15. London: Macdonald.
28. LASSWELL, H. (1960) *Psychopathology and Politics.* New York: Viking Press.
29. BARBER, J. D. *op. cit.*, p. 224.
30. Quoted in CHURCHILL, *op. cit.*, p. 241.
31. STORR, A. (1969) *Churchill: Fours Faces and the Man.* London: Allen Lane, The Penguin Press.

3

William James and the Twice-Born Sick Soul*

C. STROUT

> I became a doctor through being compelled to deviate from my original purpose; and the triumph of my life lies in my having, after a long and roundabout journey, found my way back to my earliest path.
>
> Sigmund Freud

HISTORICAL determinism was much in fashion in 1880 when William James published his essay on "Great Men and Their Environment." He had to attack the superstition, derived from Herbert Spencer, that great men were mere resultants of that "aggregate of conditions" out of which both they and their society had arisen. Spencer's method, as James pointed out, was like that of "one who would invoke the zodiac to account for the fall of the sparrow" (1). To offer the whole past as an explanation of something specific in the present was no better than explaining every event by saying "God is great." James acknowledged that society, in Darwinian terms, could preserve or reject the great man, but it did not make him before he remade it. Physiological forces, with which social conditions had no discernible connection, genetically produced the hero. Even at the level of intellectual history, the same Darwinian point applied: Society confirmed or refuted the spontaneous variations of ideas produced in great thinkers by the "functional activity of the excessively instable human brain" (2).

Certainly the movement of pragmatism cannot be explained apart from William James who became, as Ralph Barton Perry has said, "the Ambassador of American Thought to Western Europe." It is consistent with James's theory of the great man to note that social circumstances played their part in favoring the development of pragmatism into a force which influenced American philosophy, psychology, religion, political theory, education, and historiography. Voluntaristic, democratic, "tough-minded," and optimistic, pragmatism had qualities well suited to American culture at a time when science had great prestige and humanistic values needed new underpinnings because of the erosion of older theological supports. But it was James's own wide-ranging intellectual curiosity,

*Reprinted by permission of *Daedalus, Journal of the American Academy of Arts and Sciences*, **97**, 1063–1082 (edited), Boston, MA.

his familiarity with Europe and its languages, and above all his fervent conviction that pragmatism was "something quite like the protestant reformation" and destined for "definitive triumph" that made him "the revivifying force in European thought in the decade and a half preceding the outbreak of the First World War" (3). Intellectually gregarious, gifted with a talent for popular lecturing, passionately attached to American life by affection and critical commitment rather than by habitat, he was (like Franklin and Jefferson) a cosmopolitan American who could speak to the world in a voice that resonated with a specific identity.

Yet James's own struggle for forming a personal identity and finding his proper vocation was acute. His growth to greatness was precarious and painful, vulnerable to chronic debility, depression, and distress. James's theory of the great man has one conspicuous weakness: It does not cover himself. There is more to the great man than favorable social conditions, the spontaneous variations of genetics, or what James called the "seething caldron of ideas" in the "highest order of minds." He believed that the "genesis [of ideas] is sudden and, as it were, spontaneous" (4), but the history of his own development is a refutation of any such sudden spontaneity. Spontaneity was in his case a hard-won achievement of a personality threatened by imminent disorganization. What James needed to round out his theory of the great man was an ordered way of talking about the inner history of the great man's relation to himself and to the significant others in his family.

In this sense, the great man is made, in part, by that intimate society, filled with resounding echoes of the world in the significant speech, gesture, and silence of parents and siblings, which he in turn remakes by his appearance in it. If he is truly great, he conspires with circumstance to turn his private conflicts into public issues with relevance for others. He learns to speak not only to his family and his society but, in principle, to all men. Paradoxically, he might even learn to speak to all men just because on certain matters he cannot speak openly to his family. The sign of that inability would be a kind of sickness, a bafflement of development, referring to the unspeakable. For such individuals, as Erik H. Erikson has taught us in *Young Man Luther*, the identity crisis of early manhood may be a period in which endangered youths, "although suffering and deviating dangerously through what appears to be a prolonged adolescence, eventually come to contribute an original bit to an emerging style of life: the very danger which they have sensed has forced them to mobilize capacities to see and say, to dream and plan, to design and construct, in new ways" (5). Erikson suggests that "born leaders seem to fear only more consciously what in some form everybody fears in the depths of his inner life; and they convincingly claim to have an answer" (6). The conscious fear that James grappled with was the apprehension that scientific determinism, what he called "medical materialism," would leave no meaningful space for the human will. That fear was closely connected with his fears as a member of the James family. I propose to

analyze that linkage in narrative form, trying to do justice to the relevant claims
of psychoanalysis, history, and philosophy.

The historian is justified in asking the James family to sit for a portrait of
upper-class Victorian life. The bearded, revered, religious father, the domestically
devoted mother, the effusive language of family endearment, the endless trips
to Europe for convalescence — all these familiar features we recognize with the
usual smile. The intellectual issues of James's life — the conflict between science
and religion, the revolt against rationalism, and the moral cult of "the strenuous
life" — are part of the texture of that period, which writers like Walter E.
Houghton have brought to vivid life (7). James's own depressed invalidism also
had many counterparts in the lives of other eminent Victorians, like Mill, Darwin,
and Jane Addams. A pre-Freudian, James was inevitably a mystery to himself,
but he welcomed the work of Freud and his pupils on the ground that it might
shed light on "the twilight region that surrounds the clearly lighted centre of
experience." He looked forward to biographical studies that would show "the
various ways of unlocking the reserves of power" exemplified in individual
lives (8). Let us begin, therefore, with a striking peculiarity of James's career—
the long deferment of a youthful philosophical ambition, which he did not fully
commit himself to as a vocation until he was nearly sixty.

William James first decided to become a painter. As a boy he had shown a
spontaneous interest in drawing, and with his first real youthful friend shared a
hope of becoming an artist. Unfortunately, in 1859 his father whisked young
William off to Europe, away from his friend and from William Morris Hunt's
studio at Newport. The father explained to a friend:

> Newport did not give the boys what they required exactly, and we didn't relish their
> separation from us. Willy especially felt, we thought, a little too much attraction to
> painting — as I suppose from the contiguity to Mr. Hunt; let us break that up, we
> said, at all events. I hoped that his career would be a scientific one . . . and to give
> up this hope without a struggle, and allow him to tumble down into a mere painter,
> was impossible (9).

In the end, the elder James relented because his son pleaded, very respectfully
and humbly, that his life "would be embittered" if he were not allowed to try
painting. The father need not have worried; the son himself echoed his father's
judgment by declaring before entering Hunt's studio: "There is nothing on earth
more deplorable than a bad artist." For a conscientious boy who much admired
his father, this venture in vocation must have engendered a bad conscience.
Within the year he had abandoned art school, though he kept up his drawing
for several years. In 1872, he was to confess that he "regretted extremely"
letting it die out (10). Meanwhile, the Civil War was a call to action, and in
1861 both William and Henry sought to enlist in the Union Army. Once again
their father had other plans: "I have had a firm grasp upon the coat tails of my
Willy and Harry, who both vituperate me beyond measure because I won't let
them go" (11). Both boys soon developed illnesses that incapacitated them for

service anyway, and it was the younger brothers, Wilkinson and Robinson, the forgotten Jameses, who with father's blessing joined the army.

In 1861, William dutifully gave his father a plan of his future life: to study chemistry, anatomy, and medicine as preparation for spending several years with Louis Agassiz in natural history. The plan was shaped to his father's hopes for him. That fall William entered the Lawrence Scientific School in Cambridge as a student of chemistry. "Relentless Chemistry claims its hapless victim," he wryly wrote to a friend. As his teacher later recalled, nervous illness began to interfere with his work at this point (12). In 1863, he entered medical school where Jeffries Wyman taught, a man for whom James had "a filial feeling," perhaps because Wyman was also an excellent draftsman. The next year, under the spell of the "god-like" charm of Louis Agassiz, William went to Brazil as part of an exploring and collecting expedition. There he caught varioloid, a mild form of smallpox, and spent over two despondent weeks in the hospital, resting his eyes and rethinking his future. His experience convinced him that he hated collecting and was "cut out for a speculative rather than an active life." Having recovered the use of his eyes and having lost his respect for Agassiz's pretensions to omniscience, he joyfully returned home with a new resolution: "When I get home I'm going to study philosophy all my days" (13).

Privately James read philosophy voraciously, but publicly he resumed his medical studies and undertook a brief internship at the Massachusetts General Hospital. His comments on the medical profession, excepting surgery, were always contemptuous, convicting it of "much humbug." Nevertheless, his disenchantment with Agassiz and natural history forced him to consider medicine as a possible career unless he were to abandon the scientific bent of his education. In retrospect, the Brazil expedition gave him a "feeling of loneliness and intellectual and moral deadness." In the fall winter of 1866, he complained of digestive disorders, eye troubles, acute depression, and weakness of the back. His symptoms are characteristic of hypochondriasis, and in psychosomatic illness unconscious imitation often plays a part in the selection of discomforts. He revived those symptoms which he had felt in Brazil, and he now also spoke in revealing language, of a "delightful disease" in the back "which has so long made Harry so interesting" (14). Henry had developed this symptom from a trivial accident incurred while he was trying to put out a fire in 1861. When his father was thirteen, he had sustained under similar circumstances an injury that led to a leg amputation and two years in bed. William's back and eye trouble provided him with an excuse for not practicing medicine. Shortly before taking his exams for the medical degree in 1869, he wrote his brother: "I am perfectly contented that the power which gave me these facilities should recall them partially or totally when and in what order it sees fit. I don't think I should give a single damn now if I were struck blind" (15). In the winter of 1866, he felt himself on the "continual verge of suicide" and sometime during these years he was paralyzed in panic fear by the image of a greenish, withdrawn epileptic idiot whom he had seen in an asylum. *"That shape am I,* I felt, potentially," he confessed, and for months he dreaded being alone in the dark (16).

What did this paralyzing recollection mean? As a medical student he might easily have read the well-known work by the English doctor William Acton, *The Functions and Disorders of the Reproductive Organs.* Steven Marcus has pointed out in *The Other Victorians* that Acton's book is a classic statement of Victorian attitudes toward sex; indeed, one of Acton's themes is the moral need to break willfully the habit of introspection in order to ward off the temptation of masturbation, luridly imagined as a threat to sanity. Acton points up his moral by a description of inmates of an insane asylum: "The pale complexion, the emaciated form, the slouching gait, the clammy palm, the glassy or leaden eye, and the averted gaze, indicate the lunatic victim to the vice." This image resembles James's memory of the epileptic patient, and in the late 1860s he was unsuccessfully courting Fanny Dixwell, whom his friend Oliver Wendell Holmes, Jr., married in 1872. James was thirty-six when he married, and no doubt sexual frustration had plagued him, but his vocational problem persisted after 1878. That hideous figure, we may speculate, objectified not only the self-punishing guilt in his own symptoms, but also his fear of being trapped in a medical career which seemed to be his only option after his disillusionment with natural history. Neither Wyman nor Agassiz had shaken his belief that his father was, as James had written in Brazil, "the *wisest* of all men" he had ever known (17). And his father was a metaphysician – not a physician.

James defined his dilemma to a despondent friend: "I am about as little fitted by nature to be a worker in science of any sort as anyone can be, and yet . . . my only ideal of life is a scientific life" (18). His whole program, outlined to his father in 1861, had collapsed along with his health and spirits. In submitting his prospectus, he had prophesied wryly that the last stage would be "death, death, death with inflation and plethora of knowledge" (19). That jest had come symbolically true, as if he had unconsciously feared the worst in the pursuit of his scientific career. In 1867 he sailed for Europe, which served him as a psychic moratorium from commitment. Subjecting himself to the tortures of the baths and galvanic remedies, he felt ashamed not to be earning money like his brothers. He found solace in the theater, art galleries, music, novels, and glimpses of pretty *frauleins,* while he read philosophy and dutifully attended university lectures on physiology. After passing his medical exams for the degree in 1869, he wrote a sketch of his philosophical gropings which put his own pain at the center of things: "Three quantities to determine. (*1*) how much pain I'll stand; (*2*) how much other's pain I'll inflict (by existing); (*3*) how much other's pain I'll 'accept,' without ceasing to take pleasure in their existence" (20). To a friend he confessed: "I am poisoned with Utilitarian venom, and sometimes when I despair of ever doing anything, say: 'Why not step out into the green darkness?' " (21). Similarly greenish in hue was his image of the idiotic, epileptic patient, huddled in the corner of his cell. To stick to his chosen path would be, in short, a kind of suicide. He could not find himself in medicine nor the acting self in medical materialism's picture of the world. . . .

The basic clue to understanding James's search for a vocation is provided by Erikson's remark in *Young Man Luther* that it is usually a parent, who has "selected this one child, because of an inner affinity paired with an insurmountable outer distance, as the particular child who must *justify the parent*," that by an "all-pervasive presence and brutal decisiveness of judgment" precipitates the child into "a fatal struggle for his own identity" (29). If in contemporary America that parent would usually be the mother, in Victorian America it would have been the father. It is significant that James's vivid memory of the shape in the asylum closely resembles a similar experience his father suffered in 1844 when he felt "an insane and abject terror" before "some damned shape squatting invisible" to him within his room "and raying out from his fetid personality influences fatal to life" (30). Henry James, senior, had written Emerson one or two years earlier to seek help:

> What shall I do? Shall I get me a little nook in the country and communicate with my *living* kind, not my talking kind — by life only — a word, may be, of *that* communication, a fit word, once a year? Or shall I follow some commoner method, learn science and bring myself first into men's respect, that thus I may the better speak to them? I confess this last theory seems rank with earthliness — to belong to days forever past (31).

Son of a rich Calvinist merchant, William's father had been cut off without a legacy because of his worldly tastes and heretical opinions. He had temporarily fled college to work as a proofreader, made an abortive attempt to please his father by studying law, and revolted against the Presbyterian orthodoxy of Princeton Theological Seminary to become an original, if obscure and eccentric, theologian. Having broken his father's will, he was able by his inheritance to devote himself entirely to his writings and to his remarkable family, whom he shuttled constantly about in America and Europe. In 1846 he was rescued from the "endless task of conciliating a stony-hearted Deity" — *his* father's Calvinist God — by a conversion to Swedenborg, as William would be rescued from propitiating the deterministic god of medical materialism by conversion to the philosophy of Renouvier and the idea of free will.

"The children were constantly with their parents and with each other," as William's son later described his father's childhood, "and they continued all their lives to be united by much stronger attachments than usually exist between members of one family" (32). The elder James refused to send his sons to college out of contempt for a gentleman's conventional education. Depositing them briefly with a succession of instructors, he involved his sons mainly with his own spirited intellectual and moral reactions to the world. In his eldest son he must have seen an opportunity to realize his own forsaken alternative of trying to "learn science" and bring himself "into men's respect." A visionary advocate of freedom and spontaneous love, he was also a fierce polemicist. In the family circle as with strangers, the elder James spoke his mind with trenchant, witty, and brusque decisiveness. "What a passion your father has in writing and talking his religion!" exclaimed Oliver Wendell Holmes, Jr., a toughminded skeptic. "Almost he persuadeth me to be a Swedenborgian" (33). For William, his father was a vivid, perpetual presence. After his father's death in 1882, the forty-year-old son made a significant confession:

> It is singular how I'm learning every day now how the thought of his comment on my experience has hitherto formed an integral part of my daily consciousness, without my having realized it at all. I interrupt myself incessantly now in the old habit of imagining what he will say when I tell him this or that thing I have seen or heard (34).

His father was still an inner court of tribunal for him long after that is normally the case.

In this family it was easy for William to resolve his feelings and thoughts about his father because his mother had a soft spot for Henry, who was known in the family as "the Angel." Father himself, after his wife's death in 1881, felt that he had "fallen heir to all dear mother's fondness" for Henry, who had "cost us the least trouble, and given us always the most delight" (35). William, the oldest brother, had reason to be envious of Henry, who first achieved literary fame and financial independence. William's "hypochondriacal condition" — as his family called it — involved a set of highly-charged elements: his career choice, his attraction to philosophy, but fear of embracing it; his dislike of practical scientific work, whether as collector, medical student, or laboratory psychologist; and his need to become financially independent. His father was closely linked to all these issues, and because Henry was obviously the mother's favorite, it was especially important for William to feel that he was in good standing with his father. . . .

The connection between the intellectual and emotional development of William James can be followed in the growth of his work and the betterment of his health, as he successfully, but slowly, came to terms with his father's teachings and example. Four days before his father died in 1882, the son wrote him from Europe: "All my intellectual life I derive from you. . . . What my debt to you is goes beyond all my power of estimating — so early, so penetrating and so constant has been the influence." And he concluded this great and touching letter with a final benediction: "Good-night, my sacred old Father! If I don't see you again — Farewell! a blessed farewell!" (47). At the age of forty, the son would also very slowly bid farewell to his scientific career and gradually move from psychology toward those deep interests he shared with his father in religion and metaphysics. As he abandoned his image of himself as a scientist, he learned to yield to his spontaneous interest in philosophy, which had been born in his crisis of health and career in Brazil. He would increasingly see himself as well enough in body and strong enough in ego to become a philosopher by vocation, assimilating and rejecting aspects of his father's personality in a new configuration.

The father died a year after the mother. James was now the eldest in the family. He was alone in Europe, seeking respite from the burdens of his own family and having trouble getting his book under way. He was also in correspondence with Renouvier, whose philosophy had "saved" him in 1870. . . . In 1883 . . . he was undergoing a new sense of health and direction. Suffering from eye trouble, he had written but six pages of the *Psychology*. Two weeks after hearing of his father's death, he wrote his brother Henry that he felt "a different man" and was resolved to return home to his wife and children, amazed that a "change of weather could effect such a revolution."

In the winter following his father's death James wrote "The Dilemma of Determinism" – a blow for freedom against both scientific and religious monistic views of the world and the first of the characteristically Jamesian essays on the open universe which he had struggled to glimpse out of the pain of his own constricted conflicts. That same year, in filial tribute, he edited his father's *Literary Remains,* as he had promised, and in the following year he noted a definite improvement in his eyesight: "It has continued gradually, so that practically I can use them all I will. It saves my life. *Why* it should come now when, bully them as I would, it wouldn't come in in the past few years, is one of the secrets of the nervous system which the last trump . . . may reveal" (50). . . .

Having settled his intellectual accounts with his father, he was now prepared to devote himself to philosophy, writing freely "without feeling in the least degree fatigued." But he had only a few years left. "I live in apprehension lest the Avenger should cut me off," he wrote in 1906, "before I get my message out. It is an aesthetic tragedy to have a bridge begun and stopped in the middle of an arch" (55). James died with his "somewhat systematic" book unfinished. He had been able to assure Royce in 1877 that "a young man might rightfully devote himself to philosophy if he chose," an assurance James found so very difficult to achieve for himself (56). From a psychoanalytic point of view, the resolution of critical emotional issues in infancy "will determine whether an individual is apt to be dominated by a sense of autonomy, or by a sense of shame and doubt," and the way in which adults meet the child's shame and doubt "determines much of a man's future ability to combine an unimpaired will with ready self-discipline, rebellion with responsibility." Significantly, the father's crisis happened when the son was two years old, struggling to form his first sense of will. His later development illustrates the psychoanalytic point that "the neurotic ego has, by definition, fallen prey to overidentification and to faulty identifications with disturbed parents" (57). The historian must add that while the elder Henry James had made the son's struggle for identity particularly difficult, he had also made the resolution of that struggle particularly fruitful. His influence largely determined the kinds of problems that would be central for his son's intellectual development. That influence delayed the son's maturity, but it also enriched it by giving him that double focus on science and religion and that note of authenticity in dealing with the issues of freedom and determinism which stamped his work as vividly original. The father must also have engendered the son's charming tolerance of cranks and vigorous scorn for prigs of all kinds. William James had selectively assimilated and rejected what his father meant to him in a struggle of fifty years' duration.

The creative man, as Erikson has observed, has to face the risks of neurotic suffering:

> Once the issue is joined, his task proves to be at the same time intimately related to his most personal conflicts, to his superior selective perception, and to the stubbornness of his one-way will: he must court sickness, failure, or insanity, in order to test the alternative whether the established world will crush him, or whether he will disestablish a sector of this world's outworn fundaments and make a place for a new one (58).

James would have understood this point better than most philosophers. "In any minute of moral action where the path is difficult," he wrote George Santayana, "I believe a man has deeper dealings with life than he could have in libraries of philosophizing" (59). His own life was a painful, eloquent witness to this truth.

Most people, faced with such a parent as James had, learn how to evade or compromise in order finally to get their way. William's own son, "Billy," tried medical school for a melancholy year and then happily took up painting – the reverse of his father's sequence. Others make nothing distinctively great out of similar troubles. William's Swiss friend Théodore Flournoy was also depressed by his laboratory work in psychology, but could never marshal the strength to follow James's advice to give it up for philosophy. Sometimes, as Erikson has remarked, an individual feels "called upon" instead to "try to solve for all what he could not solve for himself alone" (60). By whom and by what he is called, the psychoanalyst adds, are mysteries which only theologians and bad psychologists dare to explain. James himself believed that individuality is founded in "the recesses of feeling, the darker, blinder strata of character" (61). In *The Varieties of Religious Experience,* he modified his earlier theory of the great man and offered a radical explanation for the mystery of his appearance: "Thus, when a superior intellect and a psychopathic temperament coalesce . . . in the same individual, we have the best possible condition for the kind of effective genius that gets into the biographical dictionaries" (62). Such men are possessed by their ideas, he added, and inflict them, for better or worse, upon their contemporaries. It is part of the ethical meaning of James's greatness that in this case the suffering was his, the enlightenment ours.

Looking backward, it seems an extraordinarily symbolic moment in time when James met Freud at Clark University in 1909. A decade earlier James had praised Freud's work on "the buried life of human beings" – that "unuttered inner atmosphere" in which the nervous patient "dwells alone with the secrets of its prison-house," full of "old regrets, ambitions checked by shames and aspirations obstructed by timidities," breeding "a general self-mistrust" (63).

James spoke from experience, but unlike Freud, he was never able to systematize his troubles into a revolutionary new theory of the mind. Rather, his genius was for sketching a world in which truth was profoundly human and, like action itself, a genuine addition to a reality still in the making. "Admit plurality, and time may be its form," he wrote in "The Dilemma of Determinism," a remark which points toward a profoundly historical view of the world. Pluralism characterized his life as well as his thought. Perhaps the incompleteness of his philosophy is a mark of his failure to achieve that masterful and compelling power which the greatest thinkers have, exerting their force on followers and critics alike for generations to come, as Freud certainly did. But in an age when all systems are undergoing revision, and many have collapsed beyond repair, there is still something fertile in James's critique of "the block universe" and the synoptic vision which would claim to encompass it.

Psychology itself now reflects a more existential and historically oriented mode of analysis, of which Erikson's work is a primary example. Surely the author of *The Varieties of Religious Experience: A Study in Human Nature* would have found *Young Man Luther* a deeply congenial book. It is aesthetically satisfying that the kind of study which Erikson's book illustrated and spurred a decade ago should be luminously relevant to explaining William James's troubled history. James would not have been surprised, for he knew that the discovery of the "subliminal self" — as he called it — was the door through which entered the experiences that have had emphatic influence in shaping religious history, including (we must add) his own. . . .

Notes

1. William James, *Selected Papers on Philosophy* (Everyman Edition), p. 180.
2. *Ibid.,* p. 181.
3. Letter to Henry James, May 4, 1907, *Letters of William James,* ed. Henry James (2d ed.; 2 vols; Boston, 1926), Vol. 2, p. 279; H. Stuart Hughes, *Consciousness and Society: The Reorientation of European Social Thought 1890–1930* (New York, 1958), p. 397.
4. William James, "Great Men and Their Environment," *Selected Papers,* p. 192.
5. Erik H. Erikson, *Young Man Luther: A Study in Psychoanalysis and History* (New York, 1958), pp. 14–15. Erikson's concept of the identity crisis has proved to be of great value in understanding James.
6. *Ibid.,* p. 110.
7. Walter E. Houghton, *The Victorian Frame of Mind 1830–1870* (New Haven, 1957), especially pp. 58–109.
8. Ralph Barton Perry (ed.), *The Thought and Character of William James* (Boston, 1935), Vol. 2, p. 122. Perry explains James's troubles only by reference to "morbid traits," as if they had no history.
9. *Ibid.,* Vol. 1, p. 192. (Hereafter cited as *TCWJ.*)
10. Letter to Charles Ritter, July 31, 1860. *Ibid.,* Vol. 1, p. 193; letter to Henry James, Jr., October 10, 1872. *Ibid.,* Vol. 1, p. 330.
11. Quoted by Leon Edel, *Henry James: The Untried Years, 1843–1870* (Philadelphia, 1953), pp. 174–175.
12. Letter to Katherine Temple, September, 1861. *Letters of William James,* Vol. 1, p. 40; *ibid.,* Vol. 1, p. 32. (Hereafter cited as *LWJ.*)

13. *TCWJ*, Vol. 1, p. 220. Letter to his family, May 3–10, 1865, *ibid.*, Vol. 1, p. 219.
14. Letters to Tom Ward, May 24, 1868. James Papers, Houghton Library, Harvard University; September 12, 1867, *TCWJ*, Vol. 1, p. 244.
15. Letter to Henry James, Jr., June 12, 1869, *TCWJ*, Vol. 1, p. 300.
16. Letter to Tom Ward, January, 1868, *LWJ*, Vol. 1, p. 129; *TCWJ*, Vol. 2, p. 675.
17. *TCWJ*, Vol. 1, p. 142.
18. Letter to Tom Ward, October, 1868, *ibid.*, Vol. 1, p. 287.
19. Letter to his father, November, 1861, *ibid.*, Vol. 1, p. 211.
20. *Ibid.*, Vol. 1, p. 302.
21. Letter to Tom Ward, October 9 (1868), *ibid.*, Vol. 1, p. 287.
22. February 10, 1873, *ibid.*, Vol. 1, p. 335.
23. Letter to Henry James, Jr., October 10, 1872; *ibid.*, Vol. 1, p. 341; Diary, April 10, 1873, Vol. 1, p. 343.
24. *Ibid.*, Vol. 2, p. 673.
25. Letter to Mrs. Whitman, October 15, 1890, *LWJ*, Vol. 1, p. 304.
26. *TCWJ*, Vol. 2, p. 125.
27. Letter to Théodore Flournoy, September 19, 1892, *LWJ*, Vol. 1, p. 325; to Carl Stumpf, September 10, 1899, *TCWJ*, Vol. 2, p. 195.
28. William James, *Some Problems in Philosophy* (New York, 1911), p. viii. See my "The Unfinished Arch: William James and the Idea of History," *American Quarterly*, Vol. 13 (Winter, 1961), pp. 505–15.
29. Erikson, *Young Man Luther*, p. 65.
30. Quoted by Austin Warren, *The Elder Henry James* (New York, 1934), pp. 56–57; *TCWJ*, Vol. 1, p. 21.
31. Letter to Emerson (1842?), *TCWJ*, Vol. 1, p. 43.
32. *LWJ*, Vol. 1, p. 19.
33. Letter to W. J., December 15, 1867, *TCWJ*, Vol. 1, p. 507.
34. *Ibid.*, Vol. 1, p. 142.
35. Letter to Henry James, Jr., May 9 (1882?), *TCWJ*, Vol. 1, p. 112.
36. *Ibid.*, Vol. 1, p. 171; F. O. Matthiessen, *The James Family* (New York, 1961), p. 276; *TCWJ*, Vol. 1, p. 3.
37. Letter to O. W. Holmes, Jr., May 15, 1868, *TCWJ*, Vol. 1, p. 517.
38. Letter to W. J., September 27, 1867, *ibid.*, Vol. 2, p. 711.
39. Erikson, *Young Man Luther*, p. 43.
40. *TCWJ*, Vol. 1, p. 151.
41. Letters to O. W. Holmes, Jr., May 18, 1868, *ibid.*, Vol. 1, pp. 516–517; to Tom Ward, October 9, 1868, *ibid.*, Vol. 1, p. 287.
42. Letters to Henry James, Jr., October 2, 1869, *ibid.*, Vol. 1, pp. 306–8; May 7, 1870, *LWJ*, Vol. 1, p. 158; Diary, February 1, 1870, and April 30, 1870, *TCWJ*, pp. 322–323.
43. Erik H. Erikson, "The Problem of Ego Identity," *Psychological Issues*, Vol. 1, (1959), pp. 123–124, 129.
44. Diary, April 21, 1868, James Papers, Houghton Library, Harvard University; *TCWJ*, Vol. 1, p. 164, quoted from introduction, *The Literary Remains of the Late Henry James*.
45. *TCWJ*, Vol. 1, p. 133.
46. "The Dilemma of Determinism," *Essay in Faith and Morals*, ed. R. B. Perry (New York, 1947), p. 174.
47. Letter to father, December 14, 1882, *LWJ*, Vol. 1, pp. 218–20.
48. Letters to W. J., May 28 and September 5, 1882, *TCWJ*, Vol. 1, pp. 678–679.
49. *Ibid.*, Vol. 1, p. 710.
50. Letters to Henry James, Jr., January 23, 1883, *ibid.*, Vol. 1, p. 389; April, 1885, *LWJ*, Vol. 1, pp. 242–243. He did complain again about his eyes in 1887, but not severely, and presbyopic spectacles seem to have solved the problem. *LWJ*, Vol. 1, p. 262. In his pictures he does not wear spectacles.
51. Letter to Josiah Royce, September 26, 1900, *TCWJ*, Vol. 1, p. 817.
52. Letter to G. W. Howison, July 17, 1895, *ibid.*, Vol. 2, pp. 207–208.
53. *Ibid.*, Vol. 1, p. 165.

54. William James, *The Varieties of Religious Experience: A Study in Human Nature* (New York, 1928), pp. 519, 499.
55. Letter to Théodore Flournoy, February 8, 1905, Robert C. LeClair (ed.), *The Letters of William James and Théodore Flournoy* (Madison, 1966), p. 163; to Henry James, Jr., September 10, 1906, *LWJ*, Vol. 2, p. 259.
56. *TCWJ*, Vol. 1, p. 779.
57. Erikson, *Young Man Luther*, p. 255; Erikson, "Identity and the Life Cycle," *Psychological Issues*, Vol. 1 (1959), p. 90.
58. Erikson, *Young Man Luther*, p. 46.
59. Letter to George Santayana, January 2, 1888, *TCWJ*, Vol. 1, p. 403.
60. Erikson, *Young Man Luther*, p. 67.
61. James, *Varieties of Religious Experience*, pp. 501–502.
62. *Ibid.*, pp. 23–24.
63. William James, *Talks to Teachers of Psychology* (New York, 1916), p. 203.
64. James, *Varieties of Religious Experience*, pp. 234–235.
65. *Ibid.*, p. 513.
66. William James, *Pragmatism: A New Way for Some Old Ways of Thinking* (New York, 1919), p. 295.
67. *Ibid.*, p. 296.
68. Donald Meyer, *The Positive Thinkers* (New York, 1965), p. 284.

4

A Mathematician's Apology*

G. H. HARDY

IT IS a melancholy experience for a professional mathematician to find himself writing about mathematics. The function of a mathematician is to do something, to prove new theorems, to add to mathematics, and not to talk about what he or other mathematicians have done. Statesmen despise publicists, painters despise art-critics, and physiologists, physicists, or mathematicians have usually similar feelings; there is no score more profound, or on the whole more justifiable, than that of the men who make for the men who explain. Exposition, criticism, appreciation, is work for second-rate minds.

I can remember arguing this point once in one of the few serious conversations that I ever had with Housman. Housman, in his Leslie Stephen lecture *The Name and Nature of Poetry,* had denied very emphatically that he was a "critic"; but he had denied it in what seemed to me a singularly perverse way, and had expressed an admiration for literary criticism which startled and scandalized me.

He had begun with a quotation from his inaugural lecture, delivered twenty-two years before —

> Whether the faculty of literary criticism is the best gift that Heaven has in its treasuries, I cannot say; but Heaven seems to think so, for assuredly it is the gift most charily bestowed. Orators and poets. . . , if rare in comparison with blackberries, are commoner than returns of Halley's comet: literary critics are less common. . . .

And he had continued —

> In these twenty-two years I have improved in some respects and deteriorated in others, but I have not so much improved as to become a literary critic, nor so much deteriorated as to fancy that I have become one.

It had seemed to me deplorable that a great scholar and a fine poet should write like this, and, finding myself next to him in Hall a few weeks later, I plunged in and said so. Did he really mean what he had said to be taken very seriously? Would the life of the best of critics really have seemed to him comparable with that of a scholar and a poet? We argued these questions all through dinner, and I think that finally he agreed with me. I must not seem to claim a dialectical triumph over a man who can no longer contradict me; but "Perhaps

*In G. H. Hardy, *A Mathematician's Apology.* Cambridge, Cambridge University Press, (1969), 61–73, 77–79.

not entirely" was, in the end, his reply to the first question, and "Probably no" to the second.

There may have been some doubt about Housman's feelings, and I do not wish to claim him as on my side; but there is no doubt at all about the feelings of men of science, and I share them fully. If then I find myself writing, not mathematics but "about" mathematics, it is a confession of weakness, for which I may rightly be scorned or pitied by younger and more vigorous mathematicians. I write about mathematics because, like any other mathematician who has passed sixty, I have no longer the freshness of mind, the energy, or the patience to carry on effectively with my proper job.

I propose to put forward an apology for mathematics; and I may be told that it needs none, since there are now few studies more generally recognized, for good reasons or bad, as profitable and praiseworthy. This may be true; indeed it is probable, since the sensational triumphs of Einstein, that stellar astronomy and atomic physics are the only sciences which stand higher in popular estimation. A mathematician need not now consider himself on the defensive. He does not have to meet the sort of opposition described by Bardley in the admirable defence of metaphysics which forms the introduction to *Appearance and Reality.*

A metaphysician, says Bradley, will be told that "metaphysical knowledge is wholly impossible", or that "even if possible to a certain degree, it is practically no knowledge worth the name". "The same problems," he will hear, "the same disputes, the same sheer failure. Why not abandon it and come out? Is there nothing else more worth your labour?" There is no one so stupid as to use this sort of language about mathematics. The mass of mathematical truth is obvious and imposing; its practical applications, the bridges and steam-engines and dynamos, obtrude themselves on the dullest imagination. The public does not need to be convinced that there is something in mathematics.

All this is in its way very comforting to mathematicians, but it is hardly possible for a genuine mathematician to be content with it. Any genuine mathematician must feel that it is not on these crude achievements that the real case for mathematics rests, that the popular reputation of mathematics is based largely on ignorance and confusion, and that there is room for a more rational defence. At any rate, I am disposed to try to make one. It should be a simpler task than Bradley's difficult apology.

I shall ask, then, why is it really worth while to a make a serious study of mathematics? What is the proper justification of a mathematician's life? And my answers will be, for the most part, such as are to be expected from a mathematician: I think that it is worth while, that there is ample justification. But I should say at once that my defence of mathematics will be a defence of myself, and that my apology is bound to be to some extent egotistical. I should not think it worth while to apologize for my subject if I regarded myself as one of its failures.

Some egotism of this sort is inevitable, and I do not feel that it really needs justification. Good work is not done by "humble" men. It is one of the first duties of a professor, for example, in any subject, to exaggerate a little both the importance of his subject and his own importance in it. A man who is always asking "Is what I do worth while?" and "Am I the right person to do it?" will always be ineffective himself and a discouragement to others. He must shut his eyes a little and think a little more of his subject and himself than they deserve. This is not too difficult: it is harder not to make his subject and himself ridiculous by shutting his eyes too tightly.

A man who sets out to justify his existence and his activities has to distinguish two different questions. The first is whether the work which he does is worth doing; and the second is why he does it, whatever its value may be. The first question is often very difficult, and the answer very discouraging, but most people will find the second easy enough even then. Their answers, if they are honest, will usually take one or other of two forms; and the second form is merely a humbler variation of the first, which is the only answer which we need consider seriously.

(1) "I do what I do because it is the one and only thing that I can do at all well. I am a lawyer, or a stockbroker, or a professional cricketer, because I have some real talent for that particular job. I am a lawyer because I have a fluent tongue, and am interested in legal subtleties; I am a stockbroker because my judgement of the markets is quick and sound; I am a professional cricketer because I can bat unusually well. I agree that it might be better to be a poet or a mathematician, but unfortunately I have no talent for such pursuits."

I am not suggesting that this is a defence which can be made by most people, since most people can do nothing at all well. But it is impregnable when it can be made without absurdity, as it can by a substantial minority: perhaps five or even 10 per cent of men can do something rather well. It is a tiny minority who can do anything *really* well, and the number of men who can do two things well is negligible. If a man has any genuine talent, he should be ready to make almost any sacrifice in order to cultivate it to the full.

This view was endorsed by Dr Johnson —

> When I told him that I had been to see [his namesake] Johnson ride upon three horses, he said "Such a man, sir, should be encouraged, for his performances show the extent of the human powers. . ." —

and similarly he would have applauded mountain climbers, channel swimmers, blindfold chess-players. For my own part, I am entirely in sympathy with all such attempts at remarkable achievement. I feel some sympathy even with conjurors and ventriloquists; and when Alekhine and Bradman set out to beat records, I am quite bitterly disappointed if they fail. And here both Dr Johnson and I find ourselves in agreement with the public. As W. J. Turner has said so truly, it is only the "highbrows" (in the unpleasant sense) who do not admire the "real swells".

We have of course to take account of the differences in value between different activities. I would rather be a novelist or a painter than a statesman of similar rank; and there are many roads to fame which most of us would reject as actively pernicious. Yet it is seldom that such differences of value will turn the scale in a man's choice of a career, which will almost always be dictated by the limitations of his natural abilities. Poetry is more valuable than cricket, but Bradman would be a fool if he sacrificed his cricket in order to write second-rate minor poetry (and I suppose that it is unlikely that he could do better). If the cricket were a little less supreme, and the poetry better, then the choice might be more difficult: I do not know whether I would rather have been Victor Trumper or Rupert Brooke. It is fortunate that such dilemmas occur so seldom.

I may add that they are particularly unlikely to present themselves to a mathematician. It is usual to exaggerate rather grossly the differences between the mental processes of mathematicians and other people, but it is undeniable that a gift for mathematics is one of the most specialized talents, and that mathematicians as a class are not particularly distinguished for general ability or versatility. If a man is in any sense a real mathematician, then it is a hundred to one that his mathematics will be far better than anything else he can do, and that he would be silly if he surrendered any decent opportunity of exercising his one talent in order to do undistinguished work in other fields. Such a sacrifice could be justified only by economic necessity or age.

I had better say something here about this question of age, since it is particularly important for mathematicians. No mathematician should ever allow himself to forget that mathematics, more than any other art or science, is a young man's game. To take a simple illustration at a comparatively humble level, the average age of election to the Royal Society is lowest in mathematics.

We can naturally find much more striking illustrations. We may consider, for example, the career of a man who was certainly one of the world's three greatest mathematicians. Newton gave up mathematics at fifty, and had lost his enthusiasm long before; he had recognized no doubt by the time that he was forty that his great creative days were over. His greatest ideas of all, fluxions and the law of gravitation, came to him about 1666, when he was twenty-four — "in those days I was in the prime of my age for invention, and minded mathematics and philosophy more than at any time since". He made big discoveries until he was nearly forty (the "elliptic orbit" at thirty-seven), but after that he did little but polish and perfect.

Galois died at twenty-one, Abel at twenty-seven, Ramanujan at thirty-three, Riemann at forty. There have been men who have done great work a good deal later; Gauss's great memoir on differential geometry was published when he was fifty (though he had had the fundamental ideas ten years before). I do not know an instance of a major mathematical advance initiated by a man past fifty. If a man of mature age loses interest in and abandons mathematics, the loss is not likely to be very serious either for mathematics or for himself.

On the other hand the gain is no more likely to be substantial; the later records of mathematicians who have left mathematics are not particularly encouraging. Newton made a quite competent Master of the Mint (when he was not quarrelling with anybody). Painlevé was a not very successful Premier of France. Laplace's political career was highly discreditable, but he is hardly a fair instance, since he was dishonest rather than incompetent, and never really "gave up" mathematics. It is very hard to find an instance of a first-rate mathematician who has abandoned mathematics and attained first-rate distinction in any other field. There may have been young men who would have been first-rate mathematicians if they had stuck to mathematics, but I have never heard of a really plausible example. And all this is fully borne out by my own very limited experience. Every young mathematician of real talent whom I have known has been faithful to mathematics, and not from lack of ambition but from abundance of it; they have all recognized that there, if anywhere, lay the road to a life of any distinction.

There is also what I called the "humbler variation" of the standard apology; but I may dismiss this in a very few words.

(2) "There is *nothing* that I can do particularly well. I do what I do because it came my way. I really never had a chance of doing anything else." And this apology too I accept as conclusive. It is quite true that most people can do nothing well. If so, it matters very little what career they choose, and there is really nothing more to say about it. It is a conclusive reply, but hardly one likely to be made by a man with any pride; and I may assume that none of us would be content with it. . . .

I shall assume that I am writing for readers who are full, or have in the past been full, of a proper spirit of ambition. A man's first duty, a young man's at any rate, is to be ambitious. Ambition is a noble passion which may legitimately take many forms; there was *something* noble in the ambition of Attila or Napoleon: but the noblest ambition is that of leaving behind one something of permanent value —

> Here, on the level sand,
> Between the sea and land,
> What shall I build or write
> Against the fall of night?
>
> Tell me of runes to grave
> That hold the bursting wave,
> Or bastions to design
> For longer date than mine.

Ambition has been the driving force behind nearly all the best work of the world. In particular, practically all substantial contributions to human happiness have been made by ambitious men. To take two famous examples, were not Lister and Pasteur ambitious? Or, on a humbler level, King Gillette and William Willett; and who in recent times have contributed more to human comfort than they?

Physiology provides particularly good examples, just because it is so obviously a "beneficial" study. We must guard against a fallacy common among apologists of science, the fallacy of supposing that the men whose work most benefits humanity are thinking much of that while they do it, that physiologists, for example, have particularly noble souls. A physiologist may indeed be glad to remember that his work will benefit mankind, but the motives which provide the force and the inspiration for it are indistinguishable from those of a classical scholar or a mathematician.

There are many highly respectable motives which may lead men to prosecute research, but three which are much more important than the rest. The first (without which the rest must come to nothing) is intellectual curiosity, desire to know the truth. Then, professional pride, anxiety to be satisfied with one's performance, the shame that overcomes any self-respecting craftsman when his work is unworthy of his talent. Finally, ambition, desire for reputation, and the position, even the power or the money, which it brings. It may be fine to feel, when you have done your work, that you have added to the happiness or alleviated the sufferings of others, but that will not be why you did it. So if a mathematician, or a chemist, or even a physiologist, were to tell me that the driving force in his work had been the desire to benefit humanity, then I should not believe him (nor should I think the better of him if I did). His dominant motives have been those which I have stated, and in which, surely, there is nothing of which any decent man need be ashamed.

Name Index

Acker, M.   272
Adams, J.   49, 151, 157, 158, 163
Addison, J.   1, 49, 73
Adler, A.   259, 280
Albert, R.   1, 6, 15, 24, 27, 28, 30, 31, 45, 66, 69, 74, 108, 139, 141, 142, 152
Allport, G.   129
Altus, W.   189
Ames, L.   334
Anastasi, A.   6, 7, 130, 275
Andrews, F.   194
Andry, R.   151
Angoff, W.   94
Annan, N.   60
Apperly, F.   189
Ausubel, D.   266
Archimedes   5, 287
Aristotle   5, 20, 233
Astin, A.   188, 193

Bach, J.   28, 43, 62
Bachrach, P.   189, 191
Bachtold, L.   264, 331
Bacon, F.   5, 51, 53, 57
Baird, L.   130
Bakan, D.   274
Baltes, P.   185, 196
Balzac, H.   67
Barber, B.   14, 359
Bardeen, J.   243
Barnard, J.   332, 333, 337, 341
Barron, F.   11, 14, 25, 27, 28, 67, 74, 103, 120, 121, 122, 130, 133, 190, 193, 194, 264, 269, 270, 281, 282, 331, 348
Barzun, J.   41
Beadle, G.   245
Becker, H.   2, 185
Beethoven, L.   41, 51, 53, 233
Bentham, J.   158, 160, 165
Berenson, B.   6
Berlioz, H.   41
Bernstein, J.   242
Berrington, H.   140, 345
Bett, W.   9

Bevan, A.   358
Bieri, J.   272
Bing, E.   15
Binet, A.   62
Birch, F.   15, 243
Blake, W.   309
Block, J.   312, 329
Bloom, B.   66, 67, 103
Boersma, F.   269, 271
Bordin, E.   198
Bowers, K.   105
Bramwell, B.   9
Brechbill, H.   190, 192
Bridgman, P.   243
Brimhall, D.   173, 174
Bruner, J.   194, 265, 274
Brunkan, R.   190, 196
Bullock, A.   144
Burks, B.   21, 147
Burt, C.   217, 225, 282
Bush, M.   190, 191, 194
Bushman, R.   10
Butcher, H.   130, 270, 282
Byrt, E.   221

Campbell, D.   110, 267, 268, 269, 320, 332
Canning, G.   361
Canter, S.   350
Caplow, T.   198
Carlyle, T.   49
Carpenter, B.   182, 189
Carrol, J.   28
Cattell, J.   52, 77, 155, 156, 173, 174
Cattell, R.   130, 183, 191, 194, 195, 263, 281, 282, 284, 286, 334, 335, 336, 337, 338, 342, 348
Cayley, A.   62
Chadwick, S.   347
Chambers, J.   23, 52, 183, 188, 192, 195, 270
Chandra, S.   187
Charcot, S.   258, 259
Chatterton, T.   158, 162, 165, 167, 168

398 Name Index

Sarton, G.   29
Schacters, S.   189
Schaefer, C.   130, 133, 188, 191
Schaefer, J.   233, 275
Schawlow, A.   255
Schelling, F.   49, 50
Schiller, J.   280
Schilpp, P.   64, 69
Schrodinger, E.   261
Schubert, F.   41
Schumann, R.   40
Schussel, N.   272
Schwinger, J.   244
Scott, W.   64, 187
Sears, R.   151
Segal, S.   198
Segre, E.   243, 244
Shapiro, R.   268, 275
Shakow, D.   66
Shakspeare, W.   4, 233
Shaw, G.   36, 37
Shelley, P.   280
Shotwell, A.   286
Shouksmith, G.   273
Simonton, D.   22, 27, 28, 30, 215, 234, 235, 236, 237, 238
Singer, K.   42, 104, 251
Skinner, B.   63, 68
Sloan, W.   15
Smith, A.   viii
Snow, C.   267
Soliman, A.   192, 332
Sonneborn, T.   244, 245, 246
Souief, M.   273
Southern, M.   337
Sorokin, P.   233
Sprecher, T.   281
Springer, K.   190, 194, 273, 274
Stanley, J.   21, 22, 27, 29, 74, 128
Stecklein, J.   342
Stein, M.   28, 52, 55, 73, 190, 194
Stephenson, W.   286
Stevenson, R.   280
Stierlin, H.   143, 144
Strandskov, H.   244
Strauss, S.   183, 190, 192
Strout, C.   10, 346
Suci, G.   225
Super, D.   189, 191, 197
Sutton-Smith, B.   189
Szilard, L.   261

Tafts, the   151
Tannenbaum, P.   225
Tasso, T.   158, 163

Taylor, C.   192, 194, 265, 268, 270, 272, 281, 331
Taylor, D.   87, 100, 186
Taylor, J.   15, 96, 130, 191
Teller, E.   242
Terman, L. M.   6, 7, 9, 11, 14, 15, 16, 21, 22, 28, 45, 67, 73, 74, 78, 79, 81, 82, 84, 90, 140, 141, 142, 147, 190, 191, 280, 281, 282, 315
Thompson, C. W.   15
Thorndike, R.   217, 282
Thurstone, L.   286
Tiner, L.   284
Tocqueville   37
Tolstoi, L.   67
Torrance, E.   21, 28, 235, 274
Townes, C.   255
Tyler, L. E.   7, 100, 191, 198
Tyron, R.   319

Van Zelst, R.   194
Vernon, P. E.   15, 129, 218, 219, 267, 268, 269, 274, 282
Veroff, J.   152
Virgil   3, 5
Visher, S.   188, 192
Voltaire, F.   49, 50, 53, 158, 159, 161, 280

Walberg, H.   45, 52, 191, 332
Wallace, A.   259
Wallach, M.   24, 25, 73, 74, 100, 101, 102, 103, 104, 105, 106, 108, 109, 110, 129, 266, 267, 269, 271, 274, 350, 351
Wallbrown, F.   104
Walpole, H.   167
Warburg, O.   247, 249
Ward, W.   272
Washington, G.   53
Watson, J.   64, 66, 215, 244, 245, 246, 253, 254, 255, 256, 257, 258, 260
Weber, K.   49, 157
Weiner, D.   183, 189, 192
Weisberg, P.   190, 194, 273, 274
Weiss, D.   133
Weissman, H.   272
Weitzman, R.   103
Welsh, G.   29, 130, 133, 270, 272, 314
Werner, E.   264, 331
Werts, C.   188, 189
West, S.   188, 189, 191
White, R.   10, 22, 274
Whitehead, A.   vii
Whiton, M.   104
Wieck, C.   40

Subject Index

postponement of gratification   327
pride   306, 390
recklessness   361
reflectiveness   313
self-absorbed   42
self-actualizing   284, 291
self-accepting   301, 307, 318
self-assertive   124
self-consciousness   166
staying power   59
tolerance
    for tension   127
    for being alone   181, 361
    for ambiguity   195, 336, 367
unconventionality   182, 264, 314, 318,
    353, 355
versatility   389
zeal   51
"Phaeton complex"   371
Phaeton, myth of   360
Physical traits   77
Piagetian criteria   128
Playmates   80, 162
Political fragmentation   236
Political milieu   238
Population IQ   217
Posterity   59
    see also Reputation
Precociousness   22, 69
Preference for complexity   194, 267,
    270–79, 285, 295, 305, 321
Predictors
    of eminence   15, 66
    of scientific career   187
Presidents of the United States   144, 153
Primary-process thinking   194
Prime Ministers   164, 358–72
    British   144, 345, 358–75
Princeton University   93
Principia   164
Problem-finding   249
Problems of measurement and prediction
    73
Prodigy   3, 164
Product, genius as   60
Productivity   14, 24, 62, 128, 186, 254,
    264–79, 281, 287, 311, 322, 332,
    341
Professional identity   48, 123, 126
Projective tests   116
Psychiatric patients   7, 147
Psychoanalysts   23, 25, 114, 198, 381
Psychologists   63, 66, 331–44
Psychometric study   21, 45
Psychopathology   v, ix, 9, 12, 20, 22, 37,
    40, 75, 114, 152, 258, 264, 306, 345,
    347–57, 363, 381

Psychosexual development   15
Psychosocial development   175
Public recognition   106
Publication   8, 41, 62, 101, 106
    see also Productivity

Q-sort   117, 312, 331
Q-sort descriptions of creative writers   303
Quality and quantity
    of production   see Ideational fluency

Race for priority   253–61
Racial origin   76
Rebellion   175, 206, 314, 325
Rebelliousness   126, 170
Recognition   212, 260
Rejection   206, 361
Religion   209, 325
Religious training   170
Remote associations   236, 267
Repression   152
Reputation   58, 241, 257, 311, 387, 391
Research style   327
Responsibility   115, 152, 213
Restricted range of sample   136, 273,
    304, 350
Revolution   37
Revolutionary War   163
Rhodes Scholars   89
Risk-taking   27, 43, 194, 320, 336
Role model availability   235, 242, 247,
    291
Role perception   185
Role-taking   121
Roots   143
Rorschach   178, 308

Satisfaction   212, 213
Scholastic Aptitude Test (S.A.T.)   86, 101,
    108, 172
School, age at entry   78
School adjustment   13
Schooling   see Education
Scientific elite   255
Scientists   viii, 23, 62, 170–98, 253–61
Self-awareness   259
Self-control   307, 322, 336, 337
Self-discipline   195, 270, 298, 314
Self-esteem   251, 260, 323, 325, 359, 364,
    369
Self-evaluation   96
Self-image   123, 250, 264, 291, 380
Self-regard   150
Self-reliance   27
Self-sufficiency   282